ʟʟɛNTH CENTURY

AMERICAN PLAYS

Seven Plays Including
THE BLACK CROOK

D1153710

Other Play Anthologies by
APPLAUSE THEATRE & CINEMA BOOKS:

AMAZON ALL STARS
ASIAN AMERICAN DRAMA
THE BEST AMERICAN SHORT PLAYS
BEFORE BRECHT
BLACK COMEDY
BLACK HEROES
CLASSICAL COMEDY GREEK AND ROMAN
CLASSICAL TRADGEDY GREEK AND ROMAN
ELIZABETHAN DRAMA
LIFE IS A DREAM & OTHER SPANISH CLASSICS
MEDIEVAL & TUDOR DRAMA
THE MISANTHROPE & OTHER FRENCH CLASSICS
THE MOTHER AND OTHER UNSAVORY CLASSICS
THE NATIONAL BLACK DRAMA ANTHOLOGY
PLAYS BY AMERICAN WOMEN: 1900-1930
PLAYS BY AMERICAN WOMEN: 1930-1960
THE SEEDS OF MODERN DRAMA
THE SERVANT OF TWO MASTERS & OTHER ITALIAN CLASSICS
THEATRE FOR YOUNG AUDIENCES
THE TWELVE PLAYS OF CHRISTMAS
WOMEN ON THE VERGE

NINETEENTH CENTURY
AMERICAN PLAYS

Seven Plays Including
THE BLACK CROOK

Edited by Myron Matlaw

APPLAUSE
NEW YORK • LONDON

NINETEENTH CENTURY AMERICAN PLAYS
edited by Myron Matlaw

Copyright © 1967, 2001 by Myron Matlaw

Grateful acknowledgment is made to John T. Herne for permission to publish in this anthology Margaret Fleming by his late father James A. Herne.

This material originally appeared in, and is reprinted from, The Black Crook (1967)

Library of Congress Cataloguing-in-Publication Data

Library of Congress Card Number: 2001087131

British Library Cataloguing-in-Publication Data

A catalogue record for this book is available from the British Library

ISBN: 1-55783-464-4

Printed in Canada

APPLAUSE THEATRE BOOKS
151 W46th Street, 8th Floor
New York, NY 10036
Phone: (212) 575-9265
FAX: (646) 562-5852
email: info@applausepub.com
internet: www.applausepub.com

COMBINED BOOK SERVICES LTD.
Units I/K, Paddock Wood Distribution Centre
Paddock Wood, Tonbridge, Kent TN 12 6UU
Phone: (44) 01892 837171
Fax: (44) 01892 837272

SALES & DISTRIBUTION, HAL LEONARD CORP.
7777 West Bluemound Road, P.O. Box 13819
Milwaukee, WI 53213
Phone: (414) 774-3630 Fax: (414) 774-3259
email: halinfo@halleonard.com
internet: www.halleonard.com

To Laura and John

Contents

Introduction

American drama began in the last years of the eighteenth century. In 1798 William Dunlap (1766–1839), "the Father of the American Drama," opened the Park Theatre in New York. Philadelphia was then still the theatre center of the young nation, although Baltimore, Annapolis, and even Boston, despite strong Puritanical opposition, each had at least one playhouse. The Park, however, was the most architecturally advanced theatre of its time. New York, then a city of 60,000, thus set out on its bid for the theatrical supremacy that it achieved some time before 1825 and that it has maintained, on Broadway and off, to this day.

Two plays by Americans had been performed before Dunlap's career started: Thomas Godfrey's romantic verse tragedy *The Prince of Parthia* (1767), and Royall Tyler's comedy *The Contrast* (1787). Dunlap, however, was the first professional native-born dramatist. Of his more than fifty plays, the best ones are *The Father* (1789), a comedy that became a theatrical success immediately, and *André* (1798), a poetic tragedy based on the famous Revolutionary spy story; this latter play became a hit only when Dunlap vulgarized it into a patriotic spectacle, *The Glory of Columbia* (1803). His most popular plays, however, were his adaptations of the sentimental dramas and melodramas of August von Kotzebue (1761–1819), the German playwright whose works dominated European and English stages at the turn of the century. In his *History of the American Theatre* (1832), the first record of its kind, Dunlap remarks that despite his grave financial difficulties, the successful adaptation of one of Kotzebue's many plays, *The Stranger*, "alone enabled the author to keep open the theatre." It is interesting to note the parallel with Richard Brinsley Sheridan, who at that time had the identical experience with his adaptations of Kotzebue during his management of the Drury Lane in London.

Indeed, much of the history of American drama and theatre—and written drama and living theatre were particularly interdependent in the nineteenth century, when star

rather than playwright predominated—is closely related to
English drama and London theatres. It is not surprising that
the first acting companies in America were organized by
English entrepreneurs and consisted of English actors, and
that their repertoire consisted of English drama: plays by
Shakespeare, and popular Restoration and eighteenth-century
dramas like Otway's *Venice Preserved*, Farquhar's *The Beaux'*
Stratagem, Addison's *Cato*, Steele's *The Conscious Lovers*,
Lillo's *The London Merchant*, Home's *Douglas*, and the two
English comic masterpieces of the eighteenth century, Gold-
smith's *She Stoops to Conquer* and Sheridan's *The School*
for Scandal. These plays, as well as Kotzebue's, retained their
popularity in this country throughout much of the nineteenth
century, and early American plays, such as Dunlap's and the
two that preceded his—not to mention much of the drama
that was written later—were modeled on them. It is not until
well into the nineteenth century that distinct American
characteristics, although germinal in individual early plays,
begin to predominate in our drama.

By the same token, although Americans at the beginning
of the nineteenth century were fiercely independent of
England politically, they felt very dependent culturally.
Audiences were more secure with plays that, as Dunlap puts
it in his *History*, "had been sanctioned by a London audience." A record of a successful London performance consti-
tuted a seal of approval, and some early American
playwrights, including Dunlap, were willing to have their
works advertised as having been written by Englishmen in
order to assure successful runs for them here. That audiences
persisted for many years in their defensive scorn of native
productions is evidenced by the opening lines of the Prologue
to *Fashion* (page 31).

Because of Dunlap's encouragement and the example he
provided with his own plays, however, the early years of the
century saw the composition and production of plays by
native playwrights, some of which dealt with native themes.
This trend continued after Dunlap's management of the Park
ended in 1805. Among the more successful of those plays
were Mordecai Manuel Noah's *She Would Be a Soldier*
(1819), a historic drama dealing with the War of 1812, and
a farce on the American Exchange (anticipating a topic that
would interest later playwrights), *Wall Street; or, Ten Min-*

utes Before Three (1819), probably written by Richard W. Mead. Aside from Dunlap, however, the only important playwrights born before the nineteenth century were John Howard Payne (1791–1852) and James Nelson Barker (1784–1858). Payne's immortality rests on "Home, Sweet Home," one of America's most popular songs, which he wrote for his otherwise unnotable operatic drama *Clari* (1823). Yet he was an immensely popular actor, both here and in England, and he wrote (and, even more frequently, adapted) a total of over fifty plays. Among them were heroic and romantic treatments of Roman history, and these started a vogue that resulted in the production of a host of minor historical dramas. Payne's best plays are a poetic tragedy written for and acted by Edmund Kean, *Brutus; or, The Fall of Tarquin* (1818), and a comedy written in collaboration with Washington Irving, *Charles the Second* (1824). Most of Payne's other works, although highly successful because of their great theatricality, are of no literary value; they are by and large melodramas based on contemporary German, French, and English plays. James Nelson Barker, unlike Payne, was neither a professional theatre man nor very prolific. His plays, considerably superior to the many others written at the time, deal with native themes. The best one, *Superstition* (1824)—a precursor of Arthur Miller's *The Crucible* (1953)—is based on seventeenth-century Colonial history. His *The Indian Princess* (1808), the first produced American play on an Indian theme, is a dramatization of the Pocahontas story.

Over fifty such "Indian" plays appeared before the Civil War, and the Indian character continued to remain popular for some time in minor roles, such as that of Wahnotee in *The Octoroon*. The most successful play in that genre, John Augustus Stone's *Metamora* (1829), portrayed the defeat of the Indian King Philip by the New England settlers in 1676. It was written especially for Edwin Forrest (1806–1872), who had offered a prize of $500 for the best five-act tragedy featuring an "aboriginal hero." Along with his Shakespearean and other roles, Forrest, one of America's great actors, played *Metamora* continually throughout his long stage career, and made a fortune on the play. (Stone, however, received nothing beyond his prize money; in financial despair, he eventually committed suicide.) Forrest scaled ever greater heights of popularity. An exponent of the ranting school of acting, he was at one time very popular with fashionable audiences. But he lost their support after his feud with the gentlemanly English actor William Charles Macready erupted into the Astor Place Riot—a notorious catastrophe (1849) that endeared him the more to the gallery crowds at the Bowery.

In his quest for strong parts for himself, however, Forrest helped to further the cause of native drama. He made prominent the work of a Philadelphia physician who became an important playwright, Robert Montgomery Bird (1806– 1854). Partial to the type of romantic drama in which Forrest excelled, Bird conceived for him the heroic part of the Thracian leader of gladiator-slaves in *The Gladiator* (1831), and Spartacus became another role Forrest played with immense success in England and in America throughout his career. Bird's best play was *The Broker of Bogota* (1834), a domestic prose tragedy set in eighteenth-century Colombia; Forrest (and later John McCullough) played the part of the middle-class protagonist, whose tragedy occurs when he is betrayed by the son he loves. Bird also rewrote *Metamora* for Forrest in 1836, but Forrest was as niggardly about paying for the plays written for him by Bird, his personal friend (who received but $1,000 for *The Gladiator*), as he had been with Stone. Bird gave up a successful, but unlucrative, playwriting career; the absence of copyright laws left him powerless against Forrest. But there were other native playwrights and works that became and remained popular because of Forrest. *Caius Marius* (1831), a historical verse tragedy on the Roman rebellion against political oppression, provided him with an excellent part; its author, Richard Penn Smith (1799–1854), wrote twenty plays, some of which dealt with American history. In 1852 Robert T. Conrad rewrote his *Jack Cade* (1835), whose title character led the 1450 Kentish serf rebellion; as *Aylmere*, the play provided Forrest with another favorite role.

Forrest had made his debut as Young Norval in John Home's long-popular Scottish tragedy *Douglas* (1756), in Philadelphia in 1820. Other great actors began to gain recognition in this early period: Charlotte Cushman (1816–1876), Mrs. John Drew (1820–1897), and such prominent actor families as the Booths, the Jeffersons, and the Wallacks. It was for James William Wallack that Nathaniel Parker Willis (1806–1867) wrote *Tortesa the Usurer* (1839), a poetic drama; he had won a prize two years earlier from Josephine Clifton with another poetic drama, *Bianca Visconti*, which was written for this actress. The effect on our drama by James H. Hackett (1800–1871) was more distinctively American. Although Hackett was successful as a Shakespearean actor, of greater importance to our drama were his portrayals and popularization of Yankee types. Hackett played Rip Van Winkle for years before Jefferson made that role world famous, and he rewrote the part of Solomon Gundy (in Colman's *Who Wants a Guinea?*) into that of the Yankee Solomon Swap, a part he performed in England as well as America. His best and most successful role was that of Nimrod Wildfire the frontiersman, an offshoot of the Yankee type, in James Paulding's *The Lion of the West* (1830), one of the prize plays written for him. Other famous and color-fully named Yankee characters were Lot Sap Sago in *Yankee Land* (1834) and Deuteronomy Dutiful in *The Vermont Wool Dealer* (1840), both by Cornelius A. Logan, and, of course, Adam Trueman in *Fashion*. Plays like Samuel Wood-worth's *The Forest Rose* (1825) and Joseph S. Jones's *The People's Lawyer* (1839) remained popular for many years because their stage Yankees, Jonathan Ploughboy and Solon Shingle, were performed by such once-famous comedians as George Handel Hill, Danforth Marble, John E. Owens, and Joshua Silsbee.

Apart from the Indian and rural Yankee, there were two other distinctly American stage types that gained prominence in the first half of the century. Neither gave rise to drama that can make much claim to literary pretensions, but both were so popular that no account of nineteenth-century drama can disregard them. As is true of the other stage types, actors in their performances made a great deal more of these parts than may appear from a reading of the plays.

The first of these types was the tough city lad. The B'hoy, or volunteer New York fireman (fireboy), was the most popular representative of the type. As Mose, he first appeared in Benjamin A. Baker's *A Glance at New York* (1848). F.S. Chanfrau, who was to be identified with that character until his death in 1884, was wildly cheered by audiences that consisted of many of Mose's living prototypes. The play—an almost plotless affair that existed only to enable Mose to swagger, fight, and drag a firehose across the stage—became so successful that many sequels followed soon and remained popular for years: *Mose in California, Mose in France, A Glance at Philadelphia,* and so on. The growth of urban life was also reflected in the increasingly frequent portrayal of the city merchant, in plays like *Fashion* and popular derivatives of this play, like Mrs. Sidney F. Bateman's *Self* (1856). Growing urbanization in the latter part of the century, of course, saw city types much more frequently represented in later American drama.

The final peculiarly American stage type to be noted is the most indigenous one of all. Negro minstrelsy probably began in the 1820's with T.D. Rice and his "Jim Crow" song-and-shuffle routine in which the infant Joseph Jefferson III had made one of his first stage appearances. By the 1840's, such blackface troupes as those of Dan Emmett and E.P. Christy offered full evening entertainments in major theatres. Later in the century came such famous minstrels as McIntyre and Heath, and Lew Dockstader, in whose troupe Al Jolson began his career. In the first part of the minstrel show the entertainers, grouped in a semicircular lineup, featured singing and a comic repartee among the two end men (Tambo and Bones) and the Interlocutor; the second part, the olio, was somewhat like the old vaudeville finales, and concluded with a travesty (called "burlesque") of one of the currently popular plays, including the Shakespearean and other pre-nineteenth-century drama that provided most of the theatrical staple. Scripts of such burlesques are still extant, and they furnish an interesting glimpse into the theatre of the age. The minstrel, played by white actors in blackface, was a native stage character as romantically (or unrealistically) conceived as other type characters—shiftless but jolly and good-natured. He is the only native nineteenth-century stage character, however, who remained theatrically intact well into our century. He found his way into much nineteenth-century drama, including *The Octoroon* and the readily available and most popular of all American plays, George L. Aiken's 1852 dramatization of *Uncle Tom's Cabin.*[1]

[1] This play's remarkable history may be pursued in Harry Birdoff's *The World's Greatest Hit: Uncle Tom's Cabin* (New York, 1947).

American drama and theatre before the Civil War, then, manifested considerable vitality, as it was to continue to do until the early twentieth century. However, there were few playwrights of even minor literary stature. Robert Montgomery Bird had turned away from playwriting because it was financially unrewarding at a time when stars could simply expropriate popular plays for their own sole profit. He might well have become a dramatist of note, for his few plays showed much promise. The best dramatist of the age was George Henry Boker. His *Francesca da Rimini* ranks as the finest play of the century, despite derivative poetic and dramatic conventions. Similarly *Fashion*, the best comedy of the century, was derivative of *The School for Scandal*, as Edgar Allan Poe noted in the first of his reviews of Mrs. Mowatt's popular play. In that review Poe also wrote: "We must discard all models. The Elizabethan theatre should be abandoned. We need thought of our own—principles of dramatic action drawn not from the 'old dramatists' but from the fountain of a Nature that can never grow old." These comments were to the point, but they remained unheeded for decades to come—on both sides of the Atlantic. The dominant figure in the American theatre of the 1850's, Dion Boucicault (pp. 203–256), used European models for most of his popular melodramas, although *The Octoroon* (his outstanding work) and *The Poor of New York* dealt with native themes. Ultimately of even greater importance to our drama was his work on behalf of the American copyright law of 1856, the first of its kind. It gave to dramatists some control, at least, over their own work, and paved the way for the later development of native drama.

Theatre conditions had greatly changed since Dunlap's day. The Park, periodically destroyed by fire and then rebuilt, like so many nineteenth-century theatres, dominated the American scene in the early decades. George Frederick Cooke had been the first great English star to begin his American tour there, in 1810, and he was followed at the Park by almost every contemporary star of importance, English and American. Other flourishing showplaces were Philadelphia's Chestnut Street, Washington's National, and Boston's Federal Street. By 1860, New York had many theatres, including the Bowery, the Chatham, the Olympic, and Wallack's Lyceum. Theatres had sprung up in every American city, spreading to the South, Midwest, and, beginning in the 1850's, California and other areas of the growing West. Showboats featured legitimate drama and reached areas that were otherwise difficult of access, around the Mississippi River and elsewhere. The second half of the century, of course, saw the rise of more theatres—such famous houses as the Ford in Washington, McVicker's in Chicago, and, in New York, the Fourteenth Street, Daly's Fifth Avenue, Hammerstein's Olympia, and many others.

Even before Dunlap's time, most cities had their own stock companies. The nineteenth century, however, was the century of the star system, when performers with phenomenal public followings were of far greater importance than the plays in which they were featured. Although individual stars could (and occasionally did) popularize the better plays of contemporary dramatists, the star system had distinct drawbacks as far as the drama—as well as the theatre—were concerned. Walt Whitman was but one of many observers who lamented the situation. He wrote in the Brooklyn *Eagle* (February 8, 1847): "One of the curses of the Park, and indeed of nearly all theatres now, is the *star* system. Some actor or actress flits about the country, playing a week here and a week there, bringing as his or her greatest recommendation, that of *novelty*—and very often indeed having no other. In all the intervals between the appearance of these much trumpeted people, the theatre is quite deserted, though the plays and playing are often far better than during some star engagements." Stock companies, Whitman complained, would put on excellent plays, well acted—but to empty houses, "while the next week crowds would crush each other to get a sight of some flippant well-puffed star, of no real merit, and playing a character written (for the play consists of nothing but *one* in such cases) by nobody knows whom. . . ." As the century wore on, stock companies were more and more relegated to the position of supporting local companies for touring stars, until Boucicault's (and later other) traveling companies, on tour with one New York hit, displaced them almost everywhere but in New York.

New York became the undisputed theatrical center after the Civil War. The community drama, which for so long has formed the staple of the many nonprofessional Little Theatres across the country, is indeed of great importance. Its influence, however, was not really felt before the work of Percy MacKaye in the first decades of this century. Among its early practitioners was George Melville Barker (1832–1890), who in the latter part of the nineteenth century wrote hundreds of community dramas: comedies, farces, and skits on various native topics.

The post-Civil War history of American drama, then, is largely the history of the New York stage. Paramount in the early part of this history is the career of Augustin Daly (1838–1899), its outstanding stage manager. Originally a drama critic for a number of newspapers, Daly began his career as a playwright with adaptations of French and German melodramas and popular English novels, such as those of Charles Reade and Wilkie Collins. Among the most successful of his early adaptations was his first one, *Leah the Forsaken* (1862). Based on Salomon von Mosenthal's *Deborah* (1849), a drama of eighteenth-century Austrian anti-Semitism, it was greeted with particular enthusiasm because of the timely analogy that Northerners made with anti-Negro prejudice in the South. In 1867 Daly produced his first original play, *Under the Gaslight*. Its name, like that of *Uncle Tom's Cabin*, is still a byword for nineteenth-century melodrama, and rightly so. The climax occurs at night in an almost deserted countryside. The heroine, Laura, attempts to axe her way out of a locked railway shanty to rescue Snorkey, a one-armed Civil War veteran who was tied to the tracks by the villain Byke. Tension builds up as the express train is heard in the distance, but the rescue comes in the nick of time, of course:

SNORKEY: Cut the woodwork! Don't mind the lock—cut round it! How my neck tingles! (*A blow at door is heard.*) Courage! (*Another.*) Courage! (*The steam whistle heard again—nearer, and rumble of train on track. Another blow.*) That's a true woman! Courage! (*Noise of locomotive heard—with whistle. A last blow; the door swings open, mutilated—the lock hanging—and* LAURA *appears, axe in hand.*) Here—quick! (*She runs and unfastens him. The locomotive lights glare on scene.*) Victory! Saved! Hooray! (LAURA *leans exhausted against switch.*) And these are the women who aint to have a vote! (*As* LAURA *takes his head from the track, the train of cars rushes past with roar and whistle from left to right.*)

CURTAIN

What is particularly noteworthy in these stage directions is the setting. In the beginning of the century stage settings consisted mainly of painted backdrops. Gradually these gave way to box sets and stage properties that, as the century progressed, became increasingly more realistic—and important. The dramatist Steele MacKaye (1842–1894) was to develop many technical inventions in lighting and scenic effects, and the elevator (or double) stage, which greatly accelerated and smoothed scene changes. In time came such further discoveries as hydraulic lifts and various uses of electricity that made possible even greater theatrical effects. In fact, as a scene such as the one above suggests, props themselves were often the main attraction: an actual train roaring across the stage, elaborate pyrotechnics (as in *The Octoroon* and other Boucicault plays), and so on. However misplaced, this emphasis was nonetheless a step in the direction of realism, which was carried further by Bronson Howard (pp. 377–452), whose first plays were produced by Daly and whom Daly greatly encouraged and supported in his career as one of America's foremost early dramatists.

Among Daly's greatest contributions to American drama were the shows he produced in his Fifth Avenue Theatre. He disliked the star system, and insisted that his company perform as an ensemble, with no one actor ever gaining special prominence. When Fanny Davenport, John Drew, Clara Morris, and Ada Rehan reached stellar positions, they left his company. He rigorously controlled every element of the production, and his dictatorial but sensitive directing became proverbial.[2] Daly succeeded also in effecting a new style, which dispensed at least partially with the hitherto-fashionable histrionics. Though ridiculed by some for being "underplayed," his productions gained critical acclaim and popular

[2] Eyewitness accounts of these, and, for comparison, the older slapdash rehearsals, may be found in, respectively, Clara Morris's *Life on the Stage* (New York, 1901) and Anna Cora Mowatt's *Autobiography of an Actress; or, Eight Years on the Stage* (Boston, 1854).

support. The popularity of his company, of course, increased when he took it on national tour with his great individual hits, *Frou-Frou* (1870) and *Divorce* (1871).

Although Daly adapted many foreign plays and was also a frequent and prominent producer of Shakespeare, both here and in his London theatre, he also encouraged native dramatists and favored plays with American plots. Among his own plays (nearly one hundred) were a number of "frontier" dramas, of which *Horizon* (1871) was typical of Daly's kind of realistic setting and his attempts at emotional restraint. Dramas set—and featuring the life—in various areas removed from urban or semiurban civilization ("frontier drama"), increasingly popular in the latter part of the century, found expression also in such hits and long stock favorites as *My Partner* (1879) and *The White Slave* (1882), both by Bartley Campbell (1843–1888). The most popular of all "frontier" dramas was F.H. Murdoch's *Davy Crockett* (1872). Until his death in 1896, Frank Mayo played the part of this hero of fact and fiction with enormous success. The climax of the play occurs when Davy rescues the heroine during a blizzard and bars the cabin door with his arm all night, holding off the howling wolves. ("What can save us now?" "The strong arm of a Backwoodsman.") Major literary names are associated with other "frontier" plays, but none of these achieved any real success in the theatre. Bret Harte dramatized some of his stories: with Boucicault, *The Two Men of Sandy Bar* (1876), and with T. Edgar Pemberton, *Sue* (1896). He also collaborated with Mark Twain on *Ah Sin* (1877). Mark Twain's dramatization of *The Gilded Age* (1874) was fairly successful, but a second attempt at a play with the character of Colonel Mulberry Sellers failed.

William Dean Howells collaborated with Mark Twain on this second play, *The American Claimant* (1887). As America's most distinguished champion of nineteenth-century realism, Howells encouraged "realistic" drama and wrote over thirty plays himself, ranging from farces to heroic drama. Two notable farces, *The Mouse Trap* and *The Garroters* (also produced as *A Dangerous Ruffian*), were repeatedly performed both in America and in London in the 1880's and 1890's; the latter was praised by many, including Bernard Shaw. Among Howells's other works are two comedies: *A Counterfeit Presentment* (1877), successfully produced by

Lawrence Barrett, and *The Sleeping Car* (1883). Most of
his plays were one-act farces, popular with amateur companies and readers of the magazines in which they were
published. Despite the skill of their composition, however,
none of his dramatic works achieved the popularity of
Howells's other works.

In the same genre as Howells's farces, but immensely
popular, were the Harrigan and Hart productions of the
1870's and 1880's. Edward Harrigan (1845–1911) wrote and
acted in over eighty vaudeville sketches, some of which were
developed into full-length plays. His partnership with Tony
Hart, the female impersonator of the team, produced the
famous Mulligan plays.[3] *The Mulligan Guard* (1873) was
the first in this series, which featured city types like the Irish,
Negro, Italian, and German, and sharp partisan satires of
city politics and military organizations. Some of the routines
and characters in Harrigan's works are reminiscent of minstrelsy, and the Irish are urban transpositions of Boucicault's
Irish characters. In their focus on low-life, these plays also
follow directly in the footsteps of the Mose plays, which
Chanfrau was then still playing. However, Harrigan strove
for a truer picture of contemporary life and he avoided his
predecessors' romantic characterizations. He wrote in *Harper's Weekly* (February 2, 1889): "Though I use type and
never individuals, I try to be as realistic as possible"—at
least in dress and accouterments. Also of a farcical nature and
as popular as Harrigan's plays were those of Charles Hoyt
(1860–1900). His works too are episodic in format and contemporary in content: politics, sports, women's rights, the
militia, and so on. His most popular play, *A Trip to Chinatown* (1891), holds the nineteenth-century record of a run
of 657 continuous performances; it deals with the escapades
of an assorted group of characters in San Francisco—but
mostly outside of Chinatown.

There were other plays that qualify perhaps only margin-
ally as drama but that found immense favor with theatregoers
in the late decades of the century. No account of the
American drama can ignore the musical comedy, our most
notable contribution to world theatre. *The Black Crook,*

3 See E. J. Kahn, Jr.'s *The Merry Partners: The Age and Stage
of Harrigan and Hart* (New York, 1955).

which still holds the record for its long and extravagant run, has been acclaimed the first "musical comedy," the precursor of the present-day genre. In another genre, what began as a vaudeville sketch for Denman Thompson in 1875, developed by 1886 into a four-act drama, *The Old Homestead*. Until his death in 1911, Thomas played Joshua Whitcomb, the kindly old New England farmer who goes to find and save his city-corrupted son. *The Great Diamond Robbery* (1895), a six-act detective thriller by Edward M. Alfriend and A.C. Wheeler, was one of the great hits for a decade. In the same romantic genre were the plays of the actor–dramatist William Gillette (1855–1937): *Held by the Enemy* (1886), *Secret Service* (1895), and *Sherlock Holmes* (1899). Immensely popular and frequently revived by Gillette, who played the dashing leads, these plays are among the best melodramas written after those of Boucicault; all the same, in accord with the spirit of the times, Gillette stressed the realism of his characters' actions and thoughts by inserting a profusion of details in his stage directions. Then, of course, there was *The Count of Monte Cristo*. James O'Neill began to act the Count in 1883, and eventually decided to confine his considerable acting talents to this great money-maker—a step whose agonizing consequences to himself and his family were immortalized by his son Eugene O'Neill in his masterpiece, *Long Day's Journey Into Night* (1955).

The outstanding power and personality in the theatre after Daly was David Belasco (1859–1931). He too exerted complete control over all phases of his productions and wrote and adapted plays, often with collaborators. He began his career in the 1870's and continued his professional activities until shortly before his death; his career thus spans the mid-nineteenth-century drama of Boucicault—whom he met and by whom he was greatly influenced—and the drama of the 1920's. Belasco was primarily interested in "show business," often in spectacular productions that aimed at incredible scenic realism: he went as far as reproducing, for example, a complete replica of a Childs restaurant on his stage. The scripts of the plays he wrote with Henry C. DeMille—hits like *The Wife* (1887), *Lord Chumley* (1888), and *Men and Women* (1890)—were often worked out during the production and in strict accord with effective theatre. If his nineteenth-century drama is of little permanent significance (his later dramas are historically more important, particularly because of Giacomo Puccini's use of Belasco's scripts for *Madame Butterfly* and *The Girl of the Golden West* as the librettos of his operas), he contributed considerably to the birth of modern drama by his development of realistic scenic and lighting display and, even more important, his ultimately successful struggle with the powerful Klaw-Erlanger Syndicate. In control of most of the theatres across the country, and running a central booking office that decided what productions and actors would play when and where, the Syndicate effectually dominated most of the theatrical activity for a decade at the turn of the century. The only opposition to its stranglehold came from Belasco and a few independent stars, including Sarah Bernhardt, James O'Neill, and Richard Mansfield.

It was Mansfield (who was to introduce Shaw to America in 1894 with *Arms and the Man*) who in 1889 engaged Clyde Fitch (1865–1909) to write for him *Beau Brummell*, a dramatization of the life of the famous Regency dandy who died in poverty. This play launched the career of the most popular turn-of-the-century dramatist, whose great successes came in the next century. But his *The Masked Ball*, a comedy in which John Drew and Maude Adams starred, and two historical plays, *Nathan Hale* and *Barbara Frietchie* (one of Julia Marlowe's early successes), were popular in the 1890's. In subject matter and form these typify the drama in which Fitch was to excel: comedy and history, with an emphasis on human relations but with resolutions that were constructed with a view toward audience approval and theatrical effect rather than historical fact, probability, or what is now called "psychological realism."

Augustus Thomas (1859–1934), the most distinguished playwright at the turn of the century, did most of his best work in the first two decades of this century. Although he occupied Boucicault's one-time post as adapter of foreign plays for the Madison Square Theatre, the very names of his early plays already point to the strongly American character of his works. *Alabama* (1891) deals with reconciliation after the Civil War; *In Mizzoura* (1893), an early "Western" with a love triangle, was written for Nat C. Goodwin, who played the sheriff; *The Capitol* (1895) is a deft mixture of political, economic, and love conflicts; and *Arizona* (1899) deals with the amatory intrigues of various Cavalry officers and their wives. Like Fitch, Thomas focused on human relations within his broad settings. But unlike Fitch, Thomas, despite his propensity for pseudoscience, superficiality, and melodrama, strove for truthful story and character development. He has been credited with being the first dramatist who successfully introduced New York audiences to the "drama of ideas."

"The drama of ideas," "realistic drama," and similar terms have been applied, perhaps wishfully, to various plays written before the end of the century. One of these was the domestic drama *Hazel Kirke* (1880), the most famous of some twenty plays by the stage innovator Steele MacKaye. This play was so great a hit that by 1882–83 fourteen *Hazel Kirke* road companies were touring the country. While the play is a melodrama whose main claim to realism rests on the absence of the old-fashioned villain, the dialogue is relatively constrained, reflecting the change in tastes. As has been seen, realism in scenery had begun even before the Civil War and was greatly developed by Daly and Belasco. The use of common folk like the B'hoys in place of the old-time larger-than-life heroes, and the detailed actions and gestures spelled out for the characters of Gillette's thrillers, carried realism a step further. Yet to be achieved was an inner realism that transcends the format of the "well-made play"—or its American equivalent, which Bronson Howard had defined and utilized so successfully in his dramas. It was James A. Herne—particularly in his *Margaret Fleming*—who for the first time staged drama that dispensed with the neat but conventionally contrived plot development and denouement that followed the theatrical laws of the past.

In *The Theatre Through Its Stage Door* (1919) Belasco described his own method of early scene construction as follows: "I seldom follow the stage directions on the printed page, either of my own plays or those of other dramatists. I prefer to plan the scenes myself with reference to stage values." Nothing contrasts more sharply with this method, particularly as specified in the last five words, than Herne's revision to achieve greater realism in the characters and situations of *Margaret Fleming*. Although our theatre subsequently lost the verve, buoyancy, and audience appeal it so remarkably displayed throughout the nineteenth century, it was this concern with what Herne called "Art for Truth's

Sake" that set the path American drama was to follow, and on which it was to develop and flourish in the twentieth century.

MYRON MATLAW

Queens College of the
City University of New York

FASHION

Preface to FASHION

Fashion; or, Life in New York, America's finest nineteenth-century comedy, is still fun to read—and to see. In a splendid revival in 1959 it was produced with period songs, and it became, in the words of one of the New York theatre critics, "the only successful off-Broadway musical show of the season." An even more successful revival had occurred in New York in 1924, when *Fashion* played for 235 consecutive performances.

The play's première took place at the Park Theatre on March 24, 1845, before an audience of New York's artistic, social, financial, and political *ee-light,* as the play's Mrs. Tiffany would say. In her *Autobiography,* Anna Cora Mowatt (1819–1870)—a lady with social position as well as some literary reputation—rightly alluded to the play as an "unequivocally brilliant success." The house remained packed for three weeks—an unprecedented run for a new play, and a long one for *any* play at the time; and it had equal success in other cities, here and in England. Edgar Allan Poe reviewed it in the *Broadway Journal* at great length on March 29, 1845—and then again a week later, when he had gone back to see the play every day for a total of eight times! Other New York newspapers also devoted more space to the play than they had ever devoted to drama before, rejoicing particularly in the play's American authorship.

Patriotic pride was heightened by the play's satire of affected foreign (French) manners and speech. A new idle wealthy class was rising in New York in the 1840's, and Mrs. Mowatt viewed many of its members' "parvenuisms," as she referred to them, with a mixture of irritation and humor. Both these attitudes may be seen in her characterization of Mrs. Tiffany, a composite of many people she saw about her. In the opening scene the foppish Negro servant Zeke foreshadows the pretentiousness of Mrs. Tiffany, as well as that of Augustus Fogg (the "drawing room appendage") and the daughter, Seraphina. Their model in manners and speech—

the putative French count, Jolimaitre—is, of course, the big-
gest impostor of them all.

Juxtaposed with this drawing-room mélange is the bluff
but honest farmer, Adam Trueman. This stage Yankee is a
character type that had been popular from its inception
as Jonathan in Royall Tyler's *The Contrast*, an eighteenth-
century precursor of *Fashion*. Trueman has the conventional
attributes of this type: a way of forcefully expressing democratic principles at every opportunity, a natural but noble
savagery combined with a heart of gold, New England
peddler shrewdness, and a lack of education and manners.
These attributes are not held up to ridicule; Trueman was,
on the contrary, held up for admiration as an American ideal
and the most appealing character in the play. He was the
only one of the characters who was "sketched from life,"
Mrs. Mowatt relates in her *Autobiography*, and she notes that
"the original was seen in the pit vociferously applauding
Adam Trueman's strictures on fashionable society." His con-
demnations of the hypocrisy and affectation popularly believed to be among the characteristic evils of city life are
echoed by Gertrude, who bitterly contrasts that life with
rural life and the homely virtues that were thought to char-
acterize it.

But edifying though all these sentiments may have been,
it was not they that made this play a hit in the nineteenth
century—and so superior to the many imitations that inevit-
ably sprang up soon—or that make it good reading today. It
is, rather, the vivacity and sureness of the comic touch, which
is perceptible even in the portrayal of the minor and stock
characters: the love-starved, husband-hunting spinster, Prudence; the poet manqué, T. Tennyson Twinkle, vainly trying
to declaim over the distracting household bustle, finally
blurting out his complete poem—two vapid lines; and the
servants, Mrs. Tiffany's low-comic pendant, Zeke (the re-
christened "A-dolph"), and her instructress in French, the
soubrette Millinette. Even the various melodramatic parts, all
deftly constructed, are entertaining.

Mrs. Mowatt wrote other plays, as well as poetry, stories,
and articles; but *Fashion* (first published in 1850) is her best
work. It greatly encouraged American writers by demon-
strating the possibilities inherent in the hitherto despised
native productions, and in native themes. Mrs. Mowatt's

contribution to the American theatre does not end with her authorship of *Fashion*, however, important though that contribution may be. The success of the play and her consequent fame, as well as financial need occasioned by her husband's business failure, started her out on what became a distinguished career as an actress, here and in England—the first American society lady to embark on such a career. Her unexceptionable behavior as an actress, both on stage and off, as well as her energy, dignity, beauty, and charm, were all effective in raising and making respectable the status of what was still considered a fairly disreputable profession. Her importance in our theatrical annals, therefore, transcends her authorship of what is to this day a delightful comedy.

Anna Cora Mowatt's *Autobiography of an Actress; or, Eight Years on the Stage* (1854) is a charming reminiscence; her definitive biography—and also an excellent account of her theatre and milieu—is Eric Wollencott Barnes's *The Lady of Fashion* (1954).

M.M.

FASHION;

or, LIFE IN NEW YORK. A Comedy in Five Acts
By Anna Cora Mowatt

Characters

ADAM TRUEMAN, a farmer from Catteraugus
COUNT JOLIMAITRE, a fashionable European importation
COLONEL HOWARD, an officer in the United States Army
MR. TIFFANY, a New York merchant
T. TENNYSON TWINKLE, a modern poet
AUGUSTUS FOGG, a drawing room appendage
SNOBSON, a rare species of confidential clerk
ZEKE, a colored servant
MRS. TIFFANY, a lady who imagines herself fashionable
PRUDENCE, a maiden lady of a certain age
MILLINETTE, a French lady's maid
GERTRUDE, a governess
SERAPHINA TIFFANY, a belle
LADIES and GENTLEMEN of the Ball-room

PROLOGUE[1]

(Enter a Gentleman, reading a Newspaper.)

" '*Fashion, a Comedy.*' I'll go; but stay—
Now I read farther, 'tis a native play!
Bah! homemade calicoes are well enough,
But homemade dramas *must* be stupid stuff.
Had it the *London* stamp, 'twould do—but then,
For plays, we lack the manners and the men!"
   Thus speaks one critic. Hear another's creed:—
" '*Fashion!*' What's here? (*Reads.*) It never can succeed!
What! from a woman's pen? It takes a man
To write a comedy—no woman can."
   Well, sir, and what say you, and why that frown?
His eyes uprolled, he lays the paper down:—
"Here! take," he says, "the unclean thing away!
'Tis tainted with the notice of a play!"
   But, sir!—but, gentlemen!—you, sir, who think
No comedy can flow from native ink,—
Are we such *perfect* monsters, or such *dull*,
That Wit no traits for ridicule can cull?
Have we no follies here to be redressed?
No vices gibbeted? no crimes confessed?
"But then a female hand can't lay the lash on!"
How know you that, sir, when the theme is FASHION?
   And now, come forth, thou man of sanctity!
How shall I venture a reply to thee?
The Stage—what is it, though beneath thy ban,
But a daguerreotype of life and man?
Arraign poor human nature, if you will,
But let the DRAMA have her mission still;
Let her, with honest purpose, still reflect
The faults which keeneyed Satire may detect.

----

[1] By Epes Sargent (1813–80), Boston author and journalist, and friend of the Mowatt family. He had suggested that she write the play, and later helped with some of the technical details of its composition.

For there *be* men who fear not an hereafter,
Yet tremble at the hell of public laughter!
Friends, from these scoffers we appeal to you!
Condemn the false, but O, applaud the true.
Grant that *some* wit may grow on native soil,
And Art's fair fabric rise from woman's toil.
While we exhibit but to *reprehend*
The social voices, 'tis for *you* to mend!

ACT I

SCENE 1

A *splendid Drawing Room in the House of* MRS.
TIFFANY. *Open folding doors, discovering a Conservatory.
On either side glass windows down to the ground. Doors
on right and left. Mirror, couches, ottomans, a table with
albums, beside it an arm chair.* MILLINETTE *dusting furniture.* ZEKE *in a dashing livery, scarlet coat.*

ZEKE. Dere's a coat to take de eyes ob all Broadway! Ah!
Missy, it am de fixin's dat make de natural *born* gemman.
A libery for ever! Dere's a pair ob insuppressibles to
'stonish de colored population.

MILLINETTE. (*Very politely.*) Oh, *oui*, Monsieur Zeke.
(*Aside.*) I not *comprend* one word he say!

ZEKE. I tell 'ee what, Missy, I'm 'stordinary glad to find dis
a bery 'spectabul like situation! Now, as you've made de
acquaintance ob dis here family, and dere you've had a
supernumerary advantage ob me—seeing dat I only re-
ceibed my appointment dis morning. What I wants to know
is your publicated opinion, privately expressed, ob de
domestic circle.

MILLINETTE. You mean vat *espèce*, vat kind of *personnes* are
Monsieur and Madame Tiffany? Ah! Monsieur is not de
same ting as Madame—not at all.

ZEKE. Well, I s'pose he ain't altogether.

MILLINETTE. Monsieur is man of business, Madame is lady
of fashion. Monsieur make de money, Madame spend it.

Monsieur nobody at all, Madame everybody altogether. Ah! Monsieur Zeke, de money is all dat is *necessaire* in dis country to make one lady of fashion. Oh! it is quite anoder ting in *la belle France!*

ZEKE. A bery lucifer explanation. Well, now we've disposed ob de heads ob de family, who come next?

MILLINETTE. First, dere is Mademoiselle Seraphina Tiffany. Mademoiselle is not at all one proper *personne.* Mademoiselle Seraphina is one coquette. Dat is not de mode in *la belle France*; de ladies, dere, never learn *la coquetrie* until dey do get one husband.

ZEKE. I tell 'ee what, Missy, I disreprobate dat proceeding altogeder!

MILLINETTE. Vait! I have not tell you all *la famille* yet. Dere is Ma'mselle Prudence—Madame's sister, one very *bizarre personne.* Den dere is Ma'mselle Gertrude, but she not anybody at all; she only teach Mademoiselle Seraphina *la musique.*

ZEKE. Well now, Missy, what's your own special defunctions?

MILLINETTE. I not understand, Monsieur Zeke.

ZEKE. Den I'll amplify. What's de nature ob your exclusive services?

MILLINETTE. *Ah, oui! je comprend.* I am Madame's *femme de chambre*—her lady's maid, Monsieur Zeke. I teach Madame *les modes de Paris*, and Madame set de fashion for all New York. You see, Monsieur Zeke, dat it is me, *moi-même*, dat do lead de fashion for all de American *beau monde!*

ZEKE. Yah! yah! yah! I hab de idea by de heel. Well now, p'raps you can 'lustrify my officials?

MILLINETTE. Vat you will have to do? Oh! much tings, much tings. You vait on de table—you tend de door—you clean de boots—you run de errands—you drive de carriage—you rub de horses—you take care of de flowers—you carry de water—you help cook de dinner—you wash de dishes—and den you always remember to do everyting I tell you to!

ZEKE. Wheugh, am dat *all?*

MILLINETTE. All I can tink of now. To-day is Madame's day of reception, and all her grand friends do make her one *petite* visit. You mind run fast ven de bell do ring.

ZEKE. Run? If it wasn't for dese superfluminous trimmings, I tell 'ee what, Missy, I'd run—

MRS. TIFFANY. (*Outside.*) Millinette!

MILLINETTE. Here comes Madame! You better go, Monsieur Zeke.

ZEKE. (*Aside.*) Look ahea, Massa Zeke, doesn't dis open rich!   (*Exit* ZEKE.)

(*Enter* MRS. TIFFANY, *dressed in the most extravagant height of fashion.*)

MRS. TIFFANY. Is everything in order, Millinette? Ah! very elegant, very elegant, indeed! There is a *jenny-says-quoi*[1] look about this furniture—an air of fashion and gentility perfectly bewitching. Is there not, Millinette?

MILLINETTE. Oh, *oui*, Madame!

MRS. TIFFANY. But where is Miss Seraphina? It is twelve o'clock; our visitors will be pouring in, and she has not made her appearance. But I hear that nothing is more fashionable than to keep people waiting.—None but vulgar persons pay any attention to punctuality. Is it not so, Millinette?

MILLINETTE. Quite *comme il faut.*—Great *personnes* always do make little *personnes* wait, Madame.

MRS. TIFFANY. This mode of receiving visitors only upon one specified day of the week is a most convenient custom! It saves the trouble of keeping the house continually in order and of being always dressed. I flatter myself that *I* was the first to introduce it amongst the New York *ee-light*. You are quite sure that it is strictly a Parisian mode, Millinette?

MILLINETTE. Oh, *oui*, Madame; entirely *mode de Paris.*

MRS. TIFFANY. (*Aside.*) This girl is worth her weight in gold. Millinette, how do you say *arm-chair* in French?

MILLINETTE. *Fauteuil*, Madame.

MRS. TIFFANY. *Fo-tool!* That has a foreign—an out-of-the-wayish sound that is perfectly charming—and so genteel! There is something about our American words decidedly vulgar. *Fowtool!* how refined. *Fowtool! Arm-chair!* what a difference.

[1] *Je ne sais quoi*: I know not what; a certain something. The humor stemming from Mrs. Tiffany's consistent mispronunciation of French words is suggested in the spelling here and elsewhere. Another part of the comedy consists, of course, of her overuse—and occasional misuse—of common French expressions.

MILLINETTE. Madame have one charmante pronunciation. *Fowtool* (*Mimicking aside.*) charmante, Madame!

MRS. TIFFANY. Do you think so, Millinette? Well, I believe I have. But a woman of refinement and of fashion can always accommodate herself to everything foreign! And a week's study of that invaluable work—*French Without a Master*, has made me quite at home in the court language of Europe! But where is the new valet? I'm rather sorry that he is black, but to obtain a white American for a domestic is almost impossible; and they call this a free country! What did you say was the name of this new servant, Millinette?

MILLINETTE. He do say his name is Monsieur Zeke.

MRS. TIFFANY. Ezekiel, I suppose. Zeke! Dear me, such a vulgar name will compromise the dignity of the whole family. Can you not suggest something more aristocratic, Millinette? Something *French!*

MILLINETTE. *Oh, oui,* Madame; *Adolph* is one very fine name.

MRS. TIFFANY. A-dolph! Charming! Ring the bell, Millinette! (MILLINETTE *rings the bell.*)
I will change his name immediately, besides giving him a few directions.

(*Enter* ZEKE. MRS. TIFFANY *addresses him with great dignity.*)

Your name, I hear, is *Ezekiel.*—I consider it too plebeian an appellation to be uttered in my presence. In future you are called A-dolph. Don't reply—never interrupt me when I am speaking. A-dolph, as my guests arrive, I desire that you will inquire the name of every person, and then announce it in a loud, clear tone. That is the fashion in Paris. (MILLINETTE *retires up the stage.*)

ZEKE. (*Speaking very loudly.*) Consider de officer discharged, Missus.

MRS. TIFFANY. Silence! Your business is to obey and not to talk.

ZEKE. I'm dumb, Missus!

MRS. TIFFANY. (*Pointing up stage*). A-dolph, place that *fowtool* behind me.

ZEKE. (*Looking about him.*) I habn't got dat far in de dic-

tionary yet. No matter, a genus gets his learning by nature.
(*Takes up the table and places it behind* MRS. TIFFANY,
then expresses in dumb show great satisfaction. MRS. TIF-
FANY, *as she goes to sit, discovers the mistake.*)

MRS. TIFFANY. You dolt! Where have you lived not to know
that *fow-tool* is the French for *arm-chair?* What ignorance!
Leave the room this instant.
(MRS. TIFFANY *draws forward an arm-chair and sits.*
MILLINETTE *comes forward suppressing her merriment at*
ZEKE's *mistake and removes the table.*)

ZEKE. Dem's de defects ob not having a libery education.
(*Exit.*)

(PRUDENCE *peeps in.*)

PRUDENCE. I wonder if any of the fine folks have come yet.
Not a soul—I knew they hadn't. There's Betsy all alone.
(*Walks in.*) Sister Betsy!

MRS. TIFFANY. Prudence! how many times have I desired you
to call me *Elizabeth? Betsy* is the height of vulgarity.

PRUDENCE. Oh! I forgot. Dear me, how spruce we do look
here, to be sure—everything in first rate style now, Betsy.
(MRS. TIFFANY *looks at her angrily.*)
Elizabeth, I mean. Who would have thought, when you
and I were sitting behind that little mahogany-colored
counter, in Canal Street, making up flashy hats and caps—

MRS. TIFFANY. Prudence, *what do* you mean? Millinette, leave
the room.

MILLINETTE. *Oui,* Madame. (MILLINETTE *pretends to arrange
the books upon a side table, but lingers to listen.*)

PRUDENCE. But I always predicted it—I always told you so,
Betsy—I always said you were destined to rise above your
station!

MRS. TIFFANY. Prudence! Prudence! have I not told you that—

PRUDENCE. No, Betsy, it was *I* that told *you,* when we used
to buy our silks and ribbons of Mr. Anthony Tiffany—
"talking Tony," you know we used to call him, and when
you always put on the finest bonnet in our shop to go to
his—and when you stayed so long smiling and chattering
with him, I always told you that *something* would grow
out of it—and didn't it?

MRS. TIFFANY. Millinette, send Seraphina here instantly. Leave the room.

MILLINETTE. *Oui*, Madame. (*Aside.*) So dis Americaine ladi of fashion vas one *milliner?* Oh, vat a fine country for *les marchandes des modes!* I shall send for all my relation by de next packet!

(*Exit* MILLINETTE.)

MRS. TIFFANY. Prudence! never let me hear you mention this subject again. Forget what we *have* been, it is enough to remember that we *are* of the *upper ten thousand!*

(PRUDENCE *goes up and sits down.*)

(*Enter* SERAPHINA, *very extravagantly dressed.*)

MRS. TIFFANY. How bewitchingly you look, my dear! Does Millinette say that that head dress is strictly Parisian?

SERAPHINA. Oh, yes, Mamma, all the rage! They call it a *lady's tarpaulin*, and it is the exact pattern of one worn by the Princess Clementina at the last court ball.

MRS. TIFFANY. Now, Seraphina, my dear, don't be too particular in your attentions to gentlemen not eligible. There is Count Jolimaitre, decidedly the most fashionable foreigner in town—and so refined—so much accustomed to associate with the first nobility in his own country that he can hardly tolerate the vulgarity of Americans in general. You may devote yourself to him. Mrs. Proudacre is dying to become acquainted with him. By the by, if she or her daughters should happen to drop in, be sure you don't introduce them to the Count. It is not the fashion in Paris to introduce—Millinette told me so.

(*Enter* ZEKE.)

ZEKE. (*In a very loud voice.*) Mister T. Tennyson Twinkle!

MRS. TIFFANY. Show him up.

(*Exit* ZEKE.)

PRUDENCE. I must be running away! (*Going.*)

MRS. TIFFANY. Mr. T. Tennyson Twinkle—a very literary young man and a sweet poet! It is all the rage to patronize poets! Quick, Seraphina, hand me that magazine.—Mr. Twinkle writes for it.

(SERAPHINA *hands the magazine,* MRS. TIFFANY *seats herself in an arm-chair and opens the book.*)

PRUDENCE. (*Returning.*) There's Betsy trying to make out that reading without her spectacles. (*Takes a pair of spectacles out of her pocket and hands them to* MRS. TIFFANY.) There, Betsy, I knew you were going to ask for them. Ah! they're a blessing when one is growing old!

MRS. TIFFANY. What do you mean, Prudence? A woman of fashion *never* grows old! Age is always out of fashion.

PRUDENCE. Oh, dear! what a delightful thing it is to be fashionable.

(*Exit* PRUDENCE. MRS. TIFFANY *resumes her seat.*)

(*Enter* TWINKLE. *He salutes* SERAPHINA.)

TWINKLE. Fair Seraphina! the sun itself grows dim,
Unless you aid his light and shine on him!

SERAPHINA. Ah! Mr. Twinkle, there is no such thing as answering you.

TWINKLE. (*Looks around and perceives* MRS. TIFFANY.) (*Aside.*) The *New Monthly Vernal Galaxy.* Reading my verses by all that's charming! Sensible woman! I won't interrupt her.

MRS. TIFFANY. (*Rising and coming forward.*) Ah! Mr. Twinkle, is that you? I was perfectly *abimé* at the perusal of your very *distingué* verses.

TWINKLE. I am overwhelmed, Madam. Permit me. (*Taking the magazine.*) Yes, they do read tolerably. And you must take into consideration, ladies, the rapidity with which they were written. Four minutes and a half by the stop watch! The true test of a poet is the *velocity* with which he composes. Really they do look very prettily, and they read tolerably—*quite* tolerably—*very* tolerably,—especially the first verse. (*Reads.*) "To Seraphina T——."

SERAPHINA. Oh! Mr. Twinkle!

TWINKLE. (*Reads.*) "Around my heart"—

MRS. TIFFANY. How touching! Really, Mr. Twinkle, quite tender!

TWINKLE. (*Recommencing.*) "Around my heart"—

MRS. TIFFANY. Oh, I must tell you, Mr. Twinkle! I heard the other day that poets were the aristocrats of literature.

That's one reason I like them, for I do dote on all aristocracy!

TWINKLE. Oh, Madam, how flattering! Now pray lend me your ears! (*Reads.*) "Around my heart thou weavest"—

SERAPHINA. That is such a *sweet* commencement, Mr. Twinkle!

TWINKLE. (*Aside.*) I wish she wouldn't interrupt me! (*Reads.*) "Around my heart thou weavest a spell"—

MRS. TIFFANY. Beautiful! But excuse me one moment, while I say a word to Seraphina! (*Aside to* SERAPHINA.) Don't be too affable, my dear! Poets are very ornamental appendages to the drawing room, but they are always as poor as their own verses. They don't make eligible husbands!

TWINKLE. (*Aside.*) Confound their interruptions! My dear Madam, unless you pay the utmost attention you cannot catch the ideas. Are you ready? Well, now you shall hear it to the end! (*Reads.*)
"Around my heart thou weavest a spell
"Whose"—

(*Enter* ZEKE.)

ZEKE. Mister Augustus Fogg! (*Aside.*) A bery misty lookin young gemman.

MRS. TIFFANY. Show him up, Adolph!

(*Exit* ZEKE.)

TWINKLE. This is too much!

SERAPHINA. Exquisite verses, Mr. Twinkle—exquisite!

TWINKLE. Ah, lovely Seraphina! your smile of approval transports me to the summit of Olympus.

SERAPHINA. Then I must frown, for I would not send you so far away.

TWINKLE. Enchantress! (*Aside.*) It's all over with her. (*Retire up and converse.*)

MRS. TIFFANY. Mr. Fogg belongs to one of our oldest families; to be sure, he is the most difficult person in the world to entertain, for he never takes the trouble to talk, and never notices anything or anybody—but then I hear that nothing is considered so vulgar as to betray any emotion, or to attempt to render oneself agreeable!

(*Enter* MR. FOGG, *fashionably attired but in very dark clothes.*)

FOGG. (*Bowing stiffly.*) Mrs. Tiffany, your most obedient. Miss Seraphina, yours. How d'ye do, Twinkle?

MRS. TIFFANY. Mr. Fogg, how do you do? Fine weather—delightful, isn't it?

FOGG. I am indifferent to weather, Madam.

MRS. TIFFANY. Been to the opera, Mr. Fogg? I hear that the *bow monde* make their *debutt* there every evening.

FOGG. I consider operas a bore, Madam.

SERAPHINA. (*Advancing.*) You must hear Mr. Twinkle's verses, Mr. Fogg!

FOGG. I am indifferent to verses, Miss Seraphina.

SERAPHINA. But Mr. Twinkle's verses are addressed to me!

TWINKLE. Now pay attention, Fogg! (*Reads*)—
"Around my heart thou weavest a spell
"Whose magic I"—

(*Enter* ZEKE.)

ZEKE. Mister—No, he say he ain't no Mister—

TWINKLE. "Around my heart thou weavest a spell
"Whose magic I can never tell!"

MRS. TIFFANY. Speak in a loud, clear tone, A-dolph!

TWINKLE. This is terrible!

ZEKE. Mister Count Jolly-made-her!

MRS. TIFFANY. Count Jolimaitre! Good gracious! Zeke, Zeke—A-dolph I mean. (*Aside.*) Dear me, what a mistake! Set that chair out of the way—put that table back. Seraphina, my dear, are you all in order? Dear me! dear me! Your dress is so tumbled! (*Arranges her dress.*) What are you grinning at? (*To* ZEKE.) Beg the Count to *honor* us by walking up!

(*Exit* ZEKE.)

Seraphina, my dear (*aside to her*), remember now what I told you about the Count. He is a man of the highest—good gracious! I am so flurried and nothing is so ungenteel as agitation! What will the Count think! Mr. Twinkle, pray stand out of the way! Seraphina, my dear, place yourself on my right! Mr. Fogg, the conservatory—beautiful flowers —pray amuse yourself in the conservatory.

FOGG. I am indifferent to flowers, Madam.

MRS. TIFFANY. (*Aside.*) Dear me! the man stands right in the way—just where the Count must make his *entray!* Mr. Fogg—pray—

(*Enter* COUNT JOLIMAITRE, *very dashingly dressed, wears a moustache.*)

MRS. TIFFANY. Oh, Count, this unexpected honor—

SERAPHINA. Count, this inexpressible pleasure—

COUNT. Beg you won't mention it, Madam! Miss Seraphina, your most devoted! (*Crosses.*)

MRS. TIFFANY. (*Aside.*) What condescension! Count, may I take the liberty to introduce—(*Aside.*) Good gracious! I forgot. Count, I was about to remark that we never introduce in America. All our fashions are foreign, Count.

(TWINKLE, *who has stepped forward to be introduced, shows great indignation.*)

COUNT. Excuse me, Madame, our fashions have grown antediluvian before you Americans discover their existence. You are lamentably behind the age—lamentably! 'Pon my honor, a foreigner of refinement finds great difficulty in existing in this provincial atmosphere.

MRS. TIFFANY. How dreadful, Count! I am very much concerned. If there is anything which I can do, Count—

SERAPHINA. Or I, Count, to render your situation less deplorable—

COUNT. Ah! I find but one redeeming charm in America—the superlative loveliness of the feminine portion of creation. (*Aside.*) And the wealth of their obliging papas.

MRS. TIFFANY. How flattering! Ah! Count, I am afraid you will turn the head of my simple girl here. She is a perfect child of nature, Count.

COUNT. Very possibly, for though you American women are quite charming, yet, demme, there's a deal of native rust to rub off!

MRS. TIFFANY. *Rust?* Good gracious, Count! where do you find any rust? (*Looking about the room.*)

COUNT. How very unsophisticated!

MRS. TIFFANY. Count, I am so much ashamed—pray excuse me! Although a lady of large fortune, and one, Count, who can boast of the highest connections, I blush to confess that I have never travelled, while you, Count, I presume are at home in all the courts of Europe.

COUNT. *Courts?* Eh? Oh, yes, Madam, very true. I believe I am pretty well known in some of the courts of Europe (*Aside, crossing.*)—*police courts.* In a word, Madam, I had seen enough of civilized life—wanted to refresh myself by a sight of barbarous countries and customs—had my choice between the Sandwich Islands and New York—chose New York!

MRS. TIFFANY. How complimentary to our country! And, Count, I have no doubt you speak every conceivable language? You talk English like a native.

COUNT. Eh, what? Like a native? Oh, ah, demme, yes, I am something of an Englishman. Passed one year and eight months with the Duke of Wellington, six months with Lord Brougham, two and a half with Count d'Orsay—knew them all more intimately than their best friends—no heroes to me—hadn't a secret from me, I assure you. (*Aside.*) *Especially of the toilet.*

MRS. TIFFANY. (*Aside to* SERAPHINA.) Think of that, my dear! Lord Wellington and Duke Broom!

SERAPHINA. (*Aside to* MRS. TIFFANY.) And only think of Count d'Orsay, Mamma! I am so wild to see Count d'Orsay!

COUNT. Oh! a mere man milliner. Very little refinement out of Paris! Why, at the very last dinner given at Lord—Lord Knowswho, would you believe it, Madam, there was an individual present who wore a *black* cravat and took *soup twice!*

MRS. TIFFANY. How shocking! The sight of him would have spoilt my appetite! (*Aside to* SERAPHINA.) Think what a great man he must be, my dear, to despise lords and counts in that way. (*Aside.*) I must leave them together. Mr. Twinkle, your arm. I have some really very *foreign exotics* to show you.

TWINKLE. I fly at your command. (*Aside, and glancing at the* COUNT.) I wish all her exotics were blooming in their native soil!

MRS. TIFFANY. Mr. Fogg, will you accompany us? My conservatory is well worthy a visit. It cost an immense sum of money.

FOGG. I am indifferent to conservatories, Madam; flowers are such a bore!

MRS. TIFFANY. I shall take no refusal. Conservatories are all the rage—I could not exist without mine! Let me show you —let me show you.

(*Places her arm through* MR. FOGG'S, *without his consent. Exeunt* MRS. TIFFANY, FOGG, *and* TWINKLE *into the conservatory, where they are seen walking about.*)

SERAPHINA. America, then, has no charms for you, Count?

COUNT. Excuse me, some exceptions. I find you, for instance, particularly charming! Can't say I admire your country. Ah! if you had ever breathed the exhilarating air of Paris, ate creams at Tortoni's, dined at the Café Royale, or if you had lived in London—felt at home at St. James's, and every afternoon driven a couple of Lords and a Duchess through Hyde Park, you would find America—where you have no kings, queens, lords, nor ladies—insupportable!

SERAPHINA. Not while there was a Count in it?

(*Enter* ZEKE, *very indignant.*)

ZEKE. Where's de Missus?

(*Enter* MRS. TIFFANY, FOGG, *and* TWINKLE, *from the conservatory.*)

MRS. TIFFANY. Whom do you come to announce, A-dolph?

ZEKE. He said he wouldn't trust me—no, not eben wid so much as his name; so I wouldn't trust him up stairs, den he ups wid *his stick* and I *cuts mine.*

MRS. TIFFANY. (*Aside.*) Some of Mr. Tiffany's vulgar acquaintances. I shall die with shame. A-dolph, inform him that I am *not at home.*

(*Exit* ZEKE.)

My nerves are so shattered, I am ready to sink. Mr. Twinkle, that *fow tool,* if you please!

TWINKLE. What? What do you wish, Madam?

MRS. TIFFANY. (*Aside.*) The ignorance of these Americans! Count, may I trouble you? That *fow tool,* if you please!

COUNT. (*Aside.*) She's not talking English, nor French, but
I suppose it's American.

TRUEMAN. (*Outside.*) Not at home!

ZEKE. No, Sar—Missus say she's not at home.

TRUEMAN. Out of the way, you grinning nigger!

(*Enter* ADAM TRUEMAN, *dressed as a farmer, a stout cane
in his hand, his boots covered with dust.* ZEKE *jumps out
of his way as he enters.*)
(*Exit* ZEKE.)

TRUEMAN. Where's this woman that's not *at home* in her own
house? May I be shot if I wonder at it! I shouldn't think
she'd ever feel *at home* in such a show-box as this! (*Looking round.*)

MRS. TIFFANY. (*Aside.*) What a plebeian looking old farmer!
I wonder who he is? Sir—(*Advancing very agitatedly.*)
what do you mean, Sir, by this *ow*dacious conduct? How
dare you intrude yourself into my parlor? Do you know
who I am, Sir? (*With great dignity.*) You are in the
presence of Mrs. Tiffany, Sir!

TRUEMAN. Antony's wife, eh? Well now, I might have guessed
that—ha! ha! ha! for I see you make it a point to carry
half your husband's shop upon your back! No matter; that's
being a good helpmate, for he carried the whole of it once
in a pack on his own shoulders; now you bear a share!

MRS. TIFFANY. How dare you, you impertinent, *ow*dacious,
ignorant old man! It's all an invention. You're talking of
somebody else. (*Aside.*) What will the Count think!

TRUEMAN. Why, I thought folks had better manners in the
city! This is a civil welcome for your husband's old friend,
and after my coming all the way from Catteraugus[1] to see
you and yours! First a grinning nigger tricked out in scarlet
regimentals—

MRS. TIFFANY. Let me tell you, Sir, that liveries are all the
fashion!

TRUEMAN. The fashion, are they? To make men wear the
badge of servitude in a free land, that's the fashion, is it?

[1] Catteraugus County is in the western part of the state of
New York.

Hurrah for republican simplicity! I will venture to say now that you have your coat of arms too!

MRS. TIFFANY. Certainly, Sir; you can see it on the panels of my *voyture*.[1]

TRUEMAN. Oh! no need of that. I know what your escutcheon must be! A band-box *rampant* with a bonnet *couchant*, and a peddlar's pack *passant*! Ha, ha, ha! that shows both houses united!

MRS. TIFFANY. Sir! you are most profoundly ignorant—what do you mean by this insolence, Sir? (*Aside.*) How shall I get rid of him?

TRUEMAN. (*Looking at* SERAPHINA.) I hope that is not Gertrude!

MRS. TIFFANY. Sir, I'd have you know that—Seraphina, my child, walk with the gentlemen into the conservatory.
(*Exeunt* SERAPHINA, TWINKLE, FOGG *into conservatory.*)
Count Jolimaitre, pray make due allowances for the errors of this rustic! I do assure you, Count— (*Whispers to him.*)

TRUEMAN. (*Aside.*) "Count"! She calls that critter with a shoe brush over his mouth "Count"! To look at him, I should have thought he was a tailor's walking advertisement!

COUNT. (*Addressing* TRUEMAN *whom he has been inspecting through his eyeglass.*) Where did you say you belonged, my friend? Dug out of the ruins of Pompeii, eh?

TRUEMAN. I belong to a land in which I rejoice to find that you are a foreigner.

COUNT. What a barbarian! He doesn't see the honor I'm doing his country! Pray, Madam, is it one of the aboriginal inhabitants of the soil? To what tribe of Indians does he belong—the Pawnee or Choctaw? Does he carry a tomahawk?

TRUEMAN. Something quite as useful—do you see that? (*Shaking his stick.*)
(COUNT *runs behind* MRS. TIFFANY.)

MRS. TIFFANY. Oh, dear! I shall faint! Millinette! (*Approaching.*) Millinette!

(*Enter* MILLINETTE, *without advancing into the room.*)

---

[1] *Voiture*: carriage.

MILLINETTE. *Oui,* Madame.

MRS. TIFFANY. A glass of water!

(*Exit* MILLINETTE.)

Sir, (*Crossing to* TRUEMAN.) I am shocked at your plebeian
conduct! Tis is a gentleman of the highest standing, Sir!
He is a *Count,* Sir!

(*Enter* MILLINETTE, *bearing a salver with a glass of water.
In advancing towards* MRS. TIFFANY, *she passes in front of
the* COUNT, *starts and screams. The* COUNT, *after a start of
surprise, regains his composure, plays with his eye glass,
and looks perfectly unconcerned.*)

MRS. TIFFANY. What is the matter? What *is* the matter?

MILLINETTE. Noting, noting, only— (*Looks at* COUNT *and
turns away her eyes again.*) only—noting at all!

TRUEMAN. Don't be afraid, girl! Why, did you never see a
live Count before? He's tame—I dare say your mistress
there leads him about by the ears.

MRS. TIFFANY. This is too much! Millinette, send for Mr.
Tiffany instantly!

(*Crosses to* MILLINETTE, *who is going.*)

MILLINETTE. He just come in, Madame!

TRUEMAN. My old friend! Where is he? Take me to him; I
long to have one more hearty shake of the hand!

MRS. TIFFANY. (*Crosses to him.*) Count, honor me by joining
my daughter in the conservatory; I will return immediately.
(COUNT *bows and walks towards conservatory,* MRS. TIF-
FANY *following part of the way and then returning to*
TRUEMAN.)

TRUEMAN. What a Jezebel! These women always play the
very devil with a man, and yet I don't believe such a
damaged bale of goods as *that* (*Looking at* MRS. TIFFANY.)
has smothered the heart of little Antony!

MRS. TIFFANY. This way, Sir, *sal vous plait.*

(*Exit with great dignity.*)

TRUEMAN. *Sal vous plait.* Ha, ha, ha! We'll see what Fashion
has done for him. (*Exit.*)

ACT II

SCENE 1

Inner apartment of MR. TIFFANY's *Counting House.* MR.
TIFFANY, *seated at a desk looking over papers.* MR. SNOBSON,
on a high stool at another desk, with a pen behind his ear.

SNOBSON. (*Rising, advances to the front of the stage, regards*
TIFFANY *and shrugs his shoulders. Aside.*) How the old
boy frets and fumes over those papers, to be sure! He's
working himself into a perfect fever—ex-actly; therefore
bleeding's the prescription! So here goes! Mr. Tiffany, a
word with you, if you please, Sir?

TIFFANY. (*Sitting still.*) Speak on, Mr. Snobson, I attend.

SNOBSON. What I have to say, Sir, is a matter of the first
importance to the credit of the concern—the *credit* of the
concern, Mr. Tiffany!

TIFFANY. Proceed, Mr. Snobson.

SNOBSON. Sir, you've a handsome house—fine carriage—nigger
in livery—feed on the fat of the land—everything first rate—

TIFFANY. Well, Sir?

SNOBSON. My salary, Mr. Tiffany!

TIFFANY. It has been raised three times within the last year.

SNOBSON. Still it is insufficient for the necessities of an honest
man; mark me, an *honest* man, Mr. Tiffany.

TIFFANY. (*Crossing. Aside.*) What a weapon he has made of
that word! Enough—another hundred shall be added. Does
that content you?

SNOBSON. There is one other subject, which I have before
mentioned, Mr. Tiffany: your daughter. What's the reason
you can't let the folks at home know at once that I'm to be
the man?

TIFFANY. (*Aside.*) Villain! And must the only seal upon this
scoundrel's lips be placed there by the hand of my daughter? Well, Sir, it shall be as you desire.

SNOBSON. And Mrs. Tiffany shall be informed of your resolu-
tion?

TIFFANY. Yes.

SNOBSON. Enough said! That's the ticket! The CREDIT *of the concern's safe*, Sir! (*Returns to his seat.*)

TIFFANY. (*Aside.*) How low have I bowed to this insolent rascal! To rise himself he mounts upon my shoulders, and unless I can shake him off he must crush me!

(*Enter* TRUEMAN.)

TRUEMAN. Here I am, Antony, man! I told you I'd pay you a visit in your money-making quarters. (*Looks around.*) But it looks as dismal here as a cell in the States' prison!

TIFFANY. (*Forcing a laugh.*) Ha, ha, ha! States' prison! You are so facetious! Ha, ha, ha!

TRUEMAN. Well, for the life of me I can't see anything so amusing in that! I should think the States' prison plaguy uncomfortable lodgings. And you laugh, man, as though you fancied yourself there already.

TIFFANY. Ha, ha, ha!

TRUEMAN. (*Imitating him.*) Ha, ha, ha! What on earth do you mean by that ill-sounding laugh, that has nothing of a laugh about it! This *fashion*-worship has made heathens and hypocrites of you all! *Deception* is your household God! A man laughs as if he were crying, and cries as if he were laughing in his sleeve. Everything is something else from what it seems to be. I have lived in your house only three days, and I've heard more lies than were ever invented during a Presidential election! First your fine lady of a wife sends me word that she's not at home—I walk up stairs, and she takes good care that *I* shall not be *at home*—wants to turn me out of doors. Then *you* come in—take your old friend by the hand—whisper, the deuce knows what, in your wife's ear, and the tables are turned in a tangent! Madam curtsies—says she's enchanted to see me—and orders her grinning nigger to show me a room.

TIFFANY. We were exceedingly happy to welcome you as our guest!

TRUEMAN. Happy? *You* happy? Ah, Antony! Antony! that hatchet face of yours and those criss-cross furrows tell quite another story! It's many a long day since you were *happy* at anything! You look as if you'd melted down your flesh into dollars, and mortgaged your soul in the bargain!

Your warm heart has grown cold over your ledger—your
light spirits heavy with calculation! You have traded away
your youth—your hopes—your tastes, for wealth! and now
you *have* the wealth you coveted, what does it profit you?
Pleasure it cannot buy, for you have lost your *capacity* for
enjoyment. Ease it will not bring, for the love of gain is
never satisfied! It has made your counting-house a peni-
tentiary, and your home a fashionable *museum* where
there is no niche for you! You have spent so much time
ciphering in the one, that you find yourself at last a very
cipher in the other! See me, man! Seventy-two last August!—Strong as a hickory and every whit as sound!

TIFFANY. I take the greatest pleasure in remarking your
superiority, Sir.

TRUEMAN. Bah! no man takes pleasure in remarking the
superiority of another! Why the deuce can't you speak the
truth, man? But it's not the *fashion*, I suppose! I have not
seen one frank, open face since—no, no, I can't say that
either, though lying *is* catching! There's that girl, Gertrude,
who is trying to teach your daughter music—but Gertrude
was bred in the country!

TIFFANY. A good girl; my wife and daughter find her very
useful.

TRUEMAN. Useful? Well, I must say you have queer notions
of *use!*—But come, cheer up, man! I'd rather see one of
your old smiles than know you'd realized another thousand! I hear you are making money on the true, American,
high pressure system! Better go slow and sure—the more
steam, the greater danger of the boiler's bursting! All
sound, I hope? Nothing rotten at the core?

TIFFANY. Oh, sound—quite sound!

TRUEMAN. Well, that's pleasant—though I must say you don't
look very pleasant about it!

TIFFANY. My good friend, although I am solvent, I may say,
perfectly solvent—yet you—the fact is, you can be of some
assistance to me!

TRUEMAN. That's the *fact* is it? I'm glad we've hit upon one
fact at last! Well—

(SNOBSON, *who during this conversation has been employed
in writing, but stops occasionally to listen, now gives vent
to a dry chuckling laugh.*)

TRUEMAN. Hey? What's that? Another of those deuced ill-

sounding city laughs! (*Sees* SNOBSON.) Who's that perched
up on the stool of repentance—eh, Antony?

SNOBSON. (*Aside and looking at* TIFFANY'S *seat.*) The old
boy has missed his text there—*that's* the stool of repentance!

TIFFANY. One of my clerks—my confidential clerk.

TRUEMAN. Confidential? Why he looks for all the world like
a spy—the most inquisitorial, hang-dog face—ugh! The
sight of it makes my blood run cold! Come, (*Crosses.*) let
us talk over matters where this critter can't give us the
benefit of his opinion! Antony, the next time you choose a
confidential clerk, take one that carries his credentials in
his face—those in his pocket are not worth much without!
(*Exeunt* TRUEMAN *and* TIFFANY.)

SNOBSON. (*Jumping from his stool and advancing.*) The old
prig has got the tin, or Tiff would never be so civil! All
right—Tiff will work every shiner into the concern—all the
better for me! Now I'll go and make love to Seraphina.
The old woman needn't try to knock me down with any of
her French lingo! Six months from today if I ain't driving
my two footmen tandem, down Broadway—and as fashionable as Mrs. Tiffany herself—then I ain't the trump I
thought I was, that's all! (*Looks at his watch.*) Bless me!
eleven o'clock and I haven't had my julep yet! Snobson,
I'm ashamed of you! (*Exit.*)

SCENE 2

*The interior of a beautiful conservatory; walk through the
center; stands of flower pots in bloom; a couple of rustic seats.*
GERTRUDE, *attired in white, with a white rose in her hair,
watering the flowers.* COLONEL HOWARD *regarding her.*

HOWARD. I am afraid you lead a sad life here, Miss Gertrude?

GERTRUDE. (*Turning round gaily.*) What! amongst the flowers? (*Continues her occupation.*)

HOWARD. No, amongst the thistles, with which Mrs. Tiffany
surrounds you; the tempests, which her temper raises!

GERTRUDE. They never harm me. Flowers and herbs are excellent tutors. I learn prudence from the reed, and bend
until the storm has swept over me!

HOWARD. Admirable philosophy! But still, this frigid atmosphere of fashion must be uncongenial to you? Accustomed to the pleasant companionship of your kind friends in Geneva,[1] surely you must regret this cold exchange?

GERTRUDE. Do you think so? Can you suppose that I could possibly prefer a ramble in the woods to a promenade in Broadway? A wreath of scented wild flowers to a bouquet of these sickly exotics? The odor of new-mown hay to the heated air of this crowded conservatory? Or can you imagine that I could enjoy the quiet conversation of my Geneva friends more than the edifying chit-chat of a fashionable drawing room? But I see you think me totally destitute of taste?

HOWARD. You have a merry spirit to jest thus at your grievances!

GERTRUDE. I have my *mania*—as some wise person declares that all mankind have—and mine is a love of independence! In Geneva, my wants were supplied by two kind old maiden ladies, upon whom I know not that I have any claim. I had abilities, and desired to use them. I came here at my own request; for here I am no longer *dependent!* *Voila tout*, as Mrs. Tiffany would say.

HOWARD. Believe me, I appreciate the confidence you repose in me!

GERTRUDE. Confidence! Truly, Colonel Howard, the *confidence* is entirely on your part, in supposing that I confide that which I have no reason to conceal! I think I informed you that Mrs. Tiffany only received visitors on her reception day; she is therefore not prepared to see you. Zeke—Oh! I beg his pardon—Adolph, made some mistake in admitting you.

HOWARD. Nay, Gertrude, it was not Mrs. Tiffany, nor Miss Tiffany, whom I came to see; it—it was—

GERTRUDE. The conservatory perhaps? I will leave you to examine the flowers at leisure! (*Crosses.*)

HOWARD. Gertrude—listen to me. (*Aside.*) If I only dared to give utterance to what is hovering upon my lips! Gertrude!

GERTRUDE. Colonel Howard!

HOWARD. Gertrude, I must—must—

GERTRUDE. Yes, indeed you *must*, must leave me! I think I

[1] Geneva, New York.

hear somebody coming—Mrs. Tiffany would not be well
pleased to find you here—pray, pray leave me—that door
will lead you into the street.
(*Hurries him out through door; takes up her watering pot,
and commences watering flowers, tying up branches, etc.*)
What a strange being is man! Why should he hesitate to
say—nay, why should I prevent his saying, what I would
most delight to hear? Truly man *is* strange—but woman is
quite   as   incomprehensible!   (*Walks   about   gathering
flowers.*)

(*Enter* COUNT JOLIMAITRE.)

COUNT. There she is—the bewitching little creature! Mrs.
Tiffany and her daughter are out of earshot. I caught a
glimpse of their feathers floating down Broadway, not ten
minutes ago. Just the opportunity I have been looking for!
Now for an engagement with this captivating little piece
of prudery! 'Pon honor, I am almost afraid she will not
resist a *Count* long enough to give value to the conquest.
(*Approaching her.*) *Ma belle petite*, were you gathering
roses for me?

GERTRUDE. (*Starts on first perceiving him, but instantly regains her self-possession.*) The roses here, Sir, are carefully
guarded with thorns—if you have the right to gather, pluck
for yourself!

COUNT. Sharp as ever, little Gertrude! But now that we are
alone, throw off this frigidity, and be at your ease.

GERTRUDE. Permit me to *be alone*, Sir, that I *may* be at my
ease!

COUNT. Very good, *ma belle*, well said! (*Applauding her with
his hands.*) Never yield too soon, even to a *title!* But as the
old girl may find her way back before long, we may as
well come to particulars at once. I love you; but that you
know already. (*Rubbing his eyeglass unconcernedly with
his handkerchief.*) Before long I shall make Mademoiselle
Seraphina my wife, and, of course, you shall remain in the
family!

GERTRUDE. (*Indignantly.*) Sir—

COUNT. 'Pon my honor you shall! In France we arrange these
little matters without difficulty!

GERTRUDE. But I am an *American!* Your conduct proves that you are not one! (*Going, crosses.*)

COUNT. (*Preventing her.*) Don't run away, my immaculate *petite Americaine!* Demme, you've quite overlooked my condescension—the difference of our stations—you a species of upper servant—an orphan—no friends.

(*Enter* TRUEMAN *unperceived.*)

GERTRUDE. And therefore more entitled to the respect and protection of every *true gentleman!* Had you been one, you would not have insulted me!

COUNT. My charming little orator, patriotism and declamation become you particularly! (*Approaches her.*) I feel quite tempted to taste—

TRUEMAN. (*Thrusting him aside.*) An American hickory-switch! (*Strikes him.*) Well, how do you like it?

COUNT. (*Aside.*) Old matter-of-fact! Sir, how dare you?

TRUEMAN. My stick has answered that question!

GERTRUDE. Oh! now I am quite safe!

TRUEMAN. Safe! not a bit safer than before! All women would be safe, if they knew how virtue became them! As for you, Mr. Count, what have you to say for yourself? Come, speak out!

COUNT. Sir,—aw—aw—you don't understand these matters!

TRUEMAN. That's a fact! Not having had *your* experience, I don't believe I *do* understand them!

COUNT. A piece of pleasantry—a mere joke—

TRUEMAN. A joke was it? I'll show you a joke worth two of that! I'll teach you the way we natives joke with a puppy who don't respect an honest woman! (*Seizing him.*)

COUNT. Oh! oh! demme—you old ruffian! let me go. What do you mean?

TRUEMAN. Oh! a piece of pleasantry—a mere joke—very pleasant isn't it?

(*Attempts to strike him again;* COUNT *struggles with him. Enter* MRS. TIFFANY *hastily, in her bonnet and shawl.*)

MRS. TIFFANY. What is the matter? I am perfectly *abimé* with terror. Mr. Trueman, what has happened?

TRUEMAN. Oh! we have been *joking!*

MRS. TIFFANY. (*To* COUNT, *who is re-arranging his dress.*) My dear Count, I did not expect to find you here—how kind of you!

TRUEMAN. Your *dear* Count has been showing his *kindness* in a very *foreign* manner. Too *foreign*, I think, he found it to be relished by an *unfashionable native!* What do you think of a puppy who insults an innocent girl all in the way of *kindness?* This Count of yours—this importation of—

COUNT. My dear Madam, demme, permit me to explain. It would be unbecoming—demme—particular unbecoming of you—aw—aw—to pay any attention to this ignorant person. (*Crosses to* TRUEMAN.) Anything that he says concerning a man of my standing—aw—the truth is, Madam—

TRUEMAN. Let us have the truth by all means—if it is only for novelty's sake!

COUNT. (*Turning his back to* TRUEMAN.) You see, Madam, hoping to obtain a few moments' private conversation with Miss Seraphina—with *Miss Seraphina* I say and—aw—and knowing her passion for flowers, I found my way to your very tasteful and *recherché* conservatory. (*Looks about him approvingly.*) *Very* beautifully arranged—does you great credit, Madame! Here I encountered this young person. She was inclined to be talkative; and I indulged her with—with a —aw—demme—a few *common places!* What passed between us was mere *harmless badinage*—on *my* part. You, Madame, you—so conversant with our European manners—you are aware that when a man of fashion—that is, when a woman—a man is bound—amongst noblemen, you know—

MRS. TIFFANY. I comprehend you perfectly—*parfittement*, my dear Count.

COUNT. (*Aside.*) 'Pon my honor, that's very obliging of her.

MRS. TIFFANY. I am shocked at the plebeian forwardness of this conceited girl!

TRUEMAN. (*Walking up to* COUNT.) Did you ever keep a reckoning of the lies you tell in an hour?

MRS. TIFFANY. Mr. Trueman, I blush for you! (*Crosses to* TRUEMAN.)

TRUEMAN. Don't do that—you have no blushes to spare!

MRS. TIFFANY. It is a man of rank whom you are addressing, Sir!

TRUEMAN. A rank villain, Mrs. Antony Tiffany! A *rich one* he would be, had he as much *gold* as *brass!*

MRS. TIFFANY. Pray pardon him, Count; he knows nothing of *how ton!*

COUNT. Demme, he's beneath my notice. I tell you what, old fellow—(TRUEMAN *raises his stick as* COUNT *approaches, the latter starts back.*) the sight of him discomposes me— aw—I feel quite uncomfortable—aw—let us join your charming daughter? (*To* TRUEMAN.) I can't do you the honor to shoot you, Sir—you are beneath me—a nobleman can't fight a commoner! Good bye, old Truepenny! I—aw—I'm insensible to your insolence!

(*Exeunt* COUNT *and* MRS. TIFFANY.)

TRUEMAN. You won't be insensible to a cowhide in spite of your nobility! The next time he practices any of his foreign fashions on you, Gertrude, you'll see how I'll wake up his sensibilities!

GERTRUDE. I do not know what I should have done without you, Sir.

TRUEMAN. Yes, you do—you know that you would have done well enough! Never tell a lie, girl! not even for the sake of pleasing an old man! When you open your lips let your heart speak. Never tell a lie! Let your face be the looking-glass of your soul—your heart its clock—while your tongue rings the hours! But the glass must be clear, the clock true, and then there's no fear but the tongue will do its duty in a woman's head!

GERTRUDE. You are very good, Sir!

TRUEMAN. That's as it may be!—(*Aside.*) How my heart warms towards her! Gertrude, I hear that you have no mother?

GERTRUDE. Ah! no, Sir; I wish I had.

TRUEMAN. (*Aside, and with emotion.*) So do I! Heaven knows, so do I! And you have no father, Gertrude?

GERTRUDE. No, Sir—I often wish I had!

TRUEMAN. (*Hurriedly.*) Don't do that, girl! don't do that! Wish you had a mother—but never wish that you had a father again! Perhaps the one you had did not deserve such a child!

(*Enter* PRUDENCE.)

PRUDENCE. Seraphina is looking for you, Gertrude.

GERTRUDE. I will go to her. (*Crosses.*) Mr. Trueman, you will

not permit me to thank you, but you cannot prevent my
gratitude! (*Exit.*)

TRUEMAN. (*Looking after her.*) If falsehood harbors there,
I'll give up searching after truth! (*Crosses, retires up the
stage musingly, and commences examining the flowers.*)

PRUDENCE. (*Aside.*) What a nice old man he is, to be sure! I
wish he would say something! (*Crosses, walks after him,
turning when he turns; after a pause.*)
Don't mind *me*, Mr. Trueman!

TRUEMAN. Mind you? Oh! no, don't be afraid (*Crosses.*)—I
wasn't minding you. Nobody seems to mind you much!
(*Continues walking and examining the flowers*—PRUDENCE
follows.)

PRUDENCE. Very pretty flowers, ain't they? Gertrude takes
care of them.

TRUEMAN. Gertrude? So I hear—(*advancing*) I suppose you
can tell me now who this Gertrude—

PRUDENCE. Who she's in love with? I *knew* you were going
to say that! I'll tell you all about it! Gertrude, she's in love
with—Mr. Twinkle! and he's in love with her. And Seraphina she's in love with Count Jolly—what-d'ye-call-it; but
Count Jolly don't take to her at all—but Colonel Howard—
he's the man—he's desperate about her!

TRUEMAN. Why you feminine newspaper! Howard in love
with that quintessence of affectation! Howard—the only
frank, straightforward fellow that I've met since—I'll tell
him my mind on the subject! And Gertrude hunting for
happiness in a rhyming dictionary! The girl's a greater
fool than I took her for! (*Crosses.*)

PRUDENCE. So she is; you see I know all about them!

TRUEMAN. I see you do! You've a wonderful knowledge—
wonderful—of *other people's concerns!* It may do here, but
take my word for it, in the county of Catteraugus you'd
get the name of a great *busybody.* But perhaps you know
that too?

PRUDENCE. Oh! I always know what's coming. I feel it before-
hand all over me. I knew something was going to happen
the day you came here—and what's more I can always tell
a married man from a single—I felt right off that you were
a bachelor!

TRUEMAN. Felt right off I was a bachelor did you? You were
sure of it—sure?—quite sure?

(*Prudence assents delightedly.*)
Then you felt wrong!—A bachelor and a widower are not
the same thing!

PRUDENCE. Oh! but it all comes to the same thing—a widower's as good as a bachelor any day! And besides I knew
that you were a farmer *right off.*

TRUEMAN. On the spot, eh? I suppose you saw cabbages and
green peas growing out of my hat?

PRUDENCE. No, I didn't—but I knew all about you. And I
knew—(*Looking down and fidgeting with her apron.*) I
knew you were for getting married soon! For last night I
dreamt I saw your funeral going along the streets, and the
mourners all dressed in white. And a funeral is a sure sign
of a wedding, you know! (*Nudging him with her elbow.*)

TRUEMAN. (*Imitating her voice.*) Well, I can't say that I
know any such thing! you know! (*Nudging her back.*)

PRUDENCE. Oh! it does, and there's no getting over it! For
my part, I like farmers—and I know all about setting hens
and turkeys, and feeding chickens, and laying eggs, and
all that sort of thing!

TRUEMAN. (*Aside.*) May I be shot if mistress newspaper is
not putting in an advertisement for herself! This is your
city mode of courting I suppose, ha, ha, ha!

PRUDENCE. I've been west, a little; but I never was in the
county of Catteraugus, myself.

TRUEMAN. Oh! you were not? And you have taken a particular fancy to go there, eh?

PRUDENCE. Perhaps I shouldn't object—

TRUEMAN. Oh!—ah!—so I suppose. Now pay attention to what
I am going to say, for it is a matter of great importance
to yourself.

PRUDENCE. (*Aside.*) Now it's coming—I know what he's going
to say!

TRUEMAN. The next time you want to tie a man for life to
your apron-strings, pick out one that don't come from the
county of Catteraugus—for greenhorns are scarce in those
parts, and modest women plenty! (*Exit.*)

PRUDENCE. Now who'd have thought he was going to say
that! But I won't give him up yet—I won't give him up.
(*Exit.*)

ACT III

Scene 1

MRS. TIFFANY'S *Parlor. Enter* MRS. TIFFANY, *followed by* MR. TIFFANY.

TIFFANY. Your extravagance will ruin me, Mrs. Tiffany!

MRS. TIFFANY. And your stinginess will ruin me, Mr. Tiffany! It is totally and *toot a fate* impossible to convince you of the necessity of *keeping up appearances*. There is a certain display which every woman of fashion is forced to make!

TIFFANY. And pray who made *you* a woman of fashion?

MRS. TIFFANY. What a vulgar question! All women of fashion, Mr. Tiffany—

TIFFANY. In this land are *self-constituted*, like you, Madam— and *fashion* is the cloak for more sins than charity ever covered! It was for *fashion's* sake that you insisted upon my purchasing this expensive house! It was for *fashion's* sake that you ran me in debt at every exorbitant upholsterer's and extravagant furniture warehouse in the city! It was for *fashion's* sake that you built that ruinous conservatory—hired more servants than they have persons to wait upon—and dressed your footman like a harlequin!

MRS. TIFFANY. Mr. Tiffany, you are thoroughly plebeian, and insufferably *American*, in your grovelling ideas! And, pray, what was the occasion of these very *mal-ap-pro-pos* remarks? Merely because I requested a paltry fifty dollars to purchase a new style of head-dress—a *bijou* of an article just introduced in France.

TIFFANY. Time was, Mrs. Tiffany, when you manufactured your own French headdresses—took off their first gloss at the public balls, and then sold them to your shortest-sighted customers. And all you knew about France, or French either, was what you spelt out at the bottom of your fashion plates; but now you have grown so fashionable, forsooth, that you have forgotten how to speak your mother tongue!

MRS. TIFFANY. Mr. Tiffany, Mr. Tiffany! Nothing is more positively vulgarian—more *unaristocratic*—than any allusion to the past!

TIFFANY. Why I thought, my dear, that *aristocrats* lived principally upon the past—and traded in the market of fashion with the bones of their ancestors for capital?

MRS. TIFFANY. Mr. Tiffany, such vulgar remarks are only suitable to the counting house; in my drawing room you should—

TIFFANY. Vary my sentiments with my locality, as you change your *manners* with your *dress!*

MRS. TIFFANY. Mr. Tiffany, I desire that you will purchase Count d'Orsay's *Science of Etiquette*, and learn how to conduct yourself—especially before you appear at the grand ball, which I shall give on Friday!

TIFFANY. Confound your balls, Madam; they make *footballs* of my money, while you dance away all that I am worth! A pretty time to give a ball when you know that I am on the very brink of bankruptcy!

MRS. TIFFANY. So much the greater reason that nobody should suspect your circumstances, or you would lose your credit at once. Just at this crisis a ball is absolutely *necessary* to save your reputation! There is Mrs. Adolphus Dashaway— she gave the most splendid fête of the season—and I hear on very good authority that her husband has not paid his baker's bill in three months. Then there was Mrs. Honeywood—

TIFFANY. Gave a ball the night before her husband shot himself; perhaps you wish to drive me to follow his example? (*Crosses.*)

MRS. TIFFANY. Good gracious! Mr. Tiffany, how you talk! I beg you won't mention anything of the kind. I consider black the most unbecoming color. I'm sure I've done all that I could to gratify you. There is that vulgar old torment, Trueman, who gives one the lie fifty times a day; haven't I been very civil to him?

TIFFANY. Civil to his *wealth*, Mrs. Tiffany! I told you that he was a rich, old farmer—the early friend of my father—my own benefactor—and that I had reason to think he might assist me in my present embarrassments. Your civility was *bought*, and like most of your *own* purchases has yet to be *paid* for. (*Crosses.*)

MRS. TIFFANY. And will be, no doubt! The condescension of a woman of fashion should command any price. Mr. Trueman is insupportably indecorous; he has insulted Count Jolimaitre in the most outrageous manner. If the Count was not so deeply interested, so *abimé* with Seraphina, I am sure he would never honor us by his visits again!

TIFFANY. So much the better; he shall never marry my daughter!—I am resolved on that. Why, Madam, I am told there is in Paris a regular matrimonial stock company, who fit out indigent dandies for this market. How do I know but this fellow is one of its creatures, and that he has come here to increase its dividends by marrying a fortune?

MRS. TIFFANY. Nonsense, Mr. Tiffany. The Count, the most fashionable young man in all New York—the intimate friend of all the dukes and lords in Europe—not marry my daughter? Not permit Seraphina to become a Countess? Mr. Tiffany, you are out of your senses!

TIFFANY. That would not be very wonderful, considering how many years I have been united to you, my dear. Modern physicians pronounce lunacy infectious!

MRS. TIFFANY. Mr. Tiffany, he is a man of fashion—

TIFFANY. Fashion makes fools, but cannot *feed* them. By the bye, I have a request. Since you are bent upon ruining me by this ball, and there is no help for it, I desire that you will send an invitation to my confidential clerk, Mr. Snobson.

MRS. TIFFANY. Mr. Snobson! Was there ever such an *you-nick* demand! Mr. Snobson would cut a pretty figure amongst my fashionable friends! I shall do no such thing, Mr. Tiffany.

TIFFANY. Then, Madam, the ball shall not take place. Have I not told you that I am in the power of this man? That there are circumstances which it is happy for you that you do not know, which you cannot comprehend, but which render it essential that you should be civil to Mr. Snobson? Not you merely, but Seraphina also? He is a more appropriate match for her than your foreign favorite.

MRS. TIFFANY. A match for Seraphina, indeed! (*Crosses.*) Mr. Tiffany, you are determined to make a *fow pas*.

TIFFANY. Mr. Snobson intends calling this morning. (*Crosses.*)

MRS. TIFFANY. But, Mr. Tiffany, this is not reception day— my drawing-rooms are in the most terrible disorder—

TIFFANY. Mr. Snobson is not particular; he must be admitted.

(*Enter* ZEKE.)

ZEKE. Mr. Snobson.

(*Enter* SNOBSON, *exit* ZEKE.)

SNOBSON. How dye do, Marm? (*Crosses.*) How are you? Mr. Tiffany, your most!—
MRS. TIFFANY. (*Formally.*) Bung jure. Comment vow portè vow, Monsur Snobson?
SNOBSON. Oh, to be sure—very good of you—fine day.
MRS. TIFFANY. (*Pointing to a chair with great dignity.*) Sassoyez vow, Monsur Snobson.
SNOBSON. (*Aside.*) I wonder what she's driving at? I ain't up to the fashionable lingo yet! Eh? What? Speak a little louder, Marm.
MRS. TIFFANY. (*Aside.*) What ignorance!
TIFFANY. I presume Mrs. Tiffany means that you are to take a seat.
SNOBSON. Ex-actly—very obliging of her—so I will. (*Sits.*) No ceremony amongst friends, you know, and likely to be nearer—you understand? *O.K.*, all correct. How *is* Seraphina?
MRS. TIFFANY. Miss Tiffany is not visible this morning. (*Retires up.*)
SNOBSON. (*Jumping up.*) Not visible? I suppose that's the English for can't see her? Mr. Tiffany, Sir—(*walking up to him*) what am I to understand by this *de-fal-ca-tion*, Sir? I expected your word to be as good as your bond—beg pardon, Sir—I mean *better*—considerably better—no humbug about it, Sir.
TIFFANY. Have patience, Mr. Snobson. (*Rings bell.*)

(*Enter* ZEKE.)

Zeke, desire my daughter to come here.
MRS. TIFFANY. (*Coming down.*) Adolph—I say, Adolph—
(ZEKE *straightens himself and assumes foppish airs, as he turns to* MRS. TIFFANY.)
TIFFANY. Zeke.

ZEKE. Don't know any such nigga, Boss.

TIFFANY. Do as I bid you instantly, or off with your livery and quit the house!

ZEKE. Wheugh! I'se all dismission!

(*Exit.*)

MRS. TIFFANY. A-dolph, A-dolph! (*Calling after him.*)

SNOBSON. (*Aside.*) I brought the old boy to his bearings, didn't I though! Pull that string, and he is sure to work right. Don't make any stranger of me, Marm—I'm quite at home. If you've got any odd jobs about the house to do up, I sha'n't miss you. I'll amuse myself with Seraphina when she comes; we'll get along very cosily by ourselves.

MRS. TIFFANY. Permit me to inform you, Mr. Snobson, that a French mother never leaves her daughter alone with a young man; she knows your sex too well for that!

SNOBSON. Very *dis*-obliging of her—but as we're none French—

MRS. TIFFANY. You have yet to learn, Mr. Snobson, that the American *ee-light*—the aristocracy—the *how-ton*—as a matter of conscience, scrupulously follow the foreign fashions.

SNOBSON. Not when they are foreign to their interests, Marm; for instance—

(*Enter* SERAPHINA.)

There you are at last, eh, Miss? How d'ye do? Ma said you weren't visible. Managed to get a peep at her, eh, Mr. Tiffany?

SERAPHINA. I heard you were here, Mr. Snobson, and came without even arranging my toilette; you will excuse my negligence?

SNOBSON. Of everything but *me*, Miss.

SERAPHINA. I shall never have to ask your pardon for *that*, Mr. Snobson.

MRS. TIFFANY. Seraphina—child—really—

(*As she is approaching* SERAPHINA, MR. TIFFANY *plants himself in front of his wife.*)

TIFFANY. Walk this way, Madam, if you please. (*Aside.*) To see that she fancies the surly fellow takes a weight from my heart.

MRS. TIFFANY. Mr. Tiffany, it is highly improper and not at all *distingué* to leave a young girl—

(*Enter* ZEKE.)

ZEKE. Mr. Count Jolly-made-her!

MRS. TIFFANY. Good gracious! The Count—Oh, dear!—Seraphina, run and change your dress—no there's not time!
A-dolph, admit him. (*Exit* ZEKE.) Mr. Snobson, get out
of the way, will you? Mr. Tiffany, what are you doing at
home at this hour?

(*Enter* COUNT JOLLIMAITRE, *ushered by* ZEKE.)

ZEKE. (*Aside.*) Dat's de genuine article ob a gemman. (*Exit.*)

MRS. TIFFANY. My dear Count, I am overjoyed at the very
sight of you.

COUNT. Flattered myself you'd be glad to see me, Madam—
knew it was not your *jour de reception.*

MRS. TIFFANY. But for you, Count, all days—

COUNT. I thought so. Ah, Miss Tiffany, on my honor, you're
looking beautiful. (*Crosses.*)

SERAPHINA. Count, flattery from you—

SNOBSON. What? Eh? What's that you say?

SERAPHINA. (*Aside to him.*) Nothing but what etiquette requires.

COUNT. (*Regarding* MR. TIFFANY *through his eye glass.*) Your
worthy Papa, I believe? Sir, your most obedient.

(MR. TIFFANY *bows coldly;* COUNT *regards* SNOBSON *through
his glass, shrugs his shoulders and turns away.*)

SNOBSON. (*To* MRS. TIFFANY.) Introduce me, will you? I never
knew a Count in all my life—what a strange-looking
animal!

MRS. TIFFANY. Mr. Snobson, it is not the fashion to introduce
in France!

SNOBSON. But, Marm, we're in America. (MRS. TIFFANY
crosses to COUNT. *Aside.*) The woman thinks she's somewhere else than where she is; she wants to make an *alibi?*

MRS. TIFFANY. I hope that we shall have the pleasure of seeing
you on Friday evening, Count?

COUNT. Really, Madam, my invitations—my engagements—so
numerous—I can hardly answer for myself; and you Americans take offence so easily—

MRS. TIFFANY. But Count, everybody expects you at our ball—
you are the principal attraction—

SERAPHINA. Count, you *must* come!

COUNT. Since you insist—aw—aw—there's no resisting you,
Miss Tiffany.

MRS. TIFFANY. I am so thankful. How can I repay your condescension! (COUNT *and* SERAPHINA *converse.*) Mr. Snobson, will you walk this way? I have *such* a cactus in full
bloom—remarkable flower! Mr. Tiffany, pray come here—I
have something particular to say.

TIFFANY. Then speak out, my dear. (*Aside to her.*) I thought
it was highly improper just now to leave a girl with a young
man?

MRS. TIFFANY. Oh, but the Count—that is different!

TIFFANY. I suppose you mean to say there's nothing of *the
man* about him?

(*Enter* MILLINETTE *with a scarf in her hand.*)

MILLINETTE. (*Aside.*) Adolph tell me he vas here. Pardon,
Madame, I bring dis scarf for Mademoiselle.

MRS. TIFFANY. Very well, Millinette; you know best what is
proper for her to wear.
(MR. *and* MRS. TIFFANY *and* SNOBSON *retire up; she en-
gages the attention of both gentlemen.*)
(MILLINETTE *crosses towards* SERAPHINA, *gives the* COUNT
a threatening look, and commences arranging the scarf over
SERAPHINA'S *shoulders.*)

MILLINETTE. Mademoiselle, *permettez-moi.* (*Aside to* COUNT.)
Perfide! (*To Seraphina.*) If Mademoiselle vil stand *tran-
quille* one *petit* moment. (*Turns* SERAPHINA'S *back to the*
COUNT, *and pretends to arrange the scarf. Aside to* COUNT.)
I must speak vid you to-day, or I tell all—you find me at
de foot of de stair ven you go. *Prends garde!*

SERAPHINA. What is that you say, Millinette?

MILLINETTE. Dis scarf make you so very beautiful, Mademoiselle—*Je vous salue mes dames.* (*Curtsies. Exit.*)

COUNT. (*Aside.*) Not a moment to lose! Miss Tiffany, I have
an unpleasant—a particularly unpleasant piece of intelligence. You see, I have just received a letter from my
friend—the—aw—the Earl of Airshire; the truth is, the

Earl's daughter—beg you won't mention it—has distinguished me by a tender *penchant*.

SERAPHINA. I understand—and they wish you to return and marry the young lady; but surely you will not leave us, Count?

COUNT. If *you* bid me stay—I shouldn't have the conscience—I couldn't *afford* to tear myself away. (*Aside.*) I'm sure that's honest.

SERAPHINA. Oh, Count!

COUNT. Say but one word—say that you shouldn't mind being made a Countess—and I'll break with the Earl to-morrow.

SERAPHINA. Count, this surprise—but don't think of leaving the country, Count—we could not pass the time without you! I—yes—yes, Count—I do consent!

COUNT. (*Aside, while he embraces her.*) I thought she would! Enchanted, rapture, bliss, ecstasy, and all that sort of thing—words can't express it, but you understand. But it must be kept a secret—positively it *must!* If the rumor of our engagement were whispered abroad—the Earl's daughter—the delicacy of my situation, aw—you comprehend? It is even possible that our nuptials, my charming Miss Tiffany—*our nuptials*—must take place in private!

SERAPHINA. Oh, that is quite impossible!

COUNT. It's the latest fashion abroad—the very latest. Ah, I knew that would determine you. Can I depend on your secrecy?

SERAPHINA. Oh, yes! Believe me.

SNOBSON. (*Coming forward in spite of* MRS. TIFFANY's *efforts to detain him.*) Why, Seraphina, haven't you a word to throw to a dog?

TIFFANY. (*Aside.*) I shouldn't think she had after wasting so so many upon a puppy.

(*Enter* ZEKE, *wearing a three-cornered hat.*)

ZEKE. Missus, de bran new carriage am below.

MRS. TIFFANY. Show it up—I mean, very well, A-dolph. (*Exit* ZEKE.)

Count, my daughter and I are about to take an airing in our new *voyture*—will you honor us with your company?

COUNT. Madam, I—I have a most *pressing* engagement. A

letter to write to the *Earl of Airshire*—who is at present residing in the *Isle of Skye.* I must bid you good morning.

MRS. TIFFANY. Good morning, Count.

(*Exit* COUNT.)

SNOBSON. *I'm* quite at leisure, (*Crosses to* MRS. TIFFANY.) Marm. Books balanced—ledger closed—nothing to do all the afternoon; I'm for you.

MRS. TIFFANY. (*Without noticing him.*) Come, Seraphina, come!

(*As they are going* SNOBSON *follows them.*)

SNOBSON. But, Marm—I was saying, Marm, I am quite at leisure—not a thing to do; have I, Mr. Tiffany?

MRS. TIFFANY. Seraphina, child—your red shawl, remember! Mr. Snobson, *bon swear!*

(*Exit, leading* SERAPHINA.)

SNOBSON. Swear! Mr. Tiffany, Sir, am I to be fobbed off with a *bon swear?* D—n it, I will swear!

TIFFANY. Have patience, Mr. Snobson; if you will accompany me to the counting house—

SNOBSON. Don't count too much on me, Sir. I'll make up no more accounts until these are settled! I'll run down and jump into the carriage in spite of her *bon swear.* (*Exit.*)

TIFFANY. You'll jump into a hornet's nest, if you do! Mr. Snobson, Mr. Snobson! (*Exit after him.*)

SCENE 2

Housekeeper's room.

Enter MILLINETTE.

MILLINETTE. I have set dat bête, Adolph, to vatch for him. He say he would come back so soon as Madame's voiture drive from de door. If he not come—but he vill—he vill—he *bien étourdi,* but he have *bon coeur.*

(*Enter* COUNT.)

COUNT. Ah! Millinette, my dear, you see what a good-natured dog I am to fly at your bidding—

MILLINETTE. Fly? Ah! *trompeur!* Vat for you fly from Paris?

Vat for you leave me—and I love you so much? Ven you
sick—you almost die—did I not stay by you—take care of
you—and you have no else friend? Vat for you leave Paris?
COUNT. Never allude to disagreeable subjects, *mon enfant!*
I was forced by uncontrollable circumstances to fly to the
land of liberty—
MILLINETTE. Vat you do vid all de money I give you? The
last sou I had—did I not give you?
COUNT. I dare say you did, ma petite—(*Aside.*) Wish you'd
been better supplied! Don't ask any questions here—can't
explain now—the next time we meet—
MILLINETTE. But, ah! ven shall ve meet—ven? You not deceive
me, not any more.
COUNT. Deceive you! I'd rather deceive myself. (*Aside.*) I
wish I could! I'd persuade myself you were once more
washing linen in the Seine!
MILLINETTE. I vil tell you ven ve shall meet. On Friday night
Madame give one grand ball—you come *sans doute*—den
ven de supper is served—de Americans tink of noting else
ven de supper come—den you steal out of de room, and
you find me here—and you give me one grand *explanation!*

(*Enter* GERTRUDE, *unperceived.*)

COUNT. Friday night—while supper is serving—*parole d'hon-
neur* I will be here—I will explain every thing—my sudden
departure from Paris—my—demme, my countship—every
thing! Now let me go—if any of the family should discover
us—
GERTRUDE. (*Who during the last speech has gradually advanced.*) They might discover more than you think it
advisable for them to know!
COUNT. The devil!
MILLINETTE. *Mon Dieu!* Mademoiselle Gertrude!
COUNT. (*Recovering himself.*) My dear Miss Gertrude, let me
explain—aw—aw—nothing is more natural than the situation
in which you find me—
GERTRUDE. I am inclined to believe that, Sir.
COUNT. Now—'pon my honor, that's not fair. Here is Millinette
will bear witness to what I am about to say—
GERTRUDE. Oh, I have not the slightest doubt of that, Sir.
COUNT. You see, Millinette happened to be lady's-maid in the

family of—of—the Duchess Chateau D'Espagne—and I
chanced to be a particular friend of the Duchess—*very
particular* I assure you! Of course I saw Millinette, and
she, demme, she saw me! Didn't you, Millinette?

MILLINETTE. Oh! *oui*—Mademoiselle, I knew him ver vell.

COUNT. Well, it is a remarkable fact that—being in correspondence with this very Duchess—at this very time—

GERTRUDE. That is sufficient, Sir—I am already so well acquainted with your extraordinary talents for improvisation
that I will not further tax your invention—

MILLINETTE. Ah! Mademoiselle Gertrude do not betray us—
have pity!

COUNT. (*Assuming an air of dignity.*) Silence, Millinette! My
word has been doubted—the word of a nobleman! I will
inform my friend, Mrs. Tiffany, of this young person's
audacity. (*Going.*)

GERTRUDE. (*Aside.*) His own weapons alone can foil this
villain! Sir—Sir—Count!
(*At the last word the* COUNT *turns.*) Perhaps, Sir, the least
said about this matter the better!

COUNT. (*Delightedly.*) The least said? We won't say anything
at all. (*Aside.*) She's coming round—couldn't resist me.
Charming Gertrude—

MILLINETTE. *Quoi?* Vat that you say?

COUNT. (*Aside to her.*) My sweet, adorable Millinette, hold
your tongue, will you?

MILLINETTE. (*Aloud.*) No, I vill not! If you do look so from
out your eyes at her again, I vill tell all!

COUNT. (*Aside.*) Oh, I never could manage two women at
once, jealousy makes the dear creatures so spiteful. The
only valor is in flight! Miss Gertrude, I wish you good
morning. Millinette, *mon enfant*, adieu. (*Exit.*)

MILLINETTE. But I have one word more to say. Stop, Stop!
(*Exit after him.*)

GERTRUDE. (*Musingly.*) Friday night, while supper is serving,
he is to meet Millinette here and explain—what? This man
is an impostor! His insulting me—his familiarity with Millinette—his whole conduct—prove it. If I tell Mrs. Tiffany
this she will disbelieve me, and one word may place this
so-called Count on his guard. To convince Seraphina would
be equally difficult, and her rashness and infatuation may
render her miserable for life. No—she shall be saved! I must

devise some plan for opening their eyes. Truly, if I *cannot* invent one, I shall be the first woman who was ever at a loss for a stratagem—especially to punish a villain or to shield a friend. (*Exit.*)

ACT IV

SCENE 1

Ball-room splendidly illuminated. A curtain hung at the further end. MR. *and* MRS. TIFFANY, SERAPHINA, GERTRUDE, FOGG, TWINKLE, COUNT, SNOBSON, COLONEL HOWARD, *a number of guests—some seated, some standing. As the curtain rises, a cotillion is danced;* GERTRUDE *dancing with* HOWARD, SERAPHINA *with* COUNT.

COUNT. (*Advancing with* SERAPHINA *to the front of the stage.*) To-morrow then—to-morrow—I may salute you as my bride—demme, my Countess!

(*Enter* ZEKE, *with refreshments.*)

SERAPHINA. Yes, to-morrow.
(*As the* COUNT *is about to reply,* SNOBSON *thrusts himself in front of* SERAPHINA.)
SNOBSON. You said you'd dance with me, Miss—now take my fin, and we'll walk about and see what's going on.
(COUNT *raises his eye-glass, regards* SNOBSON, *and leads* SERAPHINA *away;* SNOBSON *follows, endeavoring to attract her attention, but encountering* ZEKE, *bearing a waiter of refreshments; stops him, helps himself, and puts some in his pockets.*)
Here's the treat! get my to-morrow's luncheon out of Tiff.

(*Enter* TRUEMAN, *yawning and rubbing his eyes.*)

TRUEMAN. What a nap I've had, to be sure! (*Looks at his watch.*) Eleven o'clock, as I'm alive! (*To* TIFFANY, *who approaches.*) Just the time when country folks are com-

fortably *turned in*, and here your grand *turn-out* has hardly
begun yet.

GERTRUDE. (*Advancing.*) I was just coming to look for you,
Mr. Trueman. I began to fancy that you were paying a
visit to dreamland.

TRUEMAN. So I was, child—so I was—and I saw a face—like
yours—but brighter!—Even brighter. (*To* TIFFANY.) There's
a smile for you, man! It makes one feel that the world has
something worth living for in it yet! Do you remember a
smile like that, Antony? Ah! I see you don't—but I do—I
do! (*Much moved.*)

HOWARD. (*Advancing.*) Good evening, Mr. Trueman. (*Offers
his hand.*)

TRUEMAN. That's right, man; give me your whole hand!
When a man offers me the tips of his fingers, I know at
once there's nothing in him worth seeking beyond his
fingers' ends.

(TRUEMAN *and* HOWARD, GERTRUDE *and* TIFFANY *converse.*)

MRS. TIFFANY. (*Advancing.*) I'm in such a fidget lest that
vulgar old fellow should disgrace us by some of his plebeian
remarks! What it is to give a ball, when one is forced to
invite vulgar people!

(MRS. TIFFANY *advances towards* TRUEMAN; SERAPHINA
*stands conversing flippantly with the gentlemen who sur-
round her; amongst them is* TWINKLE, *who, having taken
a magazine from his pocket, is reading to her, much to the
undisguised annoyance of* SNOBSON.)

Dear me, Mr. Trueman, you are very late—quite in the
fashion, I declare!

TRUEMAN. Fashion! And pray what is *fashion*, madam? An
agreement between certain persons to live without using
their souls! To substitute etiquette for virtue—decorum for
purity—manners for morals! To affect a shame for the
works of their Creator! And expend all their rapture upon
the works of their tailors and dressmakers!

MRS. TIFFANY. You have the most *ow-tray* ideas, Mr. Trueman—quite rustic, and deplorably *American!* But pray walk
this way.

(MRS. TIFFANY *and* TRUEMAN *go up.*)

COUNT. (*Advancing to* GERTRUDE, HOWARD *a short distance
behind her.*) Miss Gertrude—no opportunity of speaking to
you before—in demand, you know!

GERTRUDE. (*Aside.*) I have no choice, I must be civil to him. What were you remarking, Sir?

COUNT. Miss Gertrude—charming Ger—aw—aw—(*Aside.*) I never found it so difficult to speak to a woman before.

GERTRUDE. Yes, a very charming ball—many beautiful faces here.

COUNT. Only one!—Aw—aw—one—the fact is—(*Talks to her in dumb show.*)

HOWARD. What could old Trueman have meant by saying she fancied that puppy of a Count—that paste jewel thrust upon the little finger of society.

COUNT. Miss Gertrude—aw—'pon my honor—you don't under-understand—really—aw—aw—will you dance the polka with me?

(GERTRUDE *bows and gives him her hand; he leads her to the set forming;* HOWARD *remains looking after them.*)

HOWARD. Going to dance with him, too! A few days ago she would hardly bow to him civilly—could old Trueman have had reasons for what he said? (*Retires up.*)

(*Dance, the polka;* SERAPHINA, *after having distributed her bouquet, vinaigrette and fan amongst the gentlemen, dances with* SNOBSON.)

PRUDENCE. (*Peeping in as dance concludes.*) I don't like dancing on Friday; something strange is always sure to happen! I'll be on the look out. (*Remains peeping and concealing herself when any of the company approach.*)

GERTRUDE. (*Advancing hastily.*) They are preparing the supper—now if I can only dispose of Millinette while I unmask this insolent pretender! (*Exit.*)

PRUDENCE. (*Peeping.*) What's that she said? It's coming!

(*Re-enter* GERTRUDE, *bearing a small basket filled with bouquets; approaches* MRS. TIFFANY; *they walk to the front of the stage.*)

GERTRUDE. Excuse me, Madam—I believe this is just the hour at which you ordered supper?

MRS. TIFFANY. Well, what's that to you! So you've been dancing with the Count—how dare you dance with a nobleman—*you?*

GERTRUDE. I will answer that question half an hour hence. At present I have something to propose, which I think will gratify you and please your guests. I have heard that at the most elegant balls in Paris, it is customary—

MRS. TIFFANY. What? What?

GERTRUDE. To station a servant at the door with a basket of flowers. A bouquet is then presented to every lady as she passes in. I prepared this basket a short time ago. As the company walk in to supper, might not the flowers be distributed to advantage?

MRS. TIFFANY. How *distingué!* You are a good creature, Gertrude—there, run and hand the *bokettes* to them yourself! You shall have the whole credit of the thing.

GERTRUDE. (*Aside.*) Caught in my own net! But, Madam, I know so little of fashions. Millinette, being French herself, will do it with so much more grace. I am sure Millinette—

MRS. TIFFANY. So am I. She will do it a thousand times better than you—there, go call her.

GERTRUDE. (*Giving basket.*) But, Madam, pray order Millinette not to leave her station till supper is ended; as the company pass out of the supper room she may find that some of the ladies have been overlooked.

MRS. TIFFANY. That is true—very thoughtful of you, Gertrude. (*Exit* GERTRUDE.) What a *recherché* idea!

(*Enter* MILLINETTE.)

Here, Millinette, take this basket. Place yourself there, and distribute these *bokettes* as the company pass in to supper; but remember not to stir from the spot until supper is over. It is a French fashion you know, Millinette. I am so delighted to be the first to introduce it—it will be all the rage in the *bow-monde!*

MILLINETTE. (*Aside.*) Mon Dieu! dis vill ruin all! Madame, Madame, let me tell you, Madame, dat in France, in Paris, it is de custom to present *les* bouquets ven every body first come—long before de supper. Dis vould be *outré! barbare!* not at all la mode! Ven dey do come in—dat is de fashion in Paris!

MRS. TIFFANY. Dear me! Millinette, what is the difference? Besides I'd have you to know that Americans always improve upon French fashions! Here, take the basket, and let me see that you do it in the most *you-nick* and genteel manner.

(MILLINETTE *poutingly takes the basket and retires up stage. A march. Curtain hung at the further end of the room is drawn back, and discloses a room, in the center of which stands a supper table, beautifully decorated and illuminated; the company promenade two by two into the supper room;* MILLINETTE *presents bouquets as they pass;* COUNT *leads* MRS. TIFFANY.)

TRUEMAN. (*Encountering* FOGG, *who is hurrying alone to the supper room.*) Mr. Fogg, never mind the supper, man! Ha, ha, ha! Of course you are indifferent to suppers!

FOGG. Indifferent! Suppers—oh, ah—no, Sir—suppers? No—no—I'm not indifferent to suppers! (*Hurries away towards table.*)

TRUEMAN. Ha, ha, ha! Here's a new discovery I've made in the fashionable world! Fashion don't permit the critters to have *heads* or *hearts*, but it allows them stomachs! (*To* TIFFANY, *who advances.*) So it's not fashionable to *feel*, but it's fashionable to *feed*, eh, Antony? Ha, ha, ha!
(TRUEMAN *and* TIFFANY *retire towards supper room. Enter* GERTRUDE, *followed by* ZEKE.)

GERTRUDE. Zeke, go to the supper room instantly; whisper to Count Jolimaitre that all is ready, and that he must keep his appointment without delay. Then watch him, and as he passes out of the room, place yourself in front of Millinette in such a manner that the Count cannot see her nor she him. Be sure that they do not see each other—everything depends upon that. (*Crosses.*)

ZEKE. Missey, consider dat business brought to a scientific conclusion.
(*Exit into supper room. Exit* GERTRUDE.)

PRUDENCE. (*Who has been listening.*) What can she want of the Count? I always suspected that Gertrude, because she is so merry and busy! Mr. Trueman thinks so much of her too—I'll tell him this! There's something wrong—but it all comes of giving a ball on a Friday! How astonished the dear old man will be when he finds out how much I know! (*Advances timidly towards the supper room.*)

Scene 2

Housekeeper's room; dark stage; table, two chairs.

Enter GERTRUDE, *with a lighted candle in her hand.*

GERTRUDE. So far the scheme prospers! And yet this imprudence. If I fail? Fail! To lack courage in a difficulty, or
ingenuity in a dilemma, are not woman's failings!

(*Enter* ZEKE, *with a napkin over his arm, and a bottle of
champagne in his hand.*)

Well, Zeke—Adolph!
ZEKE. Dat's right, Missey; I feels just now as if dat was my
legitimate title; dis here's de stuff to make a nigger feel
like a gemman!
GERTRUDE. But he is coming?
ZEKE. He's coming! (*Sound of a champagne cork heard.*) Do
you hear dat, Missey? Don't it put you all in a froth, and
make you feel as light as a cork? Dere's nothing like the
union brand, to wake up de harmonies ob de heart.
(*Drinks from bottle.*)
GERTRUDE. Remember to keep watch upon the outside—do
not stir from the spot; when I call you, come in quickly
with a light—now, will you be gone!
ZEKE. I'm off, Missey, like a champagne cork wid de strings
cut. (*Exit.*)
GERTRUDE. I think I hear the Count's step. (*Crosses, stage
dark; she blows out candle.*) Now if I can but disguise my
voice, and make the best of my French.

(*Enter* COUNT.)

COUNT. Millinette, where are you? How am I to see you in
the dark?
GERTRUDE. (*Imitating* MILLINETTE'S *voice in a whisper.*)
Hush! *parle bas.*
COUNT. Come here and give me a kiss.

GERTRUDE. Non—non—(*retreating alarmed*, COUNT *follows*) make haste, I must know all.

COUNT. You did not use to be so deuced particular.

ZEKE. (*Without.*) No admission, gemman! Box office closed, tickets stopped!

TRUEMAN. (*Without.*) Out of my way; do you want me to try if your head is as hard as my stick?

GERTRUDE. What shall I do? Ruined, ruined! (*She stands with her hands clasped in speechless despair.*)

COUNT. Halloa! they are coming here, Millinette! Millinette, why don't you speak? Where can I hide myself? (*Running about stage, feeling for a door.*) Where are all your closets? If I could only get out—or get in somewhere; may I be smothered in a clothes' basket if you ever catch me in such a scrape again! (*His hand accidentally touches the knob of a door opening into a closet.*) Fortune's favorite yet! I'm safe!

(*Gets into closet and closes door. Enter* PRUDENCE, TRUE- MAN, MRS. TIFFANY, *and* COLONEL HOWARD, *followed by* ZEKE, *bearing a light; lights up.*)

PRUDENCE. Here they are, the Count and Gertrude! I told you so! (*Stops in surprise on seeing only* GERTRUDE.)

TRUEMAN. And you see what a lie you told!

MRS. TIFFANY. Prudence, how dare you create this disturbance in my house? To suspect the Count, too—a nobleman!

HOWARD. My sweet Gertrude, this foolish old woman would—

PRUDENCE. Oh! you needn't talk—I heard her make the appointment—I know he's here—or he's been here. I wonder if she hasn't hid him away! (*Runs peeping about the room.*)

TRUEMAN. (*Following her angrily.*) You're what I call a confounded—troublesome—meddling—old—prying—

(*As he says the last word,* PRUDENCE *opens closet where the* COUNT *is concealed.*)

Thunder and lightning!

PRUDENCE. I told you so!

(*They all stand aghast;* MRS. TIFFANY, *with her hands lifted in surprise and anger;* TRUEMAN, *clutching his stick;* HOWARD, *looking with an expression of bewildered horror from the* COUNT *to* GERTRUDE.)

MRS. TIFFANY. (*Shaking her fist at* GERTRUDE.) You depraved
little minx! this is the meaning of your dancing with the
Count!

COUNT. (*Stepping from the closet and advancing. Aside.*) I
don't know what to make of it! Millinette not here! Miss
Gertrude. Oh! I see—a disguise—the girl's desperate about
me—the way with them all.

TRUEMAN. I'm choking—I can't speak—Gertrude—no—no—it is
some horrid mistake! (*Partly aside, changes his tone suddenly.*) The villain! I'll hunt the truth out of him, if there's
any in—(*crosses, approaches* COUNT *threateningly.*) Do you
see this stick? You made its first acquaintance a few days
ago; it is time you were better known to each other.

(*As* TRUEMAN *attempts to seize him,* COUNT *escapes, and
shields himself behind* MRS. TIFFANY, TRUEMAN *following.*)

COUNT. You ruffian! Would you strike a woman?—Madam—
my dear Madam—keep off that barbarous old man, and
I will explain! Madam, with—aw—your natural *bon
gout*—aw—your fashionable refinement—aw—your—aw—your
knowledge of *foreign customs*—

MRS. TIFFANY. Oh! Count, I hope it ain't a *foreign custom*
for the nobility to shut themselves up in the dark with
young women? We think such things *dreadful* in *America.*

COUNT. Demme—aw—hear what I have to say, Madam—I'll
satisfy all sides—I am perfectly innocent in this affair—'pon
my honor I am! That young lady shall inform you that I
am so herself!—Can't help it, sorry for her. Old matter-of-
fact won't be convinced any other way. (*Aside.*) That club
of his is so particularly unpleasant! Madam, I was summoned here *malgré moi*, and not knowing whom I was to
meet—Miss Gertrude, favor the company by saying whether
or not you directed—that—aw—aw—that colored individual
to conduct me here?

GERTRUDE. Sir, you well know—

COUNT. A simple yes or no will suffice.

MRS. TIFFANY. Answer the Count's question instantly, Miss.

GERTRUDE. I did—but—

COUNT. You hear, Madam—

TRUEMAN. I won't believe it—I can't! Here, you nigger, stop
rolling up your eyes, and let us know whether she told
you to bring that critter here?

ZEKE. I'se refuse to gib ebidence; dat's de device ob de

skilfullest counsels ob de day! Can't answer, Boss—neber git a word out ob dis child.—Yah! yah! (*Exit.*)

GERTRUDE. Mrs. Tiffany, Mr. Trueman, if you will but have patience—

TRUEMAN. Patience! Oh, Gertrude, you've taken from an old man something better and dearer than his patience—the one bright hope of nineteen years of self-denial—of nineteen years of—(*Throws himself upon a chair, his head leaning on table.*)

MRS. TIFFANY. Get out of my house, you *ow*dacious—you ruined—you *abimé* young woman! You will corrupt all my family. Good gracious! don't touch me,—don't come near me. Never let me see your face after to-morrow. Pack. (*Goes up.*)

HOWARD. Gertrude, I have striven to find some excuse for you—to doubt—to disbelieve—but this is beyond all endurance! (*Exit.*)

(*Enter* MILLINETTE *in haste.*)

MILLINETTE. I could not come before— (*Stops in surprise at seeing the persons assembled.*) Mon Dieu! vat does dis mean?

COUNT. (*Aside to her.*) Hold your tongue, fool! You will ruin everything, I will explain to-morrow. Mrs. Tiffany—Madam —my dear Madam, let me conduct you back to the ballroom. (*She takes his arm.*) You see I am quite innocent in this matter; a man of my standing, you know; aw—aw— you comprehend the whole affair.

(*Exit* COUNT *leading* MRS. TIFFANY.)

MILLINETTE. I will say to him von vord, I will! (*Exit.*)

GERTRUDE. Mr. Trueman, I beseech you—I insist upon being heard; I claim it as a right!

TRUEMAN. Right? How dare you have the face, girl, to talk of rights? (*Comes down.*) You had more rights than you thought, but you have forfeited them all! All rights to love, respect, protection, and to not a little else that you don't dream of. Go, go! I'll start for Catteraugus to-morrow; I've seen enough of what fashion can do! (*Exit.*)

PRUDENCE. (*Wiping her eyes.*) Dear old man, how he takes on! I'll go and console him! (*Exit.*)

GERTRUDE. This is too much! How heavy a penalty has my

imprudence cost me!—His esteem, and that of one dearer—
my home—my—
(*Burst of lively music from ball-room.*)
They are dancing, and I—I should be weeping, if pride
had not sealed up my tears.
(*She sinks into a chair. Band plays the polka behind till
Curtain falls.*)

ACT V

MRS. TIFFANY's *Drawing Room—same Scene as Act I.*
GERTRUDE *seated at a table, with her head leaning on her
hand; in the other hand she holds a pen. A sheet of paper
and an ink-stand before her.*

GERTRUDE. How shall I write to them? What shall I say?
Prevaricate I cannot—(*rises and comes forward*) and yet
if I write the truth—simple souls! How can they comprehend the motives for my conduct? Nay—the truly pure see
no imaginary evil in others! It is only vice that, reflecting
its own image, suspects even the innocent. I have no time
to lose—I must prepare them for my return. (*Resumes her
seat and writes.*) What a true pleasure there is in daring
to be frank! (*After writing a few lines more pauses.*) Not
so frank either; there is one name that I cannot mention.
Ah! that he should suspect—should despise me. (*Writes.*)

(*Enter* TRUEMAN.)

TRUEMAN. There she is! If this girl's soul had only been as
fair as her face! Yet she dared to speak the truth; I'll not
forget that! A woman who refuses to tell a lie has one
spark of heaven in her still. (*Approaches her.*) Gertrude,
(GERTRUDE *starts and looks up.*)
What are you writing there? Plotting more mischief, eh,
girl?
GERTRUDE. I was writing a few lines to some friends in
Geneva.
TRUEMAN. The Wilsons, eh?

GERTRUDE. (*Surprised, rising.*) Are you acquainted with them, Sir?

TRUEMAN. I shouldn't wonder if I was. I suppose you have taken good care not to mention the dark room—that foreign puppy in the closet—the pleasant surprise—and all that sort of thing, eh?

GERTRUDE. I have no reason for concealment, Sir, for I have done nothing of which I am ashamed!

TRUEMAN. Then I can't say much for your modesty.

GERTRUDE. I should not wish you to say more than I deserve.

TRUEMAN. (*Aside.*) There's a bold minx!

GERTRUDE. Since my affairs seem to have excited your interest —I will not say *curiosity*—perhaps you even feel a desire to inspect my correspondence? There, (*Handing the letter.*) I pride myself upon my good nature; you may like to take advantage of it?

TRUEMAN. (*Aside.*) With what an air she carries it off! Take advantage of it? So I will. (*Reads.*) What's this? "French chambermaid — Count — impostor — infatuation — Seraphina — Millinette—disguised myself—expose him." Thunder and lightning! I see it all! Come and kiss me, girl!

(GERTRUDE *evinces surprise.*)

No, no—I forgot—it won't do to come to that yet! She's a rare girl! I'm out of my senses with joy! I don't know what to do with myself! Tol, de rol, de rol, de ra. (*Capers and sings.*)

GERTRUDE. (*Aside.*) What a remarkable old man! Then you do me justice, Mr. Trueman?

TRUEMAN. I say I don't! Justice? You're above all dependence upon justice! Hurrah! I've found one true woman at last! *True?* (*Pauses thoughtfully.*) Humph! I didn't think of that flaw! Plotting and maneuvering—not much truth in that! An honest girl should be above stratagems!

GERTRUDE. But my *motive*, Sir, was good.

TRUEMAN. That's not enough—your *actions* must be *good* as well as your *motives*! Why could you not tell the silly girl that man was an impostor?

GERTRUDE. I did inform her of my suspicions—she ridiculed them; the plan I chose was an imprudent one, but I could not devise—

TRUEMAN. I hate devising! Give me a woman with the *firmness* to be *frank*! But no matter—I had no right to look for an angel out of Paradise; and I am as happy—as happy as a Lord! that is, ten times happier than any Lord ever was! Tol, de rol, de rol! Oh! you—you—I'll thrash every fellow that says a word against you!

GERTRUDE. You will have plenty of employment then, Sir, for I do not know of one just now who would speak in my favor!

TRUEMAN. Not *one*, eh? Why, where's your dear Mr. Twinkle? I know all about it—can't say that I admire your choice of a husband! But there's no accounting for a girl's taste.

GERTRUDE. Mr. Twinkle! Indeed you are quite mistaken!

TRUEMAN. No—really? Then you're not taken with him, eh?

GERTRUDE. Not even with his rhymes.

TRUEMAN. Hang that old mother meddle-much! What a fool she has made of me. And so you're quite free, and I may choose a husband for you myself? Heart-whole, eh?

GERTRUDE. I—I—I trust there is nothing *unsound* about my heart.

TRUEMAN. There it is again. Don't prevaricate, girl! I tell you an *evasion* is a *lie in contemplation*, and I hate lying! Out with the truth! Is your heart *free* or not?

GERTRUDE. Nay, Sir, since you *demand* an answer, permit *me* to demand by what right you ask the question?

(*Enter* HOWARD.)

Colonel Howard here!

TRUEMAN. I'm out again! What's the Colonel to her? (*Retires up.*)

HOWARD. (*Crosses to her.*) I have come, Gertrude, to bid you farewell. To-morrow I resign my commission and leave this city, perhaps forever. You, Gertrude, it is you who have exiled me! After last evening—

TRUEMAN. (*Coming forward to* HOWARD.) What the plague have you got to say about last evening?

HOWARD. Mr. Trueman!

TRUEMAN. What have you got to say about last evening? And what have you to say to that little girl at all? It's Tiffany's precious daughter you're in love with.

HOWARD. Miss Tiffany? Never! I never had the slightest pretension—

TRUEMAN. That lying old woman! But I'm glad of it! Oh!

Ah! Um! (*Looking significantly at* GERTRUDE *and then at* HOWARD.) I see how it is. So you don't choose to marry Seraphina, eh? Well now, whom do you choose to marry? (*Glancing at* GERTRUDE.)

HOWARD. I shall not marry at all!

TRUEMAN. You won't? (*Looking at them both again.*) Why you don't mean to say that you don't like— (*Points with his thumb to* GERTRUDE.)

GERTRUDE. Mr. Trueman, I may have been wrong to boast of my good nature, but do not presume too far upon it.

HOWARD. You like frankness, Mr. Trueman, therefore I will speak plainly. I have long cherished a dream from which I was last night rudely awakened.

TRUEMAN. And that's what you call speaking plainly? Well, I differ with you! But I can guess what you mean. Last night you suspected Gertrude there of—(*Angrily.*) of what no man shall ever suspect her again while I'm above ground! You did her injustice; it was a mistake! There, now that matter's settled. Go, and ask her to forgive you— she's woman enough to do it! Go, go!

HOWARD. Mr. Trueman, you have forgotten to whom you dictate.

TRUEMAN. Then you won't do it? You won't ask her pardon?

HOWARD. Most undoubtedly I will not—not at any man's bidding. I must first know—

TRUEMAN. You won't do it? Then if I don't give you a lesson in politeness—

HOWARD. It will be because you find me your *tutor* in the same science. I am not a man to brook an insult, Mr. Trueman! But we'll not quarrel in presence of the lady.

TRUEMAN. Won't we? I don't know that—

GERTRUDE. Pray, Mr. Trueman—Colonel Howard, pray desist, Mr. Trueman, for my sake! (*Taking hold of his arm to hold him back.*) Colonel Howard, if you will read this letter it will explain everything.

(*Hands letter to* HOWARD, *who reads.*)

TRUEMAN. He don't deserve an explanation! Didn't I tell him that it was a mistake? Refuse to beg your pardon! I'll teach him, I'll teach him!

HOWARD. (*After reading.*) Gertrude, how have I wronged you!

TRUEMAN. Oh, you'll beg her pardon now?
(*Between them.*)
HOWARD. Hers, Sir, and yours! Gertrude, I fear—
TRUEMAN. You needn't, she'll forgive you. You don't know
these women as well as I do: they're always ready to
pardon; it's their nature, and they can't help it. Come along,
I left Antony and his wife in the dining room; we'll go and
find them. I've a story of my own to tell! As for you,
Colonel, you may follow. Come along. Come along!
(*Leads out* GERTRUDE, *followed by* HOWARD.)

(*Enter* MR. *and* MRS. TIFFANY, MR. TIFFANY *with a bundle
of bills in his hand.*)

MRS. TIFFANY. I beg you won't mention the subject again,
Mr. Tiffany. Nothing is more plebeian than a discussion
upon economy—nothing more *ungenteel* than looking over
and fretting over one's bills!
TIFFANY. Then I suppose, my dear, it is quite as ungenteel to
pay one's bills?
MRS. TIFFANY. Certainly! I hear the *ee-light* never condescend
to do anything of the kind. The honor of their invaluable
patronage is sufficient for the persons they employ!
TIFFANY. *Patronage* then is a newly invented food upon which
the working classes fatten? What convenient appetites poor
people must have! Now listen to what I am going to say.
As soon as my daughter marries Mr. Snobson—

(*Enter* PRUDENCE, *a three-cornered note in her hand.*)

PRUDENCE. Oh, dear! Oh, dear! What shall we do! Such a
misfortune! Such a disaster! Oh, dear! Oh, dear!
MRS. TIFFANY. Prudence, you are the most tiresome creature!
What *is* the matter?
PRUDENCE (*Pacing up and down the stage.*) Such a disgrace
to the whole family! But I always expected it. Oh, dear!
Oh, dear!
MRS. TIFFANY. (*Following her up and down the stage.*) What
are you talking about, Prudence? Will you tell me what
has happened?
PRUDENCE. (*Still pacing,* MRS. TIFFANY *following.*) Oh! I
can't, I can't! You'll feel so dreadfully! How could she do

such a thing! But I expected nothing else! I never did, I never did!

MRS. TIFFANY. (*Still following.*) Good gracious! what do you mean, Prudence? Tell me, will you tell me? I shall get into such a passion! What *is* the matter?

PRUDENCE. (*Still pacing.*) Oh, Betsy, Betsy! That your daughter should have come to that! Dear me, dear me!

TIFFANY. Seraphina? Did you say Seraphina? What has happened to her? What has she done?

(*Following* PRUDENCE *up and down the stage on the opposite side from* MRS. TIFFANY.)

MRS. TIFFANY. (*Still following.*) What *has* she done? What *has* she done?

PRUDENCE. Oh! something dreadful—dreadful—shocking!

TIFFANY. (*Still following.*) Speak quickly and plainly—you torture me by this delay; Prudence, be calm, and speak! What is it?

PRUDENCE. (*Stopping.*) Zeke just told me—he carried her travelling trunk himself—she gave him a whole dollar! Oh, my!

TIFFANY. Her trunk? Where? Where?

PRUDENCE. Round the corner!

MRS. TIFFANY. What did she want with her trunk? You are the most vexatious creature, Prudence! There is no bearing your ridiculous conduct!

PRUDENCE. Oh, you will have worse to bear—worse! Seraphina's gone!

TIFFANY. Gone! Where?

PRUDENCE. Off!—Eloped—eloped with the Count! Dear me, dear me! I always told you she would!

TIFFANY. Then I am ruined! (*Stands with his face buried in his hands.*)

MRS. TIFFANY. Oh, what a ridiculous girl! And she might have had such a splendid wedding! What could have possessed her?

TIFFANY. The devil himself possessed her, for she has ruined me past all redemption! Gone, Prudence, did you say gone? Are you *sure* they are gone?

PRUDENCE. Didn't I tell you so! Just look at this note—one might know by the very fold of it—

TIFFANY. (*Snatching the note.*) Let me see it! (*Opens the note and reads.*) "My dear Ma,—When you receive this I

shall be a *countess!* Isn't it a sweet title? The Count and
I were forced to be married privately, for reasons which I
will explain in my next. You must pacify Pa, and put him
in a good humor before I come back, though now I'm to
be a countess I suppose I shouldn't care!" Undutiful huzzy!
"We are going to make a little excursion and will be back
in a week

> Your dutiful daughter—Seraphina."

A man's curse is sure to spring up at his own hearth; here
is mine! The sole curb upon that villain gone, I am wholly
in his power! Oh! The first downward step from honor—he
who takes it cannot pause in his mad descent and is sure
to be hurried on to ruin!

MRS. TIFFANY. Why, Mr. Tiffany, how you do take on! And
I dare say to elope was the most fashionable way after all!

(*Enter* TRUEMAN, *leading* GERTRUDE, *and followed by*
HOWARD.)

TRUEMAN. Where are all the folks? Here, Antony, you are the
man I want. We've been hunting for you all over the house.
Why—what's the matter? There's a face for a thriving city
merchant! Ah! Antony, you never wore such a hang-dog
look as that when you trotted about the country with your
pack upon your back! Your shoulders are no broader now—
but they've a heavier load to carry—that's plain!

MRS. TIFFANY. Mr. Trueman, such allusions are highly improper! What would my daughter, *the Countess*, say!

GERTRUDE. The Countess? Oh! Madam!

MRS. TIFFANY. Yes, the Countess! My daughter Seraphina,
the Countess *dee* Jolimaitre! What have you to say to that?
No wonder you are surprised after your *recherché, abimé*
conduct! I have told you already, Miss Gertrude, that you
were not a proper person to enjoy the inestimable advan-
tages of my patronage. You are dismissed—do you understand? Discharged!

TRUEMAN. Have you done? Very well, it's my turn now.
Antony, perhaps what I have to say don't concern you as
much as some others—but I want you to listen to me. You
remember, Antony, (*His tone becomes serious.*) a blue-
eyed, smiling girl—

TIFFANY. Your daughter, Sir? I remember her well.

TRUEMAN. None ever saw her to forget her! Give me your hand, man. There—that will do! Now let me go on. I never coveted wealth—yet twenty years ago I found myself the richest farmer in Catteraugus. This cursed money made my girl an object of speculation. Every idle fellow that wanted to feather his nest was sure to come courting Ruth. There was one—my heart misgave me the instant I laid eyes upon him—for he was a city chap, and not over fond of the truth. But Ruth—ah! She was too pure herself to look for guile! His fine words and his fair looks—the old story—she was taken with him. I said, "no"—but the girl liked her own way better than her old father's—girls always do! And one morning—the rascal robbed me; not of my money—he would have been welcome to that—but of the only treasure I cherished—my daughter!

TIFFANY. But you forgave her!

TRUEMAN. I did! I knew she would never forgive herself— that was punishment enough! The scoundrel thought he was marrying my gold with my daughter—he was mistaken! I took care that they should never want; but that was all. She loved him—what will not woman love? The villain broke her heart—mine was tougher, or it wouldn't have stood what it did. A year after they were married, he forsook her! She came back to her old home—her old father! It couldn't last long—she pined—and pined—and—then—she died! Don't think me an old fool—though I am one—for grieving won't bring her back. (*Bursts into tears.*)

TIFFANY. It was a heavy loss!

TRUEMAN. So heavy, that I should not have cared how soon I followed her, but for the child she left! As I pressed that child in my arms, I swore that my unlucky wealth should never curse it, as it had cursed its mother! It was all I had to love—but I sent it away—and the neighbors thought it was dead. The girl was brought up tenderly but humbly by my wife's relatives in Geneva. I had her taught true independence—she had hands—capacities—and should use them! Money should never buy her a husband! For I re-solved not to claim her until she had made her choice, and found the man who was willing to take her for herself alone. She turned out a rare girl! And it's time her old grandfather claimed her. Here he is to do it! And there

stands Ruth's child! Old Adam's heiress! Gertrude, Gertrude!—My child!

(GERTRUDE *rushes into his arms.*)

PRUDENCE. (*After a pause.*) Do tell; I want to know! But I
knew it! I always said Gertrude would turn out somebody,
after all!

MRS. TIFFANY. Dear me! Gertrude an heiress! My dear Gertrude, I always thought you a very charming girl—quite
YOU-NICK—an heiress! (*Aside.*) I must give her a ball! I'll
introduce her into society myself—of course an heiress must
make a sensation!

HOWARD. (*Aside.*) I am too bewildered even to wish her joy.
Ah! there will be plenty to do that now—but the gulf
between us is wider than ever.

TRUEMAN. Step forward, young man, and let us know what
you are muttering about. I said I would never claim her
until she had found the man who loved her for herself. I
have claimed her—yet I never break my word—I think I
have found that man! and here he is. (*Strikes* HOWARD *on
the shoulder.*) Gertrude's yours! There—never say a word,
man—don't bore me with your thanks—you can cancel all
obligations by making that child happy! There—take her!—
Well, girl, and what do you say?

GERTRUDE. That I rejoice too much at having found a parent
for my first act to be one of disobedience! (*Gives her hand
to* HOWARD.)

(TIFFANY *retires up—and paces the stage, exhibiting great
agitation.*)

PRUDENCE. (*To* TRUEMAN). All the *single folks* are getting
married!

TRUEMAN. No they are not. You and I are single folks, and
we're not likely to get married.

MRS. TIFFANY. My dear Mr. Trueman—my sweet Gertrude,
when my daughter, the Countess, returns, she will be
delighted to hear of this *deenooment!* I assure you that the
countess will be quite charmed!

GERTRUDE. The Countess? Pray, Madam, where *is* Seraphina?

MRS. TIFFANY. The Countess *dee* Jolimaitre, my dear, is at
this moment on her way to—to Washington! Where after
visiting all the fashionable curiosities of the day—including
the President—she will return to grace her native city!

GERTRUDE. I hope you are only jesting, Madam? Seraphina is not married?

MRS. TIFFANY. Excuse me, my dear, my daughter had this morning the honor of being united to the Count *dee* Jolimaitre!

GERTRUDE. Madam! He is an impostor!

MRS. TIFFANY. Good gracious! Gertrude, how can you talk in that disrespectful way of a man of rank? An heiress, my dear, should have better manners! The Count—

(*Enter* MILLINETTE, *crying.*)

MILLINETTE. Oh! Madame! I will tell everyting—oh! dat monstre! He break my heart!

MRS. TIFFANY. Millinette, what is the matter?

MILLINETTE. Oh! he promise to marry me—I love him much—and now Zeke say he run away vid Mademoiselle Seraphina!

MRS. TIFFANY. What insolence! The girl is mad! Count Jolimaitre marry my *femmy de chamber*!

MILLINETTE. Oh! Madame, he is not one Count, not at all! Dat is only de title he go by in dis country. De foreigners always take de large title ven dey do come here. His name *à Paris* vas Gustave Treadmill. But he not one Frenchman at all, but he do live one long time *à Paris*. First he live vid Monsieur Vermicelle—dere he vas de head cook! Den he live vid Monsieur Tire-nez, de barber! After dat he live wid Monsieur le Comte Frippon-fin—and dere he vas le Comte's valet! Dere, now I tell everyting I feel one great deal better!

MRS. TIFFANY. Oh! Good gracious! I shall faint! Not a Count! What will everybody say? It's no such thing! I say he *is* a Count! One can see the foreign *jenny says quoi* in his face! Don't you think I can tell a Count when I see one? I say he *is* a Count!

(*Enter* SNOBSON, *his hat on, his hands thrust in his pocket, evidently a little intoxicated.*)

SNOBSON. I won't stand it! I say I won't!

TIFFANY. (*Rushing up to him. Aside.*) Mr. Snobson, for heaven's sake—

SNOBSON. Keep off! I'm a hard customer to get the better of!
You'll see if I don't come out strong!

TRUEMAN. (*Quietly knocking off* SNOBSON's *hat with his stick.*)
Where are your manners, man?

SNOBSON. My business ain't with you, Catteraugus; you've
waked up the wrong passenger! (*Aside.*) Now the way
I'll put it into Tiff will be a caution. I'll make him wince!
That extra mint julep has put the true pluck in me. Now
for it! —Mr. Tiffany, Sir—you needn't think to come over
me, Sir—you'll have to get up a little earlier in the morning
before you do *that*, Sir! I'd like to know, Sir, how you came
to assist your daughter in running away with that foreign
loafer? It was a downright swindle, Sir. After the conversation I and you had on that subject she wasn't your property, Sir.

TRUEMAN. What, Antony, is that the way your city clerk
bullies his boss?

SNOBSON. You're drunk, Catteraugus—don't expose your-self—
you're drunk! Taken a little too much toddy, my old boy!
Be quiet! I'll look after you, and they won't find it out. If
you want to be busy, you may take care of my *hat*—I feel
so deuced weak in the chest, I don't think I *could* pick it
up myself. (*Aside.*) Now to put the screws to Tiff. Mr.
Tiffany, Sir—you have broken your word, as no virtuous
individual—no honorable member—of—the—com—mu—ni—
ty—

TIFFANY. (*Aside to him.*) Have some pity, Mr. Snobson, I
beseech you! I had nothing to do with my daughter's
elopement! I will agree to anything you desire—your salary
shall be doubled—trebled—

SNOBSON. (*Aloud.*) No you don't. No bribery and corruption.

TIFFANY. (*Aside to him.*) I implore you to be silent. You shall
become partner of the concern, if you please—only do not
speak. You are not yourself at this moment.

SNOBSON. Ain't I, though? I feel *twice* myself. I feel like two
Snobsons rolled into one, and I'm chock full of the spunk
of a dozen! Now Mr. Tiffany, Sir—

TIFFANY. (*Aside to him.*) I shall go distracted! Mr. Snobson,
if you have one spark of manly feeling—

TRUEMAN. Antony, why do you stand disputing with that
drunken jackass? Where's your nigger? Let him kick the
critter out, and be of use for once in his life.

SNOBSON. Better be quiet, Catteraugus. This ain't your hash, so keep your spoon out of the dish. Don't expose yourself, old boy.

TRUEMAN. Turn him out, Antony!

SNOBSON. He daren't do it! Ain't I up to him? Ain't he in my power? Can't I knock him into a cocked hat with a word? And now he's got my steam up—I *will* do it!

TIFFANY. (*Beseechingly.*) Mr. Snobson—my friend—

SNOBSON. It's no go—steam's up—and I don't stand at anything!

TRUEMAN. You won't *stand* here long unless you mend your manners—you're not the first man I've *upset* because he didn't know his place.

SNOBSON. I know where Tiff's place is, and that's in the *States' Prison!* It's bespoke already. He would have it! He wouldn't take pattern of me, and behave like a gentleman! He's a *forger*, Sir!

(TIFFANY *throws himself into a chair in an attitude of despair; the others stand transfixed with astonishment.*) He's been forging Dick Anderson's endorsements of his notes these ten months. He's got a couple in the bank that will send him to the wall anyhow—if he can't make a raise. I took them there myself! Now you know what he's worth. I said I'd expose him, and I have done it!

MRS. TIFFANY. Get out of the house! You ugly, little, drunken brute, get out! It's not true. Mr. Trueman, put him out; you have got a stick—put him out!

(*Enter* SERAPHINA, *in her bonnet and shawl—a parasol in her hand.*)

SERAPHINA. I hope Zeke hasn't delivered my note. (*Stops in surprise at seeing the persons assembled.*)

MRS. TIFFANY. Oh, here is the Countess! (*Advances to embrace her.*)

TIFFANY. (*Starting from his seat, and seizing* SERAPHINA *violently by the arm.*) Are—you—married?

SERAPHINA. Goodness, Pa, how you frighten me! No, I'm not married, *quite*.

TIFFANY. Thank heaven.

MRS. TIFFANY. (*Drawing* SERAPHINA *aside.*) What's the matter? Why did you come back?

SERAPHINA. The clergyman wasn't at home—I came back for my jewels—the Count said nobility couldn't get on without them.

TIFFANY. I may be saved yet! Seraphina, my child, you will not see me disgraced—ruined! I have been a kind father to you—at least I have tried to be one—although your mother's extravagance made a *madman* of me! The Count is an impostor—you seemed to like him—(*pointing to* SNOBSON.) (*Aside.*) Heaven forgive me!—Marry *him* and save *me*. You, Mr. Trueman, you will be my friend in this hour of extreme need—you will advance the sum which I require— I pledge myself to return it. My wife—my child—who will support them were I—the thought makes me frantic! You will aid me? You had a child yourself.

TRUEMAN. But I did not *sell* her—it was her own doings. Shame on you, Antony! Put a price on your own flesh and blood! Shame on such foul traffic!

TIFFANY. Save me—I conjure you—for my father's sake.

TRUEMAN. For your *father's* SON's sake I will *not* aid you in becoming a greater villain than you are!

GERTRUDE. Mr. Trueman—Father, I should say—save him— do not embitter our happiness by permitting this calamity to fall upon another—

TRUEMAN. Enough—I did not need your voice, child. I am going to settle this matter my own way.
(*Goes up to* SNOBSON—*who has seated himself and fallen asleep—tilts him out of the chair.*)

SNOBSON. (*Waking up.*) Eh? Where's the fire? Oh! it's you, Catteraugus.

TRUEMAN. If I comprehend aright, you have been for some time aware of your principal's forgeries?
(*As he says this, he beckons to* HOWARD, *who advances as witness.*)

SNOBSON. You've hit the nail, Catteraugus! Old chap saw that I was up to him six months ago; left off throwing dust into my eyes—

TRUEMAN. Oh, he did!

SNOBSON. Made no bones of forging Anderson's name at my elbow.

TRUEMAN. Forged at your elbow? You saw him do it?

SNOBSON. I did.

TRUEMAN. Repeatedly.

SNOBSON. Re—pea—ted—ly.

TRUEMAN. Then you, Rattlesnake, if he goes to the States' Prison, you'll take up your quarters there too. You are an accomplice, an *accessory!*

(TRUEMAN *walks away and seats himself,* HOWARD *rejoins* GERTRUDE. SNOBSON *stands for some time bewildered.*)

SNOBSON. The deuce, so I am! I never thought of that! I must make myself scarce. I'll be off! Tif, I say, Tif! (*Going up to him and speaking confidentially*) That drunken old rip has got us in his power. Let's give him the slip and be off. They want men of genius at the West—we're sure to get on! You—you can set up for a writing master, and teach copying *signatures;* and I—I'll give lectures on *temperance!* You won't come, eh? Then I'm off without you. Good bye, Catteraugus! Which is the way to California? (*Steals off.*)

TRUEMAN. There's one debt your city owes me. And now let us see what other nuisances we can abate. Antony, I'm not given to preaching; therefore I shall not say much about what you have done. Your face speaks for itself—the crime has brought its punishment along with it.

TIFFANY. Indeed it has, Sir! In *one year* I have lived a *century* of misery.

TRUEMAN. I believe you, and upon one condition I will assist you—

TIFFANY. My friend—my first, ever kind friend—only name it!

TRUEMAN. You must sell your house and all these gew-gaws, and bundle your wife and daughter off to the country. There let them learn economy, true independence, and home virtues, instead of foreign follies. As for yourself, continue your business—but let moderation, in future, be your counsellor, and let *honesty* be your confidential clerk.

TIFFANY. Mr. Trueman, you have made existence once more precious to me! My wife and daughter shall quit the city tomorrow, and—

PRUDENCE. It's all coming right! It's all coming right! We'll go to the county of Catteraugus. (*Walking up to* TRUEMAN.)

TRUEMAN. No, you won't—I make that a stipulation, Antony; keep clear of Catteraugus. None of your fashionable examples there!

(JOLIMAITRE *appears in the Conservatory and peeps into the room unperceived.*)

COUNT. What can detain Seraphina? We ought to be off!

MILLINETTE. (*Turns round, perceives him, runs and forces him into the room.*) Here he is! Ah, Gustave, mon cher Gustave! I have you now and we never part no more. Don't frown, Gustave, don't frown—

TRUEMAN. Come forward, Mr. Count! and for the edification of fashionable society confess that you're an impostor.

COUNT. An impostor? Why, you abominable old—

TRUEMAN. Oh, your feminine friend has told us all about it, the cook—the valet—barber and all that sort of thing. Come, confess, and something may be done for you.

COUNT. Well, then, I do confess I am no count; but really, ladies and gentlemen, I may recommend myself as the most capital cook.

MRS. TIFFANY. Oh, Seraphina!

SERAPHINA. Oh, Ma!

(*They embrace and retire up.*)

TRUEMAN. Promise me to call upon the whole circle of your fashionable acquaintances with your own advertisements and in your cook's attire, and I will set you up in business tomorrow. Better turn stomachs than turn heads!

MILLINETTE. But you will marry me?

COUNT. Give us your hand, Millinette! Sir, command me for the most delicate *paté*—the daintiest *croquette à la royale* —the most transcendent *omelette soufflée* that ever issued from a French pastry-cook's oven. I hope you will pardon my conduct, but I heard that in America, where you pay homage to titles while you profess to scorn them—where *Fashion* makes the basest coin current—where you have no kings, no princes, no *nobility*—

TRUEMAN. Stop there! I object to your use of that word. When justice is found only among lawyers, health among physicians, and patriotism among politicians, *then* may you say that there is no *nobility* where there are no titles! But we *have* kings, princes, and nobles in abundance—of *Nature's stamp*, if not of *Fashion's*; we have honest men, warm hearted and brave, and we have women—gentle, fair, and true, to whom no *title* could add *nobility*.

EPILOGUE

PRUDENCE. I told you so! And now you hear and see.
I told you *Fashion* would the fashion be!
TRUEMAN. Then both its point and moral I distrust.
COUNT. Sir, is that liberal?
HOWARD.   Or is it just?
TRUEMAN. The guilty have escaped!
TIFFANY.   Is, therefore, sin
Made charming? Ah! There's punishment within!
Guilt ever carries his own scourge along.
GERTRUDE. Virtue her own reward!
TRUEMAN.   You're right, I'm wrong.
MRS. TIFFANY. How we have been deceived!
PRUDENCE.   I told you so.
SERAPHINA. To lose at once a title and a beau!
COUNT. A count no more, I'm no more of *account*.
TRUEMAN. But to a nobler title you may mount,
And be in time—who knows?—an honest man!
COUNT. Eh, Millinette?
MILLINETT.   Oh, *oui*—I know you can!
GERTRUDE. (*To audience.*) But ere we close the scene, a
word with you,—
We charge you answer: Is this picture true?
Some little mercy to our efforts show,
Then let the world your honest verdict know.
Here let it see portrayed its ruling passion,
And learn to prize at its just value—*Fashion*.

FRANCESCA DA RIMINI

Preface to FRANCESCA DA RIMINI

Francesca da Rimini is one of our finest verse dramas, certainly the best American romantic tragedy written before the twentieth century. Its first run, starring E.L. Davenport as Lanciotto at the New York Broadway Theatre in 1855, lasted for a week—a respectable showing for a serious poetic drama. In 1882 Lawrence Barrett, playing Lanciotto to Otis Skinner's Paolo, began a successful revival that lasted several years. Otis Skinner himself revived the play in the 1901–1902 season, playing Lanciotto to the Paolo of Dion Boucicault's son, Aubrey. By then the reputation of the play as well as that of Boker had been firmly established.

George Henry Boker (1823–1890) was born into a wealthy Philadelphia banker's family. He began his literary career in 1848 with a book of poetry, *The Lesson of Life*. At that time he also began his lifelong friendships with Bayard Taylor and Richard Henry Stoddard who, together with Boker's childhood friend Charles Godfrey Leland, formed a literary coterie of some importance in American letters. Boker's later verse publications included *Poems of War* (1864), which was but one expression of his strong Unionist sentiments. Early during the Civil War he had left the Democratic party, with which most other well-to-do Philadelphia families were affiliated. He became an active Republican, was influential in rehabilitating the party in the city, and helped found the Union League Club, whose president he eventually became. In 1871 Boker was appointed Minister to Turkey, a post he held four years; he was then promoted to a higher ministerial rank, at the Russian court, where he remained two years. After having distinguished himself in both posts, he returned to his home in Philadelphia in 1878, where he continued his literary activities until his death.

Boker's first play, *Calaynos* (produced in 1849), like *Francesca da Rimini*, is a blank-verse tragedy with an exotic setting and romantic characters and plot: Calaynos is a Spanish nobleman, the discovery of whose Moorish taint brings about his wife's seduction and the ensuing tragedy. His other plays are, for the most part, similar in type: *Anne Boleyn* (published in 1850) reinterprets the decline and fall of Henry VIII's second wife; *Leonor de Guzman* (produced in 1853), another historical tragedy, deals with fourteenth-century Castile and the power struggle following the death of Alfonso XII; and two plays are based on Bulwer-Lytton's *The Last Days of Pompeii—Nydia* (1885) and *Glaucus* (1886), Boker's last play. He also wrote a comedy, *The Betrothal* (produced in 1850), and a number of other dramatic works.

His masterpiece is unquestionably *Francesca da Rimini*. Although it was the first (and probably is still the best) dramatization in English of the famous love story, two others had been made elsewhere before: in Germany, Johann Ludwig Uhland's fragmentary *Franceska da Rimino* (1807, never performed), and in Italy, Silvio Pellico's *Francesca da Rimini* (produced in Milan in 1818). Among later dramatizations are the English poet Stephen Phillips's *Paolo and Francesca* (1899, performed in 1902), Francis Marion Crawford's *Francesca da Rimini* (1902, written for Sarah Bernhardt), and Gabriele D'Annunzio's spectacle *Francesca da Rimini* (1902), written for Eleonora Duse, and stressing the licentiousness of society in medieval Italy. Although these and other dramatizations give very different interpretations of plot and characters, all of them were inspired by the same well-known lines of Canto V of Dante's *Inferno*. They describe Paolo and Francesca innocently reading "the rhyme of Lancelot, how love had mastered him," and how they are thereupon overwhelmed by emotion: they kiss—and "read no more that day."

Despite many legends that have grown around this poetic episode, the historical facts are very scant and somewhat less romantic. Shortly after 1275 Guido Vecchio da Polenta, of Ravenna, for political reasons had his daughter Francesca marry Gianciotto (the Lanciotto of Boker's play), the deformed son of Malatesta da Verrucchio, of Rimini. Gianciotto's younger brother Paolo at the time had been married for some years and had two children. Between seven and ten years after Francesca's marriage—she had a daughter by then—Gianciotto surprised the lovers in a room, and killed them both. In his immortal poem Dante, who knew Paolo, transformed a notorious *crime passionnel* into one of the world's great love stories.

As others have done, Boker built upon the bare narrative sketch in Dante's moving lines. His characterizations reveal strongly the influence of Boker's readings of Elizabethan tragedy. He invests Lanciotto, the protagonist of this play, with genuinely tragic proportions. Pepé, the court jester who becomes the instrument of the tragedy, is entirely Boker's invention, and in some ways the most interesting character in the play. The two lovers are sensitively portrayed; and even such relatively minor characters as the fathers, Malatesta and Guido, and Francesca's maid, Ritta, are rounded and individualized. Boker's blank verse, too, is Elizabethan in tone, and there are frequent echoes of Shakespeare in his lines. In this play, as in others, Boker followed the advice he himself had given Stoddard as early as 1850: "Get out of your age as far as you can."

There are various extant acting versions of *Francesca da Rimini*, including Barrett's (later used by Otis Skinner), which contains changes made, for stage production, by Boker himself. The text that follows is Boker's final version of the play, as printed in his *Plays and Poems* (1856, reprinted until 1891). Boker's biography is Edward S. Bradley's *George Henry Boker, Poet and Patriot* (1927).

M.M.

FRANCESCA DA RIMINI
by George Henry Boker

Characters

MALATESTA, Lord of Rimini
GUIDO DA POLENTA, Lord of Ravenna
LANCIOTTO, Malatesta's son
PAOLO, His brother
PEPÉ, Malatesta's jester
CARDINAL, Friend to Guido
RENÉ, A troubadour
FRANCESCA DA RIMINI, Guido's daughter
RITTA, Her maid

Lords, Ladies, Knights, Priests, Soldiers, Pages, Attendants,
&c.

SCENE: Rimini, Ravenna, and the neighborhood.

TIME, about 1300 A.D.

ACT I

Scene 1

Rimini. The Garden of the Palace. PAOLO *and a number of noblemen are discovered, seated under an arbor, surrounded by* RENÉ, *and other Troubadours, attendants, and so forth.*

PAOLO. I prithee, René, charm our ears again
With the same song you sang me yesterday.
Here are fresh listeners.
RENÉ.   Really, my good lord,
My voice is out of joint. A grievous cold—
(*Coughs.*)
PAOLO. A very grievous, but convenient cold,
Which always racks you when you would not sing.
RENÉ. O, no, my lord! Besides, I hoped to hear
My ditty warbled into fairer ears,
By your own lips; to better purpose, too.
(*The Noblemen all laugh.*)
FIRST NOBLEMAN. René has hit it. Music runs to waste
In ears like ours.
SECOND NOBLEMAN. Nay, nay; chaunt on, sweet Count.
PAOLO. (*Coughing.*) Alack! you hear, I've caught poor René's
cough.
FIRST NOBLEMAN. That would not be, if we wore petticoats.
(*The others laugh.*)
PAOLO. O, fie!
FIRST NOBLEMAN.   So runs the scandal to our ears.
SECOND NOBLEMAN. Confirmed by all our other senses, Count.
FIRST NOBLEMAN. Witnessed by many a doleful sigh, poured
out
By many a breaking heart in Rimini.
SECOND NOBLEMAN. Poor girls!
FIRST NOBLEMAN. (*Mimicking a lady.*) Sweet Count! sweet
Count Paolo! O!
Plant early violets upon my grave!
Thus go a thousand voices to one tune.
(*The others laugh.*)

PAOLO. 'Ods mercy! gentlemen, you do me wrong.

FIRST NOBLEMAN. And by how many hundred, more or less?

PAOLO. Ah! rogues, you'd shift your sins upon my shoulders.

SECOND NOBLEMAN. You'd bear them stoutly.

FIRST NOBLEMAN. It were vain to give
Drops to god Neptune. You're the sea of love
That swallows all things.

SECOND NOBLEMAN. We the little fish
That meanly scull about within your depths.

PAOLO. Go on, go on! Talk yourselves fairly out.
(PEPÉ *laughs without.*)
But, hark! here comes the fool. Fit company
For this most noble company of wits!
(*Enter* PEPÉ, *laughing violently.*)
Why do you laugh?

PEPÉ. I'm laughing at the world.
It has laughed long enough at me; and so
I'll turn the tables. Ho! ho! ho! I've heard
A better joke of Uncle Malatesta's
Than any I e'er uttered.
(*Laughing.*)

ALL. Tell it, fool.

PEPÉ. Why, do you know—upon my life, the best
And most original idea on earth:
A joke to put in practice, too. By Jove!
I'll bet my wit 'gainst the stupidity
Of the best gentleman among you all,
You cannot guess it.

ALL. Tell us, tell us, fool.

PEPÉ. Guess it, guess it, fools.

PAOLO. Come, disclose, disclose!

PEPÉ. He has a match afoot.—

ALL. A match!

PEPÉ. A marriage.

ALL. Who?—who?

PEPÉ. A marriage in his family.

ALL. But, who?

PEPÉ. Ah! there's the point.

ALL. Paolo?

PEPÉ. No.

FIRST NOBLEMAN. The others are well wived. Shall we turn
Turks?

PEPÉ. Why, there's the summit of his joke, good sirs.
By all the sacred symbols of my art—
By cap and bauble, by my tinkling bell—
He means to marry Lanciotto!
(*Laughs violently.*)
ALL. (*Laughing.*) Ho!—
PAOLO. Peace! peace! What tongue dare echo yon fool's
laugh?
Nay, never raise your hands in wonderment:
I'll strike the dearest friend among ye all
Beneath my feet, as if he were a slave,
Who dares insult my brother with a laugh!
PEPÉ. By Jove! ye're sad enough. Here's mirth's quick cure!
Pretty Paolo has a heavy fist,
I warn you, sirs. Ho! ho! I trapped them all;
(*Laughing.*)
(*Aside.*) Now I'll go mar old Malatesta's message.
(*Exit.*)
PAOLO. Shame on ye, sirs! I have mistaken you.
I thought I harbored better friends. Poor fops,
Who've slept in down and satin all your years,
Within the circle Lanciotto charmed
Round Rimini with his most potent sword!—
Fellows whose brows would melt beneath a casque,
Whose hands would fray to grasp a brand's rough hilt,
Who ne'er launched more than braggart threats at foes!—
Girlish companions of luxurious girls!—
Danglers round troubadours and wine-cups!—Men
Whose best parts are their clothes! bundles of silk,
Scented like summer! rag-men, nothing more!—
Creatures as generous as monkeys—brave
As hunted hares—courteous as grinning apes—
Grateful as serpents—useful as lap-dogs—
(*During this, the Noblemen, and so forth steal off.*)
                                             Ha!
I am alone at last! So let me be,
Till Lanciotto fill the vacant room
Of these mean knaves, whose friendship is but breath.
(*Exit.*)

Scene 2

The Same. A Hall in the Castle. Enter MALATESTA *and* LANCIOTTO.

MALATESTA. Guido, ay, Guido of Ravenna, son—
Down on his knees, as full of abject prayers
For peace and mercy as a penitent.
LANCIOTTO. His old trick, father. While his wearied arm
Is raised in seeming prayer, it only rests.
Anon, he'll deal you such a staggering blow,
With its recovered strength, as shall convert
You, and not him, into a penitent.
MALATESTA. No, no; your last bout levelled him. He reeled
Into Ravenna from the battle-field,
Like a stripped drunkard, and there headlong fell—
A mass of squalid misery, a thing
To draw the jeering urchins. I have this
From faithful spies. There's not a hope remains
To break the shock of his great overthrow.
I pity Guido.
LANCIOTTO. 'Sdeath! go comfort him!
I pity those who fought, and bled, and died,
Before the armies of this Ghibelin.[1]
I pity those who halted home with wounds
Dealt by his hand. I pity widowed eyes
That he set running; maiden hearts that turn,
Sick with despair, from ranks thinned down by him;
Mothers that shriek, as the last stragglers fling
Their feverish bodies by the fountain-side,
Dumb with mere thirst, and faintly point to him,
Answering the dame's quick questions. I have seen
Unburied bones, and skulls—that seemed to ask,
From their blank eye-holes, vengeance at my hand—
Shine in the moonlight on old battle-fields;

[1] Member of the party upholding the authority of the German emperors in medieval Italy, as opposed to the Guelph party that upheld the authority of the papacy.

And even these—the happy dead, my lord—
I pity more than Guido of Ravenna!
MALATESTA. What would you have?
LANCIOTTO.   I'd see Ravenna burn,
Flame into heaven, and scorch the flying clouds;
I'd choke her streets with ruined palaces;
I'd hear her women scream with fear and grief,
As I have heard the maids of Rimini.
All this I'd sprinkle with old Guido's blood,
And bless the baptism.
MALATESTA.   You are cruel.
LANCIOTTO.   Not I;
But these things ache within my fretting brain.
The sight I first beheld was from the arms
Of my wild nurse, her husband hacked to death
By the fierce edges of these Ghibelins.
One cut across the neck—I see it now,
Ay, and have mimicked it a thousand times,
Just as I saw it, on our enemies.—
Why, that cut seemed as if it meant to bleed
On till the judgment. My distracted nurse
Stooped down, and paddled in the running gore
With her poor fingers; then a prophetess,
Pale with the inspiration of the god,
She towered aloft, and with her dripping hand
Three times she signed me with the holy cross.
'Tis all as plain as noon-day. Thus she spake:
"May this spot stand till Guido's dearest blood
Be mingled with thy own!" The soldiers say,
In the close battle, when my wrath is up,
The dead man's blood flames on my vengeful brow
Like a red planet; and when war is o'er,
It shrinks into my brain, defiling all
My better nature with its slaughterous lusts.
Howe'er it be, it shaped my earliest thought,
And it will shape my last.
MALATESTA.   You moody churl!
You dismal knot of superstitious dreams!
Do you not blush to empty such a head
Before a sober man? Why, son, the world
Has not given o'er its laughing humor yet,

That you should try it with such vagaries.—Poh!
I'll get a wife to teach you common sense.
LANCIOTTO. A wife for me!
  (*Laughing.*)
MALATESTA.   Ay, sir, a wife for you.
You shall be married, to insure your wits.
LANCIOTTO. 'T is not your wont to mock me.
MALATESTA.   How now, son!
I am not given to jesting. I have chosen
The fairest wife in Italy for you.
You won her bravely, as a soldier should:
And when you'd woo her, stretch your gauntlet out,
And crush her fingers in its steely grip.
If you will plead, I ween, she dare not say—
No, by your leave. Should she refuse, howe'er,
With that same iron hand you shall go knock
Upon Ravenna's gates, till all the town
Ring with your courtship. I have made her hand
The price and pledge of Guido's future peace.
LANCIOTTO. All this is done!
MALATESTA.   Done, out of hand; and now
I wait a formal answer, nothing more.
Guido dare not decline. No, by the saints,
He'd send Ravenna's virgins here in droves,
To buy a ten days' truce.
LANCIOTTO.   Sir, let me say,
You stretch paternal privilege too far,
To pledge my hand without my own consent.
Am I a portion of your household stuff,
That you should trade me off to Guido thus?
Who is the lady I am bartered for?
MALATESTA. Francesca, Guido's daughter.—Never frown;
It shall be so!
LANCIOTTO.   By heaven, it shall not be!
My blood shall never mingle with his race.
MALATESTA. According to your nurse's prophecy,
Fate orders it.
LANCIOTTO.   Ha!
MALATESTA.   Now, then, I have struck
The chord that answers to your gloomy thoughts.
Bah! on your sibyl and her prophecy!

Put Guido's blood aside, and yet, I say,
Marry you shall.
LANCIOTTO.   'T is most distasteful, sir.
MALATESTA. Lanciotto, look ye! You brave gentlemen,
So fond of knocking out poor people's brains,
In time must come to have your own knocked out:
What, then, if you bequeath us no new hands,
To carry on your business, and our house
Die out for lack of princes?
LANCIOTTO.   Wed my brothers:
They'll rear you sons, I'll slay you enemies.
Paolo and Francesca! Note their names;
They chime together like sweet marriage-bells.
A proper match. 'T is said she's beautiful;
And he is the delight of Rimini,—
The pride and conscious centre of all eyes,
The theme of poets, the ideal of art,
The earthly treasury of Heaven's best gifts!
I am a soldier; from my very birth,
Heaven cut me out for terror, not for love.
I had such fancies once, but now—
MALATESTA.   Pshaw! son,
My faith is bound to Guido; and if you
Do not throw off your duty, and defy,
Through sickly scruples, my express commands,
You'll yield at once. No more: I'll have it so!
(Exit.)
LANCIOTTO. Curses upon my destiny! What, I—
Ho! I have found my use at last—What. I.
(Laughing.)
I, the great twisted monster of the wars,
The brawny cripple, the herculean dwarf,
The spur of panic, and the butt of scorn—
I be a bridegroom! Heaven, was I not cursed
More than enough, when thou didst fashion me
To be a type of ugliness,—a thing
By whose comparison all Rimini
Holds itself beautiful? Lo! here I stand,
A gnarléd, blighted trunk! There's not a knave
So spindle-shanked, so wry-faced, so infirm,
Who looks at me, and smiles not on himself.

And I have friends to pity me—great Heaven!
One has a favorite leg that he bewails,—
Another sees my hip with doleful plaints,—
A third is sorry o'er my huge swart arms,—
A fourth aspires to mount my very hump,
And thence harangue his weeping brotherhood!
Pah! it is nauseous! Must I further bear
The sidelong shuddering glances of a wife?
The degradation of a showy love,
That over-acts, and proves the mummer's craft
Untouched by nature? And a fair wife, too!—
Francesca, whom the minstrels sing about!
Though, by my side, what woman were not fair?
Circe looked well among her swine, no doubt;
Next me, she'd pass for Venus. Ho! ho! ho!
(*Laughing.*)
Would there were something merry in my laugh!
Now, in the battle, if a Ghibelin
Cry, "Wry-hip! hunchback!" I can trample him
Under my stallion's hoofs; or haggle him
Into a monstrous likeness of myself:
But to be pitied,—to endure a sting
Thrust in by kindness, with a sort of smile!—
'Sdeath! it is miserable!

(*Enter* PEPÉ.)

PEPÉ.   My lord—
LANCIOTTO.   My fool!
PEPÉ. We'll change our titles when your bride's bells ring—
    Ha, cousin?
LANCIOTTO. (*Aside.*) Even this poor fool has eyes,
    To see the wretched plight in which I stand.
    How, gossip, how?
PEPÉ.   I, being the court-fool,
    Am lord of fools by my prerogative.
LANCIOTTO. Who told you of my marriage?
PEPÉ.   Rimini!
    A frightful liar; but true for once, I fear.
    The messenger from Guido has returned,
    And the whole town is wailing over him.

Some pity you, and some the bride; but I,
Being more catholic, I pity both.
LANCIOTTO. (*Aside.*) Still, pity, pity!
(*Bells toll.*)
Ha! whose knell is that?
PEPÉ. Lord Malatesta sent me to the tower,
To have the bells rung for your marriage-news.
How, he said not; so I, as I thought fit,
Told the deaf sexton to ring out a knell.
(*Bells toll.*)
How do you like it?
LANCIOTTO. Varlet, have you bones,
To risk their breaking? I have half a mind
To thresh you from your motley coat!
(*Seizes him.*)
PEPÉ. Pardee!
Respect my coxcomb, cousin. Hark, ha, ha!
(*Laughing.*)
(*Bells ring a joyful peal.*)
Some one has changed my music. Heaven defend!
How the bells jangle! Yonder graybeard, now,
Rings a peal vilely. He's more used to knells,
And sounds them grandly. Only give him time,
And, I'll be sworn, he'll ring your knell out yet.
LANCIOTTO. Pepé, you are but half a fool.
PEPÉ. My lord,
I can return the compliment in full.
LANCIOTTO. So, you are ready.
PEPÉ. Truth is always so.
LANCIOTTO. I shook you rudely; here's a florin.
(*Offers money.*)
PEPÉ. No:
My wit is merchandise, but not my honor.
LANCIOTTO. Your honor, sirrah!
PEPÉ. Why not? You great lords
Have something you call lordly honor; pray,
May not a fool have foolish honor too?
Cousin, you laid your hand upon my coat—
'T was the first sacrilege it ever knew—
And you shall pay it. Mark! I promise you.
LANCIOTTO. (*Laughing.*) Ha, ha! you bluster well. Upon my
life,

You have the tilt-yard jargon to a breath.
Pepé, if I should smite you on the cheek—
Thus, gossip, thus—(*Strikes him.*) what would you then
    demand?
PEPÉ. Your life!
LANCIOTTO. (*Laughing.*) Ha, ha! there is the camp-style too—
A very cut-throat air! How this shrewd fool
Makes the punctilio of honor show!
Change helmets into coxcombs, swords to baubles,
And what a figure is poor chivalry!
Thanks for your lesson, Pepé!
(*Exit.*)
PEPÉ.   Ere I'm done,
You'll curse as heartily, you limping beast!
Ha! so we go—Lord Lanciotto, look!
(*Walks about, mimicking him.*)
Here is a leg and camel-back, forsooth,
To match your honor and nobility!
You miscreated scarecrow, dare you shake,
Or strike in jest, a natural man like me?—
You curséd lump, you chaos of a man,
To buffet one whom Heaven pronounces good!
(*Bells ring.*)
There go the bells rejoicing over you:
I'll change them back to the old knell again.
You marry, faugh! Beget a race of elves;
Wed a she-crocodile, and keep within
The limits of your nature! Here we go,
Tripping along to meet our promised bride,
Like a rheumatic elephant!—ha, ha!
(*Laughing. Exit, mimicking* LANCIOTTO.)

Scene 3

The Same. A Room in the Same. Enter LANCIOTTO, *hastily.*

LANCIOTTO. Why do these prodigies environ me?
In ancient Rome, the words a fool might drop,
From the confusion of his vagrant thoughts,
Were held as omens, prophecies; and men
Who made earth tremble with majestic deeds,

Trembled themselves at fortune's lightest threat.
I like it not. My father named this match
While I boiled over with vindictive wrath
Towards Guido and Ravenna. Straight my heart
Sank down like lead; a weakness seized on me,
A dismal gloom that I could not resist;
I lacked the power to take my stand, and say—
Bluntly, I will not! Am I in the toils?
Has fate so weakened me, to work its end?
There seems a fascination in it, too,—
A morbid craving to pursue a thing
Whose issue may be fatal. Would that I
Were in the wars again! These mental weeds
Grow on the surface of inactive peace.
I'm haunted by myself. Thought preys on thought.
My mind seems crowded in the hideous mould
That shaped my body. What a fool am I
To bear the burden of my wretched life,
To sweat and toil under the world's broad eye,
Climb into fame, and find myself—O, what?—
A most conspicuous monster! Crown my head,
Pile Caesar's purple on me—and what then?
My hump shall shorten the imperial robe,
My leg peep out beneath the scanty hem,
My broken hip shall twist the gown awry;
And pomp, instead of dignifying me,
Shall be by me made quite ridiculous.
The faintest coward would not bear all this:
Prodigious courage must be mine, to live;
To die asks nothing but weak will, and I
Feel like a craven. Let me skulk away
Ere life o'ertask me.
(*Offers to stab himself.*)

(*Enter* PAOLO.)

PAOLO. (*Seizing his hand.*) Brother! what is this?
Lanciotto, are you mad? Kind Heaven! look here—
Straight in my eyes. Now answer, do you know
How near you were to murder? Dare you bend
Your wicked hand against a heart I love?
Were it for you to mourn your wilful death,

With such a bitterness as would be ours,
The wish would ne'er have crossed you. While we're bound
Life into life, a chain of loving hearts,
Were it not base in you, the middle link,
To snap, and scatter all? Shame, brother, shame!
I thought you better metal.
LANCIOTTO.   Spare your words.
I know the seasons of our human grief,
And can predict them without almanac.
A few sobs o'er the body, and a few
Over the coffin; then a sigh or two,
Whose windy passage dries the hanging tear;
Perchance, some wandering memories, some regrets;
Then a vast influx of consoling thoughts—
Based on the trials of the sadder days
Which the dead missed; and then a smiling face
Turned on to-morrow. Such is mortal grief.
It writes its histories within a span,
And never lives to read them.
PAOLO.   Lanciotto,
I heard the bells of Rimini, just now,
Exulting o'er your coming marriage-day,
While you conspired to teach them gloomier sounds.
Why are you sad?
LANCIOTTO.   Paolo, I am wretched;
Sad's a faint word. But of my marriage-bells—
Heard you the knell that Pepé rang?
PAOLO.   'T was strange:
A sullen antic of his crabbed wit.
LANCIOTTO. It was portentous. All dumb things find tongues
Against this marriage. As I passed the hall,
My armor glittered on the wall, and I
Paused by the harness, as before a friend
Whose well-known features slack our hurried gait;
Francesca's name was fresh upon my mind,
So I half-uttered it. Instant, my sword
Leaped from its scabbard, as with sudden life,
Plunged down and pierced into the oaken floor,
Shivering with fear! Lo! while I gazed upon it—
Doubting the nature of the accident—
Around the point appeared a spot of blood,
Oozing upon the floor, that spread and spread—

As I stood gasping by in speechless horror—
Ring beyond ring, until the odious tide
Crawled to my feet, and lapped them, like the tongues
Of angry serpents! O, my God! I fled
At the first touch of the infernal stain!
Go—you may see—go to the hall!
PAOLO.   Fie! man,
You have been ever played on in this sort
By your wild fancies. When your heart is high,
You make them playthings; but in lower moods,
They seem to sap the essence of your soul,
And drain your manhood to its poorest dregs.
LANCIOTTO. Go look, go look!
PAOLO. (*Goes to the door, and returns.*) There sticks the
      sword, indeed,
Just as your tread detached it from its sheath;
Looking more like a blessed cross, I think,
Than a bad omen. As for blood—Ha, ha!
(*Laughing.*)
It sets mine dancing. Pshaw! away with this!
Deck up your face with smiles. Go trim yourself
For the young bride. New velvet, gold, and gems,
Do wonders for us. Brother, come; I'll be
Your tiring-man, for once.
LANCIOTTO.   Array this lump—
Paolo, hark! There are some human thoughts
Best left imprisoned in the aching heart,
Lest the freed malefactors should dispread
Infamous ruin with their liberty.
There's not a man—the fairest of ye all—
Who is not fouler than he seems. This life
Is one unending struggle to conceal
Our baseness from our fellows. Here stands one
In vestal whiteness with a lecher's lust;—
There sits a judge, holding law's scales in hands
That itch to take the bribe he dare not touch;—
Here goes a priest, with heavenward eyes, whose soul
Is Satan's council-chamber;—there a doctor,
With nature's secrets wrinkled round a brow
Guilty with conscious ignorance;—and here
A soldier rivals Hector's bloody deeds—
Out-does the devil in audacity—

With craven longings fluttering in a heart
That dares do aught but fly! Thus are we all
Mere slaves and alms-men to a scornful world,
That takes us at our seeming.

PAOLO.   Say 't is true;
What do you drive at?

LANCIOTTO.   At myself, full tilt.
I, like the others, am not what I seem.
Men call me gentle, courteous, brave.—They lie!
I'm harsh, rude, and a coward. Had I nerve
To cast my devils out upon the earth,
I'd show this laughing planet what a hell
Of envy, malice, cruelty, and scorn,
It has forced back to canker in the heart
Of one poor cripple!

PAOLO.   Ha!

LANCIOTTO.   Ay, now 't is out!
A word I never breathed to man before.
Can you, who are a miracle of grace,
Feel what it is to be a wreck like me?
Paolo, look at me. Is there a line,
In my whole bulk of wretched contraries,
That nature in a nightmare ever used
Upon her shapes till now? Find me the man,
Or beast, or tree, or rock, or nameless thing,
So out of harmony with all things else,
And I'll go raving with bare happiness,—
Ay, and I'll marry Helena of Greece,
And swear I do her honor!

PAOLO.   Lanciotto,
I, who have known you from a stripling up,
Never observed, or, if I did, ne'er weighed
Your special difference from the rest of men.
You're not Apollo—

LANCIOTTO.   No!

PAOLO.   Nor yet are you
A second Pluto. Could I change with you—
My graces for your nobler qualities—
Your strength, your courage, your renown—by heaven,
We'd e'en change persons, to the finest hair.

LANCIOTTO. You should be flatterer to an emperor.

PAOLO. I am but just. Let me beseech you, brother,

To look with greater favor on yourself;
Nor suffer misty phantoms of your brain
To take the place of sound realities.
Go to Ravenna, wed your bride, and lull
Your cruel delusions in domestic peace.
Ghosts fly a fireside: 't is their wont to stalk
Through empty houses, and through empty hearts.
I know Francesca will be proud of you.
Women admire you heroes. Rusty sages,
Pale poets, and scarred warriors, have been
Their idols ever; while we fair plump fools
Are elbowed to the wall, or only used
For vacant pastime.
LANCIOTTO.   To Ravenna?—no!
In Rimini they know me; at Ravenna
I'd be a new-come monster, and exposed
To curious wonder. There will be parade
Of all the usual follies of the state;
Fellows with trumpets, tinselled coats, and wands,
Would strut before me, like vain mountebanks
Before their monkeys. Then, I should be stared
Out of my modesty; and when they look,
How can I tell if 't is the bridegroom's face
Or hump that draws their eyes? I will not go.
To please you all, I'll marry; but to please
The wonder-mongers of Ravenna—Ha!
Paolo, now I have it. You shall go,
To bring Francesca; and you'll speak of me,
Not as I ought to be, but as I am.
If she draw backward, give her rein; and say
That neither Guido nor herself shall feel
The weight of my displeasure. You may say,
I pity her—
PAOLO.   For what?
LANCIOTTO.   For wedding me.
In sooth, she'll need it. Say—
PAOLO.   Nay, Lanciotto,
I'll be a better orator in your behalf,
Without your promptings.
LANCIOTTO.   She is fair, 't is said;
And, dear Paolo, if she please your eye,
And move your heart to anything like love,

Wed her yourself. The peace would stand as firm
By such a match.
PAOLO. (*Laughing.*) Ha! that is right: be gay!
Ply me with jokes! I'd rather see you smile
Than see the sun shine.
LANCIOTTO.   I am serious.
I'll find another wife, less beautiful,
More on my level, and—
PAOLO.   An empress, brother,
Were honored by your hand. You are by much
Too humble in your reckoning of yourself.
I can count virtues in you, to supply
Half Italy, if they were parcelled out.
Look up!
LANCIOTTO. I cannot: Heaven has bent me down.
To you, Paolo, I could look, however,
Were my hump made a mountain. Bless him, God!
Pour everlasting bounties on his head!
Make Crœsus jealous of his treasury,
Achilles of his arms, Endymion
Of his fresh beauties,—though the coy one lay,
Blushing beneath Diana's earliest kiss,
On grassy Latmos: and may every good,
Beyond man's sight, though in the ken of Heaven,
Round his fair fortune to a perfect end!
O, you have dried the sorrow of my eyes;
My heart is beating with a lighter pulse;
The air is musical; the total earth
Puts on new beauty, and within the arms
Of girding ocean dreams her time away,
And visions bright to-morrows!

(*Enter* MALATESTA *and* PEPÉ.)

MALATESTA.   Mount, to horse!
PEPÉ. (*Aside.*) Good Lord! he's smiling! What's the matter
    now?
Has anybody broken a leg or back?
Has a more monstrous monster come to life?
Is hell burst open?—heaven burnt up? What, what
Can make yon eyesore grin?—I say, my lord,
What cow has calved?

PAOLO.   Your mother, by the bleat.
PEPÉ. Right fairly answered—for a gentlemañ!
When did you take my trade up?
PAOLO.   When your wit
Went begging, sirrah.
PEPÉ.   Well again! My lord,
I think he'll do.
MALATESTA.   For what?
PEPÉ.   To take my place.
Once fools were rare, and then my office sped;
But now the world is overrun with them:
One gets one's fool in one's own family,
Without much searching.
MALATESTA.   Pepé, gently now.
Lanciotto, you are waited for. The train
Has passed the gate, and halted there for you.
LANCIOTTO. I go not to Ravenna.
MALATESTA.   Hey! why not?
PAOLO. For weighty reasons, father. Will you trust
Your greatest captain, hope of all the Guelfs,
With crafty Guido? Should the Ghibelins
Break faith, and shut Lanciotto in their walls—
Sure the temptation would be great enough—
What would you do?
MALATESTA.   I'd eat Ravenna up!
PEPÉ. Lord! what an appetite!
PAOLO.   But Lanciotto
Would be a precious hostage.
MALATESTA.   True; you're wise;
Guido's a fox. Well, have it your own way.
What is your plan?
PAOLO.   I go there in his place.
MALATESTA. Good! I will send a letter with the news.
LANCIOTTO. (*Apart to* PAOLO.) I thank you, brother.
PEPÉ.   Ha! ha! ha!—O! O!
(*Laughing.*)
MALATESTA. Pepé, what now?
PEPÉ.   O! lord, O!—ho! ho! ho!
(*Laughing.*)
PAOLO. Well, giggler?
PEPÉ.   Hear my fable, uncle.
MALATESTA.   Ay.

PEPÉ. Once on a time, Vulcan sent Mercury
To fetch dame Venus from a romp in heaven.
Well, they were long in coming, as he thought;
And so the god of spits and gridirons
Railed like himself—the devil. But—now mark—
Here comes the moral. In a little while,
Vulcan grew proud, because he saw plain signs
That he should be a father; and so he
Strutted through hell, and pushed the devils by,
Like a magnifico of Venice. Ere long,
His heir was born; but then—ho! ho!—the brat
Had wings upon his heels, and thievish ways,
And a vile squint, like errant Mercury's,
Which honest Vulcan could not understand;—
Can you?

PAOLO. 'Sdeath! fool, I'll have you in the stocks.
Father, your fool exceeds his privilege.

PEPÉ. (*Apart to* PAOLO.) Keep your own bounds, Paolo. In
the stocks
I'd tell more fables than you'd wish to hear.
And so ride forth. But, cousin, don't forget
To take Lanciotto's picture to the bride.
Ask her to choose between it and yourself.
I'll count the moments, while she hesitates,
And not grow gray at it.

PAOLO.   Peace, varlet, peace!

PEPÉ. (*Apart to him.*) Ah! now I have it. There's an elephant
Upon the scutcheon; show her that, and say—
Here's Lanciotto in our heraldry!

PAOLO. Here's for your counsel!
(*Strikes* PEPÉ, *who runs behind* MALATESTA.)

MALATESTA.   Son, son, have a care!
We who keep pets must bear their pecks sometimes.
Poor knave! Ha! ha! thou'rt growing villainous!
(*Laughs and pats* PEPÉ.)

PEPÉ. (*Aside.*) Another blow! another life for that!

PAOLO. Farewell, Lanciotto. You are dull again.

LANCIOTTO. Nature will rule.

MALATESTA.   Come, come!

LANCIOTTO.   God speed you, brother!
I am too sad; my smiles all turn to sighs.

PAOLO. More cause to haste me on my happy work.
(*Exit with* MALATESTA.)
PEPÉ. I'm going, cousin.
LANCIOTTO.   Go.
PEPÉ.   Pray, ask me where.
LANCIOTTO. Where, then?
PEPÉ.   To have my jewel carried home:
And, as I'm wise, the carrier shall be
A thief, a thief, by Jove! The fashion's new.
(*Exit.*)
LANCIOTTO. In truth, I am too gloomy and irrational.
Paolo must be right. I always had
These moody hours and dark presentiments,
Without mischances following after them.
The camp is my abode. A neighing steed,
A fiery onset, and a stubborn fight,
Rouse my dull blood, and tire my body down
To quiet slumbers when the day is o'er,
And night above me spreads her spangled tent,
Lit by the dying cresset of the moon.
Ay, that is it; I'm homesick for the camp.
(*Exit.*)

ACT II

Scene 1

Ravenna. A Room in Guido's Palace. Enter GUIDO *and a*
CARDINAL.

CARDINAL. I warn thee, Count.
GUIDO.   I'll take the warning, father,
On one condition: show me but a way
For safe escape.
CARDINAL.   I cannot.
GUIDO.   There's the point:
We Ghibelins are fettered hand and foot.
There's not a florin in my treasury;
Not a lame soldier, I can lead to war;

Not one to man the walls. A present siege,
Pushed with the wonted heat of Lanciotto,
Would deal Ravenna such a mortal blow
As ages could not mend. Give me but time
To fill the drainéd arteries of the land.
The Guelfs are masters, we their slaves; and we
Were wiser to confess it, ere the lash
Teach it too sternly. It is well for you
To say you love Francesca. So do I;
But neither you nor I have any voice
For or against this marriage.
CARDINAL.   'T is too true.
GUIDO. Say we refuse: Why, then, before a week,
We'll hear Lanciotto rapping at our door,
With twenty hundred ruffians at his back.
What's to say then? My lord, we waste our breath.
Let us look fortune in the face, and draw
Such comfort from the wanton as we may.
CARDINAL. And yet I fear—
GUIDO.   You fear! and so do I.
I fear Lanciotto as a soldier, though,
More than a son-in-law.
CARDINAL.   But have you seen him?
GUIDO. Ay, ay, and felt him, too. I've seen him ride
The best battalions of my horse and foot
Down like mere stubble: I have seen his sword
Hollow a square of pikemen, with the case
You'd scoop a melon out.
CARDINAL.   Report declares him
A prodigy of strength and ugliness.
GUIDO. Were he the devil—But why talk of this?—Here comes
Francesca.
CARDINAL.   Ah! unhappy child!
GUIDO. Look you, my lord! you'll make the best of it;
You will not whimper. Add your voice to mine,
Or woe to poor Ravenna!

(*Enter Francesca and Ritta.*)

FRANCESCA.   Ha! my lord—
And you, my father!—But do I intrude

Upon your counsels? How severe you look!
Shall I retire?
GUIDO.   No, no.
FRANCESCA.   You moody men
Seem leagued against me. As I passed the hall,
I met your solemn Dante, with huge strides
Pacing in measure to his stately verse.
The sweeping sleeves of his broad scarlet robe
Blew out behind, like wide-expanded wings,
And seemed to buoy him in his level flight.
Thinking to pass, without disturbing him,
I stole on tip-toe; but the poet paused,
Subsiding into man, and steadily
Bent on my face the lustre of his eyes.
Then, taking both my trembling hands in his—
You know how his God-troubled forehead awes—
He looked into my eyes, and shook his head,
As if he dared not speak of what he saw;
Then muttered, sighed, and slowly turned away
The weight of his intolerable brow.
When I glanced back, I saw him, as before,
Sailing adown the hall on out-spread wings.
Indeed, my lord, he should not do these things:
They strain the weakness of mortality
A jot too far. As for poor Ritta, she
Fled like a doe, the truant.
RITTA.   Yes, forsooth:
There's something terrible about the man.
Ugh! if he touched me, I should turn to ice.
I wonder if Count Lanciotto looks—
GUIDO. Ritta, come here.
(*Takes her apart.*)
RITTA.   My lord.
GUIDO.   'T was my command,
You should say nothing of Count Lanciotto.
RITTA. Nothing, my lord.
GUIDO.   You have said nothing, then?
RITTA. Indeed, my lord.
GUIDO.   'T is well. Some years ago,
My daughter had a very silly maid,
Who told her sillier stories. So, one day,
This maiden whispered something I forbade—

In strictest confidence, for she was sly:
What happened, think you?
RITTA.   I know not, my lord.
GUIDO. I boiled her in a pot.
RITTA.   Good heaven! my lord.
GUIDO. She did not like it. I shall keep that pot
Ready for the next boiling.
(*Walks back to the others.*)
RITTA.   Saints above!
I wonder if he ate her! Boil me—me!
I'll roast or stew with pleasure; but to boil
Implies a want of tenderness,—or rather
A downright toughness—in the matter boiled,
That's slanderous to a maiden. What, boil me—
Boil me! O! mercy, how ridiculous!
(*Retires, laughing.*)

(*Enter a Messenger.*)

MESSENGER. Letters, my lord, from great Prince Malatesta.
    (*Presents them, and exit.*)
GUIDO. (*Aside.*) Hear him, ye gods!—"from great Prince
    Malatesta!"
Greeting, no doubt, his little cousin Guido.
Well, well, just so we see-saw up and down.
(*Reads.*)
"*Fearing our treachery,*"—by heaven, that's blunt,
And Malatesta-like!—"*he will not send
His son, Lanciotto, to Ravenna, but*"—
But what?—a groom, a porter? or will he
Have his prey sent him in an iron cage?
By Jove, he shall not have her! O! no, no;
"*He sends his younger son, the Count Paolo,
To fetch Francesca back to Rimini.*"
That's well, if he had left his reasons out.
And, in a postscript—by the saints, 't is droll!—
"'*Twould not be worth your lordship's while, to shut
Paolo in a prison; for, my lord,
I'll only pay his ransom in plain steel:
Besides, he's not worth having.*" Is there one,
Save this ignoble offshoot of the Goths,
Who'd write such garbage to a gentleman?

Take that, and read it.
(*Gives letter to* CARDINAL.)
CARDINAL.   I have done the most.
She seems suspicious.
GUIDO.   Ritta's work.
CARDINAL.   Farewell!
(*Exit.*)
FRANCESCA. Father, you seem distempered.
GUIDO.   No, my child,
I am but vexed. Your husband's on the road,
Close to Ravenna. What's the time of day?
FRANCESCA. Past noon, my lord.
GUIDO.   We must be stirring, then.
FRANCESCA. I do not like this marriage.
GUIDO.   But I do.
FRANCESCA. But I do not. Poh! to be given away,
Like a fine horse or falcon, to a man
Whose face I never saw!
RITTA.   That's it, my lady.
GUIDO. Ritta, run down, and see if my great pot
Boils to your liking.
RITTA. (*Aside.*)   O! that pot again!
My lord, my heart betrays me; but you know
How true 'tis to my lady.
(*Exit.*)
FRANCESCA.   What ails Ritta?
GUIDO. The ailing of your sex, a running tongue.
Francesca, 't is too late to beat retreat:
Old Malatesta has me—you, too, child—
Safe in his clutch. If you are not content,
I must unclose Ravenna, and allow
His son to take you. Poh, poh! have a soul
Equal with your estate. A prince's child
Cannot choose husbands. Her desires must aim,
Not at herself, but at the public good.
Both as your prince and father, I command;
As subject and good daughter, you'll obey.
FRANCESCA. I knew that it must be my destiny,
Some day, to give my hand without my heart;
But—
GUIDO.   But, and I will but you back again!
When Guido da Polenta says to you,

Daughter, you must be married,—what were best?
FRANCESCA. 'T were best Francesca, of the self-same name,
  Made herself bridal-garments.
  (*Laughing.*)
GUIDO.   Right!
FRANCESCA.   My lord,
  Is Lanciotto handsome—ugly—fair—
  Black—sallow—crabbed—kind—or what is he?
GUIDO. You'll know ere long. I could not alter him,
  To please your taste.
FRANCESCA.   You always put me off;
  You never have a whisper in his praise.
GUIDO. The world reports it.—Count my soldiers' scars,
  And you may sum Lanciotto's glories up.
FRANCESCA. I shall be dutiful, to please you, father.
  If aught befall me through my blind submission,
  Though I may suffer, you must bear the sin.
  Beware, my lord, for your own peace of mind!
  My part has been obedience; and now
  I play it over to complete my task;
  And it shall be with smiles upon my lips,—
  Heaven only knows with what a sinking heart!
  (*Exeunt.*)

Scene 2

*The Same. Before the Gates of the City. The walls hung
with banners, flowers, and so forth, and crowded with citizens. At the side of the scene is a canopied dais, with chairs
of state upon it. Music, bells, shouts, and other sounds of
rejoicing, are occasionally heard. Enter* GUIDO, *the* CARDINAL,
*Noblemen, Knights, Guards, and so forth, with banners,
arms, and so forth.*

GUIDO. My lord, I'll have it so. You talk in vain.
  Paolo is a marvel in his way:
  I've seen him often. If Francesca take
  A fancy to his beauty, all the better;
  For she may think that he and Lanciotto
  Are like as blossoms of one parent branch.
  In truth, they are, so far as features go—

Heaven help the rest! Get her to Rimini,
By any means, and I shall be content.
The fraud cannot last long; but long enough
To win her favor to the family.
CARDINAL. 'T is a dull trick. Thou hast not dealt with her
Wisely nor kindly, and I dread the end.
If, when this marriage was enjoined on thee,
Thou hadst informed Francesca of the truth,
And said, Now, daughter, choose between
Thy peace and all Ravenna's; who that knows
The constant nature of her noble heart
Could doubt the issue? There'd have been some tears,
Some frightful fancies of her husband's looks;
And then she'd calmly walk up to her fate,
And bear it bravely. Afterwards, perchance,
Lanciotto might prove better than her fears,—
No one denies him many an excellence,—
And all go happily. But, as thou wouldst plot,
She'll be prepared to see a paragon,
And find a satyr. It is dangerous.
Treachery with enemies is bad enough,
With friends 't is fatal.
GUIDO.   Has your lordship done?
CARDINAL. Never, Count Guido, with so good a text.
Do not stand looking sideways at the truth;
Craft has become thy nature. Go to her.
GUIDO. I have not heart.
CARDINAL.   I have.
(Going.)
GUIDO.   Hold, Cardinal!
My plan is better. Get her off my hands,
And I care not.
CARDINAL.   What will she say of thee,
In Rimini, when she detects the cheat?
GUIDO. I'll stop my ears up.
CARDINAL.   Guido, thou art weak,
And lack the common fortitude of man.
GUIDO. And you abuse the license of your garb,
To lesson me. My lord, I do not dare
To move a finger in these marriage-rites.
Francesca is a sacrifice, I know,—
A limb delivered to the surgeon's knife,

To save our general health. A truce to this.
Paolo has the business in his hands:
Let him arrange it as he will; for I
Will give Count Malatesta no pretext
To recommence the war.

CARDINAL.   Farewell, my lord.
I'll neither help nor countenance a fraud.
You crafty men take comfort to yourselves,
Saying, deceit dies with discovery.
'T is false; each wicked action spawns a brood,
And lives in its succession. You, who shake
Man's moral nature into storm, should know
That the last wave which passes from your sight
Rolls in and breaks upon eternity!
(*Exit.*)

GUIDO. Why, that's a very grand and solemn thought:
I'll mention it to Dante. Gentlemen,
What see they from the wall?

NOBLEMAN.   The train, my lord.

GUIDO. Inform my daughter.

NOBLEMAN.   She is here, my lord.

(*Enter* FRANCESCA, RITTA, *Ladies, Attendants, and so forth.*)

FRANCESCA. See, father, what a merry face I have,
And how my ladies glisten! I will try
To do my utmost, in my love for you
And the good people of Ravenna. Now,
As the first shock is over, I expect
To feel quite happy. I will wed the Count,
Be he whate'er he may. I do not speak
In giddy recklessness. I've weighed it all,—
'T wixt hope and fear, knowledge and ignorance,—
And reasoned out my duty to your wish.
I have no yearnings towards another love:
So, if I show my husband a desire
To fill the place with which he honors me,
According to its duties, even he—
Were he less noble than Count Lanciotto—
Must smile upon my efforts, and reward
Good will with willing grace. One pang remains.
Parting from home and kindred is a thing

None but the heartless, or the miserable,
Can do without a tear. This home of mine
Has filled my heart with two-fold happiness,
Taking and giving love abundantly.
Farewell, Ravenna! If I bless thee not,
'T is that thou seem'st too blessed; and 't were strange
In me to offer what thou'st always given.
GUIDO. (*Aside.*) This is too much! If she would rail a while
At me and fortune, it could be endured.
(*Shouts, music, and so forth within*)
FRANCESCA. Ha! there's the van just breaking through the
    wood!
Music! that's well; a welcome forerunner.
Now, Ritta—here—come talk to me. Alas!
How my heart trembles! What a world to me
Lies 'neath the glitter of yon cavalcade!
Is that the Count?
RITTA.   Upon the dapple-gray?
FRANCESCA. Yes, yes.
RITTA.   No; that's his—
GUIDO. (*Apart to her.*) Ritta!
RITTA.   Ay; that's—that's—
GUIDO. (*Apart to her.*) Ritta, the pot!
RITTA. (*Aside.*) O! but this lying chokes!
Ay, that's Count Somebody, from Rimini.
FRANCESCA. I knew it was. Is that not glorious?
RITTA. My lady, what?
FRANCESCA.   To see a cavalier
Sit on his steed with such familiar grace.
RITTA. To see a man astraddle on a horse!
It don't seem much to me.
FRANCESCA.   Fie! stupid girl!
But mark the minstrels thronging round the Count!
Ah! that is more than gallant horsemanship.
The soul that feeds itself on poesy,
Is of a quality more fine and rare
Than Heaven allows the ruder multitude.
I tell you, Ritta, when you see a man
Beloved by poets, made the theme of song,
And chaunted down to ages, as a gift
Fit for the rich embalmment of their verse,
There's more about him than the patron's gold.

If that's the gentleman my father chose,
He must have picked him out from all the world.
The Count alights. Why, what a noble grace
Runs through his slightest action! Are you sad?
You too, my father? Have I given you cause?
I am content. If Lanciotto's mind
Bear any impress of his fair outside,
We shall not quarrel ere our marriage-day.
Can I say more? My blushes speak for me:
Interpret them as modesty's excuse
For the short-comings of a maiden's speech.
RITTA. (*Aside.*) Alas! dear lady!
GUIDO. (*Aside.*) 'Sdeath! my plot has failed,
By overworking its design. Come, come;
Get to your places. See, the Count draws nigh.
(GUIDO *and* FRANCESCA *seat themselves upon the dais, sur-
rounded by* RITTA, *Ladies, Attendants, Guards, and so
forth. Music, shouts, ringing of bells, and so forth. Enter
Men-at-arms, with banners, and so forth; Pages bearing
costly presents on cushions; then* PAOLO, *surrounded by
Noblemen, Knights, Minstrels, and so forth, and followed
by other Men-at-arms. They range themselves opposite the
dais.*)

GUIDO. Ravenna welcomes you, my lord, and I
Add my best greeting to the general voice.
This peaceful show of arms from Rimini
Is a new pleasure, stranger to our sense
Than if the East blew zephyrs, or the balm
Of Summer loaded rough December's gales,
And turned his snows to roses.
PAOLO.   Noble sir,
We looked for welcome from your courtesy,
Not from your love; but this unhoped for sight
Of smiling faces, and the gentle tone
In which you greet us, leave us naught to win
Within your hearts. I need not ask, my lord,
Where bides the precious object of my search;
For I was sent to find the fairest maid
Ravenna boasts, among her many fair.
I might extend my travel many a league,
And yet return, to take her from your side.

I blush to bear so rich a treasure home,
As pledge and hostage of a sluggish peace;
For beauty such as hers was meant by Heaven
To spur our race to gallant enterprise,
And draw contending deities around
The dubious battles of a second Troy.

GUIDO. Sir Count, you please to lavish on my child
The high-strained courtesy of chivalry;
Yet she has homely virtues that, I hope,
May take a deeper hold in Rimini,
After the fleeting beauty of her face
Is spoiled by time, or faded to the eye
By its familiar usage.

PAOLO.   As a man
Who ever sees Heaven's purpose in its works,
I must suppose so rare a tabernacle
Was framed for rarest virtues. Pardon me
My public admiration. If my praise
Clash with propriety, and bare my words
To cooler judgment, 't is not that I wish
To win a flatterer's grudged recompense,
And gain by falsehood what I'd win through love.
When I have brushed my travel from my garb,
I'll pay my court in more befitting style.

(*Music. Exit with his train.*)

GUIDO. (*Advancing.*) Now, by the saints, Lanciotto's deputy
Stands in this business with a proper grace,
Stretching his lord's instructions till they crack.
A zealous envoy! Not a word said he
Of Lanciotto—not a single word;
But stood there, staring in Francesca's face
With his devouring eyes.—By Jupiter,
I but half like it!

FRANCESCA. (*Advancing.*) Father?

GUIDO.   Well, my child.

FRANCESCA. How do you like—

GUIDO.   The coxcomb! I've done well!

FRANCESCA. No, no; Count Lanciotto?

GUIDO.   Well enough.
But hang this fellow—hang your deputies!
I'll never woo by proxy.

FRANCESCA.   Deputies!
And woo by proxy!
GUIDO.   Come to me anon.
I'll strip this cuckoo of his gallantry!
(*Exit with Guards, and so forth.*)
FRANCESCA. Ritta, my father has strange ways of late.
RITTA. I wonder not.
FRANCESCA.   You wonder not?
RITTA.   No, lady:
He is so used to playing double games,
That even you must come in for your share.
(*Aside.*) Plague on his boiling! I will out with it.
Lady, the gentleman who passed the gates—
FRANCESCA. Count Lanciotto? As I hope for grace,
A gallant gentleman! How well he spoke!
With what sincere and earnest courtesy
The rounded phrases glided from his lips!
He spoke in compliments that seemed like truth.
Methinks I'd listen through a summer's day,
To hear him woo.—And he must woo to me—
I'll have our privilege—he must woo a space,
Ere I'll be won, I promise.
RITTA.   But, my lady,
He'll woo you for another.
FRANCESCA.   He?—ha! ha!
(*Laughing.*)
I should not think it from the prologue, Ritta.
RITTA. Nor I.
FRANCESCA.   Nor any one.
RITTA.   'T is not the Count—
'T is not Count Lanciotto.
FRANCESCA.   Gracious saints!
Have you gone crazy? Ritta, speak again,
Before I chide you.
RITTA.   'T is the solemn truth.
That gentleman is Count Paolo, lady,
Brother to Lanciotto, and no more
Like him than—than—
FRANCESCA.   Than what?
RITTA.   Count Guido's pot,
For boiling waiting-maids, is like the bath
Of Venus on the arras.

FRANCESCA.   Are you mad,—
Quite mad, poor Ritta?
RITTA.   Yes; perhaps I am.
Perhaps Lanciotto is a proper man—
Perhaps I lie—perhaps I speak the truth—
Perhaps I gabble like a fool. O! heavens,
That dreadful pot!
FRANCESCA.   Dear Ritta!—
RITTA.   By the mass,
They shall not cozen you, my gentle mistress!
If my lord Guido boiled me, do you think
I should be served up to the garrison,
By way of pottage? Surely they would not waste me.
FRANCESCA. You are an idle talker. Pranks like these
Fit your companions. You forget yourself.
RITTA. Not you, though, lady. Boldly I repeat,
That he who looked so fair, and talked so sweet,
Who rode from Rimini upon a horse
Of dapple-gray, and walked through yonder gate,
Is not Count Lanciotto.
FRANCESCA.   This you mean?
RITTA. I do, indeed!
FRANCESCA.   Then I am more abused—
More tricked, more trifled with, more played upon—
By him, my father, and by all of you,
Than anything, suspected of a heart,
Was ever yet!
RITTA.   In Count Paolo, lady,
Perchance there was no meditated fraud.
FRANCESCA. How, dare you plead for him?
RITTA.   I but suppose:
Though in your father—O! I dare not say.
FRANCESCA. I dare. It was ill usage, gross abuse,
Treason to duty, meanness, craft—dishonor!
What if I'd thrown my heart before the feet
Of this sham husband! cast my love away
Upon a counterfeit! I was prepared
To force affection upon any man
Called Lanciotto. Anything of silk,
Tinsel, and gewgaws, if he bore that name,
Might have received me for the asking. Yes,
I was inclined to venture more than half

In this base business—shame upon my thoughts!—
All for my father's peace and poor Ravenna's.
And this Paolo, with his cavalcade,
His minstrels, music, and his pretty airs,
His showy person, and his fulsome talk,
Almost made me contented with my lot.
O! what a fool!—in faith, I merit it—
Trapped by mere glitter! What an easy fool!
Ha! ha! I'm glad it went no further, girl;
(*Laughing.*)
I'm glad I kept my heart safe, after all.
There was my cunning. I have paid them back,
I warrant you! I'll marry Lanciotto;
I'll seem to shuffle by this treachery. No!
I'll seek my father, put him face to face
With his own falsehood; and I'll stand between,
Awful as justice, meting out to him
Heaven's dreadful canons 'gainst his conscious guilt.
I'll marry Lanciotto. On my faith,
I would not live another wicked day
Here, in Ravenna, only for the fear
That I should take to lying, with the rest.
Ha! ha! it makes me merry, when I think
How safe I kept this little heart of mine!
(*Laughing. Exit, with Attendants, and so forth.*)
RITTA. So, 't is all ended—all except my boiling,
And that will make a holiday for some.
Perhaps I'm selfish. Fagot, axe, and gallows,
They have their uses, after all. They give
The lookers-on a deal of harmless sport.
Though one may suffer, twenty hundred laugh;
And that's a point gained. I have seen a man—
Poor Dora's uncle—shake himself with glee,
At the bare thought of the ridiculous style
In which some villain died. "Dancing," quoth he,
"To the poor music of a single string!
Biting," quoth he, "after his head was off!
What use of that?" Or, "Shivering," quoth he,
"As from an ague, with his beard afire!"
And then he'd roar until his ugly mouth
Split at the corners. But to see me boil—
O! that will be the queerest thing of all!

I wonder if they'll put me in a bag,
Like a great suet-ball? I'll go, and tell
Count Guido, on the instant. How he'll laugh
To think his pot has got an occupant!
I wonder if he really takes delight
In such amusements? Nay, I have kept faith:
I only said the man was not Lanciotto;
No word of Lanciotto's ugliness.
I may escape the pot, for all. Pardee!
I wonder if they'll put me in a bag!
(*Exit, laughing.*)

Scene 3

The Same. A Room in Guido's Palace. Enter GUIDO *and*
RITTA.

RITTA. There now, my lord, that is the whole of it:
I love my mistress more than I fear you.
If I could save her finger from the axe,
I'd give my head to do it. So, my lord,
I am prepared to stew.
GUIDO.   Boil, Ritta, boil.
RITTA. No; I prefer to stew.
GUIDO.   And I to boil.
RITTA. 'T is very hard, my lord, I cannot choose
My way of cooking. I shall laugh, I vow,
In the grim headsman's face, when I remember
That I am dying for my lady's love.
I leave no one to shed a tear for me;
Father nor mother, kith nor kin, have I,
To say, "Poor Ritta!" o'er my lifeless clay.
They all have gone before me, and 't were well
If I could hurry after them.
GUIDO. (*Aside.*)   Poor child!
(*Aloud.*) But, baggage, said you aught of Lanciotto?
RITTA. No, not a word; and he's so ugly, too!
GUIDO. Is he so ugly?
RITTA.   Ugly! he is worse
Than Pilate on the hangings.
GUIDO.   Hold your tongue

Here, and at Rimini, about the Count,
And you shall prosper.

RITTA. Am I not to boil?

GUIDO. No, child. But be discreet at Rimini.
Old Malatesta is a dreadful man—
Far worse than I—he bakes his people, Ritta;
Lards them, like geese, and bakes them in an oven.

RITTA. Fire is my fate, I see that.

GUIDO. Have a care
It do not follow you beyond this world.
Where is your mistress?

RITTA. In her room, my lord.
After I told her of the Count Paolo,
She flew to have an interview with you;
But on the way—I know not why it was—
She darted to her chamber, and there stays
Weeping in silence. It would do you good—
More than a hundred sermons—just to see
A single tear, indeed it would, my lord.

GUIDO. Ha! you are saucy. I have humored you
Past prudence, malpert! Get you to your room!
(*Exit* RITTA.)
More of my blood runs in yon damsel's veins
Than the world knows. Her mother to a shade;
The same high spirit, and strange martyr-wish
To sacrifice herself, body and soul,
For some loved end. All that she did for me;
And yet I loved her not. O! memory!
The darkest future has a ray of hope,
But thou art blacker than the sepulchre!
Thy horrid shapes lie round, like scattered bones,
Hopeless forever! I am sick at heart.
The past crowds on the present: as I sowed,
So am I reaping. Shadows from myself
Fall on the picture, as I trace anew
These rising spectres of my early life,
And add their gloom to what was dark before.
O! memory, memory! How my temples throb!
(*Sits.*)

(*Enter* FRANCESCA, *hastily.*)

FRANCESCA. My lord, this outrage—(*He looks up.*) Father,
are you ill?
You seem unhappy. Have I troubled you?
You heard how passionate and bad I was,
When Ritta told me of the Count Paolo.
Dear father, calm yourself; and let me ask
A child's forgiveness. 'T was undutiful
To doubt your wisdom. It is over now.
I only thought you might have trusted me
With any counsel.
GUIDO. (*Aside.*) Would I had!
FRANCESCA.   Ah! well,
I understand it all, and you were right.
Only the danger of it. Think, my lord,
If I had loved this man at the first sight:
We all have heard of such things. Think, again,
If I had loved him—as I then supposed
You wished me to—'t would have been very sad.
But no, dear sir, I kept my heart secure,
Nor will I loose it till you give the word.
I'm wiser than you thought me, you perceive.
But when we saw him, face to face, together,
Surely you might have told me then.
GUIDO.   Francesca,
My eyes are old—I did not clearly see—
Faith, it escaped my thoughts. Some other things
Came in my head. I was as ignorant
Of Count Paolo's coming as yourself.
The brothers are so like.
FRANCESCA.   Indeed?
GUIDO.   Yes, yes.
One is the other's counterpart, in fact;
(*Aside.*) And even now it may not be—O! shame!
I lie by habit.
FRANCESCA.   Then there is a hope?
He may be Lanciotto, after all?
O! joy—

(*Enter a Servant.*)

SERVANT. The Count Paolo. (*Exit.*)
FRANCESCA.   Misery!
  That name was not Lanciotto!
GUIDO.   Farewell, child.
  I'll leave you with the Count: he'll make it plain.
  It seems 't was Count Paolo.
  (*Going.*)
FRANCESCA.   Father!
GUIDO.   Well.
FRANCESCA. You knew it from the first!
  (*Exit* GUIDO.)
                               Let me begone:
  I could not look him in the face again
  With the old faith. Besides, 't would anger him
  To have a living witness of his fraud
  Ever before him; and I could not trust—
  Strive as I might—my happiness to him,
  As once I did. I could not lay my hand
  Upon his shoulder, and look up to him,
  Saying, Dear father, pilot me along
  Past this dread rock, through yonder narrow strait.
  Saints, no! The gold that gave my life away
  Might, even then, be rattling in his purse,
  Warm from the buyer's hand. Look on me, Heaven!
  Him thou didst sanctify before my eyes,
  Him thou didst charge, as thy great deputy,
  With guardianship of a weak orphan girl,
  Has fallen from grace, has paltered with his trust;
  I have no mother to receive thy charge,—
  O! take it on thyself; and when I err,
  Through mortal blindness, Heaven, be thou my guide!
  Worse cannot fall me. Though my husband lack
  A parent's tenderness, he yet may have
  Faith, truth, and honor—the immortal bonds
  that knit together honest hearts as one.
  Let me away to Rimini. Alas!
  It wrings my heart to have outlived the day
  That I can leave my home with no regret!
  (*Weeps.*)

(*Enter* PAOLO.)

PAOLO. Pray, pardon me. (*Going.*)
FRANCESCA.   You are quite welcome, Count.
A foolish tear, a weakness, nothing more:
But present weeping clears our future sight.
They tell me you are love's commissioner,
A kind of broker in the trade of hearts:
Is it your usual business? or may I
Flatter myself, by claiming this essay
As your first effort?
PAOLO.   Lady, I believed
My post, at starting, one of weight and trust;
When I beheld you, I concluded it
A charge of honor and high dignity.
I did not think to hear you underrate
Your own importance, by dishonoring me.
FRANCESCA. You are severe, my lord.
PAOLO.   No, not severe;
Say candid, rather. I am somewhat hurt
By my reception. If I feel the wound,
'T is not because I suffer from the jest,
But that your lips should deal it.
FRANCESCA.   Compliments
Appear to be the staple of your speech.
You ravish one with courtesy, you pour
Fine words upon one, till the listening head
Is bowed with sweetness. Sir, your talk is drugged;
There's secret poppy in your sugared phrase:
I'll taste before I take it.
PAOLO.   Gentle lady—
FRANCESCA. I am not gentle, or I missed my aim.
I am no hawk to fly at every lure.
You courtly gentlemen draw one broad rule—
All girls are fools. It may be so, in truth,
Yet so I'll not be treated.
PAOLO.   Have you been?
If I implied such slander by my words,
They wrong my purpose. If I compliment,
'T is not from habit, but because I thought
Your face deserved my homage as its due.
When I have clearer insight, and you spread
Your inner nature o'er your lineaments,

Even that face may darken in the shades
Of my opinion. For mere loveliness
Needs inward light to keep it always bright.
All things look badly to unfriendly eyes.
I spoke my first impression; cooler thought
May work strange changes.

FRANCESCA.   Ah! Sir Count, at length
There's matter in your words.

PAOLO.   Unpleasant stuff,
To judge by your dark brows. I have essayed
Kindness and coldness, yet you are not pleased.

FRANCESCA. How can I be?

PAOLO.   How, lady?

FRANCESCA.   Ay, sir, how?
Your brother—my good lord that is to be—
Stings me with his neglect; and in the place
He should have filled, he sends a go-between,
A common carrier of others' love;
How can the sender, or the person sent,
Please overmuch? Now, were I such as you,
I'd be too proud to travel round the land
With other people's feelings in my heart;
Even to fill the void which you confess
By such employment.

PAOLO.   Lady, 't is your wish
To nettle me, to break my breeding down,
And see what natural passions I have hidden
Behind the outworks of my etiquette.
I neither own nor feel the want of heart
With which you charge me. You are more than cruel;
You rouse my nerves until they ache with life,
And then pour fire upon them. For myself
I would not speak, unless you had compelled.
My task is odious to me. Since I came,
Heaven bear me witness how my traitor heart
Has fought against my duty; and how oft
I wished myself in Lanciotto's place,
Or him in mine.

FRANCESCA.   You riddle.

PAOLO.   Do I? Well,
Let it remain unguessed.

FRANCESCA. You wished yourself
At Rimini, or Lanciotto here?
You may have reasons.
PAOLO. Well interpreted!
The Sphinx were simple in your skilful hands!
FRANCESCA. It has become your turn to sneer.
PAOLO. But I
Have gall to feed my bitterness, while you
Jest in the wanton ease of happiness.
Stop! there is peril in our talk.
FRANCESCA. As how?
PAOLO. 'T is dangerous to talk about one's self;
It panders selfishness. My duty waits.
FRANCESCA. My future lord's affairs? I quite forgot Count
Lanciotto.
PAOLO. (*Aside.*) I, too, shame upon me!
FRANCESCA. Does he resemble you?
PAOLO. Pray drop me, lady.
FRANCESCA. Nay, answer me.
PAOLO. Somewhat—in feature.
FRANCESCA. Ha!
Is he so fair?
PAOLO. No, darker. He was tanned
In long campaigns, and battles hotly fought,
While I lounged idly with the troubadours,
Under the shadow of his watchful sword.
FRANCESCA. In person?
PAOLO. He is shorter, I believe,
But broader, stronger, more compactly knit.
FRANCESCA. What of his mind?
PAOLO. Ah! now you strike the key!
A mind just fitted to his history,
An equal balance 'twixt desert and fame.
No future chronicler shall say of him,
His fame outran his merit; or his merit
Halted behind some adverse circumstance,
And never won the glory it deserved.
My love might weary you, if I rehearsed
The simple beauty of his character;
His grandeur and his gentleness of heart,
His warlike fire and peaceful love, his faith,

His courtesy, his truth. I'll not deny
Some human weakness, to attract our love,
Harbors in him, as in the rest of us.
Sometimes against our city's enemies
He thunders in the distance, and devotes
Their homes to ruin. When the brand has fallen,
He ever follows with a healing rain,
And in his pity shoulders by revenge.
A thorough soldier, lady. He grasps crowns,
While I pick at the laurel.

FRANCESCA.   Stay, my lord!
I asked your brother's value, with no wish
To hear you underrate yourself. Your worth
May rise in passing through another's lips.
Lanciotto is perfection, then?

PAOLO.   To me:
Others may think my brother over-nice
Upon the point of honor; over-keen
To take offence where no offence is meant;
A thought too prodigal of human life,
Holding it naught when weighed against a wrong;
Suspicious of the motives of his friends;
Distrustful of his own high excellence;
And with a certain gloom of temperament,
When thus disturbed, that makes him terrible
And rash in action. I have heard of this;
I never felt it. I distress you, lady?
Perhaps I throw these points too much in shade,
By catching at an enemy's report.
But, then, Lanciotto said, "You'll speak of me,
Not as I ought to be, but as I am."
He loathes deceit.

FRANCESCA.   That's noble! Have you done?
I have observed a strange reserve, at times,
An over-carefulness in choosing words,
Both in my father and his nearest friends,
When speaking of your brother; as if they
Picked their way slowly over rocky ground,
Fearing to stumble. Ritta, too, my maid,
When her tongue rattles on in full career,
Stops at your brother's name, and with a sigh
Settles herself to dismal silence. Count,

These things have troubled me. From you I look
For perfect frankness. Is there naught withheld?
PAOLO. (*Aside.*) O, base temptation! What if I betray
His crippled person—imitate his limp—
Laugh at his hip, his back, his sullen moods
Of childish superstition?—tread his heart
Under my feet, to climb into his place?—
Use his own warrant 'gainst himself; and say,
Because I loved her, and misjudged your jest,
Therefore I stole her? Why, a common thief
Would hang for just such thinking! Ha! ha! ha!
(*Laughing.*)
I reckon on her love, as if I held
The counsels of her bosom. No, I swear,
Francesca would despise so mean a deed.
Have I no honor either? Are my thoughts
All bound by her opinion?
FRANCESCA.   This is strange!
Is Lanciotto's name a spell to all?
I ask a simple question, and straight you
Start to one side, and mutter to yourself,
And laugh, and groan, and play the lunatic,
In such a style that you astound me more
Than all the others. It appears to me
I have been singled as a common dupe
By every one. What mystery is this
Surrounds Count Lanciotto? If there be
A single creature in the universe
Who has a right to know him as he is,
I am that one.
PAOLO.   I grant it. You shall see,
And shape your judgment by your own remark.
All that my honor calls for I have said.
FRANCESCA. I am content. Unless I greatly err,
Heaven made your breast the seat of honest thoughts.
You know, my lord, that, once at Rimini,
There can be no retreat for me. By you,
Here at Ravenna, in your brother's name,
I shall be solemnly betrothed. And now
I thus extend my maiden hand to you;
If you are conscious of no secret guilt,
Take it.

PAOLO. I do.
(*Takes her hand.*)
FRANCESCA. You tremble!
PAOLO.   With the hand,
  Not with the obligation.
FRANCESCA.   Farewell, Count!
  'T were cruel to tax your stock of compliments,
  That waste their sweets upon a trammelled heart;
  Go fly your fancies at some freer game. (*Exit.*)
PAOLO. O, heaven, if I have faltered and am weak,
  'T is from my nature! Fancies, more accursed
  Than haunt a murderer's bedside, throng my brain—
  Temptations, such as mortal never bore
  Since Satan whispered in the ear of Eve,
  Sing in my ear—and all, all are accursed!
  At heart I have betrayed my brother's trust,
  Francesca's openly. Turn where I will,
  As if enclosed within a mirrored hall,
  I see a traitor. Now to stand erect,
  Firm on my base of manly constancy;
  Or, if I stagger, let me never quit
  The homely path of duty, for the ways
  That bloom and glitter with seductive sin!
  (*Exit.*)

ACT III

Scene 1

Rimini. A Room in the Castle. LANCIOTTO *discovered
reading.*

LANCIOTTO. O! fie, philosophy! This Seneca
  Revels in wealth, and whines about the poor!
  Talks of starvation while his banquet waits,
  And fancies that a two hours' appetite
  Throws light on famine! Doubtless he can tell,
  As he skips nimbly through his dancing-girls,
  How sad it is to limp about the world
  A sightless cripple! Let him feel the crutch

Wearing against his heart, and then I'd hear
This sage talk glibly; or provide a pad,
Stuffed with his soft philosophy, to ease
His aching shoulder. Pshaw! he never felt,
Or pain would choke his frothy utterance.
'T is easy for the doctor to compound
His nauseous simples for a sick man's health;
But let him swallow them, for his disease,
Without wry faces. Ah! the tug is there.
Show me philosophy in rags, in want,
Sick of a fever, with a back like mine,
Creeping to wisdom on these legs, and I
Will drink its comforts. Out! away with you!
There's no such thing as real philosophy!
(*Throws down the book.*)

(*Enter* PEPÉ.)

Here is a sage who'll teach a courtier
The laws of etiquette, a statesman rule,
A soldier discipline, a poet verse,
And each mechanic his distinctive trade;
Yet bring him to his motley, and how wide
He shoots from reason! We can understand
All business but our own, and thrust advice
In every gaping cranny of the world;
While habit shapes us to our own dull work,
And reason nods above his proper task.
Just so philosophy would rectify
All things abroad, and be a jade at home.
Pepé, what think you of the Emperor's aim
Towards Hungary?
PEPÉ.   A most unwise design;
   For mark, my lord—
LANCIOTTO.   Why, there! the fact cries out.
   Here's motley thinking for a diadem!—
   Ay, and more wisely in his own regard.
PEPÉ. You flout me, cousin.
LANCIOTTO.   Have you aught that's new?—
   Some witty trifle, some absurd conceit?
PEPÉ. Troth, no.

LANCIOTTO.   Why not give up the Emperor,
And bend your wisdom on your duties, Pepé?
PEPÉ. Because the Emperor has more need of wisdom
Than the most barren fool of wit.
LANCIOTTO.   Well said!
Mere habit brings the fool back to his art.
This jester is a rare philosopher.
Teach me philosophy, good fool.
PEPÉ.   No need.
You'll get a teacher when you take a wife.
If she do not instruct you in more arts
Than Aristotle ever thought upon,
The good old race of woman has declined
Into a sort of male stupidity.
I had a sweetheart once, she lectured grandly;
No matter on what subject she might hit,
'T was all the same, she could talk and she would.
She had no silly modesty; she dashed
Straight in the teeth of any argument,
And talked you deaf, dumb, blind. Whatever struck
Upon her ear, by some machinery,
Set her tongue wagging. Thank the Lord, she died!—
Dropped in the middle of a fierce harangue,
Like a spent horse. It was an even thing,
Whether she talked herself or me to death.
The latest sign of life was in her tongue;
It wagged till sundown, like a serpent's tail,
Long after all the rest of her was cold.
Alas! poor Zippa!
LANCIOTTO.   Were you married, fool?
PEPÉ. Married! Have I the scars upon me? No;
I fell in love; and that was bad enough,
And far enough for a mere fool to go.
Married! why, marriage is love's purgatory,
Without a heaven beyond.
LANCIOTTO.   Fie, atheist!
Would you abolish marriage?
PEPÉ.   Yes.
LANCIOTTO.   What?
PEPÉ.   Yes.
LANCIOTTO. Depopulate the world?
PEPÉ.   No fear of that.

I'd have no families, no Malatesti,
Strutting about the land, with pedigrees
And claims bequeathed them by their ancestors;
No fellows vaporing of their royal blood;
No one to seize a whole inheritance,
And rob the other children of the earth.
By Jove! you should not know your fathers, even!
I'd have you spring, like toadstools, from the soil—
Mere sons of women—nothing more nor less—
All base-born, and all equal. There, my lord,
There is a simple commonwealth for you!
In which aspiring merit takes the lead,
And birth goes begging.
LANCIOTTO.   It is so, in truth;
And by the simplest means I ever heard.
PEPÉ. Think of it, cousin. Tell it to your friends,
The statesmen, soldiers, and philosophers;
Noise it about the earth, and let it stir
The sluggish spirits of the multitudes.
Pursue the thought, scan it, from end to end,
Through all its latent possibilities.
It is a great seed dropped, I promise you,
And it must sprout. Thought never wholly dies;
It only wants a name—a hard Greek name—
Some few apostles, who may live on it—
A crowd of listeners, with the average dulness
That man possesses—and we organize;
Spread our new doctrine, like a general plague;
Talk of man's progress and development,
Wrongs of society, the march of mind,
The Devil, Doctor Faustus, and what not;
And, lo! this pretty world turns upside down,
All with a fool's idea!
LANCIOTTO.   By Jupiter,
You hit our modern teachers to a hair!
I knew this fool was a philosopher.
Pepé is right. Mechanic means advance;
Nature bows down to science' haughty tread,
And turns the wheel of smutty artifice;
New governments arise, dilate, decay,
And foster creeds and churches to their tastes:
At each advance, we cry, "Behold, the end!"

Till some fresh wonder breaks upon the age.
But man, the moral creature, midst it all
Stands still unchanged; nor moves towards virtue more,
Nor comprehends the mysteries in himself,
More than when Plato taught academies,
Or Zeno thundered from his Attic porch.

PEPÉ. I know not that; I only want my scheme
Tried for a while. I am a politician,
A wrongs-of-man man. Hang philosophy!
Let metaphysics swallow, at a gulp,
Its last two syllables, and purge itself
Clean of its filthy humors! I am one
Ready for martyrdom, for stake and fire,
If I can make my great idea take root!
Zounds! cousin, if I had an audience,
I'd make you shudder at my eloquence!
I have an itching to reform the world.

LANCIOTTO. Begin at home, then.

PEPÉ.   Home is not my sphere;
Heaven picked me out to teach my fellow-men.
I am a very firebrand of truth—
A self-consuming, doomed, devoted brand—
That burn to ashes while I light the world!
I feel it in me. I am moved, inspired,
Stirred into utterance, by some mystic power
Of which I am the humble instrument.

LANCIOTTO. A bad digestion, sage, a bilious turn,
A gnawing stomach, or a pinching shoe.

PEPÉ. O! hear, but spare the scoffer! Spare the wretch
Who sneers at the anointed man of truth!
When we reached that, I and my followers
Would rend you limb from limb. There!—ha! ha! ha!
(*Laughing.*)
Have I not caught the slang these fellows preach;
A grand, original idea, to back it;
And all the stock in trade of a reformer?

LANCIOTTO. You have indeed; nor do I wonder, Pepé.
Fool as you are, I promise you success
In your new calling, if you'll set it up.
The thing is far too simple.
(*Trumpet sounds within.*)

PEPÉ.   Hist! my lord.

LANCIOTTO. That calls me to myself.
PEPÉ.   At that alarm,
All Rimini leaped up upon its feet.
Cousin, your bridal-train. You groan! 'Ods wounds!
Here is the bridegroom sorely malcontent—
The sole sad face in Rimini. Since morn,
A quiet man could hardly walk the streets,
For flowers and streamers. All the town is gay.
Perhaps 't is merry o'er your misery.
LANCIOTTO. Perhaps; but that it knows not.
PEPÉ.   Yes, it does:
It knows that when a man's about to wed,
He's ripe to laugh at. Cousin, tell me, now,
Why is Paolo on the way so long?
Ravenna's but eight leagues from Rimini—
LANCIOTTO. That's just the measure of your tongue, good fool.
You trouble me. I've had enough of you—
Begone!
PEPÉ. I'm going; but you see I limp.
Have pity on a cripple, gentle Count.
(Limps.)
LANCIOTTO. Pepé!
PEPÉ.   A miracle, a miracle!
See, see, my lord, at Pepé's saintly name
The lame jog on.
MALATESTA. (Without.) Come, Lanciotto!
LANCIOTTO.   Hark!
My father calls.
PEPÉ.   If he were mine, I'd go—
That's a good boy!
(Pats LANCIOTTO's back.)
LANCIOTTO. (Starting.) Hands off! you'll rue it else!
(Exit.)
PEPÉ. (Laughing.) Ha! ha! I laid my hand upon his hump!
Heavens, how he squirmed! And what a wish I had
To cry, Ho! camel! leap upon his back,
And ride him to the devil! So, we've had
A pleasant flitting round philosophy!
The Count and Fool bumped heads, and struck ideas
Out by the contact! Quite a pleasant talk—
A friendly conversation, nothing more—
'Twixt nobleman and jester. Ho! my bird,

I can toss lures as high as any man.
So, I amuse you with my harmless wit?
Pepé's your friend now—you can trust in him—
An honest, simple fool! Just try it once,
You ugly, misbegotten clod of dirt!
Ay, but the hump—the touch upon the hump—
The start and wriggle—that was rare! Ha! ha!
(*Exit, laughing.*)

Scene 2

*The Same. The Grand Square before the Castle. Soldiers
on guard, with banners, and so forth. Citizens, in holiday
dresses, cross the scene. The houses are hung with trophies,
banners, garlands, and so forth. Enter* MALATESTA, *with
guards, attendants, and so forth.*

MALATESTA. Captain, take care the streets be not choked up
   By the rude rabble. Send to Cæsar's bridge
   A strong detachment of your men, and clear
   The way before them. See that nothing check
   The bride's first entrance into Rimini.
   Station your veterans in the front. Count Guido
   Comes with his daughter, and his eyes are sharp.
   Keep up a show of strength before him, sir;
   And set some laborers to work upon
   The broken bastion. Make all things look bright;
   As if we stood in eager readiness,
   And high condition, to begin a war.
CAPTAIN. I will, my lord.
MALATESTA.   Keep Guido in your eye;
   And if you see him looking over-long
   On any weakness of our walls, just file
   Your bulkiest fellows round him; or get up
   A scuffle with the people; anything—
   Even if you break a head or two—to draw
   His vision off. But where our strength is great,
   Take heed to make him see it. You conceive?
CAPTAIN. Trust me, my lord.
   (*Exit with guards.*)

(*Enter* PEPÉ.)

PEPÉ.   Room, room! A hall, a hall!
I pray you, good man, has the funeral passed?
MALATESTA. Who is it asks?
PEPÉ.   Pepé of Padua,
A learned doctor of uncivil law.
MALATESTA. But how a funeral?
PEPÉ.   You are weak of wit.
Francesca of Ravenna's borne to church,
And never issues thence.
MALATESTA.   How, doctor, pray?
PEPÉ. Now, for a citizen of Rimini,
You're sadly dull. Does she not issue thence
Fanny of Rimini? A glorious change,—
A kind of resurrection in the flesh!
MALATESTA. (*Laughing.*) Ha! ha! thou cunning villain! I
   was caught.
I own it, doctor.
PEPÉ. (*Aside.*) This old fool would laugh
To see me break a straw, because the bits
Were of unequal lengths. My character
Carries more dulness, in the guise of wit,
Than would suffice to break an ass's back.

(*Distant shouts, music, and so forth.*)

Hark! here comes Jeptha's daughter, jogging on
With timbrels and with dances.
MALATESTA.   Jeptha's daughter!
How so?
PEPÉ.   Her father's sacrifice.
MALATESTA. (*Laughing.*) Ho! ho!
You'll burst my belt! O! you outrageous wretch,
To jest at Scripture!
PEPÉ.   You outlandish heathen,
'T is not in Scripture!
MALATESTA.   Is it not?
PEPÉ.   No more
Than you are in heaven. Mere Hebrew history.

She went up to the mountains, to bewail
The too-long keeping of her honesty.
There's a woman for you! there's a character!
What man would ever think of such a thing?
Ah! we of Rimini have little cause
For such a sorrow. Would she'd been my wife!
I'll marry any woman in her case.
MALATESTA. Why, Pepé?
PEPÉ.   Why? because, in two months' time,
Along comes father Jeptha with his knife,
And there's an end. Where is your sacrifice?
Where's Isaac, Abraham? Build your altar up:
One pile will do for both.
MALATESTA.   That's Scripture, sure.
PEPÉ. Then I'm a ram, and you may slaughter me
In Isaac's stead.
MALATESTA.   Here comes the vanguard. Where,
Where is that laggard?
PEPÉ.   At the mirror, uncle,
Making himself look beautiful. He comes,
(*Looking out.*)
Fresh as a bridegroom! Mark his doublet's fit
Across the shoulders, and his hose!—
By Jove, he nearly looks like any other man!
MALATESTA. You'd best not let him hear you. Sirrah, knave
I have a mind to swinge you!
(*Seizes his ear.*)
PEPÉ.   Loose my ear!
You've got the wrong sow, swineherd! You're unjust.
Being his father, I was fool sufficient
To think you fashioned him to suit yourself,
By way of a variety. The thought
Was good enough, the practice damnable.
MALATESTA. Hush! or I'll clap you in the pillory.

(*Enter* LANCIOTTO.)

PEPÉ. (*Sings.*) Ho, ho, ho, ho!—old Time has wings—
We're born, we mourn, we wed, we bed,
We have a devilish aching head;
          So down we lie,
          And die, and fry;

And there's a merry end of things!

(*Music, and so forth, within.*)

Here come Ravenna's eagles for a roost
In Rimini! The air is black with them.
When go they thence? Wherever young bird builds,
The nest remains for ages. Have an eye,
Or Malatesta's elephant may feel
The eagle's talons.
LANCIOTTO. You're a raven, croaker.
PEPÉ. And you no white crow, to insure us luck.
MALATESTA. There's matter in his croak.
PEPÉ. There always is;
But men lack ears.
MALATESTA. Then eyes must do our work.
Old Guido shall be looked to. If his force
Appear too great, I'll camp him out of town.
LANCIOTTO. Father, you are a sorry host.
MALATESTA. Well, well,
I'm a good landlord, though. I do not like
This flight of eagles more than Pepé. S'death!
Guido was ever treacherous.
LANCIOTTO. My lord,
You mar my holiday by such a thought.
My holiday! Dear saints! it seems to me
That all of you are mocking me.
PEPÉ. So—so—
Guido was ever treacherous?—so—so!
MALATESTA. So—so! How so?
PEPÉ. What if this treachery
Run in the blood? We'll tap a vein then—so!
MALATESTA. Sew up your mouth, and mind your fooling, fool!
PEPÉ. Am I not fooling? Why, my lord, I thought
The fooling exquisite.
LANCIOTTO. (*Aside.*) This thoughtless knave
Hits near us sometimes with his random shafts.
Marriage for me! I cannot comprehend,
I cannot take it to my heart; the thing
Seems gross, absurd, ridiculous. Ah! well,
My father bears the folly of it all;
I'm but an actor in his comedy.

My part is bad, but I must through with it.
(*Retires.*)

(*Shouts, music, and so forth, within.*)

PEPÉ. Look! here's the whole parade! Mark yonder knave—
The head one with the standard. Nature, nature!
Hadst thou a hand in such a botch-work? Why,
A forest of his legs would scarcely make
A bunch of faggots. Mark old Guido, too!
He looks like Judas with his silver. Ho!
Here's news from sweet Ravenna!
MALATESTA. (*Laughing.*)   Ha! ha! ha!
PEPÉ. Ah! now the bride!—that's something—she is toothsome.
Look you, my lord—now, while the progress halts—
Cousin Paolo, has he got the dumps?
Mercy! to see him, one might almost think
'T was his own marriage. What a doleful face!
The boy is ill. He caught a fever, uncle,
Travelling across the marshes. Physic! physic!
If he be really dying, get a doctor,
And cut the matter short. 'T were merciful.
MALATESTA. For heaven's sake, cease your clamor! I shall have
No face to meet them else. 'T is strange, for all:
What ails Paolo?
PEPÉ.   Dying, by this hand!
MALATESTA. Then I will hang you.
PEPÉ.   Don't take up my craft.
Wit's such a stranger in your brain that I
Scarce knew my lodger venturing from your mouth.
Now they come on again.
MALATESTA.   Stand back!
PEPÉ. (*Looking round.*)   The bridegroom?
He flies betimes, before the bride shows fight.
(*Walks back, looking for* LANCIOTTO.)

(*Music, shouts, ringing of bells, and so forth. Enter Men-
at-arms, with banners, and so forth,* GUIDO, *Cardinal,
Knights, Attendants, and so forth; then* PAOLO, *conducting*
FRANCESCA, *followed by* RITTA, *Ladies, Pages, and so forth,
and other Men-at-arms. They file around the stage, and
halt.*)

MALATESTA. Welcome to Rimini, Count Guido! Welcome,
And fair impressions of our poor abode,
To you, my daughter! You are well returned,
My son, Paolo! Let me bless you, son.
(PAOLO *approaches.*)
(*Apart to* PAOLO.) How many spears are in old Guido's
train?
PAOLO. Some ten-score.
MALATESTA.   Footmen?
PAOLO.   Double that.
MALATESTA.   'T is well.
(*Aloud.*) Again I bid you welcome! Make no show
Of useless ceremony with us. Friends
Have closer titles than the empty name.
We have provided entertainment, Count,
For all your followers, in the midst of us.
We trust the veterans of Rimini
May prove your soldiers that our courtesy
Does not lag far behind their warlike zeal.
Let us drop Guelf and Ghibelin henceforth,
Coupling the names of Rimini and Ravenna
As bridegroom's to his bride's.
GUIDO.   Count Malatesta,
I am no rhetorician, or my words
Might keep more even with the love I feel:
Simply, I thank you. With an honest hand
I take the hand which you extend to me,
And hope our grasp may never lose its warmth.—
(*Apart to a Knight.*) You marked the bastion by the water-
side?
Weak as a bulrush.
KNIGHT.   Tottering weak, my lord.
GUIDO. Remember it; and when you're private, sir,
Draw me a plan.
KNIGHT.   I will, my lord.
GUIDO.   How's this?
(*Aloud.*) I do not see my future son-in-law.
MALATESTA. Lanciotto!
LANCIOTTO. (*Advancing.*) I am here, my lord.
FRANCESCA. (*Starting.*)   O! heaven!
(*Apart to* PAOLO.) Is that my husband, Count Paolo? You,

You then, among the rest, have played me false!
He is—
PAOLO. My brother.
LANCIOTTO. (*Aside.*) Ha! she turns from me.
PEPÉ. (*Approaching* LANCIOTTO, *sings.*)

> Around, around the lady turned,
>   She turned not to her lord;
> She turned around to a gallant, gallant knight,
>   Who ate at his father's board.

A pretty ballad! all on one string though.
LANCIOTTO. Pepé, go hence!
  (PEPÉ *retires.*)
  (*Aside.*)   I saw her start and pale,
Turn off with horror; as if she had seen—
What?—simply me. For, am I not enough,
And something over, to make ladies quail,
Start, hide their faces, whisper to their friends,
Point at me—dare she?—and perform such tricks
As women will when monsters blast their sight?
O! saints above me, have I come so low?
Yon damsel of Ravenna shall bewail
That start and shudder. I am mad, mad, mad!
I must be patient. They have trifled with her:
Lied to her, lied! There's half the misery
Of this broad earth, all crowded in one word.
Lied, lied!—Who has not suffered from a lie?
They're all aghast—all looking at me too.
Francesca's whiter than the brow of fear:
Paolo talks.—Brother, is that well meant?
What if I draw my sword, and fight my way
Out of this cursed town? 'T would be relief.
Has shame no hiding-place? I've touched the depth
Of human infamy, and there I rest.
By heaven, I'll brave this business out! Shall they
Say at Ravenna that Count Lanciotto,
Who's driven their shivering squadrons to their homes,
Haggard with terror, turned before their eyes
And slunk away? They'll look me from the field,
When we encounter next. Why should not I

Strut with my shapeless body, as old Guido
Struts with his shapeless heart? I'll do it!
(*Offers, but shrinks back.*) 'Sdeath!
Am I so false as to forswear myself?
Lady Francesca!
(*Approaches* FRANCESCA.)

FRANCESCA.   Sir—my lord—

LANCIOTTO.   Dear lady,
I have a share in your embarrassment,
And know the feelings that possess you now.

FRANCESCA. O! you do not.

PAOLO. (*Advancing.*) My lady—

LANCIOTTO.   Gentle brother,
Leave this to me.
(PAOLO *retires.*)

FRANCESCA.   Pray do not send him off.

LANCIOTTO. 'T is fitter so.

FRANCESCA.   He comforts me.

LANCIOTTO.   Indeed?
Do you need comfort?

FRANCESCA.   No, no—pardon me!
But then—he is—you are—

LANCIOTTO.   Take breath, and speak.

FRANCESCA. I am confused, 't is true. But, then, my lord,
You are a stranger to me; and Paolo
I've known so long!

LANCIOTTO.   Since yesterday.

FRANCESCA.   Ah! well:
But the relationship between us two
Is of so close a nature, while the knowledge,
That each may have of each, so slender is
That the two jar. Besides, Paolo is
Nothing to me, while you are everything.
(*Aside.*) Can I not act?

LANCIOTTO.   I scarcely understand.
You say your knowledge of me, till to-day,
Was incomplete. Has naught been said of me
By Count Paolo or your father?

FRANCESCA.   Yes;
But nothing definite.

LANCIOTTO.   Perchance, no hint

As to my ways, my feelings, manners, or—
Or—or—as I was saying—ha! ha!—or—
(*Laughing.*)
As to my person?
FRANCESCA.   Nothing, as to that.
LANCIOTTO. To what?
FRANCESCA.   Your—person.
LANCIOTTO.   That's the least of all.
(*Turns aside.*)
Now, had I Guido of Ravenna's head
Under this heel, I'd grind it into dust!
False villain, to betray his simple child!
And thou, Paolo—not a whit behind—
Helping his craft with inconsiderate love!—
Lady Francesca, when my brother left,
I charged him, as he loved me, to conceal
Nothing from you that bore on me: and now
That you have seen me, and conversed with me,
If you object to anything in me,—
Go, I release you.
FRANCESCA.   But Ravenna's peace?
LANCIOTTO. Shall not be perilled.
GUIDO. (*Coming behind, whispers her.*) Trust him not, my
     child;
I know his ways; he'd rather fight than wed.
'T is but a wish to have the war afoot.
Stand firm for poor Ravenna!
LANCIOTTO.   Well, my lady,
Shall we conclude a lasting peace between us
By truce or marriage rites?
GUIDO. (*Whispers her.*)   The devil tempts thee:
Think of Ravenna, think of me!
LANCIOTTO.   My lord,
I see my father waits you.
(GUIDO *retires.*)
FRANCESCA.   Gentle sir,
You do me little honor in the choice.
LANCIOTTO. My aim is justice.
FRANCESCA.   Would you cast me off?
LANCIOTTO. Not for the world, if honestly obtained;
Not for the world would I obtain you falsely.
FRANCESCA. The rites were half concluded ere we met.

LANCIOTTO. Meeting, would you withdraw?
FRANCESCA.   No. (*Aside.*) Bitter word!
LANCIOTTO. No! Are you dealing fairly?
FRANCESCA.   I have said.
LANCIOTTO. O! rapture, rapture! Can it be that I—
Now I'll speak plainly; for a choice like thine
Implies such love as woman never felt.
Love me! Then monsters beget miracles,
And Heaven provides where human means fall short.
Lady, I'll worship thee! I'll line thy path
With suppliant kings! Thy waiting-maids shall be
Unransomed princesses! Mankind shall bow
One neck to thee, as Persia's multitudes
Before the rising sun! From this small town,
This centre of my conquests, I will spread
An empire touching the extremes of earth!
I'll raise once more the name of ancient Rome;
And what she swayed she shall reclaim again!
If I grow mad because you smile on me,
Think of the glory of thy love; and know
How hard it is, for such a one as I,
To gaze unshaken on divinity!
There's no such love as mine alive in man.
From every corner of the frowning earth,
It has been crowded back into my heart.
Now, take it all! If that be not enough,
Ask, and thy wish shall be omnipotent!
Your hand. (*Takes her hand.*) It wavers.
FRANCESCA.   So does not my heart.
LANCIOTTO. Brave! Thou art every way a soldier's wife;
Thou shouldst have been a Cæsar's! Father, hark!
I blamed your judgment, only to perceive
The weakness of my own.
MALATESTA.   What means all this?
LANCIOTTO. It means that this fair lady—though I gave
Release to her, and to Ravenna—placed
The liberal hand, which I restored to her,
Back in my own, of her own free good-will.
Is it not wonderful?
MALATESTA.   How so?
LANCIOTTO.   How so!
PAOLO. (*Aside.*) Alas! 't is as I feared!

MALATESTA.   You're humble?—How?
LANCIOTTO. (*Aside.*) Now shall I cry aloud to all the world,
    Make my deformity my pride, and say,
    Because she loves me, I may boast of it?
    (*Aloud.*) No matter, father, I am happy; you,
    As the blessed cause, shall share my happiness.
    Let us be moving. Revels, dashed with wine,
    Shall multiply the joys of this sweet day!
    There's not a blessing in the cup of life
    I have not tasted of within an hour!
FRANCESCA. (*Aside.*) Thus I begin the practice of deceit,
    Taught by deceivers, at a fearful cost.
    The bankrupt gambler has become the cheat,
    And lives by arts that erewhile ruined me.
    Where it will end, Heaven knows; but I—
    I have betrayed the noblest heart of all!
LANCIOTTO. Draw down thy dusky vapors, sullen night—
    Refuse, ye stars, to shine upon the world—
    Let everlasting blackness wrap the sun,
    And whisper terror to the universe!
    We need ye not! we'll blind ye, if ye dare
    Peer with lack-lustre on our revelry!
    I have at heart a passion, that would make
    All nature blaze with recreated light!
    (*Exeunt.*)

ACT IV

Scene 1

The Same. An Apartment in the Castle. Enter LANCIOTTO.

LANCIOTTO. It cannot be that I have duped myself,
    That my desire has played into the hand
    Of my belief; yet such a thing might be.
    We palm more frauds upon our simple selves
    Than knavery puts upon us. Could I trust
    The open candor of an angel's brow,
    I must believe Francesca's. But the tongue

Should consummate the proof upon the brow,
And give the truth its word. The fault lies there.
I've tried her. Press her as I may to it,
She will not utter those three little words—
"I love thee." She will say, "I'll marry you;—
I'll be your duteous wife;—I'll cheer your days;—
I'll do whate'er I can." But at the point
Of present love, she ever shifts the ground,
Winds round the word, laughs, calls me "Infidel!—
How can I doubt?" So, on and on. But yet,
For all her dainty ways, she never says,
Frankly, I love thee. I am jealous—true!
Suspicious—true! distrustful of myself;—
She knows all that. Ay, and she likewise knows,
A single waking of her morning breath
Would blow these vapors off. I would not take
The barren offer of a heartless hand,
If all the Indies cowered under it.
Perhaps she loves another? No; she said,
"I love you, Count, as well as any man";
And laughed, as if she thought that precious wit.
I turn her nonsense into argument,
And think I reason. Shall I give her up?
Rail at her heartlessness, and bid her go
Back to Ravenna? But she clings to me,
At the least hint of parting. Ah! 't is sweet,
Sweeter than slumber to the lids of pain,
To fancy that a shadow of true love
May fall on this God-stricken mould of woe,
From so serene a nature. Beautiful
Is the first vision of a desert brook,
Shining beneath its palmy garniture,
To one who travels on his easy way;
What is it to the blood-shot, aching eye
Of some poor wight who crawls with gory feet,
In famished madness, to its very brink;
And throws his sun-scorched limbs upon the cool
And humid margin of its shady strand,
To suck up life at every eager gasp?
Such seems Francesca to my thirsting soul;
Shall I turn off and die?

(*Enter* PEPÉ.)

PEPÉ.   Good-morning, cousin!
LANCIOTTO. Good-morning to your foolish majesty!
PEPÉ. The same to your majestic foolery!
LANCIOTTO. You compliment!
PEPÉ.   I am a troubadour,
A ballad-monger of fine mongrel ballads,
And therefore running o'er with elegance.
Wilt hear my verse?
LANCIOTTO.   With patience?
PEPÉ.   No, with rapture.
You must go mad—weep, rend your clothes, and roll
Over and over, like the ancient Greeks,
When listening to Iliad.
LANCIOTTO.   Sing, then, sing!
And if you equal Homer in your song,
Why, roll I must, by sheer compulsion.
PEPÉ.   Nay,
You lack the temper of the fine-eared Greek.
You will not roll; but that shall not disgrace
My gallant ballad, fallen on evil times.
(*Sings.*)

    My father had a blue-black head,
      My uncle's head was reddish—maybe,
    My mother's hair was noways red,
      Sing high ho! the pretty baby!

Mark the simplicity of that! 'T is called
"The Babe's Confession," spoken just before
His father strangled him.
LANCIOTTO.   Most marvellous!
You struggle with a legend worth your art.
PEPÉ. Now to the second stanza. Note the hint
I drop about the baby's parentage:
So delicately too! A maid might sing,
And never blush at it. Girls love these songs
Of sugared wickedness. They'll go miles about,
To say a foul thing in a cleanly way.
A decent immorality, my lord,

Is art's specific. Get the passions up,
But never wring the stomach.
LANCIOTTO.   Triumphant art!
PEPÉ. (*Sings.*)

    My father combed his blue-black head,
      My uncle combed his red head—maybe,
    My mother combed my head, and said,
      Sing high ho! my red-haired baby!

LANCIOTTO. Fie, fie! go comb your hair in private.
PEPÉ.   What!
Will you not hear? Now comes the tragedy.
(*Sings.*)

    My father tore my red, red head,
      My uncle tore my father's—maybe,
    My mother tore both till they bled—
      Sing high ho! your brother's baby!

LANCIOTTO. Why, what a hair-rending!
PEPÉ.   Thence wigs arose;
A striking epoch in man's history.
But did you notice the concluding line,
Sung by the victim's mother? There's a hit!

    "Sing high ho! your brother's baby!"

Which brother's, pray you? That's the mystery,
The adumbration of poetic art,
And there I leave it to perplex mankind.
It has a moral, fathers should regard,—
A black-haired dog breeds not a red-haired cur.
Treasure this knowledge: you're about to wive;
And no one knows what accident—
LANCIOTTO.   Peace, fool!
So all this cunning thing was wound about,
To cast a jibe at my deformity?
(*Tears off* PEPÉ's *cap.*)
There lies your cap, the emblem that protects
Your head from chastisement. Now, Pepé, hark!
Of late you've taken to reviling me;

Under your motley, you have dared to jest
At God's inflictions. Let me tell you, fool,
No man e'er lived, to make a second jest
At me, before your time!
PEPÉ.   Boo! bloody-bones!
If you're a coward—which I hardly think—
You'll have me flogged, or put into a cell,
Or fed to wolves. If you are bold of heart,
You'll let me run. Do not; I'll work you harm!
I, Beppo Pepé, standing as a man,
Without my motley, tell you, in plain terms,
I'll work you harm—I'll do you mischief, man!
LANCIOTTO. I, Lanciotto, Count of Rimini,
Will hang you, then. Put on your jingling cap;
You please my father. But remember, fool,
No jests at me!
PEPÉ.   I will try earnest next.
LANCIOTTO. And I the gallows.
PEPÉ.   Well, cry quits, cry quits!
I'll stretch your heart, and you my neck—quits, quits!
LANCIOTTO. Go, fool! Your weakness bounds your malice.
PEPÉ.   Yes:
So you all think, you savage gentlemen,
Until you feel my sting. Hang, hang away!
It is an airy, wholesome sort of death,
Much to my liking. When I hang, my friend,
You'll be chief mourner, I can promise you.
Hang me! I've quite a notion to be hung:
I'll do my utmost to deserve it.—Hang!
(*Exit.*)
LANCIOTTO. I am bemocked on all sides. My sad state
Has given the licensed and unlicensed fool
Charter to challenge me at every turn.
The jester's laughing bauble blunts my sword,
His gibes cut deeper than its fearful edge;
And I, a man, a soldier, and a prince,
Before this motley patchwork of a man,
Stand all appalled, as if he were a glass
Wherein I saw my own deformity.
O Heaven! a tear—one little tear—to wash
This aching dryness of the heart away!

(*Enter* PAOLO.)

PAOLO. What ails the fool? He passed me, muttering
The strangest garbage in the fiercest tone.
"Ha! ha!" cried he, "they made a fool of me—
A motley man, a slave; as if I felt
No stir in me of manly dignity!
Ha! ha! a fool—a painted plaything, toy—
For men to kick about this dirty world!—
My world as well as theirs.—God's world, I trow!
I will get even with them yet—ha! ha!
In the democracy of death we'll square.
I'll crawl and lie beside a king's own son;
Kiss a young princess, dead lip to dead lip;
Pull the Pope's nose; and kick down Charlemagne,
Throne, crown, and all, where the old idiot sprawls,
Safe as he thinks, rotting in royal state!"
And then he laughed and gibbered, as if drunk
With some infernal ecstasy.
LANCIOTTO.   Poor fool!
That is the groundwork of his malice, then,—
His conscious difference from the rest of men?
I, of all men, should pity him the most.
Poor Pepé! I'll be kinder. I have wronged
A feeling heart. Poor Pepé!
PAOLO.   Sad again!
Where has the rapture gone of yesterday?
LANCIOTTO. Where are the leaves of Summer? Where the
     snows
Of last year's Winter? Where the joys and griefs
That shut our eyes to yesternight's repose,
And woke not on the morrow? Joys and griefs,
Huntsmen and hounds, ye follow us as game,
Poor panting outcasts of your forest-law!
Each cheers the others,—one with wild halloos,
And one with whines and howls.—A dreadful chase,
That only closes when horns sound *a mort!*
PAOLO. Thus ever up and down! Arouse yourself,
Balance your mind more evenly, and hunt
For honey in the wormwood.

LANCIOTTO.   Or find gall
Hid in the hanging chalice of the rose:
Which think you better? If my mood offend,
We'll turn to business,—to the empty cares
That make such pother in our feverish life.
When at Ravenna, did you ever hear
Of any romance in Francesca's life?
A love-tilt, gallantry, or anything
That might have touched her heart?
PAOLO.   Not lightly even.
I think her heart as virgin as her hand.
LANCIOTTO. Then there is hope.
PAOLO.   Of what?
LANCIOTTO.   Of winning her.
PAOLO. Grammercy! Lanciotto, are you sane?
You boasted yesterday—
LANCIOTTO.   And changed to-day.
Is that so strange? I always mend the fault
Of yesterday with wisdom of to-day.
She does not love me.
PAOLO.   Pshaw! she marries you:
'T were proof enough for me.
LANCIOTTO.   Perhaps, she loves you.
PAOLO. Me, Lanciotto, me! For mercy's sake,
Blot out such thoughts—they madden me! What, love—
She love—yet marry you!
LANCIOTTO.   It moves you much.
'T was but a fleeting fancy, nothing more.
PAOLO. You have such wild conjectures!
LANCIOTTO.   Well, to me
They seem quite tame; they are my bed-fellows.
Think, to a modest woman, what must be
The loathsome kisses of an unloved man—
A gross, coarse ruffian!
PAOLO.   O! good heavens, forbear!
LANCIOTTO. What shocks you so?
PAOLO.   The picture which you draw,
Wronging yourself by horrid images.
LANCIOTTO. Until she love me, till I know, beyond
The cavil of a doubt, that she is mine—
Wholly, past question—do you think that I
Could so afflict the woman whom I love?

PAOLO. You love her, Lanciotto!
LANCIOTTO.   Next to you,
Dearer than anything in nature's scope.
PAOLO. (*Aside.*) O! Heaven, that I must bear this! Yes, and
    more,—
More torture than I dare to think upon,
Spreads out before me with the coming years,
And holds a record blotted with my tears,
As that which I must suffer!
LANCIOTTO.   Come, Paolo,
Come help me woo. I need your guiding eye,
To signal me, if I should sail astray.
PAOLO. (*Aside.*) O! torture, torture!
LANCIOTTO.   You and I, perchance,
Joining our forces, may prevail at last.
They call love like a battle. As for me,
I'm not a soldier equal to such wars,
Despite my arduous schooling. Tutor me
In the best arts of amorous strategy.
I am quite raw, Paolo. Glances, sighs,
Sweets of the lip, and arrows of the eye,
Shrugs, cringes, compliments, are new to me;
And I shall handle them with little art.
Will you instruct me?
PAOLO.   Conquer for yourself.
Two captains share one honor: keep it all.
What if I ask to share the spoils?
LANCIOTTO. (*Laughing.*)   Ha! ha!
I'll trust you, brother. Let us go to her:
Francesca is neglected while we jest.
I know not how it is, but your fair face,
And noble figure, always cheer me up,
More than your words; there's healing in them, too,
For my worst griefs. Dear brother, let us in.
(*Exeunt.*)

Scene 2

The Same. A Chamber in the Same. FRANCESCA *and* RITTA
discovered at the bridal toilet.

RITTA. (*Sings.*)

>   Ring high, ring high! to earth and sky;
>   A lady goes a-wedding;
>   The people shout, the show draws out,
>   And smiles the bride is shedding.
>
>   No bell for you, ye ragged few;
>   A beggar goes a-wedding;
>   The people sneer, the thing's so queer,
>   And tears the bride is shedding.
>
>   Ring low, ring low! dull bell of woe,
>   One tone will do for either;
>   The lady glad, and beggar sad,
>   Have both lain down together.

FRANCESCA. A mournful ballad!
RITTA.   I scarce knew I sang.
  I'm weary of this wreath. These orange-flowers
  Will never be adjusted to my taste:
  Strive as I will, they ever look awry.
  My fingers ache!
FRANCESCA.   Not more than my poor head.
  There, leave them so.
RITTA.   That's better, yet not well.
FRANCESCA. They are but fading things, not worth your pains:
  They'll scarce outlive the marriage merriment.
  Ritta, these flowers are hypocrites; they show
  An outside gayety, yet die within,
  Minute by minute. You shall see them fall,
  Black with decay, before the rites are o'er.
RITTA. How beautiful you are!
FRANCESCA.   Fie, flatterer!

White silk and laces, pearls and orange-flowers,
Would do as much for any one.
RITTA.   No, no!
You give them grace, they nothing give to you.
Why, after all, you make the wreath look well;
But somewhat dingy, where it lies against
Your pulsing temple, sullen with disgrace.
Ah! well, your Count should be the proudest man
That ever led a lady into church,
Were he a modern Alexander. Poh!
What are his trophies to a face like that?
FRANCESCA. I seem to please you, Ritta.
RITTA.   Please yourself,
And you will please me better. You are sad:
I marked it ever since you saw the Count.
I fear the splendor of his victories,
And his sweet grace of manner—for, in faith,
His is the gentlest, grandest character,
Despite his—
FRANCESCA.   Well?
RITTA.   Despite his—
FRANCESCA.   Ritta, What?
RITTA. Despite his difference from Count Paolo.—
   (FRANCESCA *staggers.*)
What is the matter?
(*Supporting her.*)
FRANCESCA.   Nothing; mere fatigue.
Hand me my kerchief. I am better now.
What were you saying?
RITTA.   That I fear the Count
Has won your love.
FRANCESCA.   Would that be cause for fear?
(*Laughing.*)
RITTA. O! yes, indeed! Once—long ago—I was
Just fool enough to tangle up my heart
With one of these same men. 'T was terrible!
Morning or evening, waking or asleep,
I had no peace. Sighs, groans, and standing tears,
Counted my moments through the blessed day.
And then to this there was a dull, strange ache
Forever sleeping in my breast,—a numbing pain,

That would not for an instant be forgot.
O! but I loved him so, that very feeling
Became intolerable. And I believed
This false Giuseppe, too, for all the sneers,
The shrugs and glances, of my intimates.
They slandered me and him, yet I believed.
He was a noble, and his love to me
Was a reproach, a shame, yet I believed.
He wearied of me, tried to shake me off,
Grew cold and formal, yet I would not doubt.
O! lady, I was true! Nor till I saw
Giuseppe walk through the cathedral door
With Dora, the rich usurer's niece, upon
The very arm to which I clung so oft,
Did I so much as doubt him. Even then—
More is my shame—I made excuses for him.
"Just this or that had forced him to the course:
Perhaps, he loved me yet—a little yet.
His fortune, or his family, had driven
My poor Giuseppe thus against his heart.
The low are sorry judges for the great.
Yes, yes, Giuseppe loved me!" But at last
I did awake. It might have been with less:
There was no need of crushing me, to break
My silly dream up. In the street, it chanced,
Dora and he went by me, and he laughed—
A bold, bad laugh—right in my poor pale face,
And turned and whispered Dora, and she laughed.
Ah! then I saw it all. I've been awake,
Ever since then, I warrant you. And now
I only pray for him sometimes, when friends
Tell his base actions towards his hapless wife.—
O! I am lying—I pray every night!
(*Weeps.*)
FRANCESCA. Poor Ritta!
(*Weeping.*)
RITTA.   No! blest Ritta! Thank kind Heaven,
That kept me spotless when he tempted me,
And my weak heart was pleading with his tongue.
Pray, do not weep. You spoil your eyes for me.
But never love; O! it is terrible!
FRANCESCA. I'll strive against it.

RITTA.   Do: because, my lady,
  Even a husband may be false, you know;
  Ay, even to so sweet a wife as you.
  Men have odd tastes. They'll surfeit on the charms
  Of Cleopatra, and then turn aside
  To woo her blackamoor. 'T is so, in faith;
  Or Dora's uncle's gold had ne'er outbid
  The boundless measure of a love like mine.
  Think of it, lady, to weigh love with gold!
  What could be meaner?
FRANCESCA.   Nothing, nothing, Ritta.
  Though gold's the standard measure of the world,
  And seems to lighten everything beside.
  Yet heap the other passions in the scale,
  And balance them 'gainst that which gold outweighs—
  Against this love—and you shall see how light
  The most supreme of them are in the poise!
  I speak by book and history; for love
  Slights my high fortunes. Under cloth of state
  The urchin cowers from pompous etiquette,
  Waiving his function at the scowl of power,
  And seeks the rustic cot to stretch his limbs
  In homely freedom. I fulfil a doom.
  We who are topmost on this heap of life
  Are nearer to Heaven's hand than you below;
  And so are used, as ready instruments,
  To work its purposes. Let envy hide
  Her witless forehead at a prince's name,
  And fix her hopes upon a clown's content.
  You, happy lowly, know not what it is
  To groan beneath the crownéd yoke of state,
  And bear the goadings of the sceptre. Ah!
  Fate drives us onward in a narrow way,
  Despite our boasted freedom.

(*Enter* PAOLO, *with Pages bearing torches.*)

                                    Gracious saints!
  What brought you here?
PAOLO.   The bridegroom waits.
FRANCESCA.   He does?

Let him wait on forever! I'll not go!
O! dear Paolo—
PAOLO.   Sister!
FRANCESCA.   It is well.
I have been troubled with a sleepless night.
My brain is wild. I know not what I say.
Pray, do not call me sister: it is cold.
I never had a brother, and the name
Sounds harshly to me. When you speak to me,
Call me Francesca.
PAOLO.   You shall be obeyed.
FRANCESCA. I would not be obeyed. I'd have you do it
Because—because you love me—as a sister—
And of your own good-will, not my command,
Would please me.—Do you understand?
PAOLO. (*Aside.*)   Too well!
'T is a nice difference.
FRANCESCA.   Yet you understand?
Say that you do.
PAOLO.   I do.
FRANCESCA.   That pleases me.
'T is flattering if our—friends appreciate
Our nicer feelings.
PAOLO.   I await you, lady.
FRANCESCA. Ritta, my gloves.—Ah! yes, I have them on;
Though I'm not quite prepared. Arrange my veil;
It folds too closely. That will do; retire.
(RITTA *retires.*)
So, Count Paolo, you have come, hot haste,
To lead me to the church,—to have your share
In my undoing? And you came, in sooth,
Because they sent you? You are very tame!
And if they sent, was it for you to come?
PAOLO. Lady, I do not understand this scorn.
I came, as is my duty, to escort
My brother's bride to him. When next you're called,
I'll send a lackey.
FRANCESCA.   I have angered you.
PAOLO. With reason: I would not appear to you
Low or contemptible.
FRANCESCA.   Why not to me?
PAOLO. Lady, I'll not be catechized.

FRANCESCA.   Ha! Count!
PAOLO. No! if you press me further, I will say
A word to madden you.—Stand still! You stray
Around the margin of a precipice.
I know what pleasure 't is to pluck the flowers
That hang above destruction, and to gaze
Into the dread abyss, to see such things
As may be safely seen. 'T is perilous:
The eye grows dizzy as we gaze below,
And a wild wish possesses us to spring
Into the vacant air. Beware, beware!
Lest this unholy fascination grow
Too strong to conquer!
FRANCESCA.   You talk wildly, Count;
There's not a gleam of sense in what you say;
I cannot hit your meaning.
PAOLO.   Lady, come!
FRANCESCA. Count, you are cruel!
   (Weeps.)
PAOLO.   O! no; I would be kind.
But now, while reason over-rides my heart,
And seeming anger plays its braggart part—
In heaven's name, come!
FRANCESCA.   One word—one question more:
Is it your wish this marriage should proceed?
PAOLO. It is.
FRANCESCA. Come on! You shall not take my hand:
I'll walk alone—now, and forever!
PAOLO. (Taking her hand.)   Sister!
   (Exeunt PAOLO and FRANCESCA, with Pages.)
RITTA. O! misery, misery!—it is plain as day—
She loves Paolo! Why will those I love
Forever get themselves ensnared, and heaven
Forever call on me to succor them?
Here was the mystery, then—the sighs and tears,
The troubled slumbers, and the waking dreams!
And now she's walking through the chapel-door,
Her bridal robe above an aching heart,
Dressed up for sacrifice. 'T is terrible!
And yet she'll smile and do it. Smile, for years,
Until her heart breaks; and the nurses ask
The doctor of the cause. He'll answer too,

In hard thick Latin, and believe himself.
O! my dear mistress! Heaven, pray torture me!
Send back Giuseppe, let him ruin me,
And scorn me after; but, sweet heaven, spare her!
I'll follow her. O! what a world is this!
(*Exit.*)

Scene 3

The Same. Interior of the Cathedral. LANCIOTTO, FRAN-
CESCA, PAOLO, MALATESTA, GUIDO, RITTA, PEPÉ, *Lords,
Knights, Priests, Pages, a bridal-train of Ladies, Soldiers,
Citizens, Attendants, and so forth, discovered before the High
Altar. Organ music. The rites being over, they advance.*

MALATESTA. By heaven—
PEPÉ.   O! uncle, uncle, you're in church!
MALATESTA. I'll break your head, knave!
PEPÉ.   I claim sanctuary.
MALATESTA. Why, bridegroom, will you never kiss the bride?
We all are mad to follow you.
PEPÉ.   Yes, yes;
Here was Paolo wetting his red lips
For the last minute. Kiss, and give him room.
MALATESTA. You heaven-forsaken imp, be quiet now!
PEPÉ. Then there'd be naught worth hearing.
MALATESTA.   Bridegroom, come!
PEPÉ. Lord! he don't like it! Hey!—I told you so—
He backs at the first step. Does he not know
His trouble's just begun?
LANCIOTTO.   Gentle Francesca,
Custom imposes somewhat on thy lips:
I'll make my levy.
(*Kisses her. The others follow.*)
(*Aside.*)   Ha! she shrank! I felt
Her body tremble, and her quivering lips
Seemed dying under mine! I heard a sigh,
Such as breaks hearts—O! no, a very groan;
And then she turned a sickly, miserable look
On pale Paolo, and he shivered too!
There is a mystery hangs around her,—ay,

Paolo knows it too.—By all the saints,
I'll make him tell it, at the dagger's point!
Paolo!—here! I do adjure you, brother,
By the great love I bear you, to reveal
The secret of Francesca's grief.
PAOLO.   I cannot.
LANCIOTTO. She told you nothing?
PAOLO.   Nothing.
LANCIOTTO.   Not a word?
PAOLO. Not one.
LANCIOTTO.   What heard you at Ravenna, then?
PAOLO. Nothing
LANCIOTTO.   Here?
PAOLO.   Nothing.
LANCIOTTO.   Not the slightest hint?—
Don't stammer, man! Speak quick! I am in haste.
PAOLO. Never.
LANCIOTTO.   What know you?
PAOLO.   Nothing that concerns
Your happiness, Lanciotto. If I did,
Would I not tell unquestioned?
LANCIOTTO.   Would you not?
You ask a question for me: answer it.
PAOLO. I have.
LANCIOTTO.   You juggle, you turn deadly pale,
Fumble your dagger, stand with head half round,
Tapping your feet.—You dare not look at me!
By Satan! Count Paolo, let me say,
You look much like a full-convicted thief!
PAOLO. Brother!—
LANCIOTTO.   Pshaw! brother! You deceive me, sir:
You and that lady have a devil's league,
To keep a devil's secret. Is it thus
You deal with me? Now, by the light above,
I'd give a dukedom for some fair pretext
To fly you all! She does not love me? Well,
I could bear that, and live away from her.
Love would be sweet, but want of it becomes
An early habit to such men as I.
But you—ah! there's the sorrow—whom I loved
An infant in your cradle; you who grew
Up in my heart, with every inch you gained;

You whom I loved for every quality,
Good, bad, and common, in your natural stock;
Ay, for your very beauty! It is strange, you'll say,
For such a crippled horror to do that,
Against the custom of his kind! O! yes,
I love, and you betray me!

PAOLO.   Lanciotto,
This is sheer frenzy. Join your bride.

LANCIOTTO.   I'll not!
What, go to her, to feel her very flesh
Crawl from my touch?—to hear her sigh and moan,
As if God plagued her? Must I come to that?
Must I endure your hellish mystery
With my own wife, and roll my eyes away
In sentimental bliss? No, no! until
I go to her, with confident belief
In her integrity and candid love,
I'll shun her as a leper!
(*Alarm-bells toll.*)

MALATESTA.   What is that?

(*Enter, hastily, a Messenger in disorder.*)

MESSENGER. My lord, the Ghibelins are up—

LANCIOTTO.   And I
Will put them down again! (*Aside.*) I thank thee, Heaven,
For this unlooked-for aid!

MALATESTA.   What force have they?

LANCIOTTO. It matters not,—nor yet the time, place, cause,
Of their rebellion. I would throttle it,
Were it a riot, or a drunken brawl!

MALATESTA. Nay, son, your bride—

LANCIOTTO.   My bride will pardon me;
Bless me, perhaps, as I am going forth;—
(*Aside.*) Thank me, perhaps, if I should ne'er return.
A soldier's duty has no bridals in it.

PAOLO. Lanciotto, this is folly. Let me take
Your usual place of honor.

LANCIOTTO. (*Laughing.*)   Ha! ha! ha!
What! thou, a tilt-yard soldier, lead my troops!
My wife will ask it shortly. (*Aside.*) Not a word
Of opposition from the new-made bride?

Nay, she looks happier. O! accursed day,
That I was mated to an empty heart!
MALATESTA. But, son—
LANCIOTTO.   Well, father?
PEPÉ.   Uncle, let him go.
He'll find it cooler on a battle-field
Than in his—
LANCIOTTO.   Hark! the fool speaks oracles.
You, soldiers, who are used to follow me,
And front our charges, emulous to bear
The shock of battle on your forward arms,—
Why stand ye in amazement? Do your swords
Stick to their scabbards with inglorious rust?
Or has repose so weakened your big hearts,
That you can dream with trumpets at your ears?
Out with your steel! It shames me to behold
Such tardy welcome to my war-worn blade!
(*Draws. The Knights and Soldiers draw.*)
Ho! draw our forces out! Strike camp, sound drums,
And set us on our marches! As I live,
I pity the next foeman who relies
On me for mercy! Farewell! to you all—
To all alike—a soldier's short farewell!
(*Going.* PAOLO *stands before him.*)
Out of my way, thou juggler!
(*Exit.*)
PAOLO.   He is gone!

ACT V

Scene 1

The Same. The Garden of the Castle. Enter PEPÉ, *singing.*

PEPÉ.   'T is jolly to walk in the shady greenwood
                With a damsel by your side;
            'T is jolly to walk from the chapel-door,
                With the hand of your pretty bride;
            'T is jolly to rest your weary head,

When life runs low and hope is fled,
On the heart where you confide:
'T is jolly, jolly, jolly, they say,
They say—but I never tried.

Nor shall I ever till they dress their girls
In motley suits, and pair us, to increase
The race of fools. 'T would be a noble thing,
A motley woman, had she wit enough
To bear the bell. But there's the misery:
You may make princes out of any stuff;
Fools come by nature. She'll make fifty kings—
Good, hearty tyrants, sound, cruel governors—
For one fine fool. There is Paolo, now,
A sweet-faced fellow with a wicked heart—
Talk of a flea, and you begin to scratch.
Lo! here he comes. And there's fierce crook-back's bride
Walking beside him—O, how gingerly!
Take care, my love! that is the very pace
We trip to hell with. Hunchback is away—
That was a fair escape for you; but, then,
The devil's ever with us, and that's worse.
See, the Ravenna giglet, Mistress Ritta,
And melancholy as a cow.—How's this?
I'll step aside, and watch you, pretty folks.
(*Hides behind the bushes.*)

(*Enter* PAOLO *and* FRANCESCA, *followed by* RITTA. *He seats himself in an arbor, and reads.* RITTA *and* FRANCESCA *advance.*)

FRANCESCA. Ritta.
RITTA.   My lady.
FRANCESCA.   You look tired.
RITTA.   I'm not.
FRANCESCA. Go to your chamber.
RITTA.   I would rather stay,
   If it may please you. I require a walk
   And the fresh atmosphere of breathing flowers,
   To stir my blood. I am not very well.
FRANCESCA. I knew it, child. Go to your chamber, dear.
   Paolo has a book to read to me.

RITTA. What, the romance? I should so love to hear!
I dote on poetry; and Count Paolo
Sweetens the Tuscan with his mellow voice.
I'm weary now, quite weary, and would rest.
FRANCESCA. Just now you wished to walk.
RITTA.   Ah! did I so?
Walking, or resting, I would stay with you.
FRANCESCA. The Count objects. He told me, yesterday,
That you were restless while he read to me;
And stirred your feet amid the grass, and sighed,
And yawned, until he almost paused.
RITTA.   Indeed
I will be quiet.
FRANCESCA.   But he will not read.
RITTA. Let me go ask him.
(*Runs towards* PAOLO.)
FRANCESCA.   Stop! Come hither, Ritta.
(*She returns.*)
I saw your new embroidery in the hall.—
The needle in the midst of Argus' eyes;
It should be finished.
RITTA.   I will bring it here.—
O no! my finger's sore; I cannot work.
FRANCESCA. Go to your room.
RITTA.   Let me remain, I pray.
'T is better, lady; you may wish for me:
I know you will be sorry if I go.
FRANCESCA. I shall not, girl. Do as I order you.
Will you be headstrong?
RITTA.   Do you wish it, then?
FRANCESCA. Yes, Ritta.
RITTA.   Yet you made pretexts enough,
Before you ordered.
FRANCESCA.   You are insolent.
Will you remain against my will?
RITTA.   Yes, lady;
Rather than not remain.
FRANCESCA.   Ha! impudent!
RITTA. You wrong me, gentle mistress. Love like mine
Does not ask questions of propriety,
Nor stand on manners. I would do you good,
Even while you smote me; I would push you back,

With my last effort, from the crumbling edge
Of some high rock o'er which you toppled me.
FRANCESCA. What do you mean?
RITTA.   I know.
FRANCESCA.   Know what?
RITTA.   Too much.
Pray, do not ask me.
FRANCESCA.   Speak!
RITTA.   I know—dear lady,
Be not offended—
FRANCESCA.   Tell me, simpleton!
RITTA. You know I worship you; you know I'd walk
Straight into ruin for a whim of yours;
You know—
FRANCESCA. I know you act the fool. Talk sense!
RITTA. I know Paolo loves you.
FRANCESCA.   Should he not?
He is my brother.
RITTA.   More than brother should.
FRANCESCA. Ha! are you certain?
RITTA.   Yes, of more than that.
FRANCESCA. Of more?
RITTA.   Yes, lady; for you love him too.
I've said it! Fling me to the carrion crows,
Kill me by inches, boil me in the pot
Count Guido promised me,—but, O, beware!
Back, while you may! Make me the sufferer,
But save yourself!
FRANCESCA.   Now, are you not ashamed,
To look me in the face with that bold brow?
I am amazed!
RITTA.   I am a woman, lady;
I too have been in love; I know its ways,
Its arts, and its deceits. Your frowning face,
And seeming indignation, do not cheat.
Your heart is in my hand.
PAOLO. (*Calls.*)   Francesca!
FRANCESCA.   Hence,
Thou wanton-hearted minion! hence, I say!—
And never look me in the face again!—
Hence, thou insulting slave!
RITTA. (*Clinging to her.*)   O lady, lady—

FRANCESCA. Begone!
(*Throws her off.*)
RITTA.   I have no friends—no one to love—
O, spare me!
FRANCESCA.   Hence!
RITTA.   Was it for this I loved—
Cared for you more than my own happiness—
Ever at heart your slave—without a wish
For greater recompense than your stray smiles?
PAOLO. (*Calls.*) Francesca!
FRANCESCA.   Hurry!
RITTA.   I am gone. Alas!
God bless you, lady! God take care of you,
When I am far away! Alas, alas!
(*Exit weeping.*)
FRANCESCA. Poor girl!—but were she all the world to me,
And held my future in her tender grasp,
I'd cast her off, without a second thought,
To savage death, for dear Paolo's sake!
Paolo, hither! Now he comes to me;
I feel his presence, though I see him not,
Stealing upon me like the fervid glow
Of morning sunshine. Now he comes too near—
He touches me—O Heaven!
PAOLO.   Our poem waits.
I have been reading while you talked with Ritta.
How did you get her off?
FRANCESCA.   By some device.
She will not come again.
PAOLO.   I hate the girl:
She seems to stand between me and the light.
And now for the romance. Where left we off?
FRANCESCA. Where Lancelot and Queen Guenevra strayed
Along the forest, in the youth of May.
You marked the figure of the birds that sang
Their melancholy farewell to the sun—
Rich in his loss, their sorrow glorified—
Like gentle mourners o'er a great man's grave.
Was it not there? No, no; 't was where they sat
Down on the bank, by one impulsive wish
That neither uttered.
PAOLO. (*Turning over the book.*) Here it is.

(*Reads.*)
    "So sat
Guenevra and Sir Lancelot"—'T were well
To follow them in that.
(*They sit upon a bank.*)
FRANCESCA.   I listen: read.
Nay, do not; I can wait, if you desire.
PAOLO. My dagger frets me; let me take it off.
(*Rises.*)
In thoughts of love, we'll lay our weapons by.
(*Lays aside his dagger, and sits again.*)
Draw closer: I am weak in voice to-day.
(*Reads.*)
    "So sat Guenevra and Sir Lancelot,
        Under the blaze of the descending sun,
    But all his cloudy splendors were forgot.
    Each bore a thought, the only secret one,
        Which each had hidden from the other's heart,
        Both with sweet mystery well-nigh overrun.
    Anon, Sir Lancelot, with gentle start,
        Put by the ripples of her golden hair,
    Gazing upon her with his lips apart.
    He marvelled human thing could be so fair;
        Essayed to speak; but, in the very deed,
        His words expired of self-betrayed despair.
    Little she helped him, at his direst need,
        Roving her eyes o'er hill, and wood, and sky,
    Peering intently at the meanest weed;
        Ay, doing aught but look in Lancelot's eye.
    Then, with the small pique of her velvet shoe,
        Uprooted she each herb that blossomed nigh;
    Or strange wild figures in the dust she drew;
        Until she felt Sir Lancelot's arm around
    Her waist, upon her cheek his breath like dew.
    While through his fingers timidly he wound
        Her shining locks; and, haply, when he brushed
        Her ivory skin, Guenevra nearly swound:
    For where he touched, the quivering surface blushed,
        Firing her blood with most contagious heat,
    Till brow, cheek, neck, and bosom, all were flushed.
    Each heart was listening to the other beat.
    As twin-born lilies on one golden stalk,

Drooping with Summer, in warm languor meet,
So met their faces. Down the forest walk
Sir Lancelot looked—he looked east, west, north,
        south—
No soul was nigh, his dearest wish to balk:
She smiled; he kissed her full upon the mouth."
(*Kisses* FRANCESCA.)
I'll read no more!
(*Starts up, dashing down the book.*)
FRANCESCA.   Paolo!
PAOLO.   I am mad!
The torture of unnumbered hours is o'er,
The straining cord has broken, and my heart
Riots in free delirium! O, Heaven!
I struggled with it, but it mastered me!
I fought against it, but it beat me down!
I prayed, I wept, but Heaven was deaf to me;
And every tear rolled backward on my heart,
To blight and poison!
FRANCESCA.   And dost thou regret?
PAOLO. The love? No, no! I'd dare it all again,
Its direst agonies and meanest fears,
For that one kiss. Away with fond remorse!
Here, on the brink of ruin, we two stand;
Lock hands with me, and brave the fearful plunge!
Thou canst not name a terror so profound
That I will look or falter from. Be bold!
I know thy love—I knew it long ago—
Trembled and fled from it. But now I clasp
The peril to my breast, and ask of thee
A kindred desperation.
FRANCESCA. (*Throwing herself into his arms.*) Take me all,—
Body and soul! The women of our clime
Do never give away but half a heart:
I have not part to give, part to withhold,
In selfish safety. When I saw thee first,
Riding alone amid a thousand men,
Sole in the lustre of thy majesty,
And Guido da Polenta said to me,
"Daughter, behold thy husband!" with a bound
My heart went forth to meet thee. He deceived,
He lied to me—ah! that's the aptest word—

And I believed. Shall I not turn again,
And meet him, craft with craft? Paolo, love,
Thou'rt dull—thou'rt dying like a feeble fire
Before the sunshine. Was it but a blaze,
A flash of glory, and a long, long night?

PAOLO. No, darling, no! You could not bend me back;
My course is onward; but my heart is sick
With coming fears.

FRANCESCA.   Away with them! Must I
Teach thee to love? and reïnform the ear
Of thy spent passion with some sorcery
To raise the chilly dead?

PAOLO.   Thy lips have not
A sorcery to rouse me as this spell.
(*Kisses her.*)

FRANCESCA. I give thy kisses back to thee again:
And, like a spendthrift, only ask of thee
To take while I can give.

PAOLO.   Give, give forever!
Have we not touched the height of human bliss?
And if the sharp rebound may hurl us back
Among the prostrate, did we not soar once?—
Taste heavenly nectar, banquet with the gods
On high Olympus? If they cast us, now,
Amid the furies, shall we not go down
With rich ambrosia clinging to our lips,
And richer memories settled in our hearts?
Francesca.

FRANCESCA. Love?

PAOLO.   The sun is sinking low
Upon the ashes of his fading pyre,
And gray possesses the eternal blue;
The evening star is stealing after him,
Fixed, like a beacon, on the prow of night;
The world is shutting up its heavy eye
Upon the stir and bustle of to-day;—
On what shall it awake?

FRANCESCA.   On love that gives
Joy at all seasons, changes night to day,
Makes sorrow smile, plucks out the barbéd dart
Of moaning anguish, pours celestial balm
In all the gaping wounds of earth, and lulls

The nervous fancies of unsheltered fear
Into a slumber sweet as infancy's!
On love that laughs at the impending sword,
And puts aside the shield of caution: cries,
To all its enemies, "Come, strike me now!—
Now, while I hold my kingdom, while my crown
Of amaranth and myrtle is yet green,
Undimmed, unwithered; for I cannot tell
That I shall e'er be happier!" Dear Paolo,
Would you lapse down from misery to death,
Tottering through sorrow and infirmity?
Or would you perish at a single blow,
Cut off amid your wildest revelry,
Falling among the wine-cups and the flowers,
And tasting Bacchus when your drowsy sense
First gazed around eternity? Come, love!
The present whispers joy to us; we'll hear
The voiceless future when its turn arrives.
PAOLO. Thou art a siren. Sing, forever sing!
Hearing thy voice, I cannot tell what fate
Thou hast provided when the song is o'er;—
But I will venture it.
FRANCESCA.   In, in, my love!
(*Exeunt.*)

(PEPÉ *steals from behind the bushes.*)

PEPÉ. O, brother Lanciotto!—O, my stars!—
If this thing lasts, I simply shall go mad!
(*Laughs, and rolls on the ground.*)
O Lord! to think my pretty lady puss
Had tricks like this, and we ne'er know of it!
I tell you, Lanciotto, you and I
Must have a patent for our foolery!
"She smiled; he kissed her full upon the mouth!"—
There's the beginning; where's the end of it?
O poesy! debauch thee only once,
And thou'rt the greatest wanton in the world!
O cousin Lanciotto—ho, ho, ho!
(*Laughing.*)
Can a man die of laughter? Here we sat;
Mistress Francesca so demure and calm;

Paolo grand, poetical, sublime!—
Eh! what is this? Paolo's dagger? Good!
Here is more proof, sweet cousin Broken-back.
(*Mimicking* PAOLO.)
"In thoughts of love, we'll lay our weapons by!"
That's very pretty! Here's its counterpart:
In thoughts of hate, we'll pick them up again!
(*Takes the dagger.*)
Now for my soldier, now for crook-backed Mars!
Ere long all Rimini will be ablaze.
He'll kill me? Yes: what then? That's nothing new,
Except to me; I'll bear for custom's sake.
More blood will follow; like the royal sun,
I shall go down in purple. Fools for luck;
The proverb holds like iron. I must run,
Ere laughter smother me.—O, ho, ho, ho!
(*Exit, laughing.*)

Scene 2

A Camp among the Hills. Before LANCIOTTO's *tent. Enter, from the tent,* LANCIOTTO.

LANCIOTTO. The camp is strangely quiet. Not a sound
Breaks nature's high solemnity. The sun
Repeats again his every-day decline;
Yet all the world looks sadly after him,
As if the customary sight were new.
Yon moody sentinel goes slowly by,
Through the thick mists of evening, with his spear
Trailed at a funeral hold. Long shadows creep,
From things beyond the furthest range of sight,
Up to my very feet. These mystic shades
Are of the earth; the light that causes them,
And teaches us the quick comparison,
Is all from heaven. Ah! restless man might crawl
With patience through his shadowy destiny,
If he were senseless to the higher light
Towards which his soul aspires. How grand and vast
Is yonder show of heavenly pageantry!
How mean and narrow is the earthly stand

From which we gaze on it! Magnificent,
O God, art thou amid the sunsets! Ah!
What heart in Rimini is softened now,
Towards my defects, by this grand spectacle?
Perchance, Paolo now forgives the wrong
Of my hot spleen. Perchance, Francesca now
Wishes me back, and turns a tenderer eye
On my poor person and ill-mannered ways;
Fashions excuses for me, schools her heart
Through duty into love, and ponders o'er
The sacred meaning in the name of wife.
Dreams, dreams! Poor fools, we squander love away
On thankless borrowers; when bankrupt quite,
We sit and wonder of their honesty.
Love, take a lesson from the usurer,
And never lend but on security.
Captain!

(*Enter a* CAPTAIN.)

CAPTAIN. My lord.
LANCIOTTO.   They worsted us to-day.
CAPTAIN. Not much, my lord.
LANCIOTTO.   With little loss, indeed.
  Their strength is in position. Mark you, sir.
  (*Draws on the ground with his sword.*)
  Here is the pass; it opens towards the plain,
  With gradual widening, like a lady's fan.
  The hills protect their flanks on either hand;
  And, as you see, we cannot show more front
  Than their advance may give us. Then, the rocks
  Are sorry footing for our horse. Just here,
  Close in against the left-hand hills, I marked
  A strip of wood, extending down the gorge:
  Behind that wood dispose your force ere dawn.
  I shall begin the onset, then give ground,
  And draw them out; while you, behind the wood,
  Must steal along, until their flank and rear
  Oppose your column. Then set up a shout,
  Burst from the wood, and drive them on our spears.
  They have no outpost in the wood, I know;
  'T is too far from their centre. On the morrow,

When they are flushed with seeming victory,
And think my whole division in full rout,
They will not pause to scrutinize the wood;
So you may enter boldly. We will use
The heart to-day's repulse has given to them,
For our advantage. Do you understand?
CAPTAIN. Clearly, my lord.
LANCIOTTO.   If they discover you,
Before you gain your point, wheel, and retreat
Upon my rear. If your attack should fail
To strike them with a panic, and they turn
In too great numbers on your small command,
Scatter your soldiers through the wood:
Let each seek safety for himself.
CAPTAIN.   I see.
LANCIOTTO. Have Pluto shod; he cast a shoe to-day:
Let it be done at once. My helmet, too,
Is worn about the lacing; look to that.
Where is my armorer?
CAPTAIN.   At his forge.
LANCIOTTO.   Your charge
Must be at sunrise—just at sunrise, sir—
Neither before nor after. You must march
At moonset, then, to gain the point ere dawn.
That is enough.
CAPTAIN.   Good-even!
  (*Going.*)
LANCIOTTO.   Stay, stay, stay!
My sword-hilt feels uneasy in my grasp;
  (*Gives his sword.*)
Have it repaired; and grind the point. Strike hard!
I'll teach these Ghibelins a lesson.
  (*Loud laughter within.*)
                                   Ha!
What is that clamor?

  (*Enter hastily* PEPÉ, *tattered and travel-stained.*)

PEPÉ.   News from Rimini!
  (*Falls exhausted.*)
LANCIOTTO. Is that you, Pepé? Captain, a good-night!
  (*Exit* CAPTAIN.)

I never saw you in such straits before.
Wit without words!
PEPÉ. (*Panting.*) That's better than—O!—O!—
Words without wit.
LANCIOTTO. (*Laughing.*) You'll die a jester, Pepé.
PEPÉ. If so, I'll leave the needy all my wit.
You, you shall have it, cousin.—O! O! O!
(*Panting.*)
Those devils in the hills, the Ghibelins,
Ran me almost to death. My lord—ha! ha!
(*Laughing.*)
It all comes back to me—O! Lord 'a mercy!—
The garden, and the lady, and the Count!
Not to forget the poetry—ho! ho!
(*Laughing.*)
O! cousin Lanciotto, such a wife,
And such a brother! Hear me, ere I burst!
LANCIOTTO. You're pleasant, Pepé!
PEPÉ.   Am I?—Ho! ho! ho!
(*Laughing.*)
You ought to be; your wife's a——
LANCIOTTO.   What?
PEPÉ.   A lady—
A lady, I suppose, like all the rest.
I am not in their secrets. Such a fellow
As Count Paolo is your man for that.
I'll tell you something, if you'll swear a bit.
LANCIOTTO. Swear what?
PEPÉ.   First, swear to listen till the end.—
O! you may rave, curse, howl, and tear your hair;
But you must listen.
LANCIOTTO.   For your jest's sake? Well.
PEPÉ. You swear?
LANCIOTTO.   I do.
PEPÉ.   Next, swear to know the truth.
LANCIOTTO. The truth of a fool's story!
PEPÉ.   You mistake.
Now, look you, cousin! You have often marked—
I know, for I have seen—strange glances pass
Between Paolo and your lady wife.—
LANCIOTTO. Ha! Pepé!

PEPÉ.   Now I touch you to the quick.
I know the reason of those glances.
LANCIOTTO.   Ha!
  Speak! or I'll throttle you!
  (*Seizes him.*)
PEPÉ.   Your way is odd.
  Let go my gullet, and I'll talk you deaf.
  Swear my last oath: only to know the truth.
LANCIOTTO. But that may trouble me.
PEPÉ.   Your honor lies—
  Your precious honor, cousin Chivalry—
  Lies bleeding with a terrible great gash,
  Without its knowledge. Swear!
LANCIOTTO.   My honor? Speak!
PEPÉ. You swear?
LANCIOTTO.   I swear. Your news is ill, perchance?
PEPÉ. Ill! would I bring it else? Am I inclined
  To run ten leagues with happy news for you?
  O, Lord! that's jolly!
LANCIOTTO.   You infernal imp,
  Out with your story, ere I strangle you!
PEPÉ. Then take a fast hold on your two great oaths,
  To steady tottering manhood, and attend.
  Last eve, about this hour, I took a stroll
  Into the garden.—Are you listening, cousin?
LANCIOTTO. I am all ears.
PEPÉ.   Why, so an ass might say.
LANCIOTTO. Will you be serious?
PEPÉ.   Wait a while, and we
  Will both be graver than a church-yard. Well,
  Down the long walk, towards me, came your wife,
  With Count Paolo walking at her side.
  It was a pretty sight, and so I stepped
  Into the bushes. Ritta came with them;
  And Lady Fanny had a grievous time
  To get her off. That made me curious.
  Anon, the pair sat down upon a bank,
  To read a poem;—the tenderest romance,
  All about Lancelot and Queen Guenevra.
  The Count read well—I'll say that much for him—
  Only he stuck too closely to the text,
  Got too much wrapped up in the poesy,

And played Sir Lancelot's actions, out and out,
On Queen Francesca. Nor in royal parts
Was she so backward. When he struck the line—
"She smiled; he kissed her full upon the mouth";
Your lady smiled, and, by the saints above,
Paolo carried out the sentiment!
Can I not move you?
LANCIOTTO.   With such trash as this?
And so you ran ten leagues to tell a lie?—
Run home again.
PEPÉ.   I am not ready yet.
After the kiss, up springs our amorous Count,
Flings Queen Guenevra and Sir Lancelot
Straight to the devil; growls and snaps his teeth,
Laughs, weeps, howls, dances; talks about his love,
His madness, suffering, and the Lord knows what,
Bullying the lady like a thief. But she,
All this hot time, looked cool and mischievous;
Gave him his halter to the very end;
And when he calmed a little, up she steps
And takes him by the hand. You should have seen
How tame the furious fellow was at once!
How he came down, snivelled, and cowed to her,
And fell to kissing her again! It was
A perfect female triumph! Such a scene
A man might pass through life and never see.
More sentiment then followed,—buckets full
Of washy words, not worth my memory.
But all the while she wound his Countship up,
Closer and closer; till at last—tu!—wit!—
She scoops him up, and off she carries him,
Fish for her table! Follow, if you can;
My fancy fails me. All this time you smile!
LANCIOTTO. You should have been a poet, not a fool.
PEPÉ. I might be both.
LANCIOTTO.   You made no record, then?
Must this fine story die for want of ink?
Left you no trace in writing?
PEPÉ.   None.
LANCIOTTO.   Alas!
Then you have told it? 'T is but stale, my boy;
I'm second hearer.

PEPÉ.   You are first, in faith.

LANCIOTTO. In truth?

PEPÉ. In sadness. You have got it fresh.
I had no time; I itched to reach your ear.
Now go to Rimini, and see yourself.
You'll find them in the garden. Lovers are
Like walking ghosts, they always haunt the spot
Of their misdeeds.

LANCIOTTO.   But have I heard you out?
You told me all?

PEPÉ.   All; I have nothing left.

LANCIOTTO. Why, you brain-stricken idiot, to trust
Your story and your body in my grasp!
(*Seizes him.*)

PEPÉ. Unhand me, cousin!

LANCIOTTO.   When I drop you, Pepé,
You'll be at rest.

PEPÉ.   I will betray you—O!

LANCIOTTO. Not till the judgment day.
(*They struggle.*)

PEPÉ. (*Drawing* PAOLO's *dagger.*)   Take that!

LANCIOTTO. (*Wresting the dagger from him.*)   Well meant,
But poorly done! Here's my return.
(*Stabs him.*)

PEPÉ.   O! beast!
(*Falls.*)
This I expected; it is naught—Ha! ha!
(*Laughing.*)
I'll go to sleep; but you—what you will bear!
Hunchback, come here!

LANCIOTTO.   Fie! say your prayers.

PEPÉ.   Hark, hark!
Paolo hired me, swine, to murder you.

LANCIOTTO. That is a lie; you never cared for gold.

PEPÉ. He did, I say! I'll swear to it, by heaven!
Do you believe me?

LANCIOTTO.   No!

PEPÉ.   You lie! you lie!
Look at the dagger, cousin—Ugh!—good-night!
(*Dies.*)

LANCIOTTO. O! horrible! It was a gift of mine—
He never laid it by. Speak, speak, fool, speak!

(*Shakes the body.*)
How didst thou get it?—speak! Thou'rt warm—not dead—
Thou hast a tongue—O! speak! Come, come, a jest—
Another jest from those thin mocking lips!
Call me a cripple—hunchback—what thou wilt;
But speak to me! He cannot. Now, by heaven,
I'll stir this business till I find the truth!
Am I a fool? It is a silly lie,
Coined by yon villain with his last base breath.
What ho! without there!

(*Enter* CAPTAIN *and Soldiers.*)

CAPTAIN.   Did you call, my lord?
LANCIOTTO. Did Heaven thunder? Are you deaf, you louts?
Saddle my horse! What are you staring at?
Is it your first look at a dead man? Well,
Then look your fill. Saddle my horse, I say!
Black Pluto—stir! Bear that assassin hence.
Chop him to pieces, if he move. My horse!
CAPTAIN. My lord, he's shoeing.
LANCIOTTO.   Did I ask for shoes?
I want my horse. Run, fellow, run! Unbarbed—
My lightest harness on his back. Fly, fly!
(*Exit a Soldier. The others pick up the body.*)
Ask him, I pray you, if he did not lie!
CAPTAIN. The man is dead, my lord.
LANCIOTTO. (*Laughing.*)   Then do not ask him!
(*Exeunt Soldiers with the body.*)
By Jupiter, I shall go mad, I think!
(*Walks about.*)
CAPTAIN. (*Apart to a Soldier.*) Something disturbs him. Do
    you mark the spot
Of purple on his brow?
SOLDIER.   Then blood must flow.
LANCIOTTO. Boy, boy!
    (*Enter a Page.*)
                    My cloak and riding-staff. Quick, quick!
How you all lag! (*Exit Page.*) I ride to Rimini.
Skirmish to-morrow. Wait till my return—
I shall be back at sundown. You shall see
What slaughter is then!

CAPTAIN.   Ho! turn out a guard!—
LANCIOTTO. I wish no guard; I ride alone.

(*Re-enter Page, with a cloak and staff.*)

(*Taking them.*)   Well done!
Thou art a pretty boy.—And now my horse!

(*Enter a Soldier.*)

SOLDIER. Pluto is saddled—
LANCIOTTO.   'T is a damned black lie!
SOLDIER. Indeed, my lord—
LANCIOTTO.   O! comrade, pardon me:
I talk at random. What, Paolo too,—
A boy whom I have trotted on my knee!
Poh! I abuse myself by such a thought.
Francesca may not love me, may love him—
Indeed she ought; but when an angel comes
To play the wanton on this filthy earth,
Then I'll believe her guilty. Look you, sir!
Am I quite calm?
CAPTAIN.   Quite calm, my lord.
LANCIOTTO.   You see
No trace of passion on my face?—No sign
Of ugly humors, doubts, or fears, or aught
That may disfigure God's intelligence?
I have a grievous charge against you, sir,
That may involve your life; and if you doubt
The candor of my judgment, choose your time:
Shall I arraign you now?
CAPTAIN.   Now, if you please.
I'll trust my cause to you and innocence
At any time. I am not conscious—
LANCIOTTO.   Pshaw!
I try myself, not you. And I am calm—
That is your verdict—and dispassionate?
CAPTAIN. So far as I can judge.
LANCIOTTO.   'T is well, 't is well!
Then I will ride to Rimini. Good-night!
(*Exit. The others look after him, amazedly, and exeunt.*)

Scene 3

Rimini. The Garden of the Castle. Enter PAOLO *and* FRAN-
CESCA.

FRANCESCA. Thou hast resolved?
PAOLO. I've sworn it.
FRANCESCA. Ah! you men
Can talk of love and duty in a breath;
Love while you like, forget when you are tired,
And salve your falsehood with some wholesome saw;
But we, poor women, when we give our hearts,
Give all, lose all, and never ask it back.
PAOLO. What couldst thou ask for that I have not given?
With love I gave thee manly probity,
Innocence, honor, self-respect, and peace.
Lanciotto will return, and how shall I—
O! shame, to think of it!—how shall I look
My brother in the face? take his frank hand?
Return his tender glances? I should blaze
With guilty blushes.
FRANCESCA. Thou canst forsake me, then,
To spare thyself a little bashful pain?
Paolo, dost thou know what 't is for me,
A woman—nay, a dame of highest rank—
To lose my purity? to walk a path
Whose slightest slip may fill my ear with sounds
That hiss me out to infamy and death?
Have I no secret pangs, no self-respect,
No husband's look to bear? O! worse than these,
I must endure his loathsome touch; be kind
When he would dally with his wife, and smile
To see him play thy part. Pah! sickening thought!
From that thou art exempt. Thou shalt not go!
Thou dost not love me!
PAOLO. Love thee! Standing here,
With countless miseries upon my head,
I say, my love for thee grows day by day.
It palters with my conscience, blurs my thoughts
Of duty, and confuses my ideas

Of right and wrong. Ere long, it will persuade
My shaking manhood that all this is just.
FRANCESCA. Let it! I'll blazon it to all the world,
Ere I will lose thee. Nay, if I had choice,
Between our love and my lost innocence,
I tell thee calmly, I would dare again
The deed which we have done. O! thou art cruel
To fly me, like a coward, for thy ease.
When thou art gone, thou'lt flatter thy weak heart
With hopes and speculations; and thou'lt swear
I suffer naught, because thou dost not see.
I will not live to bear it!
PAOLO.   Die,—'t were best;
'T is the last desperate comfort of our sin.
FRANCESCA. I'll kill myself!
PAOLO.   And so would I, with joy;
But crime has made a craven of me. O!
For some good cause to perish in! Something
A man might die for, looking in God's face;
Not slinking out of life with guilt like mine
Piled on the shoulders of a suicide!
FRANCESCA. Where wilt thou go?
PAOLO.   I care not; anywhere
Out of this Rimini. The very things
That made the pleasures of my innocence
Have turned against me. There is not a tree,
Nor house, nor church, nor monument, whose face
Took hold upon my thoughts, that does not frown
Balefully on me. From their marble tombs
My ancestors scowl at me; and the night
Thickens to hear their hisses. I would pray,
But heaven jeers at it. Turn where'er I will,
A curse pursues me.
FRANCESCA.   Heavens! O, say not so!
I never cursed thee, love; I never moved
My little finger, ere I looked to thee
For my instruction.
PAOLO.   But thy gentleness
Seems to reproach me; and, instead of joy,
It whispers horror!
FRANCESCA.   Cease! cease!
PAOLO.   I must go.

FRANCESCA. And I must follow. All that I call life
Is bound in thee. I could endure for thee
More agonies than thou canst catalogue—
For thy sake, love—bearing the ill for thee!
With thee, the devils could not so contrive
That I would blench or falter from my love!
Without thee, heaven were torture!
PAOLO.   I must go.
(*Going.*)
FRANCESCA. O! no—Paolo—dearest!—
(*Clinging to him.*)
PAOLO.   Loose thy hold!
'T is for thy sake, and Lanciotto's; I
Am as a cipher in the reckoning.
I have resolved. Thou canst but stretch the time.
Keep me to-day, and I will fly to-morrow—
Steal from thee like a thief.
(*Struggles with her.*)
FRANCESCA.   Paolo—love—
Indeed, you hurt me!—Do not use me thus!
Kill me, but do not leave me. I will laugh—
A long, gay, ringing laugh—if thou wilt draw
Thy pitying sword, and stab me to the heart!

(*Enter* LANCIOTTO *behind.*)

Nay, then, one kiss!
LANCIOTTO. (*Advancing between them.*) Take it: 't will be
    the last.
PAOLO. Lo! Heaven is just!
FRANCESCA.   The last! so be it.
(*Kisses* PAOLO.)
LANCIOTTO.   Ha!
Dare you these tricks before my very face?
FRANCESCA. Why not! I've kissed him in the sight of heaven;
Are you above it?
PAOLO.   Peace, Francesca, peace!
LANCIOTTO. Paolo—why, thou sad and downcast man,
Look up! I have some words to speak with thee.
Thou art not guilty?
PAOLO.   Yes, I am. But she
Has been betrayed; so she is innocent.

Her father tampered with her. I—

FRANCESCA.   'T is false!
The guilt is mine. Paolo was entrapped
By love and cunning. I am shrewder far
Than you suspect.

PAOLO.   Lanciotto, shut thy ears;
She would deceive thee.

LANCIOTTO.   Silence, both of you!
Is guilt so talkative in its defence?
Then, let me make you judge and advocate
In your own cause. You are not guilty?

PAOLO.   Yes.

LANCIOTTO. Deny it—but a word—say no. Lie, lie!
And I'll believe.

PAOLO.   I dare not.

LANCIOTTO.   Lady, you?

FRANCESCA. If I might speak for him—

LANCIOTTO.   It cannot be:
Speak for yourself. Do you deny your guilt?

FRANCESCA. No! I assert it; but—

LANCIOTTO.   In heaven's name, hold!
Will neither of you answer no to me?
A nod, a hint, a sign, for your escape.
Bethink you, life is centred in this thing.
Speak! I will credit either. No reply?
What does your crime deserve?

PAOLO.   Death.

FRANCESCA.   Death to both.

LANCIOTTO. Well said! You speak the law of Italy;
And by the dagger you designed for me,
In Pepé's hand,—your bravo?

PAOLO.   It is false!
If you received my dagger from his hand,
He stole it.

LANCIOTTO. There, sweet heaven, I knew! And now
You will deny the rest? You see, my friends,
How easy of belief I have become!—
How easy 't were to cheat me!

PAOLO.   No; enough!
I will not load my groaning spirit more;
A lie would crush it.

LANCIOTTO.   Brother, once you gave

Life to this wretched piece of workmanship,
When my own hand resolved its overthrow.
Revoke the gift.
(*Offers to stab himself.*)
PAOLO. (*Preventing him.*) Hold, homicide!
LANCIOTTO.   But think,
You and Francesca may live happily,
After my death, as only lovers can.
PAOLO. Live happily, after a deed like this!
LANCIOTTO. Now, look ye! there is not one hour of life
Among us three. Paolo, you are armed—
You have a sword, I but a dagger: see!
I mean to kill you.
FRANCESCA. (*Whispers* PAOLO.) Give thy sword to me.
PAOLO. Away! thou'rt frantic! I will never lift
This wicked hand against thee.
LANCIOTTO.   Coward, slave!
Art thou so faint? Does Malatesta's blood
Run in thy puny veins? Take that!
(*Strikes him.*)
PAOLO.   And more:
Thou canst not offer more than I will bear.
LANCIOTTO. Paolo, what a craven has thy guilt
Transformed thee to! Why, I have seen the time
When thou'dst have struck at heaven for such thing!
Art thou afraid?
PAOLO.   I am.
LANCIOTTO.   O! infamy!
Can man sink lower? I will wake thee, though:—
Thou shalt not die a coward. See! look here!
(*Stabs* FRANCESCA.)
FRANCESCA. O!—O!—
(*Falls.*)
PAOLO.   Remorseless man, dare you do this,
And hope to live? Die, murderer!
(*Draws, rushes at him, but pauses.*)
LANCIOTTO.   Strike, strike!
Ere thy heart fail.
PAOLO.   I cannot.
(*Throws away his sword.*)
LANCIOTTO.   Dost thou see
Yon bloated spider—hideous as myself—

Climbing aloft, to reach that wavering twig?
When he has touched it, one of us must die.
Here is the dagger.—Look at me, I say!
Keep your eyes from that woman! Look, think, choose!—
Turn here to me: thou shalt not look at her!

PAOLO. O, heaven!

LANCIOTTO.   'T is done!

PAOLO. (*Struggling with him.*) O! Lanciotto, hold!
Hold, for thy sake! Thou wilt repent this deed.

LANCIOTTO. I know it.

FRANCESCA. (*Rising.*) Help!—O! murder!—help, help, help!
(*She totters towards them, and falls.*)

LANCIOTTO. Our honor, boy!
(*Stabs* PAOLO, *he falls.*)

FRANCESCA.   Paolo!

PAOLO.   Hark! she calls.
I pray thee, brother, help me to her side.
(LANCIOTTO *helps him to* FRANCESCA.)

LANCIOTTO. Why, there!

PAOLO.   God bless thee!

LANCIOTTO.   Have I not done well?
What were the honor of the Malatesti,
With such a living slander fixed to it?
Cripple! that's something—cuckold! that is damned!
You blame me?

PAOLO.   No.

LANCIOTTO.   You, lady?

FRANCESCA.   No, my lord.

LANCIOTTO. May God forgive you! We are even now:
Your blood has cleared my honor, and our name
Shines to the world as ever.

PAOLO.   O!—O!—

FRANCESCA.   Love,
Art suffering?

PAOLO.   But for thee.

FRANCESCA.   Here, rest thy head
Upon my bosom. Fie upon my blood!
It stains thy ringlets. Ha! he dies! Kind saints,
I was first struck, why cannot I die first?
Paolo, wake!—God's mercy! wilt thou go
Alone—without me? Prithee, strike again!

Nay, I am better—love—now—O!
(*Dies.*)
LANCIOTTO. (*Sinks upon his knees.*) Great heaven!
MALATESTA. (*Without.*) This way, I heard the cries.

(*Enter, with* GUIDO, *Attendants, etc.*)

GUIDO.   O! horrible!
MALATESTA. O! bloody spectacle! Where is thy brother?
LANCIOTTO. So Cain was asked. Come here, old men!
    You shrink
    From two dead bodies and a pool of blood—
    You soldiers, too! Come here!
    (*Drags* MALATESTA *and* GUIDO *forward.*)
MALATESTA.   O!—O!—
LANCIOTTO.   You groan!
    What must I do, then? Father, here it is,—
    The blood of Guido mingled with our own,
    As my old nurse predicted. And the spot
    Of her infernal baptism burns my brain
    Till reason shudders! Down, upon your knees!
    Ay, shake them harder, and perchance they'll wake.
    Keep still! Kneel, kneel! You fear them? I shall prowl
    About these bodies till the day of doom.
MALATESTA. What hast thou done?
GUIDO.   Francesca!—O! my child!
LANCIOTTO. Can howling make this sight more terrible?
    Peace! You disturb the angels up in heaven,
    While they are hiding from this ugly earth.
    Be satisfied with what you see. You two
    Began this tragedy, I finished it.
    Here, by these bodies, let us reckon up
    Our crimes together. Why, how still they lie!
    A moment since, they walked, and talked, and kissed!
    Defied me to my face, dishonored me!
    They had the power to do it then; but now,
    Poor souls, who'll shield them in eternity?
    Father, the honor of our house is safe:
    I have the secret. I will to the wars,
    And do more murders, to eclipse this one.
    Back to the battles; there I breathe in peace;

And I will take a soldier's honor back.—
Honor! what's that to me now? Ha! ha! ha!
(*Laughing.*)
A great thing, father! I am very ill.
I killed thy son for honor: thou mayst chide.
O God! I cannot cheat myself with words!
I loved him more than honor—more than life—
This man, Paolo—this stark, bleeding corpse!
Here let me rest, till God awake us all!
(*Falls on* PAOLO's *body.*)

THE OCTOROON

Preface to THE OCTOROON

The Octoroon was one of the most successful melodramas of the last half of the nineteenth century and one of the few plays that ventured to deal with the explosive subject of slavery. Its overall effect was not the same as the one Lincoln attributed to the author of its famous and oft-reprinted prototype, *Uncle Tom's Cabin*: "So this is the little woman who brought on this great war." Nonetheless, the atmosphere was charged when the New York première of *The Octoroon* took place at the packed Winter Garden on December 6, 1859, only a few days after the execution of John Brown. Referring to the slave auction scene, Agnes Robertson (Mrs. Boucicault, who had the part of Zoe) wrote: "I was solemnly warned that if I attempted to play this scene I should be shot as I stood on the table to be sold." But instead of shots and riots, there were shouts and applause for the play. The Boucicaults left the cast a week later, but the play continued to draw large audiences in American and English theatres, and it was frequently revived for over forty years.

The success of the play was in part due to Boucicault's astuteness in capitalizing on a controversial subject that would attract large crowds, and his adeptness in presenting such a subject without offending even pro-slavery partisans. As Joseph Jefferson, who played Salem Scudder, said of the play in his *Autobiography*: "The truth of the matter is, it was noncommittal. The dialogue and characters of the play made one feel for the South, but the action proclaimed against slavery, and called loudly for its abolition." *The Octoroon* also reflects its author's showmanship. The plot moves swiftly, and there is much violent action, including a chase and a bowie-knife fight, as well as a pyrotechnic spectacle when the steamer explodes. Furthermore, Boucicault artfully utilized for theatrical purposes the recently-invented camera, which he employed to unmask the villain. Accompanying these and other scenes was suitable music, which helped create suspense and set the mood. Acts ended with the tableaux so dear to audiences of the nineteenth century: groupings of actors, frozen silent and motionless in their climactic curtain positions. There were also such familiar stage characters as the Indian (played by Boucicault himself), the Yankee (a whimsical one, played by Jefferson), the hero (played by A.H. Davenport), the villain (whom Boucicault shrewdly also made a Yankee), and the loyal Negro slave "Ole Uncle" Pete. The language, too, was suitable to the genre. It strikes the modern reader as being particularly amusing when it voices now-discarded superstitions. In the love scene, for example, Zoe agonizingly reveals her Negro "taint," "the ineffaceable curse of Cain": a "bluish tinge" in the fingernails, eyewhites, and hair roots! She will not marry her still-undaunted lover, much as she loves him, for it would break the heart of his aunt, who is also her benefactress:

GEORGE: Zoe, must we immolate our lives on her prejudice?
ZOE: Yes, for I'd rather be black than ungrateful!

All these actions and speeches are, of course, characteristic of melodrama. But the story of the love of a white man and a free southern mulatto girl was deeply affecting in the theatre. A six-week revival in 1961 at the Phoenix Theatre in New York again demonstrated the theatricality of the play, which a reading can only suggest. Melodrama in a nineteenth-century format usually appears jaded to today's more sophisticated theatre audiences. But this recent performance of *The Octoroon* (which was played straight, unlike a brief burlesque revival on Broadway in 1924) proved quite successful. For, however melodramatically, Boucicault's play may still have things to say to us in our age. "The vestigial bitterness [of slavery] remains with us to be read in the daily papers," T. Edward Hambleton commented in his "Program Note" in the *Playbill*; "its remains are a part of our heritage. 'The Octoroon' is a living picture of a part of our country's past. We believe it retains today what made it significant, moving, entertaining and above all, theatrical to its first audience in 1859."

Its author, Dion Boucicault (1822?–1890), was one of the most important figures in the nineteenth-century American (as well as English) theatre. Born in Ireland, he achieved prominence in England with a comedy, *London Assurance,* in 1841. He married Agnes Robertson, who was to star in many of his plays. When he first came to this country in 1853, he was well acquainted with English novels and French drama, whose plots he freely used for his own plays. *The Octoroon,* for example, was an adaptation of an English novel, Mayne Reid's *The Quadroon* (1856). As he did with many of his other plays, however, he skilfully reshaped his source and transformed it into a highly theatrical work. In all, he wrote and adapted close to 150 plays, the most popular of which were such "Irish life" productions as *The Colleen Bawn* (1860) and *The Shaughraun* (1874); an adaptation of Dickens's *Cricket on the Hearth, Dot* (1859), in which Jefferson created his important role of Caleb Plummer; the *Rip Van Winkle* (1865) that Jefferson eventually altered into his own vehicle; and one of Boucicault's most sensational productions, *The Poor of New York* (1857), which dealt with financial panics and featured, as its *pièce de résistance,* a house going up in flames.

Boucicault was not only a prolific playwright. He was also an actor of no mean ability, whose Shaughraun, for example, was a unique creation. He was, as well, an important and influential experimenter in scenic effects and lighting, and the first entrepreneur to send a traveling company on national tour with a New York (or London) hit play. Beyond that, he succeeded, where others had failed, in securing passage of the first copyright law (1856), a law that afforded at least some protection to playwrights and generally helped raise their professional status.

There are variant acting versions of *The Octoroon.* One ends happily—in miscegenation (it was thus performed only in England), and another ends with the death of all the principal characters upon the explosion of the steamer. The text here printed was collated for this book from various acting editions and scripts, and follows the version most frequently used in American productions. For the biography of Boucicault see Townsend Walsh, *The Career of Dion Boucicault* (1915). The collection of Boucicault source material (including unproduced and unpublished scripts) was acquired by the University of South Florida Library in 1966.

M.M.

THE OCTOROON;

or, LIFE IN LOUISIANA

By Dion Boucicault

Characters

GEORGE PEYTON, Mrs. Peyton's Nephew, educated in Europe, and just returned home

JACOB M'CLOSKY, formerly Overseer of Terrebonne, but now Owner of one half of the Estate

SALEM SCUDDER, a Yankee from Massachusetts, now Overseer of Terrebonne, great on improvements and inventions, once a Photographic Operator, and been a little of everything generally

PETE, an "Ole Uncle," once the late Judge's body servant, but now "too ole to work, sa."

SUNNYSIDE, a Planter, Neighbor, and Old Friend of the Peytons

PAUL, a Yellow Boy, a favorite of the late Judge's, and so allowed to do much as he likes

RATTS, Captain of the Steamer *Magnolia*

LAFOUCHE, a Rich Planter

COLONEL POINTDEXTER, an Auctioneer and Slave Salesman

JULES THIBODEAUX
JUDGE CAILLOU   } Prospective Buyers at the Auction
JACKSON

SOLON, a Slave

WAHNOTEE, an Indian Chief of the Lepan Tribe

MRS. PEYTON, of Terrebonne Plantation, in the Attakapas, Widow of the late Judge Peyton

ZOE, an Octoroon Girl, free, the Natural Child of the late Judge by a Quadroon Slave

DORA SUNNYSIDE, only Daughter and Heiress to Sunnyside, a Southern Belle

GRACE, a Yellow Girl, a Slave
DIDO, the Cook, a Slave
MINNIE, a Quadroon Slave

PLANTERS, SLAVES, DECK HANDS

ACT I

A view of the Plantation Terrebonne, in Louisiana. A branch of the Mississippi is seen winding through the Estate. A low built but extensive Planter's Dwelling, surrounded with a veranda, and raised a few feet from the ground, occupies the left side. On the right a table and chairs. GRACE *discovered sitting at breakfast-table with children.*

SOLON *enters, from the house.*

SOLON. Yah! You bomn'ble fry—git out—a gen'leman can't pass for you.

GRACE. (*Seizing a fly whisk.*) Hee!—Ha—git out!
(*Drives the children away: in escaping they tumble against* SOLON, *who falls with the tray; the children steal the bananas and rolls that fall about.*)
(*Enter* PETE, *who is lame; he carries a mop and pail.*)

PETE. Hey! Laws a massey! Why, clar out! drop dat banana! I'll murder this yer crowd.
(*Chases children about; they leap over railing at back. Exit* SOLON.)
Dem little niggers is a judgment upon dis generation.

(*Enter* GEORGE, *from the house.*)

GEORGE. What's the matter, Pete?

PETE. It's dem black trash, Mas'r George; dis ere property wants claring; dem's getting too numerous round: when I gets time I'll kill some on 'em, sure!

GEORGE. They don't seem to be scared by the threat.

PETE. Stop, you varmin! Stop till I get enough of you in one place!

GEORGE. Were they all born on this estate?

PETE. Guess they nebber was born—dem tings! What, dem?— Get away! Born here—dem darkies? What, on Terrebonne! Don't b'lieve it, Mas'r George; dem black tings never was

208

born at all; dey swarmed one mornin' on a sassafras tree in the swamp; I cotched 'em; dey ain't no 'count. Don't believe dey'll turn out niggers when dey're growed; dey'll come out sunthin' else.

GRACE. Yes, Mas'r George, dey was born here; and old Pete is fonder on 'em dan he is of his fiddle on a Sunday.

PETE. What? Dem tings—dem?—Get away. (*Makes blow at the children.*) Born here! Dem darkies! What, on Terrebonne? Don't b'lieve it, Mas'r George,—no. One morning dey swarmed on a sassafras tree in de swamp, and I cotched 'em all in a sieve,—dat's how dey come on top of dis yearth—git out, you,—ya, ya! (*Laughs. Exit* GRACE.)

(*Enter* MRS. PEYTON, *from the house.*)

MRS. PEYTON. So, Pete, you are spoiling those children as usual!

PETE. Dat's right, missus! Gib it to ole Pete! He's allers in for it. Git away dere! Ya! if dey ain't all lighted, like coons, on dat snake fence, just out of shot. Look dar! Ya, ya! Dem debils. Ya!

MRS. PEYTON. Pete, do you hear?

PETE. Git down dar! I'm arter you! (*Hobbles off.*)

MRS. PEYTON. You are out early this morning, George.

GEORGE. I was up before daylight. We got the horses saddled, and galloped down the shell road over the Piney Patch; then coasting the Bayou Lake, we crossed the long swamps, by Paul's Path, and so came home again.

MRS. PEYTON. (*Laughing.*) You seem already familiar with the names of every spot on the estate.

(*Enter* PETE, *arranging breakfast.*)

GEORGE. Just one month ago I quitted Paris. I left that siren city as I would have left a beloved woman.

MRS. PEYTON. No wonder! I dare say you left at least a dozen beloved women there, at the same time.

GEORGE. I feel that I departed amid universal and sincere regret. I left my loves and my creditors equally inconsolable.

MRS. PEYTON. George, you are incorrigible. Ah! You remind me so much of your uncle, the judge.

GEORGE. Bless his dear old handwriting, it's all I ever saw of
him. For ten years his letters came every quarter-day[1], with
a remittance and a word of advice in his formal cavalier
style; and then a joke in the postscript, that upset the
dignity of the foregoing. Aunt, when he died, two years
ago, I read over those letters of his, and if I didn't cry like
a baby—

MRS. PEYTON. No, George; say you wept like a man. And so
you really kept those foolish letters?

GEORGE. Yes; I kept the letters, and squandered the money.

MRS. PEYTON. (*Embracing him.*) Ah! Why were you not my
son—you are so like my dear husband.

(*Enter* SALEM SCUDDER.)

SCUDDER. Ain't he! Yes—when I saw him and Miss Zoe gal-
loping through the green sugar crop, and doing ten dollars'
worth of damage at every stride, says I, how like his old
uncle he do make the dirt fly.

GEORGE. O, aunt! What a bright, gay creature she is!

SCUDDER. What, Zoe! Guess that you didn't leave anything
female in Europe that can lift an eyelash beside that gal.
When she goes along, she just leaves a streak of love
behind her. It's a good drink to see her come into the
cotton fields—the niggers get fresh on the sight of her.
If she ain't worth her weight in sunshine you may take one
of my fingers off, and choose which you like.

MRS. PEYTON. She need not keep us waiting breakfast, though.
Pete, tell Miss Zoe that we are waiting.

PETE. Yes, missus. Why, Minnie, why don't you run when
you hear, you lazy crittur?
(*Minnie runs off.*)
Dat's de laziest nigger on dis yere property. (*Sits down.*)
Don't do nuffin.

MRS. PEYTON. My dear George, you are left in your uncle's
will heir to this estate.

GEORGE. Subject to your life interest and an annuity to Zoe,
is it not so?

MRS. PEYTON. I fear that the property is so involved that the
strictest economy will scarcely recover it. My dear husband

[1] I.e., four times a year.

never kept any accounts, and we scarcely know in what condition the estate really is.

SCUDDER. Yes, we do, ma'am; it's in a darned bad condition. Ten years ago the judge took as overseer a bit of Connecticut hardware called M'Closky. The judge didn't understand accounts—the overseer did. For a year or two all went fine. The judge drew money like Bourbon whisky from a barrel, and never turned off the tap. But out it flew, free for everybody or anybody to beg, borrow, or steal. So it went, till one day the judge found the tap wouldn't run. He looked in to see what stopped it, and pulled out a big mortgage. "Sign that," says the overseer; "it's only a formality." "All right," says the judge, and away went a thousand acres; so at the end of eight years, Jacob M'Closky, Esquire, finds himself proprietor of the richest half of Terrebonne—

GEORGE. But the other half is free.

SCUDDER. No, it ain't; because, just then, what does the judge do, but hire another overseer—a Yankee—a Yankee named Salem Scudder.

MRS. PEYTON. O, no, it was—

SCUDDER. Hold on, now! I'm going to straighten this account clear out. What was this here Scudder? Well, he lived in New York by sittin' with his heels up in front of French's Hotel, and inventin'—

GEORGE. Inventing what?

SCUDDER. Improvements—anything, from a stay-lace to a fire-engine. Well, he cut that for the photographing line. He and his apparatus arrived here, took the judge's likeness and his fancy, who made him overseer right off. Well, sir, what does this Scudder do but introduces his inventions and improvements on this estate. His new cotton gins broke down, the steam sugar-mills burst up, until he finished off with his folly what Mr. M'Closky with his knavery began.

MRS. PEYTON. O, Salem! How can you say so? Haven't you worked like a horse?

SCUDDER. No, ma'am, I worked like an ass—an honest one, and that's all. Now, Mr. George, between the two overseers, you and that good old lady have come to the ground; that is the state of things, just as near as I can fix it.

(ZOE sings outside.)

GEORGE. 'T is Zoe.

SCUDDER. O, I have not spoiled that anyhow. I can't introduce any darned improvement there. Ain't that a cure for old age; it kinder lifts the heart up, don't it?

MRS. PEYTON. Poor child! What will become of her when I am gone? If you haven't spoiled her, I fear I have. She has had the education of a lady.

GEORGE. I have remarked that she is treated by the neighbors with a kind of familiar condescension that annoyed me.

SCUDDER. Don't you know that she is the natural daughter of the judge, your uncle, and that old lady thar just adored anything her husband cared for; and this girl, that another woman would 'a' hated, she loves as if she'd been her own child.

GEORGE. Aunt, I am prouder and happier to be your nephew and heir to the ruins of Terrebonne than I would have been to have had half Louisiana without you.

(*Enter* ZOE, *from the house.*)

ZOE. Am I late? Ah! Mr. Scudder, good morning.

SCUDDER. Thank'ye. I'm from fair to middlin', like a bamboo cane, much the same all the year round.

ZOE. No; like a sugar cane; so dry outside, one would never think there was so much sweetness within.

SCUDDER. Look here: I can't stand that gal! If I stop here, I shall hug her right off.
(*Sees* PETE, *who has set his pail down up stage, and goes to sleep on it.*)
If that old nigger ain't asleep, I'm blamed. Hillo!
(*Kicks pail from under* PETE, *and lets him down. Exit.*)

PETE. Hi! Debbel's in de pail! Whar's breakfass?

(*Enter* SOLON *and* DIDO *with coffee-pot and dishes.*)

DIDO. Bless'ee, Missey Zoe, here it be. Dere's a dish of pompano—jess taste, Mas'r George—and here's fried bananas; smell 'em, do, sa glosh.

PETE. Hole yer tongue, Dido. Whar's de coffee? (*He pours it out.*) If it don't stain de cup, your wicked ole life's in danger, sure! Dat right! Black as nigger; clar as ice. You may drink dat, Mas'r George. (*Looks off.*) Yah! Here's

Mas'r Sunnyside, and Missey Dora, jist drove up. Some of you niggers run and hole de hosses; and take dis, Dido. (*Gives her coffee-pot to hold, and hobbles off, followed by* SOLON *and* DIDO.)

(*Enter* SUNNYSIDE *and* DORA.)

SUNNYSIDE. Good day, ma'am. (*Shakes hands with George.*) I see we are just in time for breakfast. (*Sits.*)

DORA. O, none for me; I never eat. (*Sits.*)

GEORGE. (*Aside.*) They do not notice Zoe.—(*Aloud.*) You don't see Zoe, Mr. Sunnyside.

SUNNYSIDE. Ah! Zoe, girl; are you there?

DORA. Take my shawl, Zoe.

(ZOE *helps her.*) What a good creature she is.

SUNNYSIDE. I dare say, now, that in Europe you have never met any lady more beautiful in person, or more polished in manners, than that girl.

GEORGE. You are right, sir; though I shrank from expressing that opinion in her presence, so bluntly.

SUNNYSIDE. Why so?

GEORGE. It may be considered offensive.

SUNNYSIDE. (*Astonished.*) What? I say, Zoe, do you hear that?

DORA. Mr. Peyton is joking.

MRS. PEYTON. My nephew is not acquainted with our customs in Louisiana, but he will soon understand.

GEORGE. Never, aunt! I shall never understand how to wound the feelings of any lady; and, if that is the custom here, I shall never acquire it.

DORA. Zoe, my dear, what does he mean?

ZOE. I don't know.

GEORGE. Excuse me, I'll light a cigar. (*Goes up.*)

DORA. (*Aside to* ZOE). Isn't he sweet! O, dear, Zoe, is he in love with anybody?

ZOE. How can I tell?

DORA. Ask him, I want to know; don't say I told you to inquire, but find out. Minnie, fan me, it is so nice—and his clothes are French, ain't they?

ZOE. I think so; shall I ask him that too?

DORA. No, dear. I wish he would make love to me. When he speaks to one he does it so easy, so gentle; it isn't barroom

style; love lined with drinks, sighs tinged with tobacco—
and they say all the women in Paris were in love with him,
which I feel I shall be. Stop fanning me; what nice boots
he wears.

SUNNYSIDE. (*To* MRS. PEYTON.) Yes, ma'am, I hold a mortgage
over Terrebonne; mine's a ninth, and pretty near covers all
the property, except the slaves. I believe Mr. M'Closky has
a bill of sale on them. O, here he is.

(*Enter* M'CLOSKY.)

SUNNYSIDE. Good morning, Mr. M'Closky.

M'CLOSKY. Good morning, Mr. Sunnyside; Miss Dora, your
servant.

DORA. (*Seated.*) Fan me, Minnie.— (*Aside.*) I don't like that
man.

M'CLOSKY. (*Aside.*) Insolent as usual.—(*Aloud.*) You begged
me to call this morning. I hope I'm not intruding.

MRS. PEYTON. My nephew, Mr. Peyton.

M'CLOSKY. O, how d'ye do, sir?
(*Offers his hand,* GEORGE *bows coldly.*) (*Aside.*) A puppy—
if he brings any of his European airs here we'll fix him.—
(*Aloud.*) Zoe, tell Pete to give my mare a feed, will ye?

GEORGE. (*Angrily.*) Sir!

M'CLOSKY. Hillo! Did I tread on ye?

MRS. PEYTON. What is the matter with George?

ZOE. (*Takes fan from* MINNIE.) Go, Minnie, tell Pete; run!
(*Exit* MINNIE.)

MRS. PEYTON. Grace, attend to Mr. M'Closky.

M'CLOSKY. A julep, gal, that's my breakfast, and a bit of
cheese.

GEORGE. (*Aside to* MRS. PEYTON.) How can you ask that
vulgar ruffian to your table!

MRS. PEYTON. Hospitality in Europe is a courtesy; here, it is
an obligation. We tender food to a stranger, not because
he is a gentleman, but because he is hungry.

GEORGE. Aunt, I will take my rifle down to the Atchafalaya.
Paul has promised me a bear and a deer or two. I see my
little Nimrod yonder, with his Indian companion. Excuse
me, ladies. Ho! Paul! (*Enters house.*)

PAUL. (*Outside.*) I'ss, Mas'r George.

(*Enter* PAUL *with the Indian,* WAHNOTEE.)

SUNNYSIDE. It's a shame to allow that young cub to run over the swamps and woods, hunting and fishing his life away instead of hoeing cane.

MRS. PEYTON. The child was a favorite of the judge, who encouraged his gambols. I couldn't bear to see him put to work.

GEORGE. (*Returning with rifle.*) Come, Paul, are you ready?

PAUL. I'ss, Mas'r George. O, golly! Ain't that a pooty gun.

M'CLOSKY. See here, you imp; if I catch you, and your redskin yonder, gunning in my swamps, I'll give you rats, mind. Them vagabonds, when the game's about, shoot my pigs. (*Exit* GEORGE *into house.*)

PAUL. You gib me rattan, Mas'r Clostry, but I guess you take a berry long stick to Wahnotee. Ugh, he make bacon of you.

M'CLOSKY. Make bacon of me, you young whelp! Do you mean that I'm a pig? Hold on a bit. (*Seizes whip, and holds* PAUL.)

ZOE. O, sir! Don't, pray, don't.

M'CLOSKY. (*Slowly lowering his whip.*) Darn you, redskin, I'll pay you off some day, both of ye. (*Returns to table and drinks.*)

SUNNYSIDE. That Indian is a nuisance. Why don't he return to his nation out West?

M'CLOSKY. He's too fond of thieving and whiskey.

ZOE. No; Wahnotee is a gentle, honest creature, and remains here because he loves that boy with the tenderness of a woman. When Paul was taken down with the swamp fever the Indian sat outside the hut, and neither ate, slept, nor spoke for five days, till the child could recognize and call him to his bedside. He who can love so well is honest— don't speak ill of poor Wahnotee.

MRS. PEYTON. Wahnotee, will you go back to your people?

WAHNOTEE. Sleugh.

PAUL. He don't understand; he speaks a mash-up of Indian and Mexican. Wahnotee Patira na sepau assa wigiran?

WAHNOTEE. Weal Omenee.

PAUL. Says he'll go if I'll go with him. He calls me Omenee, the Pigeon, and Miss Zoe is Ninemoosha, the Sweetheart.

WAHNOTEE. (*Pointing to* ZOE.) Ninemoosha.

ZOE. No, Wahnotee, we can't spare Paul.

PAUL. If Omenee remain, Wahnotee will die in Terrebonne.
(*During the dialogue,* WAHNOTEE *has taken* GEORGE'S *gun.*)

(*Enter* GEORGE.)

GEORGE. Now I'm ready.
(GEORGE *tries to regain his gun;* WAHNOTEE *refuses to give
it up;* PAUL *quietly takes it from him and remonstrates with
him.*)

DORA. Zoe, he's going; I want him to stay and make love to
me; that's what I came for to-day.

MRS. PEYTON. George, I can't spare Paul for an hour or two;
he must run over to the landing; the steamer from New
Orleans passed up the river last night, and if there's a mail
they have thrown it ashore.

SUNNYSIDE. I saw the mail-bags lying in the shed this morning.

MRS. PEYTON. I expect an important letter from Liverpool;
away with you, Paul; bring the mail-bags here.

PAUL. I'm 'most afraid to take Wahnotee to the shed, there's
rum there.

WAHNOTEE. Rum!

PAUL. Come, then, but if I catch you drinkin', O, laws a
mussey, you'll get snakes! I'll gib it you! Now mind.
(*Exit with Indian.*)

GEORGE. Come, Miss Dora, let me offer you my arm.

DORA. Mr. George, I am afraid, if all we hear is true, you have
led a dreadful life in Europe.

GEORGE. That's a challenge to begin a description of my
feminine adventures.

DORA. You have been in love, then?

GEORGE. Two hundred and forty-nine times! Let me relate
you the worst cases.

DORA. No! No!

GEORGE. I'll put the naughty parts in French.

DORA. I won't hear a word! O, you horrible man! Go on.
(*Exit* GEORGE *and* DORA *to the house.*)

M'CLOSKY. Now, ma'am, I'd like a little business, if agreeable.
I bring you news; your banker, old Lafouche, of New
Orleans, is dead; the executors are winding up his affairs,
and have foreclosed on all overdue mortgages, so Terre-

bonne is for sale. Here's the *Picayune* (*Producing paper.*) with the advertisement.

ZOE. Terrebonne for sale!

MRS. PEYTON. Terrebonne for sale, and you, sir, will doubtless become its purchaser.

M'CLOSKY. Well, ma'am, I s'pose there's no law agin my bidding for it. The more bidders, the better for you. You'll take care, I guess, it don't go too cheap.

MRS. PEYTON. O, sir, I don't value the place for its price, but for the many happy days I've spent here; that landscape, flat and uninteresting though it may be, is full of charm for me; those poor people, born around me, growing up about my heart, have bounded my view of life; and now to lose that homely scene, lose their black, ungainly faces! O, sir, perhaps you should be as old as I am, to feel as I do, when my past life is torn away from me.

M'CLOSKY. I'd be darned glad if somebody would tear my past life away from *me*. Sorry I can't help you, but the fact is, you're in such an all-fired mess that you couldn't be pulled out without a derrick.

MRS. PEYTON. Yes, there is a hope left yet, and I cling to it. The house of Mason Brothers, of Liverpool, failed some twenty years ago in my husband's debt.

M'CLOSKY. They owed him over fifty thousand dollars.

MRS. PEYTON. I cannot find the entry in my husband's accounts; but you, Mr. M'Closky, can doubtless detect it. Zoe, bring here the judge's old desk; it is in the library.

(*Exit* ZOE *to the house.*)

M'CLOSKY. You don't expect to recover any of this old debt, do you?

MRS. PEYTON. Yes; the firm has recovered itself, and I received a notice two months ago that some settlement might be anticipated.

SUNNYSIDE. Why, with principal and interest this debt has been more than doubled in twenty years.

MRS. PEYTON. But it may be years yet before it will be paid off, if ever.

SUNNYSIDE. If there's a chance of it, there's not a planter round here who wouldn't lend you the whole cash, to keep your name and blood amongst us. Come, cheer up, old friend.

MRS. PEYTON. Ah! Sunnyside, how good you are; so like my poor Peyton.

(*Exit* MRS. PEYTON *and* SUNNYSIDE *to the house.*)

M'CLOSKY. Curse their old families—they cut me—a bilious, conceited, thin lot of dried up aristocracy. I hate 'em. Just because my grandfather wasn't some broken-down Virginia transplant, or a stingy old Creole, I ain't fit to sit down to the same meat with them. It makes my blood so hot I feel my heart hiss. I'll sweep these Peytons from this section of the country. Their presence keeps alive the reproach against me that I ruined them. Yet, if this money should come! Bah! There's no chance of it. Then, if they go, they'll take Zoe—she'll follow them. Darn that girl; she makes me quiver when I think of her; she's took me for all I'm worth. (*Enter* ZOE *from house, with the desk.*) O, here, do you know what the annuity the old judge left you is worth to-day? Not a picayune.

ZOE. It's surely worth the love that dictated it; here are the papers and accounts. (*Putting the desk on the table.*)

M'CLOSKY. Stop, Zoe; come here! How would you like to rule the house of the richest planter on Atchafalaya—eh? Or say the word, and I'll buy this old barrack, and you shall be mistress of Terrebonne.

ZOE. O, sir, do not speak so to me!

M'CLOSKY. Why not! Look here, these Peytons are bust; cut 'em; I am rich, jine me; I'll set you up grand, and we'll give these first families here our dust, until you'll see their white skins shrivel up with hate and rage; what d'ye say?

ZOE. Let me pass! O, pray, let me go!

M'CLOSKY. What, you won't, won't ye? If young George Peyton was to make you the same offer, you'd jump at it pretty darned quick, I guess. Come, Zoe, don't be a fool; I'd marry you if I could, but you know I can't; so just say what you want. Here, then, I'll put back these Peytons in Terrebonne, and they shall know you done it; yes, they'll have you to thank for saving them from ruin.

ZOE. Do you think they would live here on such terms?

M'CLOSKY. Why not? We'll hire out our slaves, and live on their wages.

ZOE. But I'm not a slave.

M'CLOSKY. No; if you were I'd buy you, if you cost all I'm worth.

ZOE. Let me pass!

M'CLOSKY. Stop.

(*Enter* SCUDDER.)

SCUDDER. Let her pass.
M'CLOSKY. Eh?
SCUDDER. Let her pass!
(*Takes out his knife. Exit* ZOE *to house.*)
M'CLOSKY. Is that you, Mr. Overseer? (*Examines paper.*)
SCUDDER. Yes, I'm here, somewhere, interferin'.
M'CLOSKY. (*Sitting.*) A pretty mess you've got this estate in—
SCUDDER. Yes—me and Co.—we done it; but, as you were senior partner in the concern, I reckon you got the big lick.
M'CLOSKY. What d'ye mean?
SCUDDER. Let me proceed by illustration. (*Sits.*) Look thar! (*Points with his knife off.*) D'ye see that tree?—It's called a live oak, and is a native here; beside it grows a creeper. Year after year that creeper twines its long arms round and round the tree—sucking the earth dry all about its roots—living on its life—overrunning its branches, until at last the live oak withers and dies out. Do you know what the niggers round here call that sight? They call it the Yankee hugging the Creole.
M'CLOSKY. Mr. Scudder, I've listened to a great many of your insinuations, and now I'd like to come to an understanding what they mean. If you want a quarrel—
SCUDDER. No, I'm the skurriest crittur at a fight you ever see; my legs have been too well brought up to stand and see my body abused; I take good care of myself, I can tell you.
M'CLOSKY. Because I heard that you had traduced my character.
SCUDDER. Traduced! Whoever said so lied. I always said you were the darndest thief that ever escaped a white jail to misrepresent the North to the South.
M'CLOSKY. (*Raises hand to back of his neck.*) What!
SCUDDER. Take your hand down—take it down.
(M'CLOSKY *lowers his hand.*)
Whenever I gets into company like yours, I always start with the advantage on my side.
M'CLOSKY. What d'ye mean?
SCUDDER. I mean that before you could draw that bowie-knife you wear down your back, I'd cut you into shingles. Keep quiet, and let's talk sense. You wanted to come to an under-

standing, and I'm coming thar as quick as I can. Now, Jacob M'Closky, you despise me because you think I'm a fool; I despise you because I know you to be a knave. Between us we've ruined these Peytons; you fired the judge, and I finished off the widow. Now, I feel bad about my share in the business. I'd give half the balance of my life to wipe out my part of the work. Many a night I've laid awake and thought how to pull them through, till I've cried like a child over the sum I couldn't do; and you know how darned hard 't is to make a Yankee cry.

M'CLOSKY. Well, what's that to me?

SCUDDER. Hold on, Jacob, I'm coming to that—I tell ye, I'm such a fool—I can't bear the feeling, it keeps at me like a skin complaint, and if this family is sold up—

M'CLOSKY. What then?

SCUDDER. (*Rising.*) I'd cut my throat—or yours—yours I'd prefer.

M'CLOSKY. Would you now? Why don't you do it?

SCUDDER. 'Cos I's skeered to try! I never killed a man in my life—and civilization is so strong in me I guess I couldn't do it—I'd like to, though!

M'CLOSKY. And all for the sake of that old woman and that young puppy—eh? No other cause to hate—to envy me—to be jealous of me—eh?

SCUDDER. Jealous? What for?

M'CLOSKY. Ask the color in your face: d'ye think I can't read you, like a book? With your New England hypocrisy, you would persuade yourself that it was this family alone you cared for; it ain't—you know it ain't—'t is the "Octoroon"; and you love her as I do; and you hate me because I'm your rival—that's where the tears come from, Salem Scudder, if you ever shed any—that's where the shoe pinches.

SCUDDER. Wal, I do like the gal; she's a—

M'CLOSKY. She's in love with young Peyton; it made me curse whar it made you cry, as it does now; I see the tears on your cheeks now.

SCUDDER. Look at 'em, Jacob, for they are honest water from the well of truth. I ain't ashamed of it—I do love the gal; but I ain't jealous of you, because I believe the only sincere feeling about you is your love for Zoe, and it does your heart good to have her image thar; but I believe you put it thar to spile. By fair means I don't think you can get her, and don't you try foul with her, 'cause if you do, Jacob, civilization be darned, I'm on you like a painter, and when I'm drawed out I'm pizin. (*Exit* SCUDDER *to house.*)

M'CLOSKY. Fair or foul, I'll have her—take that home with you! (*He opens desk.*) What's here—judgments? Yes, plenty of 'em; bill of costs, account with Citizens' Bank—what's this? "Judgment, $40,000, 'Thibodeaux against Peyton,' "—surely, that is the judgment under which this estate is now advertised for sale—(*Takes up paper and examines it*) yes, "Thibodeaux against Peyton, 1838." Hold on! Whew! This is worth taking to—in this desk the judge used to keep one paper I want—this should be it. (*Reads.*) "The free papers of my daughter Zoe, registered February 4th, 1841." Why, judge, wasn't you lawyer enough to know that while a judgment stood against you it was a lien on your slaves? Zoe is your child by a quadroon slave, and you didn't free her; blood! If this is so, she's mine! This old Liverpool debt—that may cross me—if it only arrive too late—if it don't come by this mail—Hold on! This letter the old lady expects—that's it; let me only head off that letter, and Terrebonne will be sold before they can recover it. That boy and the Indian have gone down to the landing for the post-bags; they'll idle on the way as usual; my mare will take me across the swamp, and before they can reach the shed, I'll have purified them bags—ne'er a letter shall show this mail. Ha, ha!—(*Calls.*) Pete, you old turkey-buzzard, saddle my mare. Then, if I sink every dollar I'm worth in her purchase, I'll own that Octoroon. (*Stands with his hand extended towards the house, and tableau.*)

ACT II

The Wharf with goods, boxes, and bales scattered about— a camera on a stand; DORA *being photographed by* SCUDDER, *who is arranging photographic apparatus,* GEORGE *and* PAUL *looking on at back.*

SCUDDER. Just turn your face a leetle this way—fix your—let's see—look here.

DORA. So?

SCUDDER. That's right. (*Putting his head under the darkening apron.*) It's such a long time since I did this sort of thing, and this old machine has got so dirty and stiff, I'm afraid it won't operate. That's about right. Now don't stir.

PAUL. Ugh! she looks as though she war gwine to have a tooth drawed!

SCUDDER. I've got four plates ready, in case we miss the first shot. One of them is prepared with a self-developing liquid that I've invented. I hope it will turn out better than most of my notions. Now fix yourself. Are you ready?

DORA. Ready!

SCUDDER. Fire!—One, two, three. (SCUDDER *takes out watch.*)

PAUL. Now it's cooking; laws mussey! I feel it all inside, as if I was at a lottery.

SCUDDER. So! (*Throws down apron.*) That's enough. (*Withdrawing slide, turns and sees* PAUL.) What! What are you doing there, you young varmint! Ain't you took them bags to the house yet?

PAUL. Now, it ain't no use trying to get mad, Mas'r Scudder. I'm gwine! I only come back to find Wahnotee; whar is dat ign'ant Injiun?

SCUDDER. You'll find him scenting round the rum store, hitched up by the nose. (*Exit into the room.*)

PAUL. (*Calling at the door.*) Say, Mas'r Scudder, take me in dat telescope?

SCUDDER. (*Inside the room.*) Get out, you cub! Clar out!

PAUL. You got four of dem dishes ready. Gosh, wouldn't I like to hab myself took! What's de charge, Mas'r Scudder? (*Runs off.*)

(*Enter* SCUDDER, *from the room.*)

SCUDDER. Job had none of them critters on his plantation, else he'd never ha' stood through so many chapters. Well, that has come out clear, ain't it? (*Showing the plate.*)

DORA. O, beautiful! Look, Mr. Peyton.

GEORGE. (*Looking.*) Yes, very fine!

SCUDDER. The apparatus can't mistake. When I travelled round with this machine, the homely folks used to sing out, "Hillo, mister, this ain't like me!" "Ma'am," says I, "the apparatus can't mistake." "But, mister, that ain't my nose." "Ma'am, your nose drawed it. The machine can't err—you mistake your phiz but the apparatus don't." "But, sir, it ain't agreeable." "No, ma'am, the truth seldom is."

(*Enter* PETE, *puffing*.)

PETE. Mas'r Scudder! Mas'r Scudder!

SCUDDER. Hillo! What are you blowing about like a steamboat with one wheel for?

PETE. *You* blow, Mas'r Scudder, when I tole you: dere's a man from Noo Aleens just arriv'd at de house, and he's stuck up two papers on de gates: "For sale—dis yer property," and a heap of oder tings—an he seen missus, and arter he shown some papers she burst out crying—I yelled; den de corious of little niggers dey set up, den de hull plantation children—de live stock reared up and created a purpiration of lamentation as did de ole heart good to har.

DORA. What's the matter?

SCUDDER. He's come.

PETE. Dass it—I saw'm!

SCUDDER. The sheriff from New Orleans has taken possession—Terrebonne is in the hands of the law.

(*Enter* ZOE.)

ZOE. O, Mr. Scudder! Dora! Mr. Peyton! Come home—there are strangers in the house.

DORA. Stay, Mr. Peyton: Zoe, a word! (*Leads her forward—aside.*) Zoe, the more I see of George Peyton the better I like him; but he is too modest—that is a very impertinent virtue in a man.

ZOE. I'm no judge, dear.

DORA. Of course not, you little fool; no one ever made love to you, and you can't understand; I mean, that George knows I am an heiress; my fortune would release this estate from debt.

ZOE. O, I see!

DORA. If he would only propose to marry me I would accept him, but he don't know that, and he will go on fooling, in his slow European way, until it is too late.

ZOE. What's to be done?

DORA. You tell him.

ZOE. What? That he isn't to go on fooling in his slow—

DORA. No, you goose! Twit him on his silence and abstraction —I'm sure it's plain enough, for he has not spoken two words to me all the day; then joke round the subject, and at last speak out.

SCUDDER. Pete, as you came here, did you pass Paul and the Indian with the letter-bags?

PETE. No, sar; but dem vagabonds neber take the 'specable straight road, dey goes by de swamp. (*Exit up the path.*)

SCUDDER. Come, sir!

DORA. (*To* ZOE.) Now's your time.—(*Aloud.*) Mr. Scudder, take us with you—Mr. Peyton is so slow, there's no getting him on.

(*Exit* DORA *and* SCUDDER.)

ZOE. They are gone!—(*Glancing at* GEORGE.) Poor fellow, he has lost all.

GEORGE. Poor child! How sad she looks now she has no resource.

ZOE. How shall I ask him to stay?

GEORGE. Zoe, will you remain here? I wish to speak to you.

ZOE. (*Aside.*) Well, that saves trouble.

GEORGE. By our ruin you lose all.

ZOE. O, I'm nothing; think of yourself.

GEORGE. I can think of nothing but the image that remains face to face with me; so beautiful, so simple, so confiding, that I dare not express the feelings that have grown up so rapidly in my heart.

ZOE. (*Aside.*) He means Dora.

GEORGE. If I dared to speak!

ZOE. That's just what you must do, and do it at once, or it will be too late.

GEORGE. Has my love been divined?

ZOE. It has been more than suspected.

GEORGE. Zoe, listen to me, then. I shall see this estate pass from me without a sigh, for it possesses no charm for me; the wealth I covet is the love of those around me—eyes that are rich in fond looks, lips that breathe endearing words; the only estate I value is the heart of one true woman, and the slaves I'd have are her thoughts.

ZOE. George, George, your words take away my breath!

GEORGE. The world, Zoe, the free struggle of minds and hands is before me; the education bestowed on me by my dear

uncle is a noble heritage which no sheriff can seize; with
that I can build up a fortune, spread a roof over the heads
I love, and place before them the food I have earned; I
will work—

ZOE. Work! I thought none but colored people worked.

GEORGE. Work, Zoe, is the salt that gives savor to life.

ZOE. Dora said you were slow; if she could hear you now—

GEORGE. Zoe, you are young; your mirror must have told you
that you are beautiful. Is your heart free?

ZOE. Free? Of course it is!

GEORGE. We have known each other but a few days, but to
me those days have been worth all the rest of my life. Zoe,
you have suspected the feeling that now commands an
utterance—you have seen that I love you.

ZOE. Me! You love *me*?

GEORGE. As my wife—the sharer of my hopes, my ambitions,
and my sorrows; under the shelter of your love I could
watch the storms of fortune pass unheeded by.

ZOE. *My* love! *My* love? George, you know not what you say!
I the sharer of your sorrows—your wife! Do you know what
I am?

GEORGE. Your birth—I know it. Has not my dear aunt forgotten it—she who had the most right to remember it?
You are illegitimate, but love knows no prejudice.

ZOE. (*Aside.*) Alas! He does not know, he does not know!
And will despise me, spurn me, loathe me, when he learns
who, what, he has so loved.—(*Aloud.*) George, O, forgive
me! Yes, I love you—I did not know it until your words
showed me what has been in my heart; each of them
awoke a new sense, and now I know how unhappy—how
very unhappy I am.

GEORGE. Zoe, what have I said to wound you?

ZOE. Nothing; but you must learn what I thought you already
knew. George, you cannot marry me; the laws forbid it!

GEORGE. Forbid it?

ZOE. There is a gulf between us, as wide as your love, as deep
as my despair; but, O, tell me, say you will pity me! That
you will not throw me from you like a poisoned thing!

GEORGE. Zoe, explain yourself—your language fills me with
shapeless fears.

ZOE. And what shall I say? I—my mother was—no, no—not her!
Why should I refer the blame to her? George, do you see

that hand you hold? Look at these fingers; do you see the nails are of a bluish tinge?

GEORGE. Yes, near the quick there is a faint blue mark.

ZOE. Look in my eyes; is not the same color in the white?

GEORGE. It is their beauty.

ZOE. Could you see the roots of my hair you would see the same dark, fatal mark. Do you know what that is?

GEORGE. No.

ZOE. That is the ineffaceable curse of Cain. Of the blood that feeds my heart, one drop in eight is black—bright red as the rest may be, that one drop poisons all the flood; those seven bright drops give me love like yours—hope like yours—ambition like yours—life hung with passions like dew-drops on the morning flowers; but the one black drop gives me despair, for I'm an unclean thing—forbidden by the laws—I'm an Octoroon!

GEORGE. Zoe, I love you none the less; this knowledge brings no revolt to my heart, and I can overcome the obstacle.

ZOE. But *I* cannot.

GEORGE. We can leave this country, and go far away where none can know.

ZOE. And your aunt, she who from infancy treated me with such fondness, she who, as you said, has most reason to spurn me, can she forget what I am? Will she gladly see you wedded to the child of her husband's slave? No! She would revolt from it, as all but you would; and if I consented to hear the cries of my heart, if I did not crush out my infant love, what would she say to the poor girl on whom she had bestowed so much? No, no!

GEORGE. Zoe, must we immolate our lives on her prejudice?

ZOE. Yes, for I'd rather be black than ungrateful! Ah, George, our race has at least one virtue—it knows how to suffer!

GEORGE. Each word you utter makes my love sink deeper into my heart.

ZOE. And I remained here to induce you to offer that heart to Dora!

GEORGE. If you bid me do so I will obey you—

ZOE. No, no! If you cannot be mine, O, let me not blush when I think of you.

GEORGE. Dearest Zoe!

(*Exit* GEORGE *and* ZOE. *As they exit,* M'CLOSKY *rises from behind a rock and looks after them.*)

M'CLOSKY. She loves him! I felt it—and how she can love! (*Advances.*) That one black drop of blood burns in her veins and lights up her heart like a foggy sun. O, how I lapped up her words, like a thirsty bloodhound! I'll have her, if it costs me my life! Yonder the boy still lurks with those mail-bags; the devil still keeps him here to tempt me, darn his yellow skin! I arrived just too late, he had grabbed the prize as I came up. Hillo! He's coming this way, fighting with his Injiun. (*Conceals himself.*)

(*Enter* PAUL, *wrestling with* WAHNOTEE.)

PAUL. It ain't no use now: you got to gib it up!

WAHNOTEE. Ugh!

PAUL. It won't do! You got dat bottle of rum hid under your blanket—gib it up now, you—. Yar! (*Wrenching it from him.*) You nasty, lying Injiun! It's no use you putting on airs; I ain't gwine to sit up wid you all night and you drunk. Hillo! War's de crowd gone? And dar's de 'paratus— O, gosh, if I could take a likeness ob dis child! Uh—uh, let's have a peep. (*Looking through camera.*) O, golly! Yar, you Wahnotee! You stan' dar, I see you. Ta demine usti.

(*Looks at* WAHNOTEE *through the camera;* WAHNOTEE *springs back with an expression of alarm.*)

WAHNOTEE. No tue Wahnotee.

PAUL. Ha, ha! He tinks it's a gun. You ign'ant Injiun, it can't hurt you! Stop, here's dem dishes—plates—dat's what he call 'em, all fix: I see Mas'r Scudder do it often—tink I can take likeness—stay dere, Wahnotee.

WAHNOTEE. No, carabine tue.

PAUL. I must operate and take my own likeness too—how debbel I do dat? Can't be ober dar an' here too—I ain't twins. Ugh. Ach! 'Top; you look, you Wahnotee; you see dis rag, eh? Well when I say go, den lift dis rag like dis, see! den run to dat pine tree up dar (*Points.*) and back ag'in, and den pull down de rag so, d'ye see?

WAHNOTEE. Hugh!

PAUL. Den you hab glass ob rum.

WAHNOTEE. Rum!

PAUL. Dat wakes him up. Coute, Wahnotee in omenee dit go Wahnotee, poina la fa, comb a pine tree, la revieut sala, la fa.

WAHNOTEE. Fire-water!

PAUL. Yes, den a glass ob fire-water; now den. (*Throwing mail-bags down and sitting on them.*) Pret, now den go.
(WAHNOTEE *raises the apron and runs off.* PAUL *sits for his picture—*M'CLOSKY *appears.*)

M'CLOSKY. Where are they? Ah, yonder goes the Indian!

PAUL. De time he gone just 'bout enough to cook dat dish plate.

M'CLOSKY. Yonder is the boy—now is my time! What's he doing; is he asleep? (*Advancing.*) He is sitting on my prize! darn his carcass! I'll clear him off there—he'll never know what stunned him. (*Takes Indian's tomahawk and steals to* PAUL.)

PAUL. Dam dat Injiun! Is dat him creeping dar? I darn't move fear to spile myself.
(M'CLOSKY *strikes him on the head—he falls dead.*)

M'CLOSKY. Hooraw; the bags are mine—now for it!—(*Opening the mail-bags.*) What's here? Sunnyside, Pointdexter, Jackson, Peyton; here it is—the Liverpool postmark, sure enough!—(*Opening letter—reads.*) "Madam, we are instructed by the firm of Mason and Co., to inform you that a dividend of forty per cent. is payable on the 1st proximo, this amount in consideration of position, they send herewith, and you will find enclosed by draft to your order, on the Bank of Louisiana, which please acknowledge—the balance will be paid in full, with interest, in three, six, and nine months—your drafts on Mason Brothers at those dates will be accepted by La Palisse and Compagnie, N. O., so that you may command immediate use of the whole amount at once, if required. Yours, etc., James Brown." What a find! This infernal letter would have saved all. (*During the reading of letter he remains nearly motionless under the focus of the camera.*) But now I guess it will arrive too late—these darned U.S. mails are to blame. The Injiun! He must not see me. (*Exit rapidly.*)
(WAHNOTEE *runs on, and pulls down the apron. He sees* PAUL, *lying on the ground and speaks to him, thinking that he is shamming sleep. He gesticulates and jabbers to him and moves him with his feet, then kneels down to rouse him. To his horror he finds him dead. Expressing great grief he raises his eyes and they fall upon the camera. Rising with a savage growl, he seizes the tomahawk and smashes the camera to pieces. Going to* PAUL *he expresses*

*in pantomime grief, sorrow, and fondness, and takes him in
his arms to carry him away. Tableau.*)

ACT III

A Room in MRS. PEYTON's *house showing the entrance on
which an auction bill is pasted.* SOLON *and* GRACE *are there.*

PETE. (*Outside.*) Dis way—dis way.

(*Enter* PETE, POINTDEXTER, JACKSON, LAFOUCHE *and*
CAILLOU.)

PETE. Dis way, gen'l'men; now, Solon—Grace—dey's hot and
tirsty—sangaree, brandy, rum.

JACKSON. Well, what d'ye say, Lafouche—d'ye smile?

(*Enter* THIBODEAUX *and* SUNNYSIDE.)

THIBODEAUX. I hope we don't intrude on the family.

PETE. You see dat hole in dar, sar? I was raised on dis yar
plantation—nebber see no door in it—always open, sar, for
stranger to walk in.

SUNNYSIDE. And for substance to walk out.

(*Enter* RATTS.)

RATTS. Fine southern style that, eh!

LAFOUCHE. (*Reading the bill.*) "A fine, well-built old family
mansion, replete with every comfort."

RATTS. There's one name on the list of slaves scratched, I see.

LAFOUCHE. Yes; No. 49, Paul, a quadroon boy, aged thirteen.

SUNNYSIDE. He's missing.

POINTDEXTER. Run away, I suppose.

PETE. (*Indignantly.*) No, sar; nigger nebber cut stick on
Terrebonne; dat boy's dead, sure.

RATTS. What, Picayune Paul, as we called him, that used to
come aboard my boat?—Poor little darkey, I hope not; many
a picayune he picked up for his dance and nigger songs,

and he supplied our table with fish and game from the Bayous.

PETE. Nebber supply no more, sar—nebber dance again. Mas'r Ratts, you hard him sing about de place where de good niggers go, de last time.

RATTS. Well!

PETE. Well, he gone dar hisself; why I tink so—'cause we missed Paul for some days, but nebber tout nothin' till one night dat Injiun Wahnotee suddenly stood right dar 'mongst us—was in his war paint, and mighty cold and grave—he sit down by de fire. "Whar's Paul?" I say—he smoke and smoke, but nebber look out ob de fire; well knowing dem critters, I wait a long time—den he say, "Wahnotee great chief"; den I say nothing—smoke anoder time—last, rising to go, he turn round at door, and say berry low—O, like a woman's voice he say, "Omenee Pangeuk," dat is, Paul is dead—nebber see him since.

RATTS. That red-skin killed him.

SUNNYSIDE. So we believe; and so mad are the folks around, if they catch the red-skin they'll lynch him sure.

RATTS. Lynch him! Darn his copper carcass, I've got a set of Irish deckhands aboard that just loved that child; and after I tell them this, let them get a sight of the red-skin, I believe they would eat him, tomahawk and all. Poor little Paul!

THIBODEAUX. What was he worth?

RATTS. Well, near on five hundred dollars.

PETE. (*Scandalized.*) What, sar! You p'tend to be sorry for Paul, and prize him like dat! Five hundred dollars! (*To* THIBODEAUX.) Tousand dollars, Massa Thibodeau.

(*Enter* SCUDDER.)

SCUDDER. Gentlemen, the sale takes place at three. Good morning, Colonel. It's near that now, and there's still the sugar-houses to be inspected. Good day, Mr. Thibodeaux— shall we drive down that way? Mr. Lafouche, why, how do you do, sir? You're looking well.

LAFOUCHE. Sorry I can't return the compliment.

RATTS. Salem's looking a kinder hollowed out.

SCUDDER. What, Mr. Ratts, are you going to invest in swamps?

RATTS. No; I want a nigger.

SCUDDER. Hush.

PETE. Eh! wass dat?

SCUDDER. Mr. Sunnyside, I can't do this job of showin' round the folks; my stomach goes agin it. I want Pete here a minute.

SUNNYSIDE. I'll accompany them certainly.

SCUDDER. (*Eagerly.*) Will ye? Thank ye; thank ye.

SUNNYSIDE. We must excuse Scudder, friends. I'll see you round the estate.

(*Enter* GEORGE *and* MRS. PEYTON.)

LAFOUCHE. Good morning, Mrs. Peyton.

(*All salute.*)

SUNNYSIDE. This way, gentlemen.

RATTS. (*Aside to Sunnyside.*) I say, I'd like to say summit soft to the old woman; perhaps it wouldn't go well, would it?

THIBODEAUX. No; leave it alone.

RATTS. Darn it, when I see a woman in trouble, I feel like selling the skin off my back.

(*Exit* THIBODEAUX, SUNNYSIDE, RATTS, POINTDEXTER, GRACE, JACKSON, LAFOUCHE, CAILLOU, SOLON.)

SCUDDER. (*Aside to Pete.*) Go outside there; listen to what you hear, then go down to the quarters and tell the boys, for I can't do it. O, get out.

PETE. He said "I want a nigger." Laws, mussey! What am goin' to cum ob us! (*Exit slowly, as if trying to conceal himself.*)

GEORGE. My dear aunt, why do you not move from this painful scene? Go with Dora to Sunnyside.

MRS. PEYTON. No, George; your uncle said to me with his dying breath, "Nellie, never leave Terrebonne," and I never *will* leave it, till the law compels me.

SCUDDER. Mr. George, I'm going to say somethin' that has been chokin' me for some time. I know you'll excuse it. Thar's Miss Dora—that girl's in love with you; yes, sir, her eyes are startin' out of her head with it: now her fortune would redeem a good part of this estate.

MRS. PEYTON. Why, George, I never suspected this!

GEORGE. I did, aunt, I confess, but—

MRS. PEYTON. And you hesitated from motives of delicacy?

SCUDDER. No, ma'am; here's the plan of it. Mr. George is in love with Zoe.

GEORGE. Scudder!

MRS. PEYTON. George!

SCUDDER. Hold on, now! Things have got so jammed in on top of us, we ain't got time to put kid gloves on to handle them. He loves Zoe, and has found out that she loves him. (*Sighing.*) Well, that's all right; but as he can't marry her, and as Miss Dora would jump at him—

MRS. PEYTON. Why didn't you mention this before?

SCUDDER. Why, because I love Zoe, too, and I couldn't take that young feller from her; and she's jist living on the sight of him, as I saw her do; and they so happy in spite of this yer misery around them, and they reproachin' themselves with not feeling as they ought. I've seen it, I tell you; and darn it, ma'am, can't you see that's what's been a hollowing me out so—I beg your pardon.

MRS. PEYTON. O, George,—my son, let me call you,—I do not speak for my own sake, nor for the loss of the estate, but for the poor people here: they will be sold, divided, and taken away—they have been born here. Heaven has denied me children; so all the strings of my heart have grown around and amongst them, like the fibres and roots of an old tree in its native earth. O, let all go, but save them! With them around us, if we have not wealth, we shall at least have the home that they alone can make—

GEORGE. My dear mother—Mr. Scudder—you teach me what I ought to do; if Miss Sunnyside will accept me as I am, Terrebonne shall be saved: I will sell myself, but the slaves shall be protected.

MRS. PEYTON. *Sell* yourself, George! Is not Dora worth any man's—

SCUDDER. Don't say that, ma'am; don't say that to a man that loves another gal. He's going to do an heroic act; don't spile it.

MRS. PEYTON. But Zoe is only an Octoroon.

SCUDDER. She's won this race agin the white, anyhow; it's too late now to start her pedigree.

(*As* DORA *enters.*)

Come, Mrs. Peyton, take my arm. Hush! Here's the other one: she's a little too thoroughbred—too much of the greyhound; but the heart's there, I believe.

(*Exeunt* SCUDDER *and* MRS. PEYTON.)

DORA. Poor Mrs. Peyton.

GEORGE. Miss Sunnyside, permit me a word: a feeling of delicacy has suspended upon my lips an avowal, which—

DORA. (*Aside.*) O, dear, has he suddenly come to his senses?

(*Enter* ZOE, *stopping at back.*)

GEORGE. In a word, I have seen and admired you!

DORA. (*Aside.*) He has a strange way of showing it. European, I suppose.

GEORGE. If you would pardon the abruptness of the question, I would ask you, Do you think the sincere devotion of my life to make yours happy would succeed?

DORA. (*Aside.*) Well, he has the oddest way of making love.

GEORGE. You are silent?

DORA. Mr. Peyton, I presume you have hesitated to make this avowal because you feared, in the present condition of affairs here, your object might be misconstrued, and that your attention was rather to my fortune than myself. (*A pause.*) Why don't he speak?—I mean, you feared I might not give you credit for sincere and pure feelings. Well, you wrong me. I don't think you capable of anything else but—

GEORGE. No, I hesitated because an attachment I had formed before I had the pleasure of seeing you had not altogether died out.

DORA. (*Smiling.*) Some of those sirens of Paris, I presume. (*Pausing.*) I shall endeavor not to be jealous of the past; perhaps I have no right to be. (*Pausing.*) But now that vagrant love is—eh, faded—is it not? Why don't you speak, sir?

GEORGE. Because, Miss Sunnyside, I have not learned to lie.

DORA. Good gracious—who wants you to?

GEORGE. I do, but I can't do it. No, the love I speak of is not such as you suppose—it is a passion that has grown up here since I arrived; but it is a hopeless, mad, wild feeling, that must perish.

DORA. Here! Since you arrived! Impossible: you have seen no one; whom can you mean?

ZOE. (*Advancing.*) Me.

GEORGE. Zoe!

DORA. You!

ZOE. Forgive him, Dora; for he knew no better until I told him. Dora, you are right. He is incapable of any but sincere and pure feelings—so are you. He loves me—what of that? You know you can't be jealous of a poor creature like me. If he caught the fever, were stung by a snake, or possessed of any other poisonous or unclean thing, you could pity, tend, love him through it, and for your gentle care he would love you in return. Well, is he not thus afflicted now? I am his love—he loves an Octoroon.

GEORGE. O, Zoe, you break my heart!

DORA. At college they said I was a fool—I must be. At New Orleans, they said, "She's pretty, very pretty, but no brains." I'm afraid they must be right; I can't understand a word of all this.

ZOE. Dear Dora, try to understand it with your heart. You love George; you love him dearly; I know it; and you deserve to be loved by him. He will love you—he must. His love for me will pass away—it shall. You heard him say it was hopeless. O, forgive him and me!

DORA. (*Weeping.*) O, why did he speak to me at all then? You've made me cry, then, and I hate you both! (*Exit through room.*)

(*Enter* MRS. PEYTON *and* SCUDDER, M'CLOSKY *and* POINT-DEXTER.)

M'CLOSKY. I'm sorry to intrude, but the business I came upon will excuse me.

MRS. PEYTON. Here is my nephew, sir.

ZOE. Perhaps I had better go.

M'CLOSKY. Wal, as it consarns you, perhaps you better had.

SCUDDER. Consarns Zoe?

M'CLOSKY. I don't know; she may as well hear the hull of it. Go on, Colonel—Colonel Pointdexter, ma'am—the mortgagee, auctioneer, and general agent.

POINTDEXTER. Pardon me, madam, but do you know these papers. (*He hands the papers to* MRS. PEYTON.)

MRS. PEYTON. (*Taking them.*) Yes, sir; they were the free papers of the girl Zoe; but they were in my husband's secretary. How came they in your possession?

M'CLOSKY. I—I found them.

GEORGE. And you purloined them?

M'CLOSKY. Hold on, you'll see. Go on, Colonel.

POINTDEXTER. The list of your slaves is incomplete—it wants one.

SCUDDER. The boy Paul—we know it.

POINTDEXTER. No, sir, you have omitted the Octoroon girl, Zoe.

MRS. PEYTON. } Zoe!
ZOE. } Me!

POINTDEXTER. At the time the judge executed those free papers to his infant slave, a judgment stood recorded against him; while that was on record he had no right to make away with his property. That judgment still exists: under it and others this estate is sold to-day. Those free papers ain't worth the sand that's on 'em.

MRS. PEYTON. Zoe a slave! It is impossible!

POINTDEXTER. It is certain, madam: the judge was negligent, and doubtless forgot this small formality.

SCUDDER. But creditors will not claim the gal?

M'CLOSKY. Excuse me; one of the principal mortgagees has made the demand.

(Exeunt M'CLOSKY and POINTDEXTER.)

SCUDDER. Hold on yere, George Peyton; you sit down there. You're trembling so, you'll fall down directly. This blow has staggered me some.

MRS. PEYTON. O, Zoe, my child! Don't think too hard of your poor father.

ZOE. I shall do so if you weep. See, I'm calm.

SCUDDER. Calm as a tombstone, and with about as much life. I see it in your face.

GEORGE. It cannot be! It shall not be!

SCUDDER. Hold your tongue—it must. Be calm—darn the things; the proceeds of this sale won't cover the debts of the estate. Consarn those Liverpool English fellers, why couldn't they send something by the last mail? Even a letter, promising something—such is the feeling round amongst the planters. Darn me, if I couldn't raise thirty thousand on the envelope alone, and ten thousand more on the postmark.

GEORGE. Zoe, they shall not take you from us while I live.

SCUDDER. Don't be a fool; they'd kill you, and then take her, just as soon as—stop: old Sunnyside, he'll buy her; that'll save her.

ZOE. No, it won't; we have confessed to Dora that we love each other. How can she then ask her father to free me?

SCUDDER. What in thunder made you do that?

ZOE. Because it was the truth, and I had rather be a slave with a free soul than remain free with a slavish, deceitful heart. My father gave me freedom—at least he thought so. May Heaven bless him for the thought, bless him for the happiness he spread around my life. You say the proceeds of the sale will not cover his debts. Let me be sold then, that I may free his name. I give him back the liberty he bestowed upon me; for I can never repay him the love he bore his poor Octoroon child, on whose breast his last sigh was drawn, into whose eyes he looked with the last gaze of affection.

MRS. PEYTON. O, my husband! I thank Heaven you have not lived to see this day.

ZOE. George, leave me! I would be alone a little while.

GEORGE. Zoe! (*Turning away overpowered.*)

ZOE. Do not weep, George. Dear George, you now see what a miserable thing I am.

GEORGE. Zoe!

SCUDDER. I wish they could sell *me!* I brought half this ruin on this family, with my all-fired improvements. I deserve to be a nigger this day—I feel like one, inside. (*Exit SCUDDER.*)

ZOE. Go now, George—leave me—take her with you.

(*Exit* MRS. PEYTON *and* GEORGE.)

A slave! A slave! Is this a dream—for my brain reels with the blow? He said so. What! Then I shall be sold!—sold! And my master—O! (*Falls on her knees, with her face in her hands.*) No—no master but one. George—George—hush —they come! Save me! No, (*Looks off.*) 't is Pete and the servants—they come this way. (*Enters the inner room.*)

(*Enter* PETE, GRACE, MINNIE, SOLON, DIDO, *and all the Negroes.*)

PETE. Cum yer now—stand round, 'cause I've got to talk to you darkies—keep dem chil'n quiet—don't make no noise, de missus up dar har us.

SOLON. Go on, Pete.

PETE. Gen'l'men, my colored frens and ladies, dar's mighty

bad news gone round. Dis yer prop'ty to be sold—old
Terrebonne—whar we all been raised, is gwine—dey's gwine
to tak it away—can't stop here nohow.

OMNES. O-o!—O-o!

PETE. Hold quiet, you trash o' niggers! Tink anybody wants
you to cry? Who's you to set up screeching?—Be quiet! But
dis ain't all. Now, my cullud brethren, gird up your lines,
and listen—hold on yer bref—it's a comin'. We tought dat
de niggers would belong to de ole missus, and if she lost
Terrebonne, we must live dere allers, and we would hire
out, and bring our wages to ole Missus Peyton.

OMNES. Ya! Ya! Well—

PETE. Hush! I tell ye, 't ain't so—we can't do it—we've got to
be sold—

OMNES. Sold!

PETE. Will you hush? She will har you. Yes! I listen dar jess
now—dar was ole lady cryin'—Mas'r George—ah! You seen
dem big tears in his eyes. O, Mas'r Scudder, he didn't cry
zackly; both ob his eyes and cheek look like de bad Bayou
in low season—so dry dat I cry for him. (*Raising his voice.*)
Den say de missus, " 'Tain't for de land I keer, but for
dem poor niggers—dey'll be sold—dat wot stagger me."
"No," say Mas'r George, "I'd rather sell myself fuss; but dey
shan't suffer, nohow,—I see 'em dam fuss."

OMNES. O, bless 'um! Bless Mas'r George.

PETE. Hole yer tongues. Yes, for you, for me, for dem little
ones, dem folks cried. Now, den, if Grace dere wid her
chil'n were all sold, she'll begin screechin' like a cat. She
didn't mind how kind old judge was to her; and Solon, too,
he'll holler, and break de ole lady's heart.

GRACE. No, Pete; no, I won't. I'll bear it.

PETE. I don't tink you will any more, but dis here will; 'cause
de family spile Dido, dey has. She nebber was worth much
a' dat nigger.

DIDO. How dar you say dat, you black nigger, you? I fetch
as much as any odder cook in Louisiana.

PETE. What's the use of your takin' it kind, and comfortin'
de missus' heart, if Minnie dere, and Louise, and Marie,
and Julie is to spile it?

MINNIE. We won't, Pete; we won't.

PETE. (*To the men.*) Dar, do ye hear dat, ye mis'able darkies;
dem gals is worth a boat load of kinder men dem is. Cum,

for de pride of de family, let every darky look his best for
the judge's sake—dat ole man so good to us and dat ole
woman—so dem strangers from New Orleans shall say,
Dem's happy darkies, dem's a fine set of niggers; every one
say when he's sold, "Lor' bless dis yer family I'm gwine
out of, and send me as good a home."

OMNES. We'll do it, Pete; we'll do it.

PETE. Hush! Hark! I tell ye dar's somebody in dar. Who is it?

GRACE. It's Missy Zoe. See! See!

PETE. Come along; she har what we say, and she's cryin' for
us. None o' ye ign'rant niggers could cry for yerselves like
dat. Come here quite: now quite.

(*Exeunt* PETE *and all the Negroes, slowly.*)

(*Enter* ZOE *who is supposed to have overheard the last
scene.*)

ZOE. O! Must I learn from these poor wretches how much I
owe, and how I ought to pay the debt? Have I slept upon
the benefits I received, and never saw, never felt, never
knew that I was forgetful and ungrateful? O, my father!
My dear, dear father! Forgive your poor child. You made
her life too happy, and now these tears will flow. Let me
hide them till I teach my heart. O, my—my heart! (*Exit,
with a low, wailing, suffocating cry.*)

(*Enter* M'CLOSKY, LAFOUCHE, JACKSON, SUNNYSIDE *and*
POINTDEXTER.)

POINTDEXTER. (*Looking at his watch.*) Come, the hour is past.
I think we may begin business. Where is Mr. Scudder?

JACKSON. I want to get to Ophelensis to-night.

(*Enter* DORA.)

DORA. Father, come here.

SUNNYSIDE. Why, Dora, what's the matter? Your eyes are red.

DORA. Are they? Thank you. I don't care, they were blue this
morning, but it don't signify now.

SUNNYSIDE. My darling! Who has been teasing you?

DORA. Never mind. I want you to buy Terrebonne.

SUNNYSIDE. Buy Terrebonne! What for?

DORA. No matter—buy it!

SUNNYSIDE. It will cost me all I'm worth. This is folly, Dora.

DORA. Is my plantation at Comptableau worth this?

SUNNYSIDE. Nearly—perhaps.

DORA. Sell it, then, and buy this.

SUNNYSIDE. Are you mad, my love?

DORA. Do you want *me* to stop here and *bid* for it?

SUNNYSIDE. Good gracious, no!

DORA. Then I'll do it if you don't.

SUNNYSIDE. I will! I will! But for Heaven's sake go—here comes
the crowd.

(*Exit* DORA.)

What on earth does that child mean or want?

(*Enter* SCUDDER, GEORGE, RATTS, CAILLOU, THIBODEAUX,
PETE, GRACE, MINNIE, *and all the Negroes. A large table is
in the center of the background.* POINTDEXTER *mounts the
table with his hammer, his clerk sitting at his feet. The
Negro mounts the table from behind. The rest sit down.*)

POINTDEXTER. Now, gentlemen, we shall proceed to business.
It ain't necessary for me to dilate, describe or enumerate;
Terrebonne is known to you as one of the richest bits of
sile in Louisiana, and its condition reflects credit on them
as had to keep it. I'll trouble you for that piece of baccy,
Judge—thank you—so, gentlemen, as life is short, we'll start
right off. The first lot on here is the estate in block, with
its sugar-houses, stock, machines, implements, good dwell-
ing-houses and furniture. If there is no bid for the estate
and stuff, we'll sell it in smaller lots. Come, Mr. Thibodeaux, a man has a chance once in his life—here's yours.

THIBODEAUX. Go on. What's the reserve bid?

POINTDEXTER. The first mortgagee bids forty thousand dollars.

THIBODEAUX. Forty-five thousand.

SUNNYSIDE. Fifty thousand.

POINTDEXTER. When you have done joking, gentlemen, you'll
say one hundred and twenty thousand. It carried that easy
on mortgage.

LAFOUCHE. Then why don't you buy it yourself, Colonel?

POINTDEXTER. I'm waiting on your fifty thousand bid.

CAILLOU. Eighty thousand.

POINTDEXTER. Don't be afraid: it ain't going for that, Judge.

SUNNYSIDE. Ninety thousand.

POINTDEXTER. We're getting on.

THIBODEAUX. One hundred—

POINTDEXTER. One hundred thousand bid for this mag—

CAILLOU. One hundred and ten thousand—

POINTDEXTER. Good again—one hundred and—

SUNNYSIDE. Twenty.

POINTDEXTER. And twenty thousand bid. Squire Sunnyside is going to sell this at fifty thousand advance to-morrow. (*Looking round.*) Where's that man from Mobile that wanted to give one hundred and eighty thousand?

THIBODEAUX. I guess he ain't left home yet, Colonel.

POINTDEXTER. I shall knock it down to the Squire—going— gone—for one hundred and twenty thousand dollars. (*Raising hammer.*) Judge, you can raise the hull on mortgage— going for half its value. (*Knocking on the table.*) Squire Sunnyside, you've got a pretty bit o' land, Squire. Hillo, darkey, hand me a smash dar.

SUNNYSIDE. I got more than I can work now.

POINTDEXTER. Then buy the hands along with the property. Now, gentlemen, I'm proud to submit to you the finest lot of field hands and house servants that was ever offered for competition: they speak for themselves, and do credit to their owners. (*Reading.*) "No. 1, Solon, a guest boy, and a good waiter."

PETE. That's my son—buy him, Mas'r Ratts; he's sure to sarve you well.

POINTDEXTER. Hold your tongue!

RATTS. Let the old darkey alone—eight hundred for that boy.

CALLIOU. Nine.

RATTS. A thousand.

SOLON. Thank you, Mas'r Ratts: I die for you, sar; hold up for me, sar.

RATTS. Look here, the boy knows and likes me, Judge; let him come my way?

CALLIOU. Go on—I'm dumb.

POINTDEXTER. One thousand bid. He's yours, Captain Ratts, Magnolia steamer.

(SOLON *goes and stands behind* RATTS.)

"No. 2, the yellow girl, Grace, with two children—Saul, aged four, and Victoria, five."

(*They get on table.*)

SCUDDER. That's Solon's wife and children, Judge.

GRACE. (*To* RATTS.) Buy me, Mas'r Ratts, do buy me, sar?

RATTS. What in thunder should I do with you and those devils on board my boat?

GRACE. Wash, sar—cook, sar—anyting.

RATTS. Eight hundred agin, then—I'll go it.

JACKSON. Nine.

RATTS. I'm broke, Solon—I can't stop the Judge.

THIBODEAUX. What's the matter, Ratts? I'll lend you all you want. Go it, if you're a mind to.

RATTS. Eleven.

JACKSON. Twelve.

SUNNYSIDE. O, O!

SCUDDER. (*To* JACKSON.) Judge, my friend. The Judge is a little deaf. Hello! (*Speaking in his ear-trumpet.*) This gal and them children belong to that boy Solon there. You're bidding to separate them, Judge.

JACKSON. The devil I am! (*Rising.*) I'll take back my bid, Colonel.

POINTDEXTER. All right, Judge; I thought there was a mistake. I must keep you, Captain, to the eleven hundred.

RATTS. Go it.

POINTDEXTER. Eleven hundred—going—going—sold! "No. 3, Pete, a house servant."

PETE. Dat's me—yer, I'm comin'—stand around dar. (*Tumbles upon the table.*)

POINTDEXTER. Aged seventy-two.

PETE. What's dat? A mistake, sar—forty-six.

POINTDEXTER. Lame.

PETE. But don't mount to nuffin—kin work cannel. Come, Judge, pick up. Now's your time, sar.

JACKSON. One hundred dollars.

PETE. What, sar? Me! For me—look ye here! (*Dances.*)

GEORGE. Five hundred.

PETE. Mas'r George—ah, no, sar—don't buy me—keep your money for some udder dat is to be sold. I ain't no 'count, sar.

POINTDEXTER. Five hundred bid—it's a good price. He's yours, Mr. George Peyton.

(PETE *goes down.*)

"No. 4, the Octoroon girl, Zoe."

(*Enter* ZOE, *very pale, and stands on table.* M'CLOSKY *who hitherto has taken no interest in the sale, now turns his chair.*)

SUNNYSIDE. (*Rising.*) Gentlemen, we are all acquainted with the circumstances of this girl's position, and I feel sure that no one here will oppose the family who desires to redeem the child of our esteemed and noble friend, the late Judge Peyton.

OMNES. Hear! Bravo! Hear!

POINTDEXTER. While the proceeds of this sale promises to realize less than the debts upon it, it is my duty to prevent any collusion for the depreciation of the property.

RATTS. Darn ye! You're a man as well as an auctioneer, ain't ye?

POINTDEXTER. What is offered for this slave?

SUNNYSIDE. One thousand dollars.

M'CLOSKY. Two thousand.

SUNNYSIDE. Three thousand.

M'CLOSKY. Five thousand.

GEORGE. Demon!

SUNNYSIDE. I bid seven thousand, which is the last dollar this family possesses.

M'CLOSKY. Eight.

THIBODEAUX. Nine.

OMNES. Bravo!

M'CLOSKY. Ten. It's no use, Squire.

SCUDDER. Jacob M'Closky, you shan't have that girl. Now, take care what you do. Twelve thousand.

M'CLOSKY. Shan't I! Fifteen thousand. Beat that any of ye.

POINTDEXTER. Fifteen thousand bid for the Octoroon.

(*Enter* DORA.)

DORA. Twenty thousand.

OMNES. Bravo!

M'CLOSKY. Twenty-five thousand.

OMNES. (*Groan.*) O! O!

GEORGE. Yelping hound—take that.

(*Rushes* M'CLOSKY. M'CLOSKY *draws his knife.*)

SCUDDER. (*Darting between them.*) Hold on, George Peyton—

stand back. This is your own house; we are under your
uncle's roof; recollect yourself. And, strangers, ain't we
forgetting there's a lady present? (*The knives disappear.*)
If we can't behave like Christians, let's try and act like
gentlemen. Go on, Colonel.

LAFOUCHE. He didn't ought to bid against a lady.

M'CLOSKY. O, that's it, is it? Then I'd like to hire a lady to go
to auction and buy my hands.

POINTDEXTER. Gentlemen, I believe none of us have two feelings about the conduct of that man; but he has the law on
his side—we may regret, but we must respect it. Mr.
M'Closky has bid twenty-five thousand dollars for the
Octoroon. Is there any other bid? For the first time,
twenty-five thousand—last time! (*Brings hammer down.*)
To Jacob M'Closky, the Octoroon girl, Zoe, twenty-five
thousand dollars. (*Tableau.*)

ACT IV

SCENE. *The Wharf. The Steamer "Magnolia," alongside; a
bluff rock.* RATTS *discovered, superintending the loading of
ship.*

Enter LAFOUCHE *and* JACKSON.

JACKSON. How long before we start, captain?

RATTS. Just as soon as we put this cotton on board.

(*Enter* PETE, *with a lantern, and* SCUDDER, *with note book.*)

SCUDDER. One hundred and forty-nine bales. Can you take
any more?

RATTS. Not a bale. I've got engaged eight hundred bales at
the next landing, and one hundred hogsheads of sugar at
Patten's Slide—that'll take my guards under—hurry up thar.

VOICE. (*Outside.*) Wood's aboard.

RATTS. All aboard then.

(*Enter* M'CLOSKY.)

SCUDDER. Sign that receipt, captain, and save me going up to the clerk.

M'CLOSKY. See here—there's a small freight of turpentine in the fore hold there, and one of the barrels leaks; a spark from your engines might set the ship on fire, and you'll go with it.

RATTS. You be darned! Go and try it, if you've a mind to.

LAFOUCHE. Captain, you've loaded up here until the boat is sunk so deep in the mud she won't float.

RATTS. (*Calling off.*) Wood up thar, you Pollo—hang on to the safety valve—guess she'll crawl off on her paddles.
(*Shouts heard.*)

JACKSON. What's the matter?

(*Enter* SOLON.)

SOLON. We got him!

SCUDDER. Who?

SOLON. The Injiun!

SCUDDER. Wahnotee? Where is he? D'ye call running away from a fellow catching him?

RATTS. Here he comes.

OMNES. Where? Where?

(*Enter* WAHNOTEE. *They are all about to rush on him.*)

SCUDDER. Hold on! Stan' round thar! No violence—the critter don't know what we mean.

JACKSON. Let him answer for the boy then.

M'CLOSKY. Down with him—lynch him.

OMNES. Lynch him!
(*Exit* LAFOUCHE.)

SCUDDER. Stan' back, I say! I'll nip the first that lays a finger on him. Pete, speak to the red-skin.

PETE. Whar's Paul, Wahnotee? What's come ob de child?

WAHNOTEE. Paul wunce—Paul pangeuk.

PETE. Pangeuk—dead!

WAHNOTEE. Mort!

M'CLOSKY. And you killed him?
(*They approach him.*)

SCUDDER. Hold on!

PETE. Um, Paul reste?

WAHNOTEE. Hugh vieu. (*Goes.*) Paul reste ci!

SCUDDER. Here, stay! (*Examining the ground.*) The earth has been stirred here lately.

WAHNOTEE. Weenee Paul. (*Points down, and shows by pantomime how he buried* PAUL.)

SCUDDER. The Injun means that he buried him there! Stop! Here's a bit of leather. (*Drawing out the mail-bags.*) The mail-bags that were lost! (*Sees the tomahawk in* WAHNOTEE's *belt—draws it out and examines it.*) Look! Here are marks of blood—look thar, red-skin, what's that?

WAHNOTEE. Paul! (*Makes a sign that* PAUL *was killed by a blow on the head.*)

M'CLOSKY. He confesses it; the Indian got drunk, quarrelled with him, and killed him.

(*Re-enter* LAFOUCHE, *with smashed apparatus.*)

LAFOUCHE. Here are evidences of the crime; this rum-bottle half emptied—this photographic apparatus smashed—and there are marks of blood and footsteps around the shed.

M'CLOSKY. What more d'ye want—ain't that proof enough? Lynch him!

OMNES. Lynch him! Lynch him!

SCUDDER. Stan' back, boys! He's an Injiun—fair play.

JACKSON. Try him, then—try him on the spot of his crime.

OMNES. Try him! Try him!

LAFOUCHE. Don't let him escape!

RATTS. I'll see to that. (*Drawing revolver.*) If he stirs, I'll put a bullet through his skull, mighty quick.

M'CLOSKY. Come, form a court then, choose a jury—we'll fix this varmin.

(*Enter* THIBODEAUX *and* CAILLOU.)

THIBODEAUX. What's the matter?

LAFOUCHE. We've caught this murdering Injiun, and are going to try him.

(WAHNOTEE *sits, rolled in blanket.*)

PETE. Poor little Paul—poor little nigger!

SCUDDER. This business goes agin me, Ratts—'t ain't right.

LAFOUCHE. We're ready; the jury's impanelled—go ahead—who'll be accuser?

RATTS. M'Closky.

M'CLOSKY. Me?

RATTS. Yes; you was the first to hail Judge Lynch.

M'CLOSKY. Well, what's the use of argument whar guilt sticks out so plain; the boy and Injiun were alone when last seen.

SCUDDER. Who says that?

M'CLOSKY. Everybody—that is, I heard so.

SCUDDER. Say what you know—not what you heard.

M'CLOSKY. I know then that the boy was killed with that tomahawk—the redskin owns it—the signs of violence are all round the shed—this apparatus smashed—ain't it plain that in a drunken fit he slew the boy, and when sober concealed the body yonder?

OMNES. That's it—that's it.

RATTS. Who defends the Injiun?

SCUDDER. I will; for it is agin my natur' to b'lieve him guilty; and if he be, this ain't the place, nor you the authority to try him. How are we sure the boy is dead at all? There are no witnesses but a rum bottle and an old machine. Is it on such evidence you'd hang a human being?

RATTS. His own confession.

SCUDDER. I appeal against your usurped authority. This lynch law is a wild and lawless proceeding. Here's a pictur' for a civilized community to afford; yonder, a poor, ignorant savage, and round him a circle of hearts, white with revenge and hate, thirsting for his blood: you call yourselves judges—you ain't—you're a jury of executioners. It is such scenes as these that bring disgrace upon our Western life.

M'CLOSKY. Evidence! Evidence! Give us evidence. We've had talk enough; now for proof.

OMNES. Yes, yes! Proof, proof!

SCUDDER. Where am I to get it? The proof is here, in my heart.

PETE. (*Who has been looking about the camera.*) 'Top, sar! 'Top a bit! O, laws-a-mussey, see dis! Here's a pictur' I found stickin' in that yar telescope machine, sar! Look, sar!

SCUDDER. A photographic plate.

(PETE *holds his lantern up.*) What's this, eh? Two forms! The child—'t is he! Dead—and above him—Ah! ah! Jacob M'Closky, 't was you murdered that boy!

M'CLOSKY. Me?

SCUDDER. You! You slew him with that tomahawk; and as you stood over his body with the letter in your hand, you thought that no witness saw the deed, that no eye was on you—but there was, Jacob M'Closky, there was. The eye of the Eternal was on you—the blessed sun in heaven, that, looking down, struck upon this plate the image of the deed. Here you are, in the very attitude of your crime!

M'CLOSKY. 'T is false!

SCUDDER. 'T is true! The apparatus can't lie. Look there, jurymen. (*Showing plate to jury.*) Look there. O, you wanted evidence—you called for proof—Heaven has answered and convicted you.

M'CLOSKY. What court of law would receive such evidence? (*Going.*)

RATTS. Stop! *This* would! You called it yourself; you wanted to make us murder that Injiun; and since we've got our hands in for justice, we'll try it on *you*. What say ye? Shall we have one law for the red-skin and another for the white?

OMNES. Try him! Try him!

RATTS. Who'll be accuser?

SCUDDER. I will! Fellow-citizens, you are convened and assembled here under a higher power than the law. What's the law? When the ship's abroad on the ocean, when the army is before the enemy, where in thunder's the law? It is in the hearts of brave men, who can tell right from wrong, and from whom justice can't be bought. So it is here, in the wilds of the West, where our hatred of crime is measured by the speed of our executions—where necessity is law! I say, then, air you honest men? Air you true? Put your hands on your naked breasts, and let every man as don't feel a real American heart there, bustin' up with freedom, truth, and right, let that man step out—that's the oath I put to ye—and then say, Darn ye, go it!

OMNES. Go on! Go on!

SCUDDER. No! I won't go on; that man's down. I won't strike him, even with words. Jacob, your accuser is that picture of the crime—let that speak—defend yourself.

M'CLOSKY. (*Drawing knife.*) I will, quicker than lightning.

RATTS. Seize him, then!

(*They rush on* M'CLOSKY, *and disarm him.*)

He can fight though he's a painter: claws all over.

SCUDDER. Stop! Search him, we may find more evidence.

M'CLOSKY. Would you rob me first, and murder me afterwards?

RATTS. (*Searching him.*) That's his program—here's a pocketbook.

SCUDDER. (*Opening it.*) What's here? Letters! Hello! To "Mrs. Peyton, Terrebonne, Louisiana, United States." Liverpool postmark. Ho! I've got hold of the tail of a rat—come out. (*Reading.*) What's this? A draft for eighty-five thousand dollars, and credit on Palisse and Co., of New Orleans, for the balance. Hi! The rat's out. You killed the boy to steal this letter from the mail-bags—you stole this letter, that the money should not arrive in time to save the Octoroon; had it done so, the lien on the estate would have ceased, and Zoe be free.

OMNES. Lynch him! Lynch him! Down with him!

SCUDDER. Silence in the court: stand back, let the gentlemen of the jury retire, consult, and return their verdict.

RATTS. I'm responsible for the crittur—go on.

PETE. (*To* WAHNOTEE.) See, Injiun; look dar (*Showing him the plate.*), see dat innocent; look, dar's de murderer of poor Paul.

WAHNOTEE. Ugh! (*Examining the plate.*)

PETE. Ya! As he? Closky tue Paul—kill de child with your tomahawk dar: 't wasn't you, no—ole Pete allus say so. Poor Injiun lub our little Paul.

(WAHNOTEE *rises and looks at* M'CLOSKY—*he is in his war paint and fully armed.*)

SCUDDER. What say ye, gentlemen? Is the prisoner guilty, or is he not guilty?

OMNES. Guilty!

SCUDDER. And what is to be his punishment?

OMNES. Death!

(*All advance.*)

WAHNOTEE. (*Crosses to* M'CLOSKY.) Ugh!

SCUDDER. No, Injiun; we deal out justice here, not revenge. 'T ain't you he has injured, 't is the white man, whose laws he has offended.

RATTS. Away with him—put him down the aft hatch, till we rig his funeral.

M'CLOSKY. Fifty against one! O! If I had you one by one alone in the swamp, I'd rip ye all. (*He is borne off in boat struggling.*)

SCUDDER. Now, then, to business.

PETE. (*Re-enters from boat.*) O, law, sir, dat debil Closky, he tore hisself from de gen'lam, knock me down, take my light, and trows it on de turpentine barrels, and de shed's all afire! (*Fire seen.*)

JACKSON. (*Re-entering.*) We are catching fire forward: quick, cut free from the shore.

RATTS. All hands aboard there—cut the starn ropes—give her headway!

ALL. Ay, ay!

(*Cry of "Fire" heard—Engine bells heard—steam whistle noise.*)

RATTS. Cut all away, for'ard—overboard with every bale afire. (*The Steamer moves off with the fire still blazing.*)

(M'CLOSKY *re-enters, swimming.*)

M'CLOSKY. Ha! Have I fixed ye? Burn! Burn! That's right. You thought you had cornered me, did ye? As I swam down, I thought I heard something in the water, as if pursuing me— one of them darned alligators, I suppose—they swarm hereabout—may they crunch every limb of ye. (*Exit.*)

(WAHNOTEE *is seen swimming. He finds trail and follows* M'CLOSKY. *The Steamer floats on at back, burning.*)

ACT V

Scene 1

Negroes' Quarters.

Enter ZOE.

ZOE. It wants an hour yet to daylight—here is Pete's hut— (*Knocks.*) He sleeps—no: I see a light.

DIDO. (*Enters from hut.*) Who dat?

ZOE. Hush, aunty! 'T is I—Zoe.

DIDO. Missey Zoe? Why you out in de swamp dis time ob night; you catch de fever sure—you is all wet.

ZOE. Where's Pete?

DIDO. He gone down to de landing last night wid Mas'r Scudder; not come back since—kint make it out.

ZOE. Aunty, there is sickness up at the house; I have been up all night beside one who suffers, and I remembered that when I had the fever you gave me a drink, a bitter drink, that made me sleep—do you remember it?

DIDO. Didn't I? Dem doctors ain't no 'count; dey don't know nuffin.

ZOE. No; but you, aunty, you are wise—you know every plant, don't you, and what it is good for?

DIDO. Dat you drink is fust rate for red fever. Is de folks' head bad?

ZOE. Very bad, aunty; and the heart aches worse, so they can get no rest.

DIDO. Hold on a bit, I get you de bottle. (*Exit.*)

ZOE. In a few hours that man, my master, will come for me: he has paid my price, and he only consented to let me remain here this one night, because Mrs. Peyton promised to give me up to him to-day.

DIDO. (*Re-enters with phial.*) Here 't is—now you give one timble-full—dat's nuff.

ZOE. All there is there would kill one, wouldn't it?

DIDO. Guess it kill a dozen—nebber try.

ZOE. It's not a painful death, aunty, is it? You told me it produced a long, long sleep.

DIDO. Why you tremble so? Why you speak so wild? What you's gwine to do, missey?

ZOE. Give me the drink.

DIDO. No. Who dat sick at de house?

ZOE. Give it to me.

DIDO. No. You want to hurt yourself. O, Miss Zoe, why you ask old Dido for dis pizen?

ZOE. Listen to me. I love one who is here, and he loves me— George. I sat outside his door all night—I heard his sighs— his agony—torn from him by my coming fate; and he said, "I'd rather see her dead than his!"

DIDO. Dead!

ZOE. He said so—then I rose up, and stole from the house, and ran down to the bayou: but its cold, black, silent stream terrified me—drowning must be so horrible a death. I could not do it. Then, as I knelt there, weeping for courage, a

snake rattled beside me. I shrunk from it and fled. Death
was there beside me, and I dared not take it. O! I'm afraid
to die; yet I am more afraid to live.

DIDO. Die!

ZOE. So I came here to you; to you, my own dear nurse; to
you, who so often hushed me to sleep when I was a child;
who dried my eyes and put your little Zoe to rest. Ah! Give
me the rest that no master but One can disturb—the sleep
from which I shall awake free! You can protect me from
that man—do let me die without pain.

DIDO. No, no—life is good for young ting like you.

ZOE. O! good, good nurse: you will, you will.

DIDO. No—g'way.

ZOE. Then I shall never leave Terrebonne—the drink, nurse;
the drink; that I may never leave my home—my dear, dear
home. You will not give me to that man? Your own Zoe,
that loves you, aunty, so much, so much. (*Gets the phial.*)
Ah! I have it.

DIDO. No, missey. O! No—don't.

ZOE. Hush! (*Runs off.*)

DIDO. Here, Solon, Minnie, Grace.

(*They enter.*)

ALL. Was de matter?

DIDO. Miss Zoe got de pizen. (*Exit.*)

ALL. O! O! (*Exeunt.*)

Scene 2

In a Cane-brake Bayou, on a bank, with a canoe near by,
M'CLOSKY *is seen asleep.*

M'CLOSKY. Burn, burn! Blaze away! How the flames crack.
I'm not guilty; would ye murder me? Cut, cut the rope—
I choke—choke!—Ah! (*Waking.*) Hello! Where am I? Why,
I was dreaming—curse it! I can never sleep now without
dreaming. Hush! I thought I heard the sound of a paddle
in the water. All night, as I fled through the cane-brake, I
heard footsteps behind me. I lost them in the cedar swamp
—again they haunted my path down the bayou, moving as

I moved, resting when I rested—hush! There again!—No; it was only the wind over the canes. The sun is rising. I must launch my dug-out, and put for the bay, and in a few hours I shall be safe from pursuit on board of one of the coasting schooners that run from Galveston to Matagorda. In a little time this darned business will blow over, and I can show again. Hark! There's that noise again! If it was the ghost of that murdered boy haunting me! Well—I didn't mean to kill him, did I? Well, then, what has my all-cowardly heart got to skeer me so for?

(*Gets in canoe and rows off.* WAHNOTEE *appears in another canoe. Gets out and finds trail and paddles off after* M'CLOSKY.)

Scene 3

A cedar Swamp.

Enter SCUDDER *and* PETE.

SCUDDER. Come on, Pete, we shan't reach the house before midday.

PETE. Nebber mind, sa, we bring good news—it won't spile for de keeping.

SCUDDER. Ten miles we've had to walk, because some blamed varmin onhitched our dug-out. I left it last night all safe.

PETE. P'r'aps it floated away itself.

SCUDDER. No; the hitching line was cut with a knife.

PETE. Say, Mas'r Scudder, s'pose we go in round by de quarters and raise de darkies, den dey cum long wid us, and we 'proach dat ole house like Gin'ral Jackson when he took London out dar.

SCUDDER. Hello, Pete, I never heard of that affair.

PETE. I tell you, sa—hush!

SCUDDER. What?

PETE. Was dat?—A cry out dar in the swamp—dar again!

SCUDDER. So it is. Something forcing its way through the undergrowth—it comes this way—it's either a bear or a runaway nigger.

(*Draws a pistol.* M'CLOSKY *rushes on, and falls at* SCUDDER's *feet.*)

SCUDDER. Stand off—what are ye?

PETE. Mas'r Clusky.

M'CLOSKY. Save me—save me! I can go no farther. I heard voices.

SCUDDER. Who's after you?

M'CLOSKY. I don't know, but I feel it's death! In some form, human, or wild beast, or ghost, it has tracked me through the night. I fled; it followed. Hark! There it comes—it comes—don't you hear a footstep on the dry leaves!

SCUDDER. Your crime has driven you mad.

M'CLOSKY. D'ye hear it—nearer—nearer—ah!

(WAHNOTEE *rushes on, and attacks* M'CLOSKY.)

SCUDDER. The Injiun! By thunder.

PETE. You'se a dead man, Mas'r Clusky—you got to b'lieve dat.

M'CLOSKY. No—no. If I must die, give me up to the law; but save me from the tomahawk. You are a white man; you'll not leave one of your own blood to be butchered by the red-skin?

SCUDDER. Hold on now, Jacob; we've got to figure on that— let us look straight at the thing. Here we are on the selvage of civilization. It ain't our side, I believe, rightly; but Nature has said that where the white man sets his foot, the red man and the black man shall up sticks and stand around. But what do we pay for that possession? In cash? No—in kind—that is, in protection, forbearance, gentleness, in all them goods that show the critters the difference between the Christian and the savage. Now, what have you done to show them the distinction? For, darn me, if I can find out.

M'CLOSKY. For what I have done, let me be tried.

SCUDDER. You have been tried—honestly tried and convicted. Providence has chosen your executioner. I shan't interfere.

PETE. O, no; Mas'r Scudder, don't leave Mas'r Closky like dat—don't, sa—'t ain't what good Christian should do.

SCUDDER. D'ye hear that, Jacob? This old nigger, the grandfather of the boy you murdered, speaks for you—don't that go through you? D'ye feel it? Go on, Pete, you've waked up the Christian here, and the old hoss responds. (*Throws bowie-knife to* M'CLOSKY.) Take that, and defend yourself. (*Exeunt* SCUDDER *and* PETE. WAHNOTEE *faces him. They fight.* M'CLOSKY *runs off,* WAHNOTEE *follows him.—Screams outside.*)

Scene 4

Parlor at Terrebonne.

Enter ZOE.

ZOE. My home, my home! I must see you no more. Those little
flowers can live, but I cannot. To-morrow they'll bloom
the same—all will be here as now, and I shall be cold. O!
My life, my happy life; why has it been so bright?

(*Enter* MRS. PEYTON *and* DORA.)

DORA. Zoe, where have you been?
MRS. PEYTON. We felt quite uneasy about you.
ZOE. I've been to the Negro quarters. I suppose I shall go
before long, and I wished to visit all the places, once again,
to see the poor people.
MRS. PEYTON. Zoe, dear, I'm glad to see you more calm this
morning.
DORA. But how pale she looks, and she trembles so.
ZOE. Do I?

(*Enter* GEORGE.)

Ah! He is here.
DORA. George, here she is.
ZOE. I have come to say good-by, sir; two hard words—so
hard, they might break many a heart; mightn't they?
GEORGE. O, Zoe! Can you smile at this moment?
ZOE. You see how easily I have become reconciled to my
fate—so it will be with you. You will not forget poor Zoe!
But her image will pass away like a little cloud that ob-
scured your happiness a while—you will love each other;
you are both too good not to join your hearts. Brightness
will return amongst you. Dora, I once made you weep;
those were the only tears I caused anybody. Will you
forgive me?
DORA. Forgive you—(*Kisses her.*)

ZOE. I feel you do, George.

GEORGE. Zoe, you are pale. Zoe!—She faints!

ZOE. No; a weakness, that's all—a little water.

(DORA *gets some water.*)

I have a restorative here—will you pour it in the glass?

(DORA *attempts to take it.*)

No; not you—George. (GEORGE *pours the contents of the phial into glass.*) Now, give it to me. George, dear George, do you love me?

GEORGE. Do you doubt it, Zoe?

ZOE. No! (*Drinks.*)

DORA. Zoe, if all I possess would buy your freedom, I would gladly give it.

ZOE. I am free! I had but one Master on earth, and he has given me my freedom!

DORA. Alas! But the deed that freed you was not lawful.

ZOE. Not lawful—no—but I am going to where there is no law—where there is only justice.

GEORGE. Zoe, you are suffering—your lips are white—your cheeks are flushed.

ZOE. I must be going—it is late. Farewell, Dora. (*Retiring.*)

PETE. (*Outside.*) Whar's Missus—whar's Mas'r George?

GEORGE. They come.

(*Enter* SCUDDER.)

SCUDDER. Stand around and let me pass—room thar! I feel so big with joy, creation ain't wide enough to hold me! Mrs. Peyton, George Peyton, Terrebonne is yours. It was that rascal M'Closky—but he got rats, I swow—he killed the boy, Paul, to rob this letter from the mail-bags—the letter from Liverpool you know—he sot fire to the shed—that was how the steamboat got burned up.

MRS. PEYTON. What d'ye mean?

SCUDDER. Read—read that. (*Gives letter to them.*)

GEORGE. Explain yourself.

(*Enter* SUNNYSIDE.)

SUNNYSIDE. Is it true?

SCUDDER. Every word of it, Squire. Here, you tell it, since you know it. If I was to try, I'd bust.

MRS. PEYTON. Read, George. Terrebonne is yours.

(*Enter* PETE, DIDO, SOLON, MINNIE, *and* GRACE.)

PETE. Whar is she—whar is Miss Zoe?

SCUDDER. What's the matter?

PETE. Don't ax me. Whar's de gal? I say.

SCUDDER. Here she is—Zoe!—Water—she faints.

PETE. No—no. 'T ain't no faint—she's a dying, sa: she got pizon from old Dido here, this mornin'.

GEORGE. Zoe!

SCUDDER. Zoe! Is this true?—No, it ain't—darn it, say it ain't. Look here, you're free, you know; nary a master to hurt you now: you will stop here as long as you're a mind to, only don't look so.

DORA. Her eyes have changed color.

PETE. Dat's what her soul's gwine to do. It's going up dar, whar dere's no line atween folks.

GEORGE. She revives.

ZOE. (*On the sofa.*) George—where—where—

GEORGE. O, Zoe! What have you done?

ZOE. Last night I overheard you weeping in your room, and you said, "I'd rather see her dead than so!"

GEORGE. Have I then prompted you to this?

ZOE. No; but I loved you so, I could not bear my fate; and then I stood between your heart and hers. When I am dead she will not be jealous of your love for me, no laws will stand between us. Lift me; so—(GEORGE *raises her head.*)—let me look at you, that your face may be the last I see of this world. O! George, you may, without a blush, confess your love for the Octoroon.

(*Dies.* GEORGE *lowers her head gently and kneels beside her.*)

SCUDDER. Poor child; she is free. (*Tableau.*)

RIP VAN WINKLE

Preface to RIP VAN WINKLE

Despite the appeal of *Rip Van Winkle* to many nineteenth-century actors and playwrights, its name is most closely associated with that of Joseph Jefferson (1829–1905). Jefferson achieved and maintained success in other roles; but popular demand as well as personal inclination consistently made him return to Rip, the fabulous Dutch-American comic hero. For years he devoted his career almost exclusively to this play, performing it in England and in practically every part of the United States, much as James O'Neill (the father of Eugene O'Neill) did so successfully with *The Count of Monte Cristo.*

He first played his Rip Van Winkle in 1865. Both his father and his grandfather had acted in the play, perhaps in John Kerr's dramatization of the Washington Irving story, which was first published in 1819 and is still among the best-known tales in the English language. It was Kerr, an Anglo-American actor, who had invented Rip's toast—"Here's your good health and your family's good health and may you all live long and prosper"—which was retained by subsequent adaptors of the play, including Jefferson. In 1850 Jefferson himself had played the part of Seth Slough, the innkeeper, to his half-brother Charles Burke's Rip, in the latter's own dramatization of the play. That version of the increasingly popular and frequently redramatized story eventually supplanted Kerr's, even in some of James Hackett's later performances, and contained Rip's oft-quoted line, "Are we so soon forgot when we are gone?" (Act IV, Scene 3). The next dramatization of interest was the first one that Jefferson himself made—a three-act play that was for the most part a collation of other versions. Produced in Washington in 1859, it was neither successful nor was Jefferson satisfied with it.

But his interest in the play continued. When he visited England in June 1865, after his four-year tour of Australia and South America, he asked Dion Boucicault to rework it for him. The resultant play, a three-act adaptation, was pro-

duced at the Adelphi Theatre in London on September 4,
and it was an immediate and enormous success. Jefferson
played in it for 170 nights in London and then repeated his
triumph, first briefly in Manchester, then in New York
and in other parts of America. Through the years he con-
stantly kept altering and developing his role. He succeeded
in producing a play that is a curious and appealing mixture
of comedy, fantasy, and pathos—a "tall tale," Constance
Rourke notes in her *American Humor* (1931), that "lived
again in a transmuted mythology of death and dream and
thunder." The text of the play that follows—first printed in
1895, thirty years after that of Boucicault—is Jefferson's
acting script, and he continued to play it substantially in
this form until the end of his career.

Joseph Jefferson was the most illustrious member of an
illustrious theatre family. Its progenitor, an Englishman who
acted with David Garrick at the Drury Lane, was Thomas
Jefferson (1732?–1807). His son, the first Joseph Jefferson
(1774–1832), sailed to America when he was twenty-one,
and achieved fame on the New York stage. Among his seven
children, all of whom became actors, was the second Joseph
Jefferson (1804–1842). He did not inherit his father's considerable thespian talents (and he certainly lacked those of
his son), although he had artistic talents and often did the
scene painting in his theatre. He married an actress who was
also an accomplished singer, Cornelia Frances Thomás
(Charles Burke's mother by her first marriage), and they
had four children; two of them survived infancy, the older
being the third—and most famous—Joseph Jefferson.

In his *Autobiography* Jefferson tells about his early stage
appearances—the first as the infant in the melodramatic
rescue scene of Sheridan and Kotzebue's *Pizarro*, where, in
a panic, he inadvertently scalped the Indian hero by pulling
off the balding tragedian's wig; the second, at the age of
four, when, carried onstage in a sack by T.D. Rice, he was
emptied out at the end of the act to mimic the famous Jim
Crow's dance and song:

> First on de heel tap, den on de toe,
> Ebery time I wheel about I jump Jim Crow.
> Wheel about and turn about and do jis so,
> And ebery time I wheel about I jump Jim Crow.

He first became successful in 1857 with 'his portrayals of Dr. Pangloss in George Colman's *The Heir at Law* and, the following year, Asa Trenchard in Tom Taylor's *Our American Cousin*, the play Lincoln was watching when he was assassinated. Later famous characterizations by Jefferson included Bob Acres in Richard Brinsley Sheridan's *The Rivals*, Caleb Plummer in Charles Dickens's *The Cricket on the Hearth*, and Salem Scudder in Boucicault's *The Octoroon*. He also lectured widely and with much acclaim on acting, drama, and the theatre. Performing for a total of more than seventy years, he reached the pinnacle of his profession when he succeeded Edwin Booth as President of the Players' Club in 1893. He retired in 1904, a year before his death on April 23, 1905.

The Autobiography of Joseph Jefferson (1890) was republished in 1949 as *Rip Van Winkle*. Biographies include William Winter's *Life and Art of Joseph Jefferson* (1894) and Montrose J. Moses's *Famous Actor-Families in America* (1906).

M.M.

RIP VAN WINKLE
as played by
Joseph Jefferson

Characters

RIP VAN WINKLE
DERRICK VON BEEKMAN, Village capitalist
NICHOLAS ("NICK") VEDDER, Innkeeper
HENDRICK, his son
COCKLES, Derrick's nephew
JACOB STEIN, Rip's drinking companion
SETH SLOUGH, Innkeeper

GRETCHEN, Rip's wife, later Derrick's wife
MEENIE, Rip's daughter
KÄTCHEN, Seth's wife
DEMONS AND VILLAGERS

ACT I

The village of Falling Waters, set amid familiar and un-mistakable Hudson River scenery, with the shining river itself and the noble heights of the Catskills visible in the distance. In the foreground, to the left of the stage, is a country inn bearing the sign of George III. *In the wall of the inn, a window closed by a solid wooden shutter. To the right of the stage, an old cottage with a door opening into the interior; before the cottage stands a bench holding a wash-tub, with a washboard, soap and clothes in the tub. In the center of the stage, a table and chairs, and on the table a stone pitcher and two tin cups.*

As the curtain rises, GRETCHEN *is discovered washing, and little* MEENIE *sitting nearby on a low stool. The sound of a chorus and laughter comes from the inn.*

GRETCHEN. Shouting and drinking day and night.

(*Laughter is heard from the inn.*)

Hark how they crow over their cups while their wives are working at home, and their children are starving.

(*Enter* DERRICK *from the inn with a green bag, followed by* NICK VEDDER. DERRICK *places his green bag on the table.*)

DERRICK. Not a day, not an hour. If the last two quarters' rent be not paid by this time tomorrow, out you go!

NICK. Oh, come, Derrick, you won't do it. Let us have a glass, and talk the matter over; good liquor opens the heart. Here, Hendrick! Hendrick!

(*Enter* HENDRICK.)

HENDRICK. Yes, Father.

DERRICK. So that is your brat?

NICK. Yes, that is my boy.

DERRICK. Then the best I can wish him is that he won't take after his father, and become a vagabond and a penniless outcast.

NICK. Those are hard words to hear in the presence of my child.

HENDRICK. Then why don't you knock him down, Father?

GRETCHEN. I'll tell you why—

DERRICK. Gretchen!

GRETCHEN. (*Wiping her arms and coming to front of tub.*) It is because your father is in that man's power. And what's the use of getting a man down, if you don't trample on him?

NICK. Oh, that is the way of the world.

GRETCHEN. (*To* HENDRICK.) Go in, boy. I want to speak to your father, and my words may not be fit for you to hear. Yonder is my little girl; go and play with her.

(HENDRICK *and* MEENIE *exeunt into the cottage.*)

GRETCHEN. Now, Derrick, Vedder is right; you won't turn him out of his house yonder.

DERRICK. And why not? Don't he owe me a year's rent?

GRETCHEN. And what do you owe him? Shall I sum up your accounts for you? Ten years ago, this was a quiet village, and belonged mostly to my husband, Rip Van Winkle, a foolish, idle fellow. That house yonder has since been his ruin. Yes; bit by bit, he has parted with all he had, to fill the mouths of sots and boon companions, gathered around him in yonder house. And you, Derrick—you supplied him with the money to waste in riot and drink. Acre by acre, you've sucked in his land to swell your store. Yonder miserable cabin is the only shelter we have left; but that is mine. Had it been his, he would have sold it you, Derrick, long ago, and wasted its price in riot.

(NICK, *who has been enjoying* DERRICK's *discomfiture during this speech, is unable to control himself, and at the end of the speech bursts into a loud laugh.*)

Aye, and you too, Nick Vedder; you have ruined my husband between you.

NICK. Oh, come, Mrs. Van Winkle, you're too hard. I couldn't refuse Rip's money in the way of business; I had my rent to pay.

GRETCHEN. And shall I tell you why you can't pay it? It is because you have given Rip credit, and he has ended by drinking you out of house and home. Your window-shutter is not wide enough to hold the score against him; it is full of chalk. Deny it if you can.

NICK. I do deny it. There now!

GRETCHEN. Then why do you keep that shutter closed? I'll show you why. (*Goes to inn, opens shutter, holds it open, pointing at* RIP's *score.*) That's why! Nick Vedder, you're a good man in the main, if there is such a thing. (DERRICK *laughs.*) Aye, and I doubt it. (*Turning on him.*) But you are the pest of this village; and the hand of every woman in it ought to help pull down that drunkard's nest of yours, stone by stone.

NICK. Come, Dame Van Winkle, you're too hard entire; now a man must have his odd time, and he's none the worse for being a jolly dog.

GRETCHEN. No, none the worse. He sings a good song; he tells a good story—oh, he's a glorious fellow! Did you ever see the wife of a jolly dog? Well, she lives in a kennel. Did you ever see the children of a jolly dog? They are the street curs, and their home is the gutter. (*Goes up to the washtub, and takes revenge on the clothing she scrubs.*)

NICK. (*Getting up and approaching* GRETCHEN *timidly.*) I tell you what it is, Dame Van Winkle. I don't know what your home may be, but judging from the rows I hear over there, and the damaged appearance of Rip's face after having escaped your clutches—

(GRETCHEN *looks up angrily;* NICK *retreats a few paces hastily.*)

—I should say that a gutter was a luxurious abode compared with it, and a kennel a peaceful retreat.

(*Exit hurriedly, laughing, to the inn.* GRETCHEN *looks up angrily, and throws the cloth she has been wringing after him, then resumes washing.* DERRICK *laughs at* NICK's *exit, walks up to* GRETCHEN, *and puts one foot on the bench.*)

DERRICK. Is it true, Gretchen? Are you truly miserable with Rip?

GRETCHEN. Ain't you pleased to hear it? Come then and warm your heart at my sorrow. Ten years ago I might have had you, Derrick. But I despised you for your miserly ways, and threw myself away on a vagabond.

DERRICK. You and I shared him between us. I took his estate, and you took his person. Now, I've improved my half. What have you done with yours?

GRETCHEN. I can't say that I have prospered with it. I've tried every means to reclaim him, but he is as obstinate and perverse as a Dutch pig. But the worst in him—and what I can't stand—is his good-humor. It drives me frantic when, night after night, he comes home drunk and helplessly good-humored! Oh, I can't stand that!

DERRICK. Where is he now?

GRETCHEN. We had a tiff yesterday, and he started. He has been out all night. Only wait until he comes back! The longer he stops out, the worse it will be for him.

DERRICK. Gretchen, you've made a great mistake, but there is time enough to repair it. You are comely still, thrifty, and that hard sort of grain that I most admire in woman. (*Looks cautiously around. Leans on tub.*) Why not start Rip for ever, and share my fortune?

GRETCHEN. Oh, no, Derrick; you've got my husband in your clutches, but you can't get them around me. If Rip would only mend his ways, he would see how much I love him; but no woman could love you, Derrick; for woman is not a domestic animal, glad to serve and fawn upon a man for the food and shelter she can get; and that is all she would ever get from you, Derrick. (*Piling the clothes on the washboard, and shouldering it.*)

DERRICK. The time may come when you'll change your tune.

GRETCHEN. Not while Rip lives, bad as he is. (*Exit into cottage.*)

DERRICK. Then I'll wait until you've killed him. Her spirit is not broken yet. But patience, Derrick, patience; in another month I'll have my claws on all that remains of Rip's property—yonder cottage and grounds; then I'll try you again my lady.

(*Enter* COCKLES, *with papers in his hand, running towards the inn.*)

How now, you imp? What brings you here so full of a hurry? Some mischief's in your head, or your heels would not be so busy.

COCKLES. I've brought a letter for you from my employer. There it is.

DERRICK. (*Examining letter.*) Why, the seal is broken!

COCKLES. Yes, I read it as I came along.

DERRICK. Now I apprenticed this vagabond to my lawyer, and this is his gratitude.

COCKLES. Don't waste your breath, Nunky,[1] for you'll want it; for when you read that, if it don't take you short in the wind, I'll admire you.

DERRICK. (*Reads.*) "You must obtain from Rip van Winkle a proper conveyance of the lands he has sold to you. The papers he has signed are in fact nothing but mortgages on his estate. If you foreclose, you must sell the property, which has lately much advanced in value; and it would sell for enough to pay off your loan, and all your improvements would enure to the benefit of Rip Van Winkle."

COCKLES. There, now, see what you've been doing—wasting your money and my expectations on another chap's property! Do you want to leave me a beggar?

DERRICK. (*Reads.*) "I enclose a deed for him to sign that will make him safe."

COCKLES. Of course he'll sign it; he won't wait to be asked—he'll be in such a hurry.

DERRICK. All my savings—all my money—sunk in improving this village!

COCKLES. Yes, instead of physicking[2] Rip, as you thought, you've been coddling him all the while.

DERRICK. All these houses I've built are on another man's land. What shall I do?

COCKLES. Pull them down again; pull them down.

DERRICK. Ass!—Dolt that I have been!

COCKLES. Calling yourself names won't mend it, Nunky.

DERRICK. The imp is right. Rip must be made to sign this paper. But how—how?

COCKLES. How? How? How's a big word sometimes, ain't it, Nunky?

DERRICK. Rip would not do it if he knew what he was about. But he can't read—nor write, for the matter of that. But he can make his cross, and I can cajole him.

COCKLES. Look sharp, Nunky. The man that's looking round for a fool and picks up Rip Van Winkle, will let him drop again very quick.

[1] Uncle.

[2] "Bleeding"; relieving someone of his money.

DERRICK. He is poor; I'll show him a handful of money. He's a drunkard; I'll give him a stomachful of liquor. Go in, boy, and leave me to work this; and let this be a lesson to you hereafter: beware of the fatal effects of poverty and drink.

COCKLES. Yes—and parting with my money on bad security. (*Exit. Laughter outside.*)

DERRICK. Here he comes now, surrounded by all the dogs and children in the district. They cling around him like flies around a lump of sugar.

(RIP *enters, running and skipping, carrying one small child pickaback, and surrounded by a swarm of others hanging on the skirts of his coat. He is laughing like a child himself, and his merry blue eyes twinkle with delight. He is dressed in an old deerskin coat, a pair of breeches which had once been red, now tattered, patched, and frayed, leather gaiters and shoes equally dilapidated, a shapeless felt hat with a bit of the brim hanging loose—the whole stained and weather-worn to an almost uniform clay-color, except for the bright blue of his jean shirt and the scarlet of his long wisp of a necktie. One of the boys carries his gun.*)

RIP. (*Taking his gun from the boy.*) There, run along mit you; run along.

DERRICK. (*The children scamper off.*) The vagabond looks like the father of the village.

RIP. (*Who has stood laughing and watching the children, suddenly calls after them.*) Hey! You let my dog Schneider alone there; you hear that, Sock der Jacob der bist eine for donner spits poo—yah—

DERRICK. Why, what's the matter, Rip?

RIP. (*Coming down and shaking hands with* DERRICK.) Oh, how you was, Derrick? How you was?

DERRICK. You seem in trouble.

RIP. Oh, yah; you know them fellers. Vell, I tole you such a funny thing. (*Laughing.*) Just now, as me and Schneider was comin' along through the willage—Schneider's my dawg; I don't know whether you know him? (RIP *always speaks of Schneider as if he were a person, and one in whom his hearer took as profound an interest as he does himself.*) Well, them fellers went and tied a tin kettle mit Scneider's tail, and how he did run then, mit the kettle banging about. Well, I didn't hi him comin'. He run betwixt me and my legs, an' spilt me an' all them children in the mud;—yah, that's a fact.

(RIP *leans his gun against the cottage.*)

DERRICK. (*Aside.*) Now's my time. (*Aloud.*) Vedder! Vedder! (NICK *appears at the door of the inn.*) Bring us a bottle of liquor. Bring us your best, and be quick.

NICK. What's in the wind now? The devil's to pay when Derrick stands treat! (*Exit. Re-enters, with bottle and cups in left hand. Hands bottle to* DERRICK. RIP *lounges forward, and perches on the corner of the table.*)

DERRICK. (*Rising and approaching* RIP.) Come, Rip, what do you say to a glass?

RIP. (*Takes a cup and holds it to be filled.*) Oh, yah; now what do I generally say to a glass? I say it's a fine thing— when there's plenty in it. (Ve gates! Ve gates!) (*Shakes hands with* NICK.) And then I says more to what's in it than I do to the glass. Now you wouldn't believe it—that's the first one I've had today.

DERRICK. How so?

RIP. (*Dryly.*) Because I couldn't get it before, I suppose.

DERRICK. Then let me fill him up for you.

RIP. No, that is enough for the first one.

NICK. Come, Rip, a bumper for the first one.

RIP. That is enough for the first one.

DERRICK. Come, Rip, let me fill him up for you.

RIP. (*With ludicrous decision and dignity.*) I believe I know how much to drink. When I says a thing, I mean it.

DERRICK. Oh, well—(*Turns aside, and starts to fill his own cup.*)

RIP. All right; come along. (*Holding out his glass, and laughing at his own inconsistency.*) Here's your good health and your family's, and may they live long and prosper! (*They all drink. At the end,* NICK *smacks his lips and exclaims "Ah!"* DERRICK *repeats the same and* RIP *repeats after* DERRICK.)

(*To* NICK, *sadly.*) Ah, you may well go "Ah!" and smack your chops over that. You don't give me such schnapps when I come. Derrick, my score is too big now. (*Jerking his head towards the shutter, he notices for the first time that it is open.*) What you go and open that window for? —That's fine schnapps, Nick. Where you got that?

NICK. That's high Dutch, Rip—high Dutch, and ten years in bottle. Why, I had that in the very day of your wedding. We broached the keg under yonder shed. Don't you recollect?

RIP. Is that the same?

NICK. Yes.

RIP. I thought I knowed that licker. You had it ten years ago? (*Laughing suddenly.*) I would not have kept it so long. But stop, mein freund; that's more than ten years ago.

NICK. No, it ain't.

RIP. It's the same day I got married?

NICK. Yes.

RIP. Well, I know by that. You think I forgot the day I got married? Oh, no, my friend; I remember that day long as I live. (*Serious for a moment. Takes off his hat, and puts it on the table.*)

DERRICK. Ah! Rip, I remember Gretchen then, ten years ago.—Zounds, how I envied you!

RIP. (*Looking up, surprised.*) Did you? (*Winks at* NICK. *Then, suddenly remembering.*) So did I. You didn't know what was comin', Derrick.

DERRICK. She was a beauty.

RIP. What, Gretchen?—Yes, she was. She was a pretty girl. My! My! Yah, we was a fine couple altogether. Well, come along.

(*Holding out his cup to* DERRICK, *who fills it from the bottle.*)

NICK. Yes, come along.

(*Takes water pitcher from the table, and starts to fill up* RIP's *cup.* RIP *stops him.*)

RIP. (*Who has been lounging against the table, sits on it, and puts his feet on the chair.*) Stop! I come along mitout that, Nick Vedder. (*Sententiously.*) Good licker and water is like man and wife.

DERRICK *and* NICK. How's that, Rip?

RIP. (*Laughing.*) They don't agree together. I always like my licker single. Well, here's your good health, and your family's, and may they live long and prosper!

(*They all drink.*)

NICK. That's right, Rip; drink away, and drown your sorrow.

RIP. (*Drolly.*) Yes; but she won't drown. My wife is my sorrow, and you cannick drown her. She tried it once, but couldn't do it.

DERRICK *and* NICK. Why, how so?

RIP. (*Puts down his cup and clasps his knee, still perched on the corner of the table.*) Didn't you know that Gretchen like to got drown?

DERRICK *and* NICK. No.

RIP. (*Puts hat on.*) That's the funniest thing of the whole of it. It's the same day I got married; she was comin' across the river there in the ferry-boat to get married mit me—

DERRICK *and* NICK. Yes.

RIP. Well, the boat she was comin' in got upsetted.

DERRICK *and* NICK. Ah!

RIP. Well, but she wasn't in it.

DERRICK *and* NICK. Oh!

RIP. (*Explaining quite seriously.*) No, that's what I say; if she had been in the boat what got upsetted, maybe she might have got drowned. (*More and more reflective.*) I don't know how it was she got left somehow or other. Women is always behind that way—always.

DERRICK. But surely, Rip, you would have risked your life to save such a glorious creature as she was.

RIP. (*Incredulously.*) You mean I would yump in and pull Gretchen out?

DERRICK. Yes.

RIP. Oh, would I? (*Suddenly remembering.*) Oh, you mean then—yes, I believe I would then. (*With simple conviction.*) But it would be more my duty now than it was then.

DERRICK. How so?

RIP. (*Quite seriously.*) Why, you see when a feller gets married a good many years mit his wife, he gets very much attached to her.

NICK. (*Pompously*). Ah, he does indeed.

RIP. (*Winks at* DERRICK, *and points at* NICK *with his thumb.*) But if Mrs. Van Winkle was a-drowning in the water now, an' she says to me, "Rip, come an' save your wife!" I would say, "Mrs. Van Winkle, I will yust go home and think about it." Oh, no, Derrick, if ever Gretchen tumbles in the water, she's got to swim now, you mind that.

DERRICK. She was here just now, anxiously expecting you home.

RIP. I know she's keeping it hot for me.

NICK. What, your dinner, Rip?

RIP. No, the broomstick.

(*Exit* NICK *into house, laughing.*)

(*Confidentially.*) Derrick, whenever I come back from the mountains, I always stick the game-bag in the window and creep in behind.

DERRICK. (*Seating himself on the table by the side of* RIP.) Have you anything now?

RIP. (*Dropping into the chair* DERRICK *has just left. Leaning back, and putting hands behind his head.*) What, for game? No, not a tail, I believe, not a feather. (*With humorous indifference.*)

DERRICK. (*Touching* RIP *on the shoulder and shaking a bag of money.*) Rip, suppose you were to hang this bagful of money inside, don't you think it would soothe her down, eh?

RIP. (*Sitting up.*) For me, is that?

DERRICK. Yes.

RIP. (*With a shrewd glance.*) Ain't you yokin' mit me?

DERRICK. No, Rip, I've prospered with the lands you've sold me, and I'll let you have a loan on easy terms. I'll take no interest.

RIP. (*Getting up and walking forward, with decision.*) No, I'm afraid I might pay you again some day, Derrick.

DERRICK. And so you shall, Rip, pay me when you please. (*Puts the bag in* RIP's *hands, and forces his fingers over it, turns, and goes to the table, speaking as he goes.*) Say in twenty years—twenty years from this day. Ah, where shall we be then?

RIP. (*Quizzically, and half to himself.*) I don't know about myself; but I think I can guess where you'll be about that time. (*Takes chair and sits down.*)

DERRICK. Well, Rip, I'll just step into the inn and draw out a little acknowledgement.

RIP. (*Who has been sitting, leaning forward with his elbows on his knees, softly chinking the bag of money in his hand, looks up suddenly.*) 'Knowledgment—for what is that?

DERRICK. Yes, for you to put your cross to.

RIP. (*Indifferently.*) All right; bring it along.

DERRICK. No fear of Gretchen now, eh, Rip?

RIP. (*Plunged in thought.*) Oh, no.

DERRICK. You feel quite comfortable now, don't you, Rip? (*Exit to inn.*)

RIP. Oh, yah! (*Suddenly becoming serious and much mystified at* DERRICK's *conduct.*) Well, I don't know about that Derrick! Derrick! (*Holding up the bag and chinking it.*) It don't chink like good money neither. (*Grimly.*) It rattles like a snake in a hole.

GRETCHEN. (*Inside the cottage.*) Out with that lazy, idle cur! I won't have him here. Out, I say!

RIP. I'm glad I'm not in there now. I believe that's Schneider what she's lickin'; he won't have any backbone left in him. (*Sadly.*) I would rather she would lick me than the dog; I'm more used to it than he is. (*Gets up, and looks in at the window.*) There she is at the washtub. (*Admiring her energy, almost envying it.*) What a hard-workin' woman that is! Well, somebody must do it, I suppose. (*With the air of a profound moral reflection.*) She's comin' here now; she's got some broomstick mit her, too. (RIP *snatches up his gun and slinks off around the corner of the house.*)

(*Enter* GRETCHEN *with broomstick, followed by* HENDRICK *and* MEENIE, *carrying clothes-basket.*)

GRETCHEN. Come along, children. Now, you take the washing down to Dame Van Sloe's, then call at the butcher's and tell him that my husband has not got back yet, so I will have to go down myself to the marsh, and drive up the bull we have sold to him. Tell him the beast shall be in his stable in half an hour; so let him have the money ready to pay me for it.

(*During this,* RIP *has crept in and sat on the bench by the side of the tub behind* GRETCHEN.)

Ah, it is the last head of cattle we have left. Houses, lands, beasts, everything gone—everything except a drunken beast who nobody would buy or accept as a gift. Rip! Rip! wait until I get you home!

(*Threatening an imaginary* RIP *with broomstick. With a comical grimace,* RIP *tiptoes back behind the house.*)

Come, children, to work, to work! (*Exit.*)

(*Re-enter* RIP, *cautiously.*)

RIP. (*Laughing to himself.*) She gone to look after the bull.
She better not try the broomstick on him; he won't stand
it. (*Drops into the chair, with his back to the audience.*)
HENDRICK. Oh, Meenie, there's your father.
RIP. (*Holds out his arms, and* MEENIE *runs into them. Taking
her in his arms, and embracing her with great tenderness.*)
Ah, little gorl, was you glad to see your father come home?
MEENIE. Oh, yes!
RIP. (*Holding her close.*) I don't believe it, was you? Come
here. (*Getting up and leading her to the chair by the side
of the table.*) Let me look at you; I don't see you for such
a long time; come here. I don't deserve to have a thing
like that belong to me. (*Takes his hat off as if in reverence.*) You're too good for a drunken, lazy feller like me,
that's a fact. (*Bites his underlip, looks up, and brushes
away a tear.*)
MEENIE. (*Kneeling by him.*) Oh, no, you are a good papa!
RIP. (*Makes this confession with a childlike simplicity. The
tears come, and he brushes them away once or twice.
When he asks for the cup, at the end, it seems but the
natural conclusion of his speech.*) No, I wasn't: no good
father would go and rob his child; that's what I've done.
Why, don't you know, Meenie, all the houses and lands in
the village was mine—they would all have been yours
when you grew up? Where they gone now? I gone drunk
'em up, that's where they gone. Hendrick, you just take
warnin' by that; that's what licker do; see that? (*Holds
up the skirt of coat.*) Bring a man to hunger and rags. Is
there any more in that cup over there? Give it to me.
(*Drinks.*)
HENDRICK. (*Hands him cup.*) Don't cry, Rip; Meenie does
not want your money, for when I'm a big man I shall work
for her, and she shall have all I get.
MEENIE. Yes, and I'll have Hendrick too.
RIP. (*Greatly amused.*) You'll have Hendrick, too. (*With
mock gravity.*) Well, is this all settled?
HENDRICK. Yes, Meenie and me have made it all up.
RIP. I didn't know, I only thought you might speak to me
about it, but if it's all settled, Meenie, then git married

mit him. (*Laughing silently, and suddenly.*) You goin' to
marry my daughter? Well, now, that's very kind of you.
Marry one another? (*The children nod.* RIP, *with immense
seriousness.*) Well, here's your good health, and your
family, may they live long and prosper. (*To* HENDRICK.)
What you goin' to do when you get married, and grow
up and so? (*Leans forward.*)

HENDRICK. I'm not going to stop here with Father; oh, no,
that won't do. I'm going with Uncle Hans in his big ship
to the North Pole, to catch whales.

RIP. Goin' to cotch wahales mit the North Pole? That's a long
while away from here.

HENDRICK. Yes, but Uncle will give me ten shillings a month,
and I will tell him to pay it all to Meenie.

RIP. There! He's goin' to pay it all to you; that's a good boy,
that's a good boy.

MEENIE. Yes, and I'll give it all to you to keep for us.

RIP. (*With one of his little explosive laughs.*) I wouldn't
do that, my darlin'; maybe if you give it to me, you don't
get it back again. Hendrick! (*Suddenly earnest.*) You shall
marry Meenie when you grow up, but you mustn't drink.

HENDRICK. (*Slapping* RIP *on the knee.*) I'll never touch a
drop.

RIP. (*Quite seriously.*) You won't, nor me either; shake hands
upon it. Now we swore off together. (*With a change of
tone.*) I said so so many times, and never kept my word
once, never. (*Drinks.*)

HENDRICK. I've said so once, and I'll keep mine.

DERRICK. (*Outside.*) Well, bring it along with you.

RIP. Here comes Derrick; he don't like some children; run
along mit you.

(*Exit children with basket.*)

(*Enter* DERRICK *from inn with document.*)

DERRICK. There, Rip, is the little acknowledgement. (*Handing it to him.*)

RIP. 'Knowledgment. (*Putting on hat.*) For what is that?

DERRICK. That is to say I loaned you the money.

RIP. (*Lounging back in his chair.*) I don't want that; I would
lose it if I had it. (*Fills his cup from the bottle. Blandly.*)
I don't want it.

DERRICK. Don't you? But I do.

RIP. (*With simple surprise.*) For what?

DERRICK. Why, for you to put your cross to. Why, bless me, I've forgotten my pen and ink.

(*Enter* COCKLES.)

But luckily here comes my nephew with it. (*Aside.*) And in time to witness the signature.

RIP. Say, Derrick, have you been writing all that paper full in the little time you been in the house there? (*Turns the paper about curiously. Pours out more schnapps.*)

DERRICK. Yes, every word of it.

RIP. Have you? Well, just read it out loud to me. (*With an air of great simplicity.*)

DERRICK. (*Aside.*) Does he suspect? (*Aloud.*) Why, Rip, this is the first time you ever wanted anything more than the money.

RIP. (*Clasping his hands behind his head with an air of lordly indifference.*) Yes, I know; but I got nothing to do now. I'm a little curious about that, somehow.

COCKLES. (*Aside to* DERRICK.) The fish has taken the ground bait, but he's curious about the hook.

DERRICK. (*Aside.*) I dare not read a word of it.

COCKLES. (*Aside.*) Nunkey's stuck.

DERRICK. Well, Rip, I suppose you don't want to hear the formalities.

RIP. The what?

DERRICK. The preliminaries.

RIP. (*Indolently.*) I'll take it all—Bill, Claws, and Feathers. (*Leans forward and rests his head on his hand, and looks at the ground.*)

DERRICK. "Know all men by these presents, that I, Rip Van Winkle, in consideration of the sum of sixteen pounds received by me from Derrick Von Beekman"—(*Looks around at* COCKLES; *they wink knowingly at each other. Continues as if reading. Watching* RIP.)—"Do promise and undertake to pay the same in twenty years from date." (RIP *looks up; as he does so,* DERRICK *drops his eyes on document, then looks as if he had just finished reading.*) There, now are you satisfied?

RIP. (*Takes the document. In childlike surprise.*) Well, well, and does it take all that pen and ink to say such a little thing like that?

DERRICK. Why, of course it does.

COCKLES. (*Aside to* DERRICK.) Oh, the fool! he swallows it whole, hook and all.

RIP. (*Spreading the paper on the table.*) Where goes my cross, Derrick?

DERRICK. (*Pointing.*) There, you see I've left a nice little white corner for you.

RIP. (*Folds up paper in a leisurely manner and puts it in gamebag.*) W-e-l-l, I'll yust think about it. (*Looks up at* DERRICK *innocently.*)

DERRICK. Think about it? Why, what's the matter, Rip, isn't the money correct?

RIP. Oh, yes, I got the money all right. (*Chuckling.*) Oh! you mean about signing it. (*Rising. At a loss for a moment.*) Stop, yesterday was Friday, wasn't it?

DERRICK. So it was.

RIP. (*With an air of conviction.*) Well, I never do nothing like that the day after Friday, Derrick. (*Walks away towards his cottage.*)

DERRICK. (*Aside.*) The idiot! what can that signify? But I must not arouse his suspicions by pressing him. (*Aloud.*) You are right, Rip; sign it when you please; but I say, Rip, now that you're in funds, won't you help your old friend Nick Vedder, who owes me a year's rent?

RIP. (*Coming back to the table.*) Oh, yah, I will wipe off my schore, and stand treat to the whole willage.

DERRICK. Run, boy, and tell all the neighbors that Rip stands treat.

RIP. (*Leans on back of chair.*) An', Cockles, tell them we'll have a dance.

COCKLES. A dance! (*Runs off.*)

DERRICK. And I'll order the good cheer for you. (*Exit.*)

RIP. So do! So do! (*Cogitating dubiously.*) I don't understand it.

(*Re-enter* HENDRICK *with the basket over his head, followed by* MEENIE.)

Oh, you've come back?

HENDRICK. Yes, we've left the clothes.

RIP. Meenie, you take in the basket.

(*Exit* MEENIE *with the basket into the cottage.* HENDRICK *is following.*)

Hendrick, come here.

(HENDRICK *kneels between* RIP's *knees.*) So you are going to marry my daughter?

(HENDRICK *nods.*)

So, so. That's very kind of yer. (*Abruptly.*) Why you don't been to school today? You go to school some times, don't you?

HENDRICK. Yes, when father can spare me.

RIP. What do you learn mit that school,—pretty much something? (*Laughing at his mistake.*) I mean, everything?

HENDRICK. Yes; reading, writing and arithmetic.

RIP. Reading, and what?

HENDRICK. And writing, and arithmetic.

RIP. (*Puzzled.*) Writing and what?

HENDRICK. Arithmetic.

RIP. (*More puzzled.*) What meticks is that?

HENDRICK. Arithmetic.

RIP. (*With profound astonishment and patting* HENDRICK's *head.*) I don't see how the little mind can stand it all. Can you read?

HENDRICK. Oh, yes!

RIP. (*With a serious affectation of incredulity.*) I don't believe it; now, I'm just goin' to see if you can read. If you can't read, I won't let you marry my daughter. No, sir. (*Very drolly.*) I won't have nobody in my family what can't read. (*Taking out the paper that* DERRICK *has given him.*) Can you read ritmatics like that?

HENDRICK. Yes, that's writing.

RIP. (*Nonplussed.*) Oh! I thought it was reading.

HENDRICK. It's reading and writing, too.

RIP. What, both together. (*Suspiciously looking at the paper.*) Oh, yes; I didn't see that before; go long with it.

HENDRICK. (*Reads.*) "Know all men by these presents"—

RIP. (*Pleased, leaning back in his chair.*) Yah! that's right, what a wonderful thing der readin' is; why you can read it pretty nigh as good as Derrick, yes you do; go long.

HENDRICK. "That I, Rip Van Winkle"—

RIP. (*Taking off his hat, and holding it with his hands behind his head.*) Yah, that's right; you read it yust as well as Derrick; go long.

HENDRICK. "In consideration of the sum of sixteen pounds received do hereby sell and convey to Derrick Von Beekman all my estate, houses, lands whatsoever"— (*Hat drops.*)

RIP. (*Almost fiercely.*) What are you readin', some ritmatics what ain't down there: where you got that? (*Looking sharply at* HENDRICK.)

HENDRICK. (*Pointing.*) There. "Houses, lands, whatsoever."

RIP. (*Looking not at the paper but at* HENDRICK *very earnestly, as if turning over in his mind whether the boy has read it correctly. Then satisfied of the deception* DERRICK *has practiced upon him and struck by the humor of the way in which he has discovered it, he laughs exultantly and looks towards the inn-door through which* DERRICK *disappeared a short time before.*) Yes, so it is. Go long mit the rest. (*He leans forward, and puts his ear close to* HENDRICK, *so as not to miss a word.*)

HENDRICK. "Whereof he now holds possession by mortgaged deeds, from time to time executed by me."

RIP. (*Takes paper, and looks towards the inn fiercely exultant.*) You read it better than Derrick, my boy, much better. (*After a moment's pause, recollects himself. Kindly to* HENDRICK.) That will do, run along mit you. (*Exit* HENDRICK.)

RIP. Aha, my friend, Derrick! I guess you got some snakes in the grass. Now keep sober, Rip; I don't touch another drop so long what I live; I swore off now, that's a fixed fact.

(*Enter* DERRICK, NICK, STEIN, *and villagers.*)

DERRICK. Come, Rip, we'll have a rouse.

RIP. (*Seriously; half fiercely still.*) Here, Nick Vedder, here is the gelt; wipe off my score, and drink away. I don't join you; I swore off.

NICK. Why, Rip, you're king of the feast.

RIP. (*Absently, still intent on* DERRICK.) Am I dat?

OMNES. Swore off? What for?

RIP. I don't touch another drop.

JACOB STEIN. (*Coming down towards* RIP *with cup.*) Come, Rip, take a glass.

RIP. (*Turning on him, almost angry.*) Jacob Stein, you hear what I said?

STEIN. Yes.

RIP. (*Firmly.*) Well, when I said a thing, I mean it. (*Leans back in his chair with his hands behind his head.*)

STEIN. Oh, very well.

(*Turns away;* NICK *comes down and holds cup under* RIP's *nose.* RIP *looks to see if they are watching him. He can resist no longer, and takes the cup.*)

RIP. (*Laughing.*) Well, I won't count this one. Here's your good health and your family's, may they all live long and prosper.

DERRICK. Here come the fiddlers and the girls.

(*Enter girls.* RIP *walks over and closes the shutter which has held his score, then returns and seats himself on a low stool, and keeps time to the music as the villagers dance. Finally, the rhythm fires his blood. He jumps to his feet, snatches one of the girls away from her partner, and whirls into the dance. After a round or two, he lets go of her, and pirouettes two or three times by himself. Once more he catches her in his arms, and is in the act of embracing her, when he perceives* GRETCHEN *over her shoulder. He drops the girl, who falls on her knees at* GRETCHEN's *feet. There is a general laugh at his discomfiture, in which he joins half-heartedly. As the curtain descends,* RIP *is seen pointing at the girl as if seeking, like a modern Adam, to put the blame on her.*)

ACT II

The dimly lighted kitchen of RIP's *cottage. The door and window are at the back. It is night, and through the window a furious storm can be seen raging, with thunder, lightning, and rain. A fire smoulders on the hearth, to the right, and a candle gutters on the table in the center; a couple of chairs, a low stool, and a little cupboard, meagerly provided with cups and plates, complete the furniture of the room. Between the door and the window a clothes-horse, with a few garments hanging on it, forms a screen. To the left is a small door leading to the other rooms of the cottage.*

As the curtain rises, MEENIE *is seen sitting by the window, and* GRETCHEN *enters, takes off cloak, and throws a broomstick on the table.*

GRETCHEN. Meenie! Has your father come yet?

MEENIE. No, Mother.

GRETCHEN. So much the better for him. Never let him show his face in these doors again—never!

MEENIE. Oh, Mother, don't be so hard on him.

GRETCHEN. I'm not hard; how dare you say so?
(MEENIE *approaches her.*)
There, child, that father of yours is enough to spoil the temper of an angel. I went down to the marsh to drive up the bull. I don't know what Rip has been doing to the beast; he was howling and tearing about. I barely escaped with my life.
(*A crash outside.*)
What noise is that?

MEENIE. That's only Schneider, father's dog.

GRETCHEN. (*Picking up broomstick.*) Then I'll Schneider him. I won't have him here. (*Exit through the door leading to the rest of the cottage.*) Out, you idle, vagabond cur; out, I say!

MEENIE. (*Following her to the door, and crying.*) Oh, don't, don't hurt the poor thing!

(*Re-enter* GRETCHEN.)

GRETCHEN. He jumped out of the window before I could catch him. He's just like his master. Now, what are you crying for?

MEENIE. Because my poor father is out in all this rain.
(*A peal of thunder is heard.*)
Hark, how it thunders!

GRETCHEN. Serve him right—do him good. Is the supper ready?

MEENIE. Yes, Mother; it is there by the fireside. (*Pointing to the soup-bowl by the fire.*) Shall I lay the table?

GRETCHEN. Yes.
(*Again it thunders.*)
It's a dreadful night; I wonder where Rip is?

MEENIE. (*Bringing the cups and platters from the sideboard, together with a loaf of bread.*) Shall I lay the table for two, Mother, or for three?

GRETCHEN. For two, girl; he gets no supper here tonight. (*Another peal of thunder.*)

Mercy, how the storm rages! the fool, to stop out in such a downpour. I hope he's found shelter. I must take out the old suit I washed and mended for him last week, and put them by the fire to air. The idiot, to stop out in such a downpour! I'll have him sick on my hands next; that's all I want to complete my misery. (*She fetches clothes from the horse and hangs them on the back of the chair in front of the fire.*) He knows what I am suffering now, and that's what keeps him out. (*Lightning.*) Mercy, what a flash that was! The wretch will be starved with the cold! Meenie!

MEENIE. Yes, mother.

GRETCHEN. You may lay the table for three. (*There is a knock at the outer door.*)

There he is now!

(*Enter* HENDRICK, *who shakes rain from his hat.*)

Where's Rip? Is he not at your father's?

HENDRICK. No; I thought he was here.

GRETCHEN. He's gone back to the mountain. He's done it on purpose to spite me.

HENDRICK. (*Going to the fire.*) Shall I run after him, and bring him home? I know the road. We've often climbed it together.

GRETCHEN. No; I drove Rip from his house, and it's for me to bring him back again.

MEENIE. (*Still arranging the supper table.*) But, Mother— (*She pauses, with embarrassment.*) If he hears your voice behind him, he will only run away the faster.

GRETCHEN. Well, I can't help it; I can't rest under cover, while he is out in the storm. I shall feel better when I'm outside sharing the storm with him. Sit down, and take your suppers. I'll take my cloak along with me. (*Exit.* MEENIE *has seated herself by the window.* HENDRICK *carries stool to the center of the stage, in front of the table.*)

HENDRICK. Meenie! Meenie!

MEENIE. Eh?

(HENDRICK *beckons to her. She runs to him. He stops her suddenly, then puts the stool down with great deliberation, and sits on it, while* MEENIE *kneels beside him.*)

HENDRICK. (*In a very solemn tone.*) I hope your father ain't gone to the mountains tonight, Meenie!

MEENIE. (*In distress.*) Oh, dear! He will die of the cold there.

HENDRICK. (*Suddenly.*) Sh! (MEENIE *starts.*) It ain't for that. (*Mysteriously.*) I've just heard old Clausen, over at father's, saying, that on this very night, every twenty years, the ghosts—

MEENIE. (*Catching his wrist.*) The what?

HENDRICK. (*In an awed tone.*) The ghosts of Hendrick Hudson, and his pirate crew, visit the Catskills above here.

(*The two children look around, frightened.*)

MEENIE. Oh, dear! Did he say so?

HENDRICK. Sh! (*Again they look around, frightened.*) Yes; and the spirits have been seen there smoking, drinking, and playing at tenpins.

MEENIE. Oh, how dreadful!

HENDRICK. Sh!

(*He goes cautiously to the chimney, and looks up, while* MEENIE *looks under the table; then he returns to the stool, speaking as he comes.*)

Yes; and every time that Hendrick Hudson lights his pipe there's a flash of lightning.

(*Lightning and* MEENIE *gives a gasp of fear.*)

And when he rolls the balls along, there is a peal of thunder.

(*Loud rumbles of thunder.* MEENIE *screams and throws herself into* HENDRICK's *arms.*)

Don't be frightened, Meenie; I'm here. (*In a frightened tone, but with a manly effort to be courageous.*)

(*Re-enter* GRETCHEN *with her cloak.*)

GRETCHEN. Here, stop that!

(*The children separate quickly.* HENDRICK *looks up at the ceiling and whistles, with an attempt at unconsciousness, and* MEENIE *assumes an innocent and unconcerned expression.*)

Now, don't you be filling that child's head with nonsense,
but remain quietly here until I return. Hush, what noise
is that? There is someone outside the window.

(*She steps behind the clothes-horse.* RIP *appears at the
window, which he opens, and leans against the frame.*)

RIP. Meenie!

MEENIE *and* HENDRICK. (*Trying to make him perceive*
GRETCHEN, *by a gesture in her direction.*) Sh!

(RIP *turns, and looks around outside to see what they
mean, then, discovering nothing, drops his hat in at the
window, and calls again, cautiously.*)

RIP. Meenie!

MEENIE *and* HENDRICK. (*With the same warning gesture.*)
Sh!

(GRETCHEN *shakes her fist at the children, who assume an
air of innocence.*)

RIP. What's the matter? Meenie, has the wildcat come home?
(RIP *reaches in after his hat.* GRETCHEN *catches him by his
hair, and holds his head down.*) Och, my darlin', don't
do that, eh!

HENDRICK *and* MEENIE. (*Who run towards* GRETCHEN.) Don't,
Mother! Don't, Mother! Don't!

RIP. (*Imitating their tone.*) Don't, Mother, don't! Don't you
hear the children? (*Getting angry.*) Let go my head, won't
you?

GRETCHEN. No; not a hair.

RIP. (*Bantering.*) Hold on to it then, what do I care?

HENDRICK *and* MEENIE. (*Catching* GRETCHEN's *dress.*) Don't,
Mother! Don't, Mother! Don't!

(GRETCHEN *lets go of* RIP, *and turns upon them. They
escape, and disappear through the door to the left.*)

RIP. (*Getting in through the window, and coming forward,
apparently drunk, but jolly; and his resentment for the
treatment he has just received is half humorous.*) For what
you do dat, hey? You must want a bald-headed husband,
I reckon!

(GRETCHEN *picks up chair, and bangs it down;* RIP *imitates
her with the stool. She sits down angrily, and slaps the
table.* RIP *throws down his felt hat with a great show of
violence, and it makes no noise; then seats himself on the
stool.*)

GRETCHEN. Now, then!

RIP. Now, den; I don't like it den, neider. (*When* RIP *is drunk,
his dialect grows more pronounced.*)

GRETCHEN. Who did you call a wildcat?

RIP. (*With a sudden little tipsy laugh, and confused.*) A
wildcat—dat's when I come in at the window?

GRETCHEN. Yes; that's when you came in the window.

RIP. (*Rising, and with a tone of finality.*) Yes; that's the time
I said it.

GRETCHEN. Yes; and that's the time I heard it.

RIP. (*With drunken assurance.*) That's all right; I was afraid
you wouldn't hear it.

GRETCHEN. Now who did you mean by that wildcat?

RIP. (*Confused.*) Who did I mean? Now, let me see.

GRETCHEN. Yes; who did you mean?

RIP. How do I know who-oo I mean? (*With a sudden inspiration.*) Maybe it's the dog Schneider, I call that.

GRETCHEN. (*Incredulously.*) The dog Schneider; that's not
likely.

RIP. (*Argumentatively.*) Of course it is likely; he's my dog.
I'll call him a wildcat much as I please. (*Conclusively. He
sits down in the chair on which his clothes are warming,
in front of the fire.*)

GRETCHEN. And then, there's your disgraceful conduct this
morning. What have you got to say to that?

RIP. How do I know what I got to say to that, when I don't
know what I do-a, do-a? (*Hiccoughs.*)

GRETCHEN. Don't know what you do-a-oo! Hugging and kissing the girls before my face; you thought I wouldn't see
you.

RIP. (*Boldly.*) I knowed you would—I knowed you would;
because, because—(*Losing the thread of his discourse.*)
Oh-h, don' you bodder me. (*He turns and leans his head
against the back of the chair.*)

GRETCHEN. You knew I was there?

RIP. (*Laughing.*) I thought I saw you.

GRETCHEN. I saw you myself, dancing with the girl.

RIP. You saw the girl dancin' mit me.

(GRETCHEN *remembers* RIP's *clothes, and goes over to see
if he is wet, and pushes him towards the center of the
stage.* RIP *mistakes her intention.*)

You want to pull some more hair out of my head?

GRETCHEN. Why, the monster! He isn't wet a bit! He's as dry
as if he'd been aired!

RIP. Of course I'm dry. (*Laughing.*) I'm always dry—always dry.

GRETCHEN. (*Examines game-bag, and pulls out a flask, which she holds under* RIP's *nose.*) Why, what's here? Why, it's a bottle—a bottle!

RIP. (*Leaning against the table.*) Yes; it's a bottle. (*Laughs.*) You think I don't know a bottle when I see it?

GRETCHEN. That's pretty game for your game-bag, ain't it?

RIP. (*Assuming an innocent air.*) Somebody must have put it there.

GRETCHEN. (*Putting the flask in her pocket.*) Then, you don't get it again.

RIP. (*With a show of anger.*) Now mind, If I don't get it again—well—all there is about it—(*Breaking down.*) I don't want it. I have had enough. (*With a droll air of conviction.*)

GRETCHEN. I'm glad you know when you've had enough.

RIP. (*Still leaning against the table.*) That's the way mit me. I'm glad I know when I got enough—(*Laughs.*) An' I'm glad when I've got enough, too. Give me the bottle; I want to put it in the game-bag.

GRETCHEN. For what?

RIP. (*Lounging off the table, and coming forward and leaning his arms on* GRETCHEN's *shoulders.*) So that I can't drink it. Here's the whole business—(*He slides his hand down to* GRETCHEN's *pocket and tries to find the bottle while he talks to her.*) Here's the whole business about it. What is the use of anybody—well—wash the use of anybody, anyhow—well—oh(*Missing the pocket.*) What you talkin' 'bout. (*Suddenly his hand slips in her pocket, and he begins to pull the bottle out, with great satisfaction.*) Now, now I can tell you all 'bout it.

GRETCHEN. (*Discovering his tactics, and pushing him away.*) Pshaw!

RIP. If you don't give me the bottle, I just break up everything in the house.

GRETCHEN. If you dare!

RIP. If I dare! Haven't I done it two or three times before? I just throw everything right out of the window.

(RIP *throws the plates and cups on the floor and overturns a chair, and seats himself on the table.* GRETCHEN *picks them up again.*)

GRETCHEN. Don't Rip; don't do that! Now stop, Rip, stop! (GRETCHEN *bangs down a chair by the table and seats herself.*) Now, then, perhaps you will be kind enough to tell where you've been for the last two days. Where have you been? Do you hear?

RIP. Where I've been? Well, it's not my bottle, anyhow. I borrowed that bottle from another feller. You want to know where I been?

GRETCHEN. Yes; and I will know.

RIP. (*Good-humoredly.*) Let's see. Last night I stopped out all night.

GRETCHEN. But why?

RIP. Why? You mean the reason of it?

GRETCHEN. Yes, the reason.

RIP. (*Inconsequently.*) The reason is why. Don't bother me.

GRETCHEN. (*Emphasizing each word with a bang on the table.*) Why—did—you—stop—out—all—night?

RIP. (*Imitating her tone.*) Because—I—want—to—get—up—early—in—the—morning. (*Hiccough.*) Come don't get so mad mit a feller. Why, I've been fillin' my game-bag mit game.

(*Rip gets down off the table, and* GRETCHEN *comes towards him and feels his game-bag.*)

GRETCHEN. Your game-bag is full of game, isn't it?

RIP. (*Taking her hand and holding it away from her pocket.*) That? Why, that wouldn't hold it. (*Finding his way into* GRETCHEN's *pocket.*) Now I can tell you all about it. You know last night I stopped out all night—

GRETCHEN. Yes; and let me catch you again.

(*He is pulling the bottle out, when* GRETCHEN *catches him, and slaps his hand.*)

You paltry thief!

RIP. Oh, you ain't got no confidence in me. Now what do you think was the first thing I saw in the morning? (*Dragging a chair to the front of the stage.*)

GRETCHEN. I don't know. What?

RIP. (*Seating himself.*) A rabbit.

GRETCHEN. (*Pleased.*) I like a rabbit. I like it in a stew.

RIP. (*Looking at her, amused.*) I guess you like everything in a stew—everything what's a rabbit I mean. Well, there was a rabbit a-feedin' mit the grass; you know they always come out early in der mornin' and feed mit the grass?

GRETCHEN. Never mind the grass. Go on.

RIP. Don't get so patient; you wait till you get the rabbit. (*Humorously.*) Well, I crawl up—

GRETCHEN. Yes, yes!

RIP. (*Becoming interested in his own powers of invention.*) An' his little tail was a-stickin' up so—(*With a gesture of his forefinger.*)

GRETCHEN. (*Impatiently.*) Never mind his tail. Go on.

RIP. (*Remonstrating at her interruption.*) The more fatter the rabbit, the more whiter is his tail—

GRETCHEN. Well, well, go on.

RIP. (*Taking aim.*) Well, I haul up—

GRETCHEN. Yes, yes!

RIP. And his ears was a-stickin' up so—(*Making the two ears with his two forefingers.*)

GRETCHEN. Never mind his ears. Go on.

RIP. I pull the trigger.

GRETCHEN. (*Eagerly.*) Bang went the gun, and—

RIP. (*Seriously.*) And the rabbit run away.

GRETCHEN. (*Angrily.*) And so you shot nothing?

RIP. How will I shot him when he run away? (*He laughs at her disappointment.*) There, don't get so mad mit a feller. Now I'm going to tell you what I did shot; that's what I didn't shot. You know that old forty-acre field of ours?

GRETCHEN. (*Scornfully.*) Ours! Ours, did you say?

RIP. (*Shamefacedly.*) You know the one I mean well enough. It used to be ours.

GRETCHEN. (*Regretfully.*) Yes; it used, indeed!

RIP. It ain't ours now, is it?

GRETCHEN. (*Sighing.*) No, indeed, it is not.

RIP. No? Den I won't bodder about it. Better let somebody bodder about that field what belongs to it. Well, in that field there's a pond; and what do you think I see in that pond?

GRETCHEN. I don't know. Ducks?

RIP. Ducks! More an' a thousand.

GRETCHEN. (*Walking to where broomstick is.*) More than a thousand ducks?

RIP. I haul up again—

GRETCHEN. (*Picking up broomstick.*) Yes, and so will I. And if you miss fire this time—(*She holds it threateningly over* RIP's *shoulder.*)

RIP. (*Looking at it askance out of the corner of his eye, then putting up his hand and pushing it aside.*) You will scare the ducks mit that. Well, I take better aim this time as I did before. I pull the trigger, and—bang!

GRETCHEN. How many down?

RIP. (*Indifferently.*) One.

GRETCHEN. (*Indignantly.*) What! only one duck out of a thousand?

RIP. Who said one duck?

GRETCHEN. You did!

RIP. (*Getting up and leaning on the back of the chair.*) I didn't say anything of the kind.

GRETCHEN. You said "one."

RIP. Ah! *One.* But I shot more as one duck.

GRETCHEN. Did you?

RIP. (*Crosses over, and sits on the low stool, laughing silently.*) I shot our old bull.

(GRETCHEN *flings down the broomstick, and throws herself into the chair at the right of the table, in dumb rage.*)

I didn't kill him. I just sting him, you know. Well, then the bull come right after me; and I come right away from him. O, Gretchen, how you would laugh if you could see that— (*With a vain appeal to her sense of humor.*) the bull was a-comin', and I was a-goin'. Well, he chased me across the field. I tried to climb over the fence so fast what I could,—(*Doubles up with his silent laugh.*) an' the bull come up an' save me the trouble of that. Well, then, I rolled over on the other side.

GRETCHEN. (*With disgust.*) And then you went fast asleep for the rest of the day.

RIP. That's a fact. That's a fact.

GRETCHEN. (*Bursting into tears, and burying her head in her arms on the table.*) O, Rip, you'll break my heart! You will.

RIP. Now she's gone crying mit herself! Don't cry, Gretchen, don't cry. My d-a-r-l-i-n', don't cry.

GRETCHEN. (*Angrily.*) I will cry.

RIP. Cry 'way as much as you like. What do I care? All the better soon as a woman gets cryin'; den all the danger's over. (RIP *goes to* GRETCHEN, *leans over, and puts his arm around her.*) Gretchen, don't cry; my angel, don't. (*He succeeds in getting his hand into her pocket, and steals the bottle.*) Don't cry, my daarlin'. (*Humorously.*)

Gretchen won't you give me a little drop out of that bottle what you took away from me? (*He sits on the table, just behind her, and takes a drink from the bottle.*)

GRETCHEN. Here's a man drunk, and asking for more.

RIP. I wasn't. I swore off. (*Coaxingly.*) You give me a little drop an' I won't count it.

GRETCHEN. (*Sharply.*) No!

RIP. (*Drinking again.*) Well, den, here's your good health, an' your family's, and may they live long and prosper! (*Puts bottle in his bag.*)

GRETCHEN. You unfeeling brute. Your wife's starving. And, Rip, your child's in rags.

RIP. (*Holding up his coat, and heaving a sigh of resignation.*) Well, I'm the same way; you know dat.

GRETCHEN. (*Sitting up, and looking appealingly at* RIP.) Oh, Rip, if you would only treat me kindly!

RIP. (*Putting his arms around her.*) Well, den, I will. I'm going to treat you kind. I'll treat you kind.

GRETCHEN. Why, it would add ten years to my life.

RIP. (*Over her shoulder, and after a pause.*) That's a great inducement; it is, my darlin'. I know I treat you too bad, an' you deserve to be a widow.

GRETCHEN. (*Getting up, and putting her arms on* RIP's *shoulder.*) Oh, Rip, if you would only reform!

RIP. Well, den, I will. I won't touch another drop so long as I live.

GRETCHEN. Can I trust you?

RIP. You mustn't suspect me.

GRETCHEN. (*Embracing him.*) There, then, I will trust you. (*She takes the candle and goes to fetch the children.*) Here, Hendrick, Meenie? Children, where are you? (*Exit through the door on the left.*)

RIP. (*Seats himself in the chair to the right of the table, and takes out flask.*) Well, it's too bad; but it's all a woman's fault anyway. When a man gets drinkin' and that, they ought to let him alone. So soon as they scold him, he goes off like a sky-rocket.

(*Re-enter* GRETCHEN *and the children.*)

GRETCHEN. (*Seeing the flask in* RIP's *hand.*) I thought as much.

RIP. (*Unconscious of her presence.*) How I did smooth her down! I must drink her good health. Gretchen, here's your good health. (*About to drink.*)

GRETCHEN. (*Snatching the bottle, and using it to gesticulate with.*) Oh, you paltry thief!

RIP. (*Concerned for the schnapps.*) What you doin'? You'll spill the licker out of the bottle. (*He puts in the cork.*)

GRETCHEN. (*Examining the flask.*) Why, the monster, he's emptied the bottle!

RIP. That's a fac'. That's a fac'.

GRETCHEN. (*Throwing down the flask.*) Then that is the last drop you drink under my roof!

RIP. What! What!

(MEENIE *approaches her father on tiptoe, and kneels beside him.*)

GRETCHEN. Out, you drunkard! Out, you sot! You disgrace to your wife and to your child! This house is mine.

RIP. (*Dazed, and a little sobered.*) Yours! Yours!

GRETCHEN. (*Raising her voice above the storm, which seems to rage more fiercely outside.*) Yes, mine, mine! Had it been yours to sell, it would have gone along with the rest of your land. Out then, I say— (*Pushing open the door.*) for you have no longer any share in me or mine. (*A peal of thunder.*)

MEENIE. (*Running over, and kneeling by* GRETCHEN.) Oh, mother, hark at the storm!

GRETCHEN. (*Pushing her aside.*) Begone, man, can't you speak? Are you struck dumb? You sleep no more under my roof.

RIP. (*Who has not moved, even his arm remaining outstretched, as it was when* MEENIE *slipped from his side, murmurs in a bewildered, incredulous way.*) Why, Gretchen, are you goin' to turn me out like a dog? (GRETCHEN *points to the door.* RIP *rises and leans against the table with a groan. His conscience speaks.*) Well, maybe you are right. (*His voice breaks, and with a despairing gesture.*) I have got no home. I will go. But mind, Gretchen, after what you say to me tonight, I can never darken your door again—never— (*Going towards the door.*) I will go.

HENDRICK. (*Running up to* RIP.) Not into the storm, Rip. Hark, how it thunders!

RIP. (*Putting his arm around him.*) Yah, my boy; but not as bad to me as the storm in my home. I will go. (*At the door by this time.*)

MEENIE. (*Catching* RIP's *coat.*) No, Father, don't go!

RIP. (*Bending over her tenderly, and holding her close to him.*) My child! Bless you, my child, bless you!

(MEENIE *faints.* RIP *gives a sobbing sigh.*)

GRETCHEN. (*Relenting.*) No, Rip—I—

RIP. (*Waving her off.*) No, you have drive me from your house. You have opened the door for me to go. You may never open it for me to come back. (*Leaning against the doorpost, overcome by his emotion. His eyes rest on* MEENIE, *who lies at his feet.*) You say I have no share in this house. (*Points to* MEENIE *in profound despair.*) Well, see, then, I wipe the disgrace from your door. (*He staggers out into the storm.*)

GRETCHEN. No, Rip! Husband, come back! (GRETCHEN *faints, and the curtain falls.*)

ACT III

A steep and rocky clove in the Catskill Mountains, down which rushes a torrent, swollen by the storm. Overhead, the hemlocks stretch their melancholy boughs. It is night.

RIP *enters, almost at a run, with his head down, and his coat-collar turned up, beating his way against the storm. With the hunter's instinct, he protects the priming of his gun with the skirt of his jacket. Having reached a comparatively level spot, he pauses for breath, and turns to see what has become of his dog.*

RIP. (*Whistling to the dog.*) Schneider! Schneider! What's the matter with Schneider? Something must have scared that dog. There he goes head over heels down the hill. Well, here I am again—another night in the mountains! Heigho! these old trees begin to know me, I reckon. (*Taking off his hat.*) How are you, old fellows? Well, I like the trees; they keep me from the wind and the rain, and they never blow me up; and when I lay me down on the broad of my back, they seem to bow their heads to me, an' say: "Go to sleep, Rip, go to sleep." (*Lightning.*) My, what a flash that was! Old Hendrick Hudson's lighting his pipe in the mountains tonight; now, we'll hear him roll the big balls along. (*Thunder.* RIP *looks back over the path he has come and whistles again for his dog.*) Well, I—no—Schneider! No; whatever it is, it's on two legs. Why, what a funny thing is that a comin' up the hill? I thought nobody but me ever come nigh this place.

(*Enter a strange dwarfish figure, clad all in gray like a Dutch seaman of the seventeenth century, in short-skirted doublet, hose and high-crowned hat drawn over his eyes. From beneath the latter his long gray beard streams down till it almost touches the ground. He carries a keg on his shoulder. He advances slowly towards* RIP, *and, by his gesture, begs* RIP *to set the keg down for him.* RIP *does so, and the dwarf seats himself upon it.*)

(*With good-humored sarcasm.*) Sit down, and make yourself comfortable. (*A long pause and silence.*) What? What's the matter? Ain't ye goin' to speak to a feller? I don't want to speak to you, then. Who you think you was, that I want to speak to you, any more than you want to speak to me; you hear what I say?
(RIP *pokes the dwarf in the ribs, who turns, and looks up.* RIP *retreats hastily.*)
Donner an' Blitzen! What for a man is das? I have been walking over these mountains ever since I was a boy, an' I never saw a queer looking codger like that before. He must be an old sea-snake, I reckon.
(*The dwarf approaches* RIP, *and motions* RIP *to help him up the mountain with the keg.*)
Well, why don't you say so, den? You mean you would like me to help you up with that keg?
(*The dwarf nods in the affirmative.*)
Well, sir, I don't do it.
(*The dwarf holds up his hands in supplication.*)
No, there's no good you speakin' like that. I never seed you before, did I?
(*The dwarf shakes his head,* RIP, *with great decision, walking away, and leaning against a tree.*)

I don't want to see you again, needer. What have you got
in that keg, schnapps?
(*The dwarf nods.*)
I don't believe you.
(*The dwarf nods more affirmatively.*)
Is it good schnapps?
(*The dwarf again insists.*)
Well, I'll help you. Go 'long; pick up my gun, there, and
I follow you mit that keg on my shoulder. I'll follow you,
old broadchops.
(*As* RIP *shoulders the keg, a furious blast whirls up the
valley, and seems to carry him and his demon companion
before it. The rain that follows blots out the landscape.
For a few moments, all is darkness. Gradually, the topmost
peak of the Catskill Mountains becomes visible, far above
the storm. Stretching below, the country lies spread out
like a map. A feeble and watery moonlight shows us a
weird group, gathered upon the peak—Hendrick Hudson,
and his ghostly crew. In the foreground, one of them poises
a ball, about to bowl it, while the others lean forward in
attitudes of watchful expectancy. Silently he pitches it;
and, after a momentary pause, a long and rumbling peal
of thunder reverberates among the valleys below. At this
moment, the demon, carrying* RIP's *gun, appears over the
crest of the peak in the background, and* RIP *toils after
with the keg on his shoulder. Arrived at the summit, he
drops the keg on his knee, and gasps for breath.*)
(*Glancing out over the landscape.*) I say, old gentleman,
I never was so high up in the mountains before. Look
down into the valley there; it seems more as a mile. I—
(*Turning to speak to his companion, and perceiving another of the crew.*) You're another feller!
(*The second demon nods assent.*)
You're that other chap's brother?
(*The demon again assents.* RIP *carries the keg a little
further, and comes face to face with a third.*)
You're another brother?
(*The third demon nods assent.* RIP *takes another step, and
perceives* HENDRICK HUDSON *in the center, surrounded by
many demons.*)
You're his old gran'father?
(HUDSON *nods.* RIP *puts down the keg in perplexity, not
untinged with alarm.*)

Donner and Blitzen! here's the whole family; I'm a dead man to a certainty.
(*The demons extend their arms to* HUDSON, *as if inquiring what they should do. He points to* RIP, *they do the same.*)
My, my, I suppose they're speakin' about me! (*Looking at his gun, which the first demon has deposited on the ground, and which lies within his reach.*) No good shootin' at 'em; family's to big for one gun.
(HENDRICK HUDSON *advances, and seats himself on the keg facing* RIP. *The demons slowly surround the two.*)
(*Looking about him with growing apprehension.*) My, my, I don't like that kind of people at all! No, sir! I don't like any sech kind. I like that old gran'father worse than any of them. (*With a sheepish attempt to be genial, and appear at his ease.*) How you was, old gentleman? I didn't mean to intrude on you, did I?
(HUDSON *shakes his head.*) What? (*No reply.*) I'll tell you how it was; I met one of your gran'children, I don't know which is the one— (*Glancing around.*) They're all so much alike. Well— (*Embarrassed and looking at one demon.*) That's the same kind of a one. Anyway, this one, he axed me to help him up the mountain mit dat keg. Well, he was an old feller, an' I thought I would help him. (*Pauses, troubled by their silence.*) Was I right to help him? (HUDSON *nods.*) I say, was I right to help him?
(HUDSON *nods again.*)
If he was here, he would yust tell you the same thing any way, because— (*Suddenly perceiving the demon he had met below.*) Why, dat's the one, ain't it?
(*The demon nods.*)
Yes; dat is the one, dat's the same kind of a one dat I met. Was I right to come? (HUDSON *nods approval.*) I didn't want to come here, anyhow; no, sir, I didn't want to come to any such kind of a place. (*After a pause, seeing that no one has anything to say.*) I guess I better go away from it.
(RIP *picks up his gun, and is about to return by the way he came; but the demons raise their hands threateningly, and stop him. He puts his gun down again.*)
I didn't want to come here, anyhow— (*Grumbling to himself, then pulling himself together with an effort, and facing* HUDSON.) Well, old gentleman, if you mean to do me any harm, just speak it right out— (*Then with a little*

laugh.) Oh! I will die game—(*Glancing around for a means of escape, and half to himself.*) If I can't run away.

(HUDSON *extends a cup to* RIP, *as if inviting him to drink.*)

(*Doubtfully.*) You want me to drink mit you?

(HUDSON *nods.* RIP *approaches him cautiously, unable to resist the temptation of a drink.*)

Well, I swore off drinkin'; but as this is the first time I see you, I won't count this one—

(*He takes the cup.* HUDSON *holds up another cup.* RIP *is reassured, and his old geniality returns.*)

You drink mit me? We drink mit one another?

(HUDSON *nods affirmatively.* RIP *feels at home under these familiar circumstances, and becomes familiar and colloquial again.*)

What's the matter mit you, old gentleman, anyhow? You go and make so (*Imitating the demon.*) mit your head every time; was you deaf?

(HUDSON *shakes his head.*)

Oh, nein. (*Laughing at his error.*) If you was deaf, you wouldn't hear what I was sayin'. Was you dumb?

(HUDSON *nods yes.*)

So? You was dumb?

(HUDSON *nods again.*)

Has all of your family the same complaint?

(HUDSON *nods.*)

All the boys dumb, hey? All the boys dumb.

(*All the demons nod. Then, suddenly, as if struck with an idea.*)

Have you got any girls?

(HUDSON *shakes his head.*)

Don't you? Such a big family, and all boys?

(HUDSON *nods.*)

(*With profound regret.*) That's a pity; my, that's a pity. Oh, my, if you had some dumb girls, what wives they would make— (*Brightening up.*) Well, old gentleman, here's your good health, and all your family—(*Turning, and waving to them.*)—may they live long and prosper.

(RIP *drinks. As he does so, all the demons lean forward, watching the effect of the liquor.* RIP *puts his hand to his head. The empty cup falls to the ground.*)

(*In an awed and ecstatic voice.*) What for licker is that! (*As he turns, half reeling, he sees* HUDSON *holding out to him another cup. He snatches it with almost frantic eager-*

ness.) Give me another one! (*He empties it at a draught.
A long pause follows during which the effect of the liquor
upon* RIP *becomes apparent; the light in his eyes fades,
his exhilaration dies out, and he loses his grasp on the
reality of his surroundings. Finally, he clasps his head with
both hands, and cries in a muffled, terrified voice.*) Oh,
my, my head was so light, and now, it's heavy as lead!
(*He reels, and falls heavily to the ground. A long pause.
The demons begin to disappear.* RIP *becomes dimly conscious of this, and raises himself on his elbow.*)
Are you goin' to leave me, boys? Are you goin' to leave
me all alone? Don't leave me; don't go away. (*With a last
effort.*) I will drink your good health, and your family's—
(*He falls back heavily, asleep*)

CURTAIN

ACT IV

Scene 1

*As the curtain rises, the same high peaks of the Catskills,
and the far-stretching valley below, are disclosed in the gray
light of dawn.*

RIP *is still lying on the ground, as in the last act, but he is
no longer the* RIP *we knew. His hair and beard are long and
white, bleached by the storms that have rolled over his head
during the twenty years he has been asleep.*

*As he stirs and slowly rises to a half-sitting posture, we see
that his former picturesque rags have become so dilapidated
that it is a matter of marvel how they hold together. They
have lost all traces of color, and have assumed the neutral
tints of the moss and lichens that cover the rocks. His
voice, when he first speaks, betrays even more distinctly
than his appearance the lapse of time. Instead of the full
round tones of manhood, he speaks in the high treble of
feeble old age. His very hands have grown old and weather-
beaten.*

RIP. (*Staring vacantly around.*) I wonder where I was. On
  top of the Catskill Mountains as sure as a gun! Won't my
  wife give it to me for stopping out all night? I must get

up and get home with myself. (*Trying to rise.*) Oh, I feel
very bad! Vat is the matter with my elbow? (*In trying to
rub it, the other one gives him such a twinge that he cries
out.*) Oh! the other elbow is more badder than the other
one. I must have cotched the rheumatix a-sleepin' mit the
wet grass. (*He rises with great difficulty.*) Och! I never
had such rheumatix like that. (*He feels himself all over,
and then stands for a moment pondering, and bewildered
by a strange memory.*) I wasn't sleeping all the time,
needer. I know I met a queer kind of a man, and we got
drinkin' and I guess I got pretty drunk. Well, I must pick
up my gun, and get home mit myself. (*After several painful attempts, he succeeds in picking up his gun, which
drops all to pieces as he lifts it.* RIP *looks at it in amazement.*) My gun must have cotched the rheumatix too.
Now, that's too bad. Them fellows have gone and stole my
good gun, and leave me this rusty old barrel. (RIP *begins
slowly to climb over the peak towards the path by which
he had ascended, his memory seeming to act automatically.
When he reaches the highest point, where he can look out
over the valley, he stops in surprise.*) Why, is that the
village of Falling Waters that I see? Why, the place is
more than twice the size it was last night. I—(*He sinks
down.*) I don't know whether I am dreaming, or sleeping,
or waking. (*Then pulling himself together with a great
effort, and calling up the image of his wife to act as whip
and spur to his waning powers, with humorous conviction,
as he gets up painfully again.*) I go home to my wife.
She'll let me know whether I'm asleep or awake or not.
(*Almost unable to proceed.*) I don't know if I will ever
get home, my k-nees are so stiff. My backbone, it's broke
already. (*As the curtain falls,* RIP *stands leaning on the
barrel of his gun as on a staff, with one hand raised, looking out over the valley.*)

Scene 2

A comfortable-looking room in DERRICK'S *house. As the
curtain rises,* MEENIE *and* GRETCHEN *enter.* MEENIE *is a tall
young woman of twenty-six, and* GRETCHEN *is a matronly
figure with white hair. They are well dressed, and have every
appearance of physical and material prosperity.*

GRETCHEN. I am sent to you by your father, Meenie.

MEENIE. Oh, don't call him so; he is not my father! He is your husband, Mother; but I owe him no love. And his cruel treatment of you—

GRETCHEN. Hush, child! Oh, if he heard you, he would make me pay for every disrespectful word you utter.

MEENIE. Yes; he would beat you, starve and degrade you. You are not his wife, Mother, but his menial.

GRETCHEN. My spirit is broken, Meenie. I cannot resent it. Nay, I deserve it; for as Derrick now treats me, so I treated your poor father when he was alive.

MEENIE. You, Mother? You, so gentle? You, who are weakness and patience itself?

GRETCHEN. Yes; because for fifteen years I have been Derrick's wife. But it was my temper, my cruelty, that drove your father from our home twenty years ago. You were too young then to remember him.

MEENIE. No, Mother, I recollect dear Father taking me on his knee, and saying to Hendrick that I should be his wife; and I promised I would.

GRETCHEN. Poor Rip! Poor, good-natured, kind creature that he was! How gently he bore with me; and I drove him like a dog from his home. I hunted him into the mountains, where he perished of hunger or cold, or a prey to some wild beast.

MEENIE. Don't cry, Mother!

(*Enter* DERRICK, *now grown old and bent over his cane, and infinitely more disagreeable than before. He, too, has thriven, and is dressed in a handsome full suit of black silk.*)

DERRICK. Snivelling again, eh? Teaching that girl of yours to be an obstinate hypocrite?

MEENIE. Oh, sir, she—

DERRICK. Hold your tongue, Miss. Speak when you're spoken to. I'll have you both to understand that there's but one master here. Well, mistress, have you told her my wishes, and is she prepared to obey them?

GRETCHEN. Indeed, sir, I was trying to—

DERRICK. Beating about the bush, prevaricating, and sneaking, as you usually do.

MEENIE. If you have made her your slave, you must expect
her to cringe.

DERRICK. (*Approaching her threateningly.*) What's that?

GRETCHEN. Meenie! Meenie! For Heaven's sake, do not anger
him!

DERRICK. (*Raising his cane.*) She had better not.

MEENIE. (*Defiantly.*) Take care how you raise your hand to
me, for I'll keep a strict account of it. And when Hendrick
comes back from sea, he'll make you smart for it, I promise
you.

DERRICK. Is the girl mad?

MEENIE. He thrashed your nephew once for being insolent to
me. Go and ask him how Hendrick pays my debts; and
then when you speak to me you'll mind your stops.

DERRICK. (*To* GRETCHEN.) Oh, you shall pay for this!

GRETCHEN. No, Derrick, indeed, indeed I have not urged her
to this! O, Meenie, do not speak so to him; for my sake
forbear!

MEENIE. For your sake, yes, dear Mother. I forgot that he
could revenge himself on you.

DERRICK. As for your sailor lover, Hendrick Vedder, I've got
news of him at last. His ship, the *Mayflower*, was lost three
years ago, off Cape Horn.

MEENIE. No, no. Not lost?

DERRICK. If you doubt it, there's the *Shipping Gazette*, in on
my office table. You can satisfy yourself that your sailor
bully has gone to the bottom.

GRETCHEN. Oh, sir, do not convey the news to her so cruelly.

DERRICK. That's it. Because I don't sneak and trick and lie
about it, I'm cruel. The man's dead, has been dead and
gone these two years or more. The time of mourning is
over. Am I going to be nice about it this time of day?

MEENIE. Then all my hope is gone, gone forever!

DERRICK. So much the better for you. Hendrick's whole
fortune was invested in that ship. So there's an end of him
and your expectations. Now you are free, and a beggar.
My nephew has a fancy for you. He will have a share of
my business now, and my money when—when I die.

GRETCHEN. Do not ask her to decide now!

DERRICK. Why not? If she expects to make a better bargain
by holding off, she's mistaken.

GRETCHEN. How can you expect her to think of a husband
at this moment?

DERRICK. Don't I tell you the other one is dead these two years?

GRETCHEN. (*Leading* MEENIE *away.*) Come, my child. Leave her to me, sir; I will try and persuade her.

DERRICK. Take care that you do; for if she don't consent to accept my offer, she shall pack bag and baggage out of this house. Aye, this very day! Not a penny, not a stitch of clothes but what she has on her back, shall she have! Oh, I've had to deal with obstinate women before now, and I've taken them down before I've done with them. You know who I mean? Do you know who I mean? Stop. *Answer me! Do you know who I mean?*

GRETCHEN. (*Submissively.*) Yes, sir.

DERRICK. Then why didn't you say so before? Sulky, I suppose. There, you may be off.

(*Exeunt.*)

Scene 3

The village of Falling Waters, which has grown to be a smart and flourishing town, but whose chief features remain unchanged.

To the left, as of yore, is the inn, bearing scarcely any mark of the lapse of time, save that the sign of George III has been replaced by a portrait of George Washington. To the right, where RIP's *cottage used to stand, nothing remains, however, but the blackened and crumbling ruins of a chimney. A table and chairs stand in front of the inn porch.*

Into this familiar scene RIP *makes his entrance, but not as before, in glee, with children clinging about him. Faint, weak, and weary, he stumbles along, followed by a jeering, hooting mob of villagers; while the children hide from him in fear, behind their elders. His eyes look dazed and uncomprehending, and he catches at the back of a chair as if in need of physical as well as mental support.*

KÄTCHEN. (*As* RIP *enters.*) Why, what queer looking creature is this, that all the boys are playing—

SETH. Why, he looks as though he's been dead for fifty years, and dug up again!

RIP. My friends, *Kannst du Deutsch sprechen?*[1]

FIRST VILLAGER. I say, old fellow, you ain't seen anything of an old butter-tub with no kiver[2] on, no place about here, have you?

RIP. (*Bewildered, but with simplicity.*) What is that? I don't know who that is.

SECOND VILLAGER. I say, old man, who's your barber?

(*The crowd laughs, and goes off repeating, "Who's your barber?" Some of the children remain to stare at* RIP; *but when he holds out his hand to them, they, too, run off frightened.*)

RIP. Who's my barber; what dey mean by dat? (*Noticing his beard.*) Why is that on me? I didn't see that before. My beard and hair is so long and white. Gretchen won't know me with that, when she gets me home. (*Looking towards the cottage.*) Why, the home's gone away! (RIP *becomes more and more puzzled, like a man in a dream who sees unfamiliar things amid familiar surroundings, and cannot make out what has happened; and as in a dream a man preserves his individuality, so* RIP *stumbles along through his bewilderment, exhibiting flashes of his old humor, wit, and native shrewdness. But with all this he never laughs.*)

SETH. I say, old man, hadn't you better go home and get shaved?

RIP. (*Looking about for the voice.*) What?

SETH. Here, this way. Hadn't you better go home and get shaved?

RIP. My wife will shave me when she gets me home. Is this the village of "Falling Waters" where we was?

SETH. Yes.

RIP. (*Still more puzzled, not knowing his face.*) Do you live here?

SETH. Well, rather. I was born here.

RIP. (*Reflectively.*) Then you live here?

SETH. Well, rather; of course I do.

RIP. (*Feeling that he has hold of something certain.*) Do you know where I live?

SETH. No; but I should say you belong to Noah's Ark.

RIP. (*Putting his hand to his ear.*) That I belong mit vas?

SETH. Noah's Ark.

[1] "Do you speak German?"
[2] Cover.

RIP. (*Very much hurt.*) Why will you say such thing like that? (*Then, with a flash of humor, and drawing his beard slowly through his fingers.*) Well, look like it, don't I? (*Beginning all over again to feel for his clue.*) My friend, did you never hear of a man in this place whose name was Rip Van Winkle?

SETH. Rip Van Winkle, the laziest, drunken vagabond in the country?

RIP. (*Somewhat taken aback by this description, but obliged to concur in it.*) Yah, that is the one; there is no mistaking him, eh?

SETH. I know all about him.

RIP. (*Hopefully.*) Do you?

SETH. Yes.

RIP. (*Quite eagerly.*) Well, if you know all about him; well, what has become of him?

SETH. What has become of him? Why, bless your soul, he's been dead these twenty years!

RIP. (*Looking at* SETH.) Then I am dead, I suppose. So Rip Van Winkle was dead, eh?

SETH. Yes; and buried.

RIP. (*Humorously.*) I'm sorry for that; for he was a good fellow, so he was.

SETH. (*Aside.*) There appears to be something queer about this old chap; I wonder who he is. (*Rising and taking chair over to* RIP.) There, old gentleman, be seated.

RIP. (*Seating himself with great difficulty, assisted by* SETH.) Oh, thank you; every time I move a new way, I get another pain. My friend, where is the house what you live in?

SETH. (*Pointing at inn.*) There.

RIP. Did you live there yesterday?

SETH. Well, rather.

RIP. No, it is Nick Vedder what live in that house. Where is Nick Vedder?

SETH. Does he? Then I wish he'd pay the rent for it. Why, Nick Vedder has been dead these fifteen years.

RIP. Did you know Jacob Stein, what was with him?

SETH. No; but I've heard of him. He was one of the same sort as Rip and Nick.

RIP. Yes, them fellows was all pretty much alike.

SETH. Well, he went off the hooks a short time after Rip.

RIP. Where has he gone?

SETH. Off the hooks.

RIP. What is that, when they go off the hooks?

SETH. Why, he died.

RIP. (*With an air of hopelessness.*) Is there anybody alive
here at all? (*Then, with a sudden revulsion of feeling, convinced of the impossibility of what he hears.*) That man is
drunk what talks to me.

SETH. Ah, they were a jolly set, I reckon.

RIP. Oh, they was. I knowed them all.

SETH. Did you?

RIP. Yes, I know Jacob Stein, and Nick Vedder, and Rip Van
Winkle, and the whole of them. (*A new idea strikes him,
and he beckons to* SETH, *whom he asks, very earnestly.*)
Oh, my friend, come and see here. Did you know
Schneider?

SETH. Schneider! Schneider! No, I never heard of him.

RIP. (*Simply.*) He was a dog. I thought you might know him.
Well, if dat is so, what has become of my child Meenie,
and my wife Gretchen? Are they gone, too? (*Turning to
look at the ruins of the house.*) Yah, even the house is
dead.

SETH. Poor, old chap! He seems quite cast down at the loss
of his friends. I'll step in and get a drop of something to
cheer him up. (*Exit.*)

RIP. (*Puzzling it out with himself.*) I can't make it out how
it all was; because if this here is me, what is here now, and
Rip Van Winkle is dead, then who am I? That is what I
would like to know. Yesterday, everybody was here; and
now they was all gone. (*Very forlorn.*)

(*Re-enter* SETH, *followed by the villagers.*)

SETH. (*Offering* RIP *the cup.*) There, old gent, there's a drop
of something to cheer you up.

RIP. (*Shaking hands with* SETH *and* KÄTCHEN.) Oh, thank
you. I—I—I swore off; but this is the first time what I see
you. I won't count this one. (*His voice breaks.*) My friend,
you have been very kind to me. Here is your good health,
and your family's, and may they all live long and prosper!

SETH. I say, wife, ain't he a curiosity fit for a show?

RIP. (*Aside.*) That gives me courage to ask these people
anodder question. (*He begins with difficulty.*) My friend, I
don't know whether you knowed it or not, but there was
a child of Rip—Meenie her name was.

SETH. Oh, yes; that's all right.

RIP. (*With great emotion, leaning forward.*) She is not gone? She is not dead? No, no!

SETH. No; she is alive.

RIP. (*Sinking back with relief.*) Meenie is alive. It's all right now—all right now.

SETH. She's the prettiest girl in the village.

RIP. I know dat.

SETH. But if she wastes her time waiting on Hendrick Vedder, she'll be a middle-aged woman before long.

RIP. (*Incredulously.*) She's a little child, only six years old.

SETH. Six-and-twenty, you mean.

RIP. (*Thinking they are making fun of him.*) She's a little child no bigger than that. Don't bodder me; I don't like that.

SETH. Why she's as big as her mother.

RIP. (*Very much surprised that* SETH *knows* GRETCHEN.) What, Gretchen?

SETH. Yes, Gretchen.

RIP. Isn't Gretchen dead?

SETH. No. She's alive.

RIP. (*With mixed emotions.*) Gretchen is alive, eh! Gretchen's alive!

SETH. Yes; and married again.

RIP. (*Fiercely.*) How would she do such a thing like that?

SETH. Why, easy enough. After Rip died, she was a widow, wasn't she?

RIP. Oh, yes. I forgot about Rip's being dead. Well, and then?

SETH. Well, then Derrick made love to her.

RIP. (*Surprised, and almost amused.*) What for Derrick? Not Derrick Von Beekman?

SETH. Yes, Derrick Von Beekman.

RIP. (*Still more interested.*) Well, and then?

SETH. Well, then her affairs went bad; and at last she married him.

RIP. (*Turning it over in his mind.*) Has Derrick married Gretchen?

SETH. Yes.

RIP. (*With a flash of his old humor, but still with no laughter.*) Well, I didn't think he would come to any good; I never did. So she cotched Derrick, eh? Poor Derrick!

SETH. Yes.

RIP. Well, here's their good health, and their family's, and may they all live long and prosper! (*Drinks.*)

SETH. Now, old gent, hadn't you better be going home, wherever that is?

RIP. (*With conviction.*) Where my home was? Here's where it is.

SETH. What, here in this village? Now do you think we're going to keep all the half-witted strays that choose to come along here? No; be off with you. Why, it's a shame that those you belong to should allow such an old tramp as you to float around here.

VILLAGERS. (*Roughly, and trying to push him along.*) Yes; away with him!

RIP. (*Frightened, and pleading with them.*) Are you going to drive me away into the hills again?

FIRST VILLAGER. Yes; away with him! He's an old tramp.

(*Enter* HENDRICK, *with stick and bundle, followed by some of the women of the village.*)

VILLAGERS. Away with him!

HENDRICK. (*Throwing down bundle.*) Avast there, mates. Where are you towing that old hulk to? What, you won't? (*Pushing crowd aside, and going forward.*) Where are you towing that old hulk to?

SETH. Who are you?

HENDRICK. I'm a man, every inch of me; and if you doubt it, I'll undertake to remove the suspicions from any two of you in five minutes. Ain't you ashamed of yourselves? Don't you see the poor old creature has but half his wits?

SETH. Well, this is no asylum for worn out idiots.

VILLAGERS. (*Coming forward.*) No, it ain't!

HENDRICK. Ain't it?

OMNES. No, it ain't.

HENDRICK. Then I'll make it a hospital for broken heads if you stand there much longer. Clear the decks, you lubberly swabs! (*Drives them aside. Turns to* RIP, *who stands bewildered.*) What is the cause of all this?

RIP. (*Helplessly.*) I don't know, do you?

HENDRICK. (*To villagers.*) Do any of you know him?

FIRST VILLAGER. No; he appears to be a stranger.

HENDRICK. (*To* RIP.) You seem bewildered. Can I help you?

RIP. (*Feebly.*) Just tell me where I live.

HENDRICK. And don't you know?

RIP. No; I don't.

HENDRICK. Why, what's your name?

RIP. (*Almost childishly.*) I don't know; but I believe I know
vat it used to be. My name, it used to be Rip Van Winkle.

VILLAGERS. (*In astonishment.*) Rip Van Winkle?

HENDRICK. Rip Van Winkle? Impossible!

RIP. (*Pathetically feeble, and old.*) Well, I wouldn't swear to
it myself. I tell you how it was: Last night, I don't know
about the time, I went away up into the mountains, and
while I was there I met a queer kind o' man, and we got
drinkin'; and I guess I got pretty drunk. And then I went
to sleep; and when I woke up this morning, I was dead.
(*All laugh.*)

HENDRICK. Poor old fellow; he's crazy. Rip Van Winkle has
been dead these twenty years. I knew him when I was a
child.

RIP. (*Clutching at a faint hope.*) You don't know me?

HENDRICK. No; nor anybody else here, it seems.
(*The villagers, finding that there is to be no amusement
for them straggle off to their occupations.*)

SETH. (*As he goes into the inn.*) Why, wife, he's as cracked
as our old teapot.

RIP. (*With simple pathos.*) Are we so soon forgot when we
are gone? No one remembers Rip Van Winkle.

HENDRICK. Come, cheer up, my old hearty, and you shall
share my breakfast. (*Assists* RIP *to sit at the table.* RIP *has
fallen into a dream again. To* KÄTCHEN.) Bring us enough
for three, and of your best.

KÄTCHEN. That I will. (*Exit into inn.*)

HENDRICK. So here I am, home again. And yonder's the very
spot where, five years ago, I parted from Meenie.

RIP. (*Roused by the name.*) What, Meenie Van Winkle?

HENDRICK. And she promised to remain true to Hendrick
Vedder.

RIP. Oh, yah; that was Nick Vedder's son.

HENDRICK. (*Turning to* RIP.) That's me.

RIP. (*Resentfully.*) That was you! You think I'm a fool? He's
a little child, no bigger than that, the one I mean.

HENDRICK. How mad he is!

(*Enter* KÄTCHEN *from inn with tray, on which is laid a breakfast. She puts it on table, and exits into inn.*)

There, that's right. Stow your old locker full while I take a cruise around yonder house where, five years ago, I left the dearest bit of human nature that was ever put together. I'll be back directly. Who comes here? It's surely Derrick and his wife. Egad, I'm in luck; for now the old birds are out, Meenie will surely be alone. I'll take advantage of the coast being clear, and steer into harbor alongside. (*Exit.*)

(*Enter* DERRICK, *followed by* GRETCHEN.)

DERRICK. So you have come to that conclusion, have you?
GRETCHEN. I cannot accept this sacrifice.
RIP. (*Starting from his reverie, and turning to look at her.*) Why, that is Gretchen's voice. (*As he recognizes her, and sees how aged she is.*) My, my! Is that my wife?
DERRICK. Oh, you can't accept! Won't you kindly allow me a word on the subject?
RIP. (*Aside, humorously.*) No, indeed, she will not. Now, my friend, you are going to cotch it.
GRETCHEN. There is a limit even to my patience. Don't drive me to it.
RIP. (*Aside, drolly.*) Take care, my friend; take care.
DERRICK. Look you, woman; Meenie has consented to marry my nephew. She has pledged her word to do so on condition that I settle an annuity on you.
GRETCHEN. I won't allow my child to break her heart.
DERRICK. You won't allow? Dare to raise your voice, dare but to speak except as I command you, you shall repent it to the last hour of your life.
RIP. (*Expectantly.*) Now she'll knock him down, flat as a flounder.
DERRICK. (*Sneeringly.*) You won't allow? This is something new. Who are you; do you think you are dealing with your first husband?
GRETCHEN. Alas, no; I wish I was.
RIP. (*Lost in wonderment.*) My, my, if Rip was alive, he never would have believed it!
DERRICK. So you thought to get the upper hand of me, when you married me; didn't you?

GRETCHEN. I thought to get a home for my little girl—shelter, and food; want drove me to your door, and I married you for a meal's victuals for my sick child.

DERRICK. So you came to me as if I was a poorhouse, eh? Then you can't complain of the treatment you received. You sacrificed yourself for Meenie, and the least she can do now is to do the same for you. In an hour the deeds will be ready. Now, just you take care that no insolent interference of yours spoils my plans; do you hear?

GRETCHEN. Yes, sir.

DERRICK. Why can't you be kind and affectionate to her, as I am to you. There, go and blubber over her; that's your way. You are always pretending to be miserable.

GRETCHEN. Alas, no sir! I am always pretending to be happy.

DERRICK. Don't cry. I won't have it; come now, none of that. If you come home today with red eyes, and streaky cheeks, I'll give you something to cry for; now you know what's for supper. (*Exit.*)

RIP. (*Still amazed.*) Well, if I hadn't seen it, I never would have believed it!

GRETCHEN. (*Absorbed in her grief.*) Oh, wretch that I am, I must consent, or that man will surely thrust her out of doors to starve, to beg, and to become—(*Seeing* RIP.) Yes, to become a thing of rags and misery, like that poor soul.

RIP. She always drived the beggars away; I suppose I must go. (*Getting up, and starting to go.*)

GRETCHEN. (*Taking penny from her pocket.*) Here, my poor man, take this. It is only a penny; but take it, and may God bless you, poor wanderer, so old, so helpless. Why do you come to this strange place, so far from home?

RIP. (*Keeping his face turned away from her.*) She don't know me; she don't know me!

GRETCHEN. Are you alone in the world?

RIP. (*Trying to bring himself to look directly at* GRETCHEN.) My wife asks me if I'm alone.

GRETCHEN. Come with me. How feeble he is; there, lean on me. Come to yonder house, and there you shall rest your limbs by the fire.

(GRETCHEN *takes his arm, and puts it in her own. As they move towards her house,* RIP *stops, and, with an effort, turns and looks her full in the face, with a penetrating gaze, as if imploring recognition, but there is none; and,*

*sadly shaking his head, he shrinks into himself, and allows
her to lead him tottering off.)*

Scene 4

The same room in DERRICK's *home as in Scene 2.*

Enter DERRICK.

DERRICK. I don't know what women were invented for, except
to make a man's life miserable. I can get a useful, hard-
working woman to keep my house clean, and order my
dinner for me, for half that weak, snivelling creature costs
me.

(*Enter* COCKLES.)

COCKLES. Well, uncle, what news; will she have me?
DERRICK. Leave it to me; she must, she shall.
COCKLES. If she holds out, what are we to do? It was all very
well, you marrying Rip's widow, that choked off all inquiry
into his affairs; but here's Meenie, Rip's heiress, who
rightly owns all this property; if we don't secure her, we're
not safe.
DERRICK. You've got rid of Hendrick Vedder; that's one obstacle removed.
COCKLES. I'm not so sure about that. His ship was wrecked
on a lonely coast; but some of the crew may have, unfor-
tunately, been saved.
DERRICK. If he turns up after you're married, what need you
care?
COCKLES. I'd like nothing better; I'd like to see his face when
he saw my arm around his sweetheart—my wife. But if he
turns up before our marriage—
DERRICK. I must put the screw on somewhere.
COCKLES. I'll tell you, Meenie will do anything for her
mother's sake. Now you are always threatening to turn
her out, as she turned out Rip. That's the tender place.
Meenie fears more for her mother than she cares for herself.
DERRICK. Well, what am I to do?
COCKLES. Make Gretchen independent of you; settle the little

GRETCHEN. That is my daughter.

RIP. (*Looking timidly at* MEENIE, *as* GRETCHEN *helps him into a chair.*) I thought you was a child.

GRETCHEN. (*Crossing to go into another room, and speaking to* MEENIE, *who starts to follow her.*) Stay with him until I get some food to fill his wallet. Don't be frightened, child, he is only a simple, half-witted creature whose misery has touched my heart.

(*Exit.* MEENIE *takes her workbasket and starts to follow.*)

RIP. (*Holding out his hand to detain her, and speaking with hardly suppressed excitement.*) One moment, my dear. Come here, and let me look at you. (*Pathetically.*) Are you afraid? I won't hurt you. I only want to look at you; that is all. Won't you come? (MEENIE *puts down her workbasket, and* RIP *is relieved of his great fear that she might leave him. His excitement increases as he goes on in his struggle to make her recognize him.*) Yes, I thought you would. Oh, yah, that is Meenie! But you are grown!

(MEENIE *smiles.*)

But see the smile and the eyes! That is just the same Meenie. You are a woman, Meenie. Do you remember something of your father? (*He looks at her eagerly and anxiously, as if on her answer hung his reason and his life.*)

MEENIE. I do. I do. Oh, I wish he was here now!

RIP. (*Half rising in his chair, in his excitement.*) Yah? But he isn't? No? No?

MEENIE. No; he's dead. I remember him so well. No one ever loved him as I did.

RIP. No; nobody ever loved me like my child.

MEENIE. Never shall I forget his dear, good face. Tell me—

RIP. (*Eagerly and expectantly.*) Yah?—

MEENIE. Did you know him?

RIP. (*Confused by her question, and afraid to answer.*) Well —I thought I did. But I— When I say that here, in the village, the people all laugh at me.

MEENIE. He is wandering. (*She starts to go.*)

RIP. (*Making a great effort of will, and resolved to put the question of his identity to the test.*) Don't go away from me. I want you to look at me now, and tell me if you have ever seen me before.

MEENIE. (*Surprised.*) No.

RIP. (*Holding out his arms to her.*) Try, my darlin', won't you?

fortune on her, that you are always talking about doir
but never keeping your word. The girl will sell herself
secure her mother's happiness.

DERRICK. And it would be a cheap riddance for me. I w
just talking about it to Gretchen this morning. You sh
have the girl; but I hope you are not going to marry h
out of any weak feeling of love. You're not going to let h
make a fool of you by and by?

COCKLES. I never cared for her until she was impudent to n
and got that sailor lover of hers to thrash me; and ther
began to feel a hunger for her I never felt before.

DERRICK. That's just the way I felt for Gretchen.

COCKLES. 'T ain't revenge that I feel; it's enterprise. I wa
to overcome a difficulty.

DERRICK. (*Chuckling.*) And so you shall. Come, we'll p
your scheme in train at once; and let this be a warni
to you hereafter: never marry another man's widow.

COCKLES. No, uncle; I'll take a leaf out of your book, and
it be a warning to her.
(*Exeunt.*)

Scene 5

A plain sitting-room in DERRICK's *house. A table stands
the center with several chairs around it. There are cu*
a jug, and a workbasket on the table. As the curtain ris
MEENIE *is discovered seated by the table.*

MEENIE. Why should I repine? Did my mother hesitate
sacrifice her life to make a home for me? No; these te
are ungrateful, selfish.
(*The door at the back opens.*)

(GRETCHEN *enters, leading* RIP, *who seems very feeble a
a little wild.*)

GRETCHEN. Come in and rest a while.

RIP. This your house, your home?

GRETCHEN. Yes. Meenie, Meenie, bring him a chair.

RIP. (*Turning aside so as to shield his face from* MEENIE
Is that your daughter?

MEENIE. (*Frightened.*) What do you mean? Why do you gaze so earnestly and fondly on me?

RIP. (*Rising from his chair, in trembling excitement, and approaching her.*) I am afraid to tell you, my dear, because if you say it is not true, it may be it would break my heart. But, Meenie, either I dream, or I am mad; but I am your father.

MEENIE. My father!

RIP. Yes; but hear me, my dear, and then you will know. (*Trying to be logical and calm, but laboring under great excitement.*) This village here is the village of Falling Waters. Well, that was my home. I had here in this place my wife, Gretchen, and my child Meenie—little Meenie— (*A long pause, during which he strives to reassemble his ideas and memories more accurately.*) and my dog Schneider. That's all the family what I've got. Try and remember me. Dear, won't you? (*Pleadingly.*) I don't know when it was.— This night there was a storm; and my wife drove me from my house; and I went away—I don't remember any more till I come back here now. And see, I get back now, and my wife is gone, and my home is gone. My home is gone, and my child—my child looks in my face, and don't know who I am!

MEENIE. (*Rushing into his arms.*) I do! Father!

RIP. (*Sobbing.*) Ah, my child! Somebody knows me now! Somebody knows me now!

MEENIE. But can it be possible?

RIP. Oh, yah; it is so, Meenie! (*With a pathetic return of his uncertainty.*) Don't say it is not, or you will kill me if you do.

MEENIE. No. One by one your features come back to my memory. Your voice recalls that of my dear father, too. I cannot doubt; yet it is so strange.

RIP. Yah, but it is me, Meenie; it is me.

MEENIE. I am bewildered. Surely mother will know you.

RIP. (*Smiling.*) No, I don't believe she'll know me.

MEENIE. She can best prove your identity. I will call her.

RIP. No. You call the dog Schneider. He'll know me better than my wife.

(*They retire to a sofa in the background, where* RIP *sits with his arm around* MEENIE.)

(*Enter* DERRICK, *with documents.*)

DERRICK. What old vagabond is this?

(MEENIE *starts to resent insult.*)

DERRICK. Here, give him a cold potato, and let him go.
(*To* GRETCHEN, *who has entered, followed by* COCKLES.
GRETCHEN *seats herself in the chair at the right of the
table.*)
Come you here, mistress. Here are the papers for the
young couple to sign.

COCKLES. (*Aside.*) And the sooner, the better. Hush, Uncle,
Hendrick is here.

DERRICK. Young Vedder? Then we must look sharp. (*To*
GRETCHEN.) Come, fetch that girl of yours to sign this
deed.

GRETCHEN. Never shall she put her name to that paper with
my consent. Never.

DERRICK. Dare you oppose me in my own house? Dare you
preach disobedience under my roof?

GRETCHEN. I dare do anything when my child's life's at stake.
No, a thousand times, no! You shall not make of her what
you have of me. Starvation and death are better than such
a life as I lead.

DERRICK. (*Raising cane.*) Don't provoke me.

GRETCHEN. (*Kneeling.*) Beat me, starve me. You can only
kill me. After all, I deserve it. (*Rising.*) But Meenie has
given her promise to Hendrick Vedder, and she shall not
break her word.

COCKLES. (*Seated at right of table.*) But Hendrick Vedder is
dead.

(*The door is flung open, and* HENDRICK *enters.*)

HENDRICK. That's a lie! He's alive!

GRETCHEN *and* MEENIE. (*Rushing to him.*) Alive!

HENDRICK. (*To* MEENIE). I've heard all about it. They made
you believe that I was dead. (*To* DERRICK.) Only wait till
I get through here. (*Embracing* MEENIE.) What a pleasure
I've got to come! (*To* DERRICK.) And what a thrashing I've
brought back for you two swabs.

DERRICK. (*Angrily.*) Am I to be bullied under my own roof
by a beggarly sailor? Quit my house all of you. (*Seizes*
GRETCHEN, *and drags her away from the crowd.*) As for

you, woman, this is your work, and I'll make you pay for
it.

GRETCHEN. Hendrick, save me from him. He will kill me.

HENDRICK. Stand off!

DERRICK. (*Raising cane.*) No; she is my wife, mine.

GRETCHEN. Heaven help me, I am!

(RIP *has risen from the sofa, and comes forward, and leans
against the center of the table, with one hand in his game-
bag. He is fully awake now, and has recovered all his old
shrewdness.*)

RIP. Stop. I am not so sure about that. If that is so, then
what has become of Rip Van Winkle?

COCKLES. He's dead.

RIP. That's another lie. He's no more dead than Hendrick
Vedder. Derrick Von Beekman, you say this house and
land was yours?

DERRICK. Yes.

RIP. Where and what is the paper what you wanted Rip Van
Winkle to sign when he was drunk, but sober enough not
to do it? (*Taking an old paper out of game-bag, and turning to* HENDRICK.) Have you forgot how to read?

HENDRICK. No.

RIP. Then you read that.

(HENDRICK *takes the document from* RIP, *and looks it
over.*)

DERRICK. What does this mad old vagabond mean to say?

RIP. I mean, that is my wife, Gretchen Van Winkle.

GRETCHEN. (*Rushing to* RIP.) Rip! Rip!

COCKLES. I say, Uncle, are you going to stand that? That old
impostor is going it under your nose in fine style.

DERRICK. I'm dumb with rage. (*To the villagers, who have
come crowding in.*) Out of my house, all of you! Begone,
you old tramp!

HENDRICK. Stay where you are. (*To* DERRICK.) This house
don't belong to you. Not an acre of land, not a brick in
the town is yours. They have never ceased to belong to
Rip Van Winkle; and this document proves it.

DERRICK. 'Tis false. That paper is a forgery.

HENDRICK. Oh, no, it is not; for I read it to Rip twenty years
ago.

RIP. Clever boy! Clever boy! Dat's the reason I didn't sign
it then, Derrick.

DERRICK. (*Approaching* HENDRICK.) And do you think I'm fool enough to give up my property in this way?

HENDRICK. No. You're fool enough to hang on to it, until we make you refund to Rip every shilling over and above the paltry sum you loaned him upon it. Now, if you are wise, you'll take a hint. There's the door. Go! And never let us see your face again.

RIP. Yah; give him a cold potato, and let him go.

(*Exit* DERRICK *in a great rage. All the villagers laugh at him.* HENDRICK *follows him to the door.*)

COCKLES. (*Kneeling to* MEENIE.) O, Meenie! Meenie!

HENDRICK. (*Coming down, and taking him by the ear.*) I'll Meenie you!

(*Takes him and pushes him out. All the villagers laugh.* MEENIE *gives* RIP *a chair.*)

GRETCHEN. (*Kneeling by the side of* RIP.) O, Rip! I drove you from your home; but do not desert me again. I'll never speak an unkind word to you, and you shall never see a frown on my face. And Rip—

RIP. Yah.

GRETCHEN. You may stay out all night, if you like.

RIP. (*Leaning back in his chair.*) No, thank you. I had enough of that.

GRETCHEN. And, Rip, you can get tight as often as you please.

RIP. (*Taking bottle, and filling the cup from it.*) No; I don't touch another drop.

MEENIE. (*Kneeling by the other side of* RIP.) Oh, yes, you will, Father. For see, here are all the neighbors come to welcome you home.

(GRETCHEN *offers* RIP *the cup.*)

RIP. (*With all his old kindliness and hospitality.*) Well, bring in all the children, and the neighbors, and the dogs, and— (*Seeing the cup which* GRETCHEN *is offering to him.*) I swore off, you know. Well, I won't count this one; for this will go down with a prayer. I will take my cup and pipe and tell my strange story to all my friends. Here is my child Meenie, and my wife Gretchen, and my boy Hendrick. I'll drink all your good health, and I'll drink your good health, and your families', and may they all live long and prosper!

CURTAIN

THE BLACK CROOK

Preface to THE BLACK CROOK

American musical comedy, most theatre historians say, began on September 12, 1866. At Niblo's Garden that evening, *The Black Crook* took New York by a storm that soon swept through the whole country and lasted for decades. Its author had been totally unknown, and the production featured no popular stars. What *The Black Crook* offered, instead, was something of timeless delight to audiences: beautiful girls who, as *The New York Times* review noted, "wear no clothes to speak of." For whatever else may be claimed for it, *The Black Crook* was first of all a lavishly-produced girlie show. Though it has become renowned as America's first musical comedy, *The Black Crook* perhaps with even greater justification may be cited as the foremost precursor of American burlesque.

The play itself, as its chronicler, Joseph Whitton of the Niblo's Garden management, frankly admitted later, had no "literary merit" whatever. It was simply "a clothes-line" on which to hang the ballet, costumes, and scenery. The plot, he confessed with equal candor, was "a medley made up of the Naiad Queen, Undine, Lurline, and two or three other spectacular dramas of like nature." Enterprising producers had recently returned from Europe, where they had assembled a ballet corps for an extravaganza at New York's Academy of Music. That house burned down, however, and William Wheatley, the manager and lessee of Niblo's Garden, thereupon bought the troupe of beautiful dancers as well as the already-assembled wardrobe and scenery. The only thing he lacked was a play. When Charles M. Barras submitted *The Black Crook*, Wheatley and his associates immediately realized its potentialities.

The plot of *The Black Crook* is both convoluted and flimsy, a hodgepodge of the melodramas of the age and the ever-popular *Faust* and *Der Freischütz*. A rich count falls in love with a poor girl, the fiancée of a starving artist whom he throws into a dungeon. An aging sorcerer, the "Black Crook"

Hertzog, makes a pact with the Arch Fiend: for every soul
he delivers, Hertzog is granted a year of life. He tempts the
incarcerated artist, Rodolphe, with tales of a buried treasure
and a vision of his betrothed. Freed of bondage, Rodolphe
sallies forth to acquire the treasure and to punish the count.
Accidentally he saves the metamorphosed Fairy Queen, who
thereupon becomes Rodolphe's guardian angel. She helps him
defeat the count and saves him from the Black Crook, who
thus loses his pact with the Arch Fiend—and is borne off to
hell.

Neither the story nor the often hackneyed dialogue is im-
pressive. What made the play successful were its theatricality
and its lavish production. There is ample and still effective
comedy in the heroine's foster-mother, the preening old
Dame Barbara; her bibulous old suitor, Von Puffengruntz;
the Black Crook's "drudge" Greppo, who later becomes
Rodolphe's "Sancho Panza"; and the saucy maid, Carline. Of
even greater appeal was the stage spectacle, which can
merely be suggested in the text. Almost every scene gives
ample scope for theatre magic: displays of fire, water, transformations of all sorts, phantasmagorias of horror, caverns,
grottos, necromancy and conjury, and most important of all,
the ballet extravaganzas. No expense was spared to make it
the most magnificent show imaginable.

While newspaper reviews praised such a "gorgeous" and
"magnificent" spectacle, they fulminated against the "immorality" of the ballet. The fourteen- or fifteen-year-old
première danseuse, Mlle. Marie Bonfant (as Stalacta), and
thirty other dancers were announced in the original bill—
plus "fifty Auxiliary Ladies selected from the principal
theatres" of Europe. Scantily clad in flesh-colored tights,
they created a sensation. "Nothing in any other Christian
country, or in modern times, has approached the indecent
and demoralizing exhibition," a leading daily commented
editorially, and ministers thundered from the pulpit—so
vividly describing the sinful doings on stage that their
parishioners eagerly went to examine these "abominations"
for themselves.

The production opened, after extensive advertising, to an
overflowing house that was assembled by curtain time at
7:45 and remained to gape and cheer until the last scene,
which ended at 1:15 in the morning. It cost the then-

astounding amount of $55,000, but the net profits were even more astounding: $660,000 in little more than a year. Though Barras sold the New York run of *The Black Crook* for a mere $2,000, he collected in the first few months alone some $60,000 in royalties from across the country. The play was produced almost continuously for thirty years—certainly the longest run for a musical. George W.H. Griffin's *The Black Crook Burlesque*, produced by Christy's Minstrels, concurrently played to a filled house for three months. A songbook of *The Black Crook* was published, with some of Barras's lyrics and snatches from the original score by Operti and others. In 1873 Barras published a novel based on *The Black Crook*. The play received a major revival in Hoboken, New Jersey, as late as 1929, with lyrics by Christopher Morley and the ballet by Agnes De Mille (as Stalacta). In 1934 The People's Theatre (formerly The Bowery) in New York prepared and repeatedly advertised another *The Black Crook* revival, but finally canceled its plans. Two years later, however—in 1936—the Federal Theatre in Los Angeles did revive the play.

Accounts of *The Black Crook* are abundant, and may be found in every history of the American theatre. Yet little was written or is known about its author, Charles M. Barras. He was born in Philadelphia in 1820 or 1821, learned the carpenter's trade, and served in the U.S. Navy for about three years. The remainder of his life Barras spent in the theatre: as comedian, agent, scriptwriter for a variety team, and adapter of plays. He was unsuccessful in all these endeavors. It was as a "desperate old trouper" that he wrote *The Black Crook*, his only hit. Bitterly he noted that it came too late to save his ailing wife Sallie St. Clair, a fairly well-known actress. To many, Barras himself appeared somewhat grotesque with his wig (he had lost his hair when a youth) and stammer, and he was considered haughty and pugnacious. When he became wealthy Barras was generous to the poor and a delight as a wit to his many friends. After his wife's death he sold his Connecticut mansion to Edwin Booth, and lived in a New York hotel suite. Barras died in an accident (some thought it was a suicide) in 1873.

"*The Black Crook*, an Original Magical and Spectacular Drama in Four Acts by Charles M. Barras," was copyrighted in 1863, but remained unpublished; only a few scripts and

prompt copies are extant. The most complete and authoritative account of the play's history is Joseph Whitton's *"The
Naked Truth!" An Inside History of The Black Crook* (Philadelphia, 1897). Further information about the play and its
author may be found in Christopher Morley's column in *The
Saturday Review of Literature* (March 2, 1929), in Seabury
Quinn's "Charley One-Hit" in *Esquire* (January 1947), and
in Julian Mates's "The *Black Crook* Myth" in *Theatre Survey*
(May 1966).

M.M.

THE BLACK CROOK
An Original Magical and Spectacular Drama
in Four Acts
by Charles M. Barras

Characters

COUNT WOLFENSTEIN
RODOLPHE, a poor artist
VON PUFFENGRUNTZ, the Count's steward
HERTZOG, surnamed the Black Crook, an alchymist and
sorcerer
GREPPO, his drudge
WULFGAR, a gypsy ruffian
BRUNO, his companion
CASPER
JAN

AMINA, betrothed to Rodolphe
DAME BARBARA, her foster-mother
CARLINE
ROSETTA

VILLAGERS, PEASANTS, CHORESTERS, GUARDS, ATTENDANTS, etc.

Immortals

STALACTA, Queen of the Golden Realm
CRYSTALINE, RUBYBLOSSOM, SAPPHIRA, EMERALDINE, SCIN-
TILLA, AMETHYSTA, CORALBUD, GARNET, her attendants
FAIRIES, SPRITES, NAIADS, SUBMARINE MONSTERS, etc.

Amphibea

DRAGONFIN, HACKLETOOTH, SHARKSKIN, SPLAYFOOT, STICKLE-
BACK, MULLETMUG, EELEYE, CUTTLEKONK

Gnomes

GOLDDUST,   NUGGETNOSE,   YELLOWSCALE,   SPANGLENECK,
SMELTERFACE, PINCHBACK

Infernals

ZAMIEL, the arch-fiend
SKULDAWELP, familiar to Hertzog
REDGLARE, the recording demon
SKELETONS, APPARITIONS, DEMONS, MONSTERS, etc.

Scene: In and around the Hartz Mountains. Time: 1600.

Note: Hertzog is a hideous deformity, with leaden complexion, humped back, knotted limbs, crooked body, and lame. Von Puffengruntz is corpulent and rubicund.

ACT I

Scene 1

A quiet valley at the foot of the Hartz Mountains. Cottage of DAME BARBARA, *with upper windows and balcony. Tree beside cottage at back, arbor, broken water [i.e., partly obstructed view of brook] and mystic stone bridge, a long rocky tail-piece with platform backed by an extended range of hills or mountain spurs above which light clouds appear, illuminated by the reflected light of the moon. Shortly after rise of curtain, the moonbeams grow faint and ruddy glow of the rising sun diffuses itself over the clouds and horizon. Music.*

Enter RODOLPHE *at back; he descends, comes forward, and after looking cautiously around, claps his hands three times beneath the window. The upper window opens and* AMINA *appears on balcony.*

AMINA. Surely I heard his well-known signal. Hist, who's there?

RODOLPHE. It is I—Rodolphe.

AMINA. Rodolphe! Hush, speak low. If my foster-mother still sleeps, I will join you. (*Exits.*)

(*Music.* RODOLPHE *goes up-stage and looks cautiously off, then comes down.* AMINA *re-enters from cottage.*)

AMINA. (*Throwing herself into his arms.*) Rodolphe, Rodolphe, my own!

RODOLPHE. My own!

AMINA. When did you return?

RODOLPHE. 'Twas past midnight. Although wearied and foot-sore, I could not sleep until I had seen you.

AMINA. Oh how wearily the days and nights have passed since you left me! What kept you so long?

RODOLPHE. Ill fortune, Amina. After reaching Göttingen and finding my purchaser for my picture, I heard that there was a wealthy traveler at Kassel, collecting works of art.

I had but four silver florins in my pocket, yet I hopefully set out to meet him. After journeying five whole days, I arrived at Kassel, only to find that the traveler had departed two days before.

AMINA. And your beautiful picture, upon which so much of our future was built—you have brought it back?

RODOLPHE. No. Crushed in my last hope to obtain the means necessary to our union, I left it with a remorseless agent for a pittance barely sufficient for subsistence during my journey homeward. And here I am, without a single guilder in my pocket, and what is worse, if I fail to return my pledge at the end of two months, it is lost to me forever.

AMINA. (*Aside.*) Poor dear Rodolphe, he knows not the worst. The heaviest blow is yet to come. How shall I break it to him? (*Aloud.*) Dear Rodolphe, my great joy at seeing you made me forget for a moment that which I fear to tell you.

(*The moonlight begins to fade and the horizon grows ruddy with the rising sun.*)

RODOLPHE. Fear to tell me! Speak, what has happened?

AMINA. Be calm and listen. Last week I attended the Festival of St. John in company with the other members of the village choir. Upon raising my eyes after we had finished the anthem I found a dark strange man gazing upon me. A moment after, he quitted the spot. I enquired who he was and learned that it was the Count Wolfenstein, the all-powerful lord of this wide domain.

RODOLPHE. Well—

AMINA. Although I met his gaze but for a moment, I felt that it boded evil to me—to us.

RODOLPHE. Evil! Evil to us?

AMINA. Yes, evil, Rodolphe, nor were my fears idle. The next day brought him here to our humble abode. He told my foster-mother that he loved me.

RODOLPHE. (*Starting.*) Loved! —You?

AMINA. Yes, and that we should no longer dwell in obscurity —that we should be removed to the castle, that masters should be provided for my suitable education, and in a year I should take the place of the late Countess of Wolfenstein.

RODOLPHE. And Dame Barbara?

AMINA. Joyfully consented. This very day is set apart for our removal. The escort will be here at sunrise.

RODOLPHE. And you, Amina? You?

AMINA. I supplicated, wept, remonstrated, but you know, dear Rodolphe, I am powerless.

RODOLPHE. (*Vehemently.*) By heaven, you shall not go!

AMINA. Hush, be calm, dear Rodolphe.

(DAME BARBARA *appears on the balcony.*)

RODOLPHE. I say you shall not! Were he twenty times more potent, I would oppose his power to the last.

BARBARA. Eh, what, varlet, hussy, only wait till I get down. (*Music. She disappears from balcony and enters from door.*) What jade, ingrate! How dare you! Is this your gratitude? Where is your pride? You, the most noble Countess of Wolfenstein that-is-to-be, meeting young men in secret—and on the very day of your betrothal! Oh, if his High-Mightiness, the Count, should find it out!

AMINA. But Mother—

BARBARA. Not a word—how dare you? In with you—into the house, I say! (*Forces her into the cottage, closes the door, then turns to Rodolphe.*) So, beggar, you've come back, have you? How dare you show your unlucky face here at such a time as this? I had hoped you had fallen into the hands of the conscript officers and gone for a soldier, or better still been carried off by the demons of the Brocken.

RODOLPHE. And yet, you see I have escaped both. Hark ye, Dame, I love Amina. She loves me. You yourself promised that she should be mine as soon as I could command one hundred silver crowns.

BARBARA. Pah—that was before I knew her value, but now— that I *do* know it—and others know it too, I changed my mind. But where are the hundred crowns? Where is the fortune you were to get for your great painting? I warrant me you haven't got a single groschen of it. Come, let me see the hundred crowns.

RODOLPHE. My picture is not yet sold.

BARBARA. Ha-ha! Didn't I say so? Not yet sold, eh? Here's a pretty fellow, that would take a young girl from her comfortable home, good bed, sweet milk and egg pudding, to

lodge her on pea-straw, and feed her at best on black
bread and sour cheese. Oh, was there ever such villainy?

RODOLPHE. Nay, but listen to me!

BARBARA. Not a word! Begone! Do you think people of
quality have nothing to do but listen to beggars' com-
plaints, and above all at such a time as this. Begone, I
say! This is to be a festival day. The maidens of the village
will be here soon. The grand escort will be here, headed
by the Count's chamberlain, aye, and his Lordship the
Count, himself, will be here, to bear the Countess that-is-
to-be, and her right honorable foster-mother that-is-to-be,
to the castle.

(*Music.*)

Hark, here come the villagers, already. Out of the way,
I say! (*Pushes him rudely aside. Goes up and looks off.*
RODOLPHE *retires into the arbor.*)

(*Enter lively from back female villagers with garlands,
followed by males, two of whom bear a rustic chair festooned with flowers. They descend and come forward,
greeting* BARBARA. *The sun appears above one of the spurs
of the mountain.*)

Ah—you are early, friends.

CARLINE. Yes, but not earlier than the sun, for see, it is
already peeping over the great-toe of the Brocken. But
where's Amina?

BARBARA. (*Drawing herself up.*) The Countess that-is-to-be
is preparing to receive his Lordship the Count; but never
mind her Ladyship. Enjoy yourselves until she is ready.
Here, Casper, here I am, come with me and bring some
refreshments while I help to prepare her Ladyship.

(*Goes into the cottage, followed by* CASPER *and* JAN. *The
two latter re-enter with white cloths, wine, fruits, etc.,
which they arrange on the table beneath the tree.*)

CARLINE. Bless me, how grand Dame Barbara has grown, to
be sure! If she goes on at this rate, the wide halls of the
grand old castle of Wolfenstein will be a world too small
to hold her. I hope this piece of good fortune does not
make such a fool of dear 'Mina.

ROSETTA. I don't understand this, I thought 'Mina was betrothed to the handsome young painter, Rodolphe. Whatever could have become of him?

CARLINE. Oh, 'tis said he has gone for a soldier; but come, while 'Mina is making ready, let us rehearse our festival dance.

(*Music. Grand Garland Dance by principals and full ballet, during which the males gather around the table and eat and drink.*)

(*After dance,* BARBARA *enters, extravagantly dressed, wearing a monstrous cap ridiculously trimmed.*)

BARBARA. There! Having completed her Ladyship's toilet, I have attended to my own, and if I know anything about dress, I flatter myself that my appearance would do honor to any occasion. (*Displays herself.*)

CARLINE. (*Aside to* ROSETTA.) Mercy on us—was there ever such a fright! Why, she looks for all the world like a great horned owl dressed up in the cast-off finery of a peacock. Ha, ha, ha—did you ever? Observe me tickle the old buzzard. (*Aloud, and with affected admiration.*) Why, Dame Barbara, is that you?

BARBARA. (*Drawing herself up.*) Of course it is, child, who else could it be? (*Aside.*) I knew I should make them open their eyes.

CARLINE. Why you've almost taken away my breath. I declare, Dame, you're looking gorgeous. So young and girlish, too. Indeed, if I were 'Mina—I beg pardon, I mean, her Ladyship—I wouldn't care to have you in the way when his Lordship, the Count, arrives.

BARBARA. And why not, pray?

CARLINE. Because I should consider you a dangerous rival.

BARBARA. Nonsense, girl, you don't think so?

CARLINE. Indeed, Dame Barbara, I was never more serious in my life. (*Laughingly confers with* ROSETTA *and Villagers.*)

BARBARA. It is strange, I never noticed before. But that girl Carline is a very sensible person.

(*Music.*)

Ah, here comes the escort!

(*All go up and look off,* RODOLPHE *glides from the arbor into the cottage unobserved.*)

(*Enter from back and descending* VON PUFFENGRUNTZ *bearing his wand of office. He is preceded by two servants of the Count's household. As he comes down the male villagers take off their caps and the females curtsy.*)

VON PUFFENGRUNTZ. (*With pompous condescension.*) Be covered, good people, be covered; the air of the valley is yet damp. We never insist upon ceremony at the expense of health. (*Aside.*) Ahem—it is the true policy of greatness to occasionally waive a point of etiquette in dealing with inferiors.

BARBARA. What a courtly gentleman!

VON PUFFENGRUNTZ. What an imposing female!

BARBARA. (*Curtsying.*) Your Excellency is welcome.

VON PUFFENGRUNTZ. (*Bowing.*) I cannot be mistaken. I was just about to inquire, but that stately presence and graceful dignity tell me that I am addressing Madam Barbara.

BARBARA. (*Curtsying.*) O sir! (*Aside.*) How one's manner will betray one. I always said I belonged to a higher sphere.

VON PUFFENGRUNTZ. I come, Madame, by the Count's order to announce that the cavalcade has arrived and is now resting on the plateau, beyond the ravine. His Lordship will be here presently and in person conduct your fair foster-daughter to her palfrey that waits without, impatient for the honor to be mounted by her.

BARBARA. (*Curtsying.*) Oh, sir, his Lordship is so considerate. But may I inquire if *I* have been thought of? Am *I also* to be provided with a becoming escort? Is there any palfrey without, impatient for the honor to be ridden by *me?*

VON PUFFENGRUNTZ. That shall be my privilege.

BARBARA. (*Astonished.*) Eh?

VON PUFFENGRUNTZ. That is, I have charged myself with the especial happiness of being your escort.

BARBARA. (*Curtsying very low.*) Oh!
(*Music.*)

VON PUFFENGRUNTZ. He comes! Room there for his Lordship. (*Villagers range themselves to receive the Count, who enters preceded by Guards and followed by* WULFGAR *and* BRUNO. *When down, Villagers shout and raise their caps.*)

WOLFENSTEIN. Salutations to the good Dame Barbara.

BARBARA. (*Curtsying very low.*) Oh, your Lordship.

WOLFENSTEIN. And how fares your lovely charge?

BARBARA. Well, may it please your Lordship—quite well. A little nervous from over-anxiety to see your Lordship, but that is quite natural for us poor silly things. I suffered *dreadfully* in that way when my poor dear, dead and gone Christopher courted me. Many and many a time—

WOLFENSTEIN. (*Impatiently interrupting her.*) But the fair Amina?

BARBARA. Is quite ready and dying to see you. I will present her to your Lordship at once.

(*She is going into the cottage when* RODOLPHE *appears and comes forward, leading Amina by the hand. Chord.*)

RODOLPHE. Allow *me*, Dame Barbara, to do the honors.

ALL THE VILLAGERS. Rodolphe! (*Picture of astonishment.*)

RODOLPHE. My Lord Count Wolfenstein, permit me, Rodolphe Werner, a poor artist, to present to you Amina, foster-daughter to Dame Barbara, a free maiden of this valley and my affianced bride.

WOLFENSTEIN. Who is this madman?

BARBARA. N-n-n-nobody, your Lordship. —That is—a poor, weak simpleton, who imagines he is betrothed to every girl in the village. As your Lordship *truly* says, a madman.

VON PUFFENGRUNTZ. A madman! Mercy on us, we shall all be murdered. Seize him, secure him, somebody, everybody.

(*Music.* WULFGAR *and* BRUNO *seize* RODOLPHE, *and after a struggle overpower him.* AMINA *screams, clings to him for a moment, then throws herself at the Count's feet. He raises her and passes her to* BARBARA, *then turns to Guards.*)

WOLFENSTEIN. Release him.

(*They release him.*)

His misfortune claims our pity. Let some of his fellows conduct him hence and see that no harm comes to him.

RODOLPHE. (*Defiantly.*) My Lord Count—

WOLFENSTEIN. Begone—sirrah!

CASPER. Come, Rodolphe, come with me. (*Aside.*) Are you indeed mad to brave the tiger in his lair? (*Leads him off.*) Come I say, this is neither time nor place to right your wrong. Be calm, I say, be calm!

RODOLPHE. (*Shaking him by the hand.*) You are right, Casper, you are right. (*Looks scornfully at Wolfenstein.*) Come, my friend—come.
(*Exit with* CASPER.)

WOLFENSTEIN. (*Aside.*) 'Tis he, the lover. He braves me, too. (*Aloud.*) Wulfgar!
(WULFGAR *advances. Speaks apart to him.*)
Track yonder knave, take Bruno with you. Seize him, but let no eye see you. Place him in the secret vault beneath the eastern wing. Once there—you know the rest.

WULFGAR. (*Nods meaningly.*) I understand. (*Gives a sign to* BRUNO, *and is going.*)

WOLFENSTEIN. Stay—not now, it will be noted; when the procession moves, then steal away by the upper path.
(WULFGAR *nods, turns up-stage, and confers with* BRUNO. WOLFENSTEIN *confers with* VON PUFFENGRUNTZ *at back.*)

BARBARA. (*Leading* AMINA *forward, and aside, to her.*) Silence, on your life. Not a word that you have ever seen him before! If the Count were to know—mercy on me! I tremble to think of it—there would not be a head left on any of our shoulders.
(*Birds heard singing, till scene closes.*)

VON PUFFENGRUNTZ. (*Waving his wand.*) Let the procession move.
(*Music.*)
(WOLFENSTEIN *joins* AMINA. *Villagers bring forward the festooned chair.* WOLFENSTEIN *assists* AMINA *into the seat. The chair is borne by four Villagers. The others form in procession,* WOLFENSTEIN *beside the chair,* VON PUFFENGRUNTZ *pompously leading* BARBARA *by the hand.* WULFGAR *and* BRUNO *loiter behind and when unobserved, steal off. The procession, after making a circle of the stage, ascends the rocks, and crosses to the right, the Villagers singing the following chorus.*)

VILLAGERS' CHORUS. Hark, hark, hark,
                Hark the birds with tuneful voices
                Vocal for our lady fair
                And the lips of op'ning flowers
                Breathe their incense on the air,
                Breathe their incense on the air.

See, see, see,
See the sun in orient splendor
Gilding every glittering spray,
Busy weaving jeweled chaplets
For our lovely Queen of May,
For our lovely Queen of May.

Mark, mark, mark,
Mark the plumes of mighty Brocken
Waving in the fragrant air,
Proudly nodding salutation
To our charming lady fair,
To our charming lady fair.

Scene 2

A dark woody or rocky pass.
Music.
Enter WULFGAR *and* BRUNO.

WULFGAR. So, we've reached the pass a good five minutes
before him.

BRUNO. But if he should cross the bridge?

WULFGAR. Aye, *if*; but he'll not. I watched him from behind
The Devil's Hump and saw him part company with that
lout at the foot of the old cross. I tell you, his path lies
this way. (*Crosses.*) Hark, someone comes. (*Looks cautiously off.*) Ha, I was right, 'tis he. Quick, conceal yourself, and when I hood the hawk, stand ready to clip his
claws.
(*Music.*)
(WULFGAR *and* BRUNO *conceal themselves.*)

(*Enter* RODOLPHE.)

RODOLPHE. Deeper, let me plunge deeper still into the heart
of the mountain. The light of the sun falls like molten lead
upon my aching eyeballs. My heart's on fire, my brain is
in a whirl. I strive to think, but thought becomes a chaos.
Am I awake or is this some horrible dream? Water, water,

my throat is flaming. Ha, yonder is a rill trickling from the rock.

(*Music.*)

(*He is going when* WULFGAR, *who has stolen from his concealment, throws a cloak over his head, while* BRUNO *at the same moment pinions his arms*—RODOLPHE *struggling violently.*)

WULFGAR. Quick, quick, the cord, the cord—he has the strength of a lion!

(BRUNO *draws a cord tightly over his arms.*)

Go away, away!

(*Music. They force* RODOLPHE *off.*)

Scene 3

Study and laboratory of the Black Crook. HERTZOG *discovered, seated at table poring over a large cabalistic book.* GREPPO, *pinched and starved, asleep on stool, before a retort furnace. An antique lamp illuminates the characters of the book upon the table, upon which is a skull and hour-glass.*
Music at opening of scene.

HERTZOG. (*Rising in pain and with difficulty. He closes the book and comes forward.*) Vain, vain, some subtle spell is hovering in the air that mocks my power and makes the charms that once were potent a jabbering, idle sound. And shall I yield to the invisible? I, Hertzog, the Crook, whom men call SORCERER? I, at whose name the strong man trembles and the weak grows faint? I, whose whole life of long, laborious years hath well-nigh run its course, gleaning dark knowledge in forbidden paths? Shall I now seek the light? My eyes are old and dim and could not brave the glare. No, no, I'll work new mines, new mines, and plumb the depths of darker mysteries still!

(GREPPO *snores loudly.* HERTZOG, *turning.*)

How now, knave?

(GREPPO *starts from his sleep and uses the bellows rapidly at the mouth of the furnace.*)

Come hither, varlet.

GREPPO. Yes, Master. (*Rises from stool, puts down bellows and comes forward, yawning.*)

HERTZOG. What, drone, sluggard, drowsing again?

GREPPO. N-n-no, good master, no.

HERTZOG. Out, lying knave. Did I not hear thee snore?

GREPPO. Snore? Aye, granted, but 'twas in *thy* service, Master. Much fasting and long watching caused this left, rebellious eye to wink, and so I snored, to wake it up again.

HERTZOG. Bah. Shuffling crow, thy drowsing comes of overfeeding.

GREPPO. (*Viewing himself.*) Overfeeding? Look I as if I were overfed? A scanty chopin of weak sour beer with one poor groschen's-worth of musty beans is all the banquet this shrunk belly knows from week to week.

HERTZOG. What, rogue, dost grumble?

GREPPO. No, good Master, no.

(*Rumbling thunder. Music—tremulo, piano.*)

HERTZOG. Ha, the night grows foul. 'Tis all the better. Bring me my cloak and staff.

GREPPO. (*Bringing forward crutch stick and short black hooded cloak.*) They are here. (*Places cloak on* HERTZOG's *shoulders.*)

HERTZOG. (*Drawing the hood over his head.*) So, now, thine own.

GREPPO. My cloak? I have none, master.

HERTZOG. Thy cap.

GREPPO. Mine?

HERTZOG. Thine.

(*Thunder.*)

GREPPO. Oh, Lord, what a night. (*Brings his cap from peg beside the furnace.*)

HERTZOG. Bring with thee yonder brazen casket.

GREPPO. Th-th-the brazen casket?

HERTZOG. Aye, echoing fool.

(*Thunder.*)

GREPPO. (*Trembling, goes to table and takes casket. Aside.*) The Devil's tool chest. (*Aloud.*) Whither go we, dread Master?

HERTZOG. To the Serpents' Glen.

(*Loud thunder.*)

GREPPO. (*Starting.*) Oh, Lord, the Serpents' Glen! Beelzebub's favorite chapel! Surely, Good Master, you would not, and above all, on such a night as this?

(*Thunder and lightning, the latter showing itself on transparent window.*)

Hark, how the tempest howls! Strong pines are toppling

down the mountainsides. 'Twere certain death to go
abroad tonight.

HERTZOG. Silence, and follow.

(*Goes toward door. Lightning and loud thunder.*)

GREPPO. (*Who has made a movement to follow, starts back,
trembling violently.*) Master, I cannot.

HERTZOG. (*Turning fiercely.*) What, ingrate, do you rebel?

GREPPO. No, master, no. My spirit's willing, but my legs are
weak.

HERTZOG. Wretch, did I not snatch thee drowning from the
whirling gulf, bind thy torn limbs with rare medicaments
and stanch the current of thy ebbing life that fast was
running out?

GREPPO. You did, good Master, you did. (*Aside.*) Out of the
water into the fire.

HERTZOG. Begone.

(*Music forte. Throws open the door. Loud, crashing thunder and vivid lightning. Greppo starts back.*)

Fool—begone, I say.

(*Seizes and hurls him towards the open door. Heavy
thunder and lightning.* GREPPO *in doorway, entreats—*
HERTZOG *raises his staff.*)

Away, away.

(*Thunder and lightning. Exeunt.*)

Scene 4

An apartment in the castle of WOLFENSTEIN. *Low thunder,
lights up.*

Enter CARLINE.

CARLINE. Bless me, what a night to welcome her Ladyship
that-is-to-be to her new home! I declare, the old castle
trembles and shakes like a great ship at sea.

(*Loud thunder.*)

Mercy on us, what a crash. But pshaw, why should I care
how the tempest rages without, am I not safe within and
in rare good luck, too? Only to think that I should be
chosen from among all the girls in the village to become
Amina's companion and own particular waiting-maid. Old
Hagar, the gypsy fortune-teller whose palm I crossed with
a new quarter-florin last week, told me that good fortune

awaited me and sure enough, here it is. Only to think of it, that I, Carline Brenner, who for ten long years have been chained to a stupid spinning-wheel day and night, should become confidential companion to the future mistress of Wolfenstein! Was there ever such good fortune? I declare, I am so happy I could sing for a month! (*Song, and exit.*)

Scene 5

A wild glen in the heart of the Brocken. Perilous rocky pathway, leading from above at back, returning, crosses over a rock five feet high with blasted tree back of it. Large, working raven on limb, and vampire doors in trunk. A rock piece in center bearing a general resemblance in outline to a rude altar. Trick plants, with serrated leaves.

The whole stage is much broken up with rocky sets, leaving the center back of the altar generally open.

Lights down.

Music—at opening.

HERTZOG *appears above, followed by* GREPPO, *tremblingly. They cross and re-cross on rock in front of blasted tree, and descend slowly.* GREPPO *making several efforts to turn back is checked by a gesture from* HERTZOG.

GREPPO. (*Coming forward when down.*) Oh Lord, what a place!
  (*Music—the raven croaks, flaps its wings and shows red illuminated eyes. Starting.*)
  What's that? (*Turns.*) 'Twas the croaking of yonder monk-raven. Didst hear, Master? 'Tis an evil sign. Let's begone.
HERTZOG. Silence, fool, set down the casket. (*Goes upstage.*)
GREPPO. I will. (*Places the casket on the ground.*) Thank St. Michael I'm rid of that pleasant companion. As I have an empty belly and hope someday to have it filled, I could swear before the Burgomaster that when we passed over the bridge of "Beelzebub's Nose" I heard voices laughing inside that very casket, saw blue blazes come out of the keyhole, and smelled a strong smell of brimstone.
  (*Music. Raven croaks as before. Looking fearfully around.*)

Oh Lord, Oh Lord, what a pleasant place for an uninter-
rupted funeral! Ugh!

HERTZOG. Knave!

GREPPO. Master!

HERTZOG. Bring hither fuel.

GREPPO. I obey. (*Aside.*) Here's a chance! If I can only get
out of this, may the Fiend singe me if he catches me back.
I'd rather be on the raging flood than serve him an hour
longer. (*Is about to ascend the rocks.*)

HERTZOG. Whither go you, Varlet?

GREPPO. For fuel, Master. This around us is wet with the
storm and will not burn. As we came along I noted beneath the shelter of a crag hard by many dry faggots. I will
fetch them. (*Going.*)

HERTZOG. Come back!

(GREPPO *groans and returns.*)

(*Pointing.*) The dead branches of yon blasted larch will
serve.

GREPPO. But, master—

HERTZOG. Dolt, obey me.

GREPPO. I am gone. (*Groans and exits.*)

(*Music.* HERTZOG *goes slowly up to set altar and smites it
three times with his crutch-stick. Blue flame issues from
the top of the altar and continues throughout the scene.*
GREPPO (*re-entering with an armload of faggots.*) Here are
the faggots, master.

HERTZOG. 'Tis well, feed yonder flame.

GREPPO. A flame. How came we by a flame? I'll swear I
brought no tinder-box. More brimstone, I suppose. Oh
Lord, Oh Lord!

HERTZOG. Fool, dc as I command.

GREPPO. I fly.

(*Music. He goes slowly and timidly up to and behind altar
with faggots.*)

Now for some devil's cookery.

HERTZOG. So! Pluck me an inner leaf from yonder adder-
plant. (*Points to trick plant.*)

GREPPO. I knew it, vegetable broth.

(*Music. He approaches the plant, and is about to pluck a
leaf when it opens suddenly and discovers a dwarf demon,
around whose body is twined a huge green serpent with
flaming eyes, distended jaws, and forked tongue. As the*

leaves open the head darts at GREPPO *viciously. He starts back, uttering a cry of alarm. The leaves close.*)

HERTZOG. Ha! (*Stamps his foot angrily and points to the plant.*)

(GREPPO *tremblingly crosses and is about to pluck a leaf from the plant, when it opens and the same action of dwarf-demon, serpent, and* GREPPO *as before. Leaves close.*)

(*Chafing.*) So—so—bring me the green flagon from yonder casket.

(*Music.* GREPPO *goes to casket, and raises the lid, when fire flashes from the box. He starts back in an agony of fright, and crossing, sits upon a small rock-piece, when flames shoot from this stone, and he springs into the air, uttering a sharp cry of pain.*)

(HERTZOG *is enraged.*) Baffled at every turn! Begone, knave! Thy presence mars my work.

GREPPO. Most willingly. (*Is about to ascend the rocks.*)

HERTZOG. Not there.

(GREPPO *groans and returns.*)

Keep watch without, from yonder crag that overhangs the gorge. (*Points.*) Should struggling footsteps bend this way, give timely warning.

GREPPO. (*Aside.*) Struggling footsteps! Struggling indeed to be abroad on such a night, and least of all in such a place as this!

HERTZOG. Didst hear me?

GREPPO. I vanish. (*Exit.*)

(*Music.* HERTZOG *describes a circle and figures on the ground with his crutch-stick, after which the end of the stick ignites and burns with a faint blue flame. He then describes figures in the air, during which latter action he speaks.*)

HERTZOG. Skuldawelp, familiar, slave of my power, I invoke thee!

(*Music. A spectre in filmy drapery, with death head, luminous eyes, moveable jaw, and skeleton hands appears, illuminated by light from calcium.*)

SKULDAWELP. Your will!

HERTZOG. Break the malignant spells that thwart and mock me. Bind fast my hidden enemies. Restore to me my lost power.

SKULDAWELP. I cannot, an adverse spell has crossed me. My power is spent. All that was mine is thine. Zamiel alone can serve thee.

HERTZOG. (*Shrinking.*) Zamiel!

SKULDAWELP. Zamiel! Dismiss me.

HERTZOG. (*Waving his staff.*) Begone!

(*Music.* SKULDAWELP *glides off.*)

Zamiel! No, no. I dare not invoke his fearful aid.

(*Music—tremulo piano.*)

I—I—Ha! What tremor's this? My blood grows icy cold. My limbs are failing, a film is gathering in my eyes. (*Falls.*) Can this be death? Death? No, no, I cannot, I will not die. Save me, save me! Zamiel, Zamiel!

(*Music—Forte. He drags himself toward the casket, seizes it, rises with difficulty, and totters to the altar, at the foot of which he places the casket, opens it and brings forth a packet containing four lesser packets and begins the following incantation.*)

"By a bloody murder done
'Gainst a mother by her son:"

(*He casts red ingredient into the fire. Wild blast of demoniacal music. A huge green serpent, with moveable jaw, rises from the flame behind the altar and strikes viciously at* HERTZOG. *The raven croaks, flaps its wings and shows red illuminated eyes. The leaves of the adder-plant open and disclose demon and serpent as before. Skeleton forms appear above on rocks, pointing to* HERTZOG. *Music changes to tremulo-piano.*)

(*The adder-plant remains open during remainder of scene.*)

"By the venomed tongue that 'stills
Poisoned slender 'till it kills"

(*Casts green ingredient into the fire. Wild blast of demoniacal music and same action as before.*)

(*Music changes to tremulo-piano.*)

"By the thief with skulking tread
Who breaks the grave and robs the dead."

(*Casts blue ingredient into the fire. Wild blast and same action as before.*)

(*Music changes to tremulo-piano.*)

"By all the crimes men hate and fear
Zamiel, Master, now appear."

(*Casts red ingredient into the fire.*)

"Zamiel, appear, appear!"

(*Wild blast and same action as before. In addition to this, loud crashing thunder and vivid lightning, the latter showing itself in luminous forks in backing. Huge serpents writhe to and fro across the stage.*)

(ZAMIEL, *bearing a scepter around which is twined a green serpent, suddenly appears from trunk of blasted tree with strong light from calcium thrown upon him. He holds the picture a moment, before speaking.* HERTZOG *kneeling down. Music stops.*)

ZAMIEL. Arise.

(HERTZOG *rises.*)

Why am I summoned?

HERTZOG. My life is waning. Give me to live, feed the dull currents of my sluggish veins. Give me fresh charms and potencies.

ZAMIEL. Wherefore?

HERTZOG. Men hate, and did they not fear, would despise me. I would repay their hate with hate. I would live on, on, on, and in that life rival thy dread power of evil.

ZAMIEL. What wilt thou give for such a boon?

HERTZOG. Whatever thou wilt, give me but life, and all I have is thine.

ZAMIEL. 'Tis not enough. What's thine is mine already.

HERTZOG. What else?

ZAMIEL. Listen. A soul, younger, fresher, whiter than thine, must, on each recurring year be, by your arts, turned to my account.

HERTZOG. I hear, dread master, and will pay the price.

ZAMIEL. For every soul thus lost to good and gained to me, a year's new life is thine. A single soul, a single year, a hundred souls, a hundred years. 'Tis with thyself to live forever.

HERTZOG. Forever!

ZAMIEL. Forever! But should the stroke of midnight fall a twelve-month hence and no lost soul by you betrayed within that time come waiting at my gates, perdition closes on your dark career. Is't a compact?

HERTZOG. It is.

(*Music.* ZAMIEL *waves his scepter. Thunder and lightning. A fiend*—REDGLARE—*arises from below, bearing a large red book, pen and ink-horn.*)

ZAMIEL. (*Pointing to book.*) Sign!

(*Music. Thunder and lightning. Sheeted spectres arise at back and appear from behind rocks.* SKULDAWELP *reappears. Demons and skeletons appear, all pointing at* HERTZOG, *who takes the pen and dips it in the horn.*)

(*The pen ignites and flames blue. He writes in the book, during which the raven croaks, flaps its wings, etc. Serpents writhe, and demoniacal laughter is heard outside and above. After he has signed,* ZAMIEL *waves his scepter. Gong sounds. And* REDGLARE *descends with book, etc., amid red fire. Music stops.*)
'Tis well. Listen, slave. Within a dungeon of the eastern wing of gray and gloomy Wolfenstein, there lies enchained a youth called Rodolphe. His fortune's desperate, and desperate souls, like drowning men, will catch at straws. Begin with him.

HERTZOG. Dread Power, I hear thy mandate, and thy will obey. (*Bows low before* ZAMIEL.)
(*Music. Thunder, lightning and all the action as before. Red fire from behind altar and at the sides.* REDGLARE *reappears, pointing to* HERTZOG. *Winged serpents above, and fiery dragon enters. Simultaneous with which* GREPPO, *very white, with hair on end, rushes in as if to communicate something.*)

GREPPO. Master, I— (*Is appalled at the sight before him. Utters a loud cry, falls upon his knees clasping his hands and moving his lips as if in prayer.*)

ACT II

Scene 1

A subterranean vault beneath the castle of Wolfenstein.
WULFGAR *discovered chaining* RODOLPHE *to wall.*
Music at rise of curtain.

WULFGAR. There, my fine fellow, I think you are both safe and comfortable. No intruders, neither light nor sound, ever come here.
RODOLPHE. Wretch.

WULFGAR. When you want exercise or change of air and you can manage to get rid of yonder little encumbrance—(*Pointing to chains.*)—you can take it in the vault beneath; yonder trap leads to it. You may find it a little mouldy and may stumble over the skeleton of the last lodger, but that's nothing. Any change is better than no change at all.

RODOLPHE. Monster, begone.

WULFGAR. (*Taking up lamp.*) Oh, certainly, anything to oblige. In the meantime, if your exercise should give you an appetite and you should want food, cry out for it. Cry loud, and it won't come. Ha, ha, ha. Goodnight! (*Exit.*)

RODOLPHE. (*Alone.*) Alone. So end in darkness and in death all my bright dreams of the future. And must I perish thus, I who have but entered the portal of life? No, no, it cannot be. I must, I will burst these bonds.
(*Music.*)
(*He makes an effort to break the chains.*) 'Tis vain. They defy even the strength of despair. (*Shuddering.*) How awful is the chill of this noxious vault! Its very vapors press upon my brow like the hand of death, and freeze my very marrow.
(*Music.* HERTZOG *enters with dark-lantern.*)
(RODOLPHE, *starts.*) Who's there?

HERTZOG. Thy friend.

RODOLPHE. Who are you?

HERTZOG. (*Turning the light of the lantern upon his own face.*) Behold!
(*Chord.*)

RODOLPHE. (*Starting.*) Hertzog—the Crook!

HERTZOG. Aye, so men call me. (*Puts lantern up.*)

RODOLPHE. Ill-omened bird, what brings *you* here? Yet why should I ask? You are the monster of death. 'Tis well, 'tis merciful. Begin your work.

HERTZOG. Out, foolish boy. I serve no human master.

RODOLPHE. Then why are you here?

HERTZOG. I come to give thee liberty.

RODOLPHE. Liberty!

HERTZOG. Aye. Listen, I hate thine enemy. Thou lov'st a maid of whom thou hast been robbed. Wouldst win her back? I have the power to aid thee.

RODOLPHE. Begone, tempter! I know your power and guess

from whence it comes. Men say you deal in dark and
necromantic spells that warp the senses and enthrall the
soul.

HERTZOG. Pah! Art thou, too, tainted with the vulgar fear
that calls philosophy—the natural working of great Nature's laws—a spell of darkness? It is the light, weak boy,
the light which we sage men, who waste our lives o'er
midnight lamps, glean from dull vapors for the sluggards'
use. Fools sneer the most when least they understand, and
brand as foul what nature stamps as fair. Thy chains gall
thee; let me loose them. (*He touches them with his staff.
They fall to the ground.*)

RODOLPHE. (*Coming forward.*) What is your purpose?

HERTZOG. Again I say, to serve thee.

RODOLPHE. How?

HERTZOG. Listen—I will tell thee a secret. She whom thou
lovest is of noble birth.

RODOLPHE. Amina?

HERTZOG. Aye, yet not Amina, but the only child and heiress
of the noble house of Wellenstein, stolen when but an infant by a revengeful gypsy whom her father scourged, and
given to gabbling Barbara.

RODOLPHE. Amina—noble?

HERTZOG. Aye, and thou of humble birth—but gold can buy
nobility, nay more, can give thee power to cross thine
enemy.

RODOLPHE. Why talk to me of gold—to me—the poorest of
the poor, whose purse contains not half so much as one
poor silver mark.

HERTZOG. Thou'rt poor indeed, but thou art poor because
thou wilt be poor. 'Tis with thyself to shame the wealth of
mighty Croesus.

RODOLPHE. How?

HERTZOG. Hast thou not heard of glittering gold in massive
piles fast locked within these mountains?

RODOLPHE. An idle tale. A senseless fable told by crowing
gossips. A treasure often sought but never found, and
some do say 'tis death to seek it.

HERTZOG. I tell thee, boy, the story's true. This gold is pal-
pable to sight and touch, and may be garnered, too, if thou
art bold enough.

RODOLPHE. I'll hear no more. Thou'dst take advantage of my

desperate strait to work some juggle to entrap my soul. Begone, I say, begone!

HERTZOG. And leave thee to thy doom?

RODOLPHE. Aye.

HERTZOG. And thy affianced bride? Would'st thou—so like a craven—yield her up unto thine enemy?

RODOLPHE. Oh, agony!

HERTZOG. 'Tis true she loves thee, but bethink thee, boy. She is but woman and she may be won. Her noble birth is known to Wolfenstein, who means to wed her and with her fortune prop his falling house. Already flattered by his serpent-tongue, she dries her tears and listens to his suit.

RODOLPHE. 'Tis false.

HERTZOG. 'Tis true.

RODOLPHE. The proof?

HERTZOG. Behold.

(*Music. He waves his staff.* WOLFENSTEIN *and* AMINA *are revealed; the former is clasping the hand and kneeling at the feet of the latter whose face is averted.*)

RODOLPHE. (*Starting toward it.*) By Heaven, he shall not.

HERTZOG. (*Waves his staff to interpose.*) Bravely said, bravely said.

RODOLPHE. (*Turning quickly.*) What dev'lish compact would you have me sign? Propose it while my reason whirls and desperation aids your damn'd design. If by the act I snatch her from his grasp, I'll pay the ransom though it reach my soul.

(HERTZOG, *with face averted, chuckles sardonically.*)

Come, philosopher, or fiend—whate'er thou art—the price, I say the price!

HERTZOG. Pah! I ask no compact. I would serve thee gratis. I but demand that thou shalt serve thyself. Be rich and thou'lt be powerful. In thy revenge upon thine enemy and *mine* thou'lt pay thy debt to me with interest.

RODOLPHE. Where lies this wondrous treasure?

HERTZOG. Listen. Amid the fastnesses of the Hartz, beyond the outlet of the Black Gorge, lies a small lake whose waters few have ever gazed upon, for vulgar fear and superstitious dread have long since marked it for enchanted ground.

RODOLPHE. I've heard the story.

HERTZOG. Trace carefully its northern shore until a rock—

rising like a wall—bars further passage. Beneath a fringe
of tangled vines you'll find a boat concealed. Behold this
talismanic ring. (*Takes a large ring from his finger.*) 'Tis
a magnet of wondrous power. When thou hast found the
boat, step boldly in. This ring will guide thee safely to
the entrance of the golden cavern, within the compass of
whose glittering walls thy wondering eyes may feast on
wealth far greater than the coffers of the world can boast.

RODOLPHE. Give me the ring.

HERTZOG. 'Tis thine. (*Gives ring.*) Stay, thou'lt need a
henchman. (*Stamps his foot.*) Varlet, come forth.
(*Music.*)

(GREPPO *enters.*)

(*Aside.*) He, too, shall perish.

GREPPO. Your will, master?

HERTZOG. To part with thee.

GREPPO. (*Aside.*) Oh, if this should be true. (*Aloud.*) With
me?

HERTZOG. With thee, knave.

GREPPO. Wherefore?

HERTZOG. I weary with thine appetite.

GREPPO. (*Aside.*) Here is a chance. Oh, here *is* a chance, if
he but stick to it. I must seem unwilling, lest he repent.
(*Aloud.*) Dear Master, I will reform, believe me, I will
reform. Allowance me to what would starve a mouse, nay
more, to pleasure you, I will not eat at all. I'll live on air,
but do not cast me off.

HERTZOG. I am resolved. Behold thy future master. (*To*
RODOLPHE.) Thou'lt find him faithful, but he breeds a
famine. Take for thy present need this purse of gold.
(*Offers purse.* RODOLPHE *by a gesture refuses it.*)
Nay, when thou'rt rich thou can'st repay it.

RODOLPHE. (*Taking purse.*) Nay, more, if what you say be
true, eternal gratitude—

HERTZOG. Nay, you trifle time. (*Waves staff.*) Yonder lies
your path, it is a golden one. Begone.

RODOLPHE. Farewell, Come boy, come.
(*Music. Exit,* GREPPO *following. Turns to entreat* HERTZOG,
who raises his staff threateningly. GREPPO *exits hurriedly.*)

HERTZOG. (*Stands on opening and, chuckling, gazes after*

them.) The thought of vengeance stirs within his heart—the lust of gold is rising in his soul—the path that leads to where 'tis hoarded ends in death. He's mine—ha, ha—he's mine!

Scene 2

A lobby in the castle of WOLFENSTEIN. *Enter* BARBARA, *followed by* CARLINE.

BARBARA. Don't talk to me, girl. Remember your station and consider mine. Who *am* I and *what* am I that I should be lodged in a wing of the castle overlooking the dog-kennels?

CARLINE. Your Ladyship is quite right to rebel, and when I advised your Ladyship to calm yourself, it was out of consideration for your Ladyship's eyes. Any little flurry does so spoil the natural beauty of their expression.

BARBARA. Carline, you're a good girl, you're a considerate girl and I forgive you, but eyes or no eyes, I'll not be imposed upon. Where's Mynheer von Puffengruntz? Where's his Lordship's chamberlain?

CARLINE. Here he comes down the great stairway, as full of flesh and scant of breath as ever. (*Aside.*) And as the waddling old porpoise appears to have a licorice tooth for this silly old buzzard, I'll leave them to bill and coo, while I run off to comfort dear 'Mina, who has passed the whole night in tears for poor Rodolphe.

(VON PUFFENGRUNTZ *enters.* CARLINE *curtsies and exits.*)

VON PUFFENGRUNTZ. Eh, what? Madam Barbara, stirring so early. Why, bless my soul, the mist of the mountain is yet hanging upon the turrets of the castle.

BARBARA. There let it hang and be hanged to it—stirring indeed! Haven't I been stirring all night, and wouldn't the seven sleepers have been stirring all night, too, if they had lodged where I did?

VON PUFFENGRUNTZ. Surely nothing has had the audacity to disturb the quiet of your slumber?

BARBARA. Nothing? To begin with, do you call such a storm

as that of last night nothing? Why, the thunder crashed over the castle loud enough to wake the dead. That was bad enough, but only to think that I, the right honorable foster-mother that-is-to-be, to her right honorable Ladyship that-is-to-be, passing the night in apartments overlooking a dog-kennel!

VON PUFFENGRUNTZ. A dog-kennel?

BARBARA. Aye, a kennel of great savage hounds, fed late at night on raw meat, on purpose, to give them the nightmare and make them dream all night long of chasing wild bears in the forest. Ugh! I shall never get their horrible yelping out of my head.

VON PUFFENGRUNTZ. Believe me, my dear Madam Barbara, it is the first time the brutes were ever known to have been unruly. I promise that they shall be soundly punished and instantly removed. But I, too, am criminal. The apartments were selected by me, because they command the best view of the mountain.

BARBARA. But I don't want to look at the mountain. I got a glimpse of it from one of the north windows last night during the storm, and it looked for all the world as if Beelzebub and his imps were holding a jubilee there.

VON PUFFENGRUNTZ. Enough, my dear Madam Barbara, enough. If the mountain is unpleasant, it shall be removed. No, no. I mean *you* shall be removed. (*Approaching her in a wheedling manner.*) Will it please you to accompany me and choose for yourself?

BARBARA. (*Simperingly.*) Really, Mynheer von Puffengruntz, you have such mollifying ways that—that—

VON PUFFENGRUNTZ. (*Taking her hand.*) Oh—a—a—o.

BARBARA. Would it be prudent? Dare I trust myself? We poor silly things are so weak and you men are so naughty that—that—(*Leans her head upon his shoulder, looks up into his face and sighs.*)

VON PUFFENGRUNTZ. Confiding innocence—rely upon the honor of a von Puffengruntz.

(*Looks around, sighs, kisses her. She utters a faint scream, and hiding her face in her fan, is led off by* VON PUFFEN-GRUNTZ, *chuckling.*)

Scene 3

A wild pass in the Hartz Mountains.
Music.
Enter RODOLPHE *and* GREPPO, *each bearing an alpine staff.*
GREPPO *in improved condition.*

RODOLPHE. A strange, weird place, and one it seems not often
trod by human footsteps. I fear we've missed the way—
what think you, Master Greppo?

GREPPO. (*Aside.*) *Master* Greppo! *Master* Greppo. He calls
me *Master* Greppo! Here's an honor, and here's a master.
Oh *such* a master, such a liberal master as this—stuffed
belly, tight as any drum with goodly provender and generous wine will testify! (*To* RODOLPHE.) What think I,
princely Master?

RODOLPHE. Aye.

GREPPO. Why, since you honor me with consultation and
give me leave to think at all, a privilege grown rusty from
great lack of use, I say we're right, and that the lake we
seek is near at hand.

RODOLPHE. Why think you so?

GREPPO. Because just now I heard a bittern cry and twice
ere that I heard a marsh frog croak, and as they're both
accounted water-fowl, 'twere safe to say we're near the
water.

RODOLPHE. Then let us on. Ere long the rising moon will
pierce this veil of mist and light us to our golden haven.
Come. (*Exit.*)

GREPPO. I follow. (*Exit.*)

Scene 4

The grotto of Golden Stalactites. A grand and comprehen-
sive water-cavern of gold, deeply perspective, with stalacti-
form, arched roof. Vistas, running parallel and harmonizing
with the main Grotto, the mouth of which discloses an open
lake and distant shore at back. Transparent silver waters, in
which are seen sporting fishes and nondescript amphibea.

Diminutive fairies asleep on the waters of the Grotto in golden shells. Ground- or shore-piece, richly studded with gold and jewels. Masses of emerald and gold, upon and at the foot of which are reclining gnomes and amphibea.

Fairies asleep in poses. The moon, seen through the opening at back and over the distant shore of the lake, shows red upon its face at opening of scene.

Music.

DRAGONFIN, *who has been asleep on a jeweled mass on the shore, slowly awakens, rises and stretches himself. Upon turning, he sees the red upon the face of the moon.*

Music—chord.

DRAGONFIN. (*Uttering a cry of alarm.*) Awake. Awake.

(*Music—hurry. Gnomes and amphibea spring to their feet. Fairies and water nymphs enter hurriedly. Diminutive sprites in shells and fairies in poses, awaken.*)

Behold, there's blood upon the face of the moon—our Queen's in danger! To arms, to arms!

(*Music. The sprites in the shells disappear. The gnomes, amphibea and fairies rush off and immediately re-enter armed, the first-named with knotted clubs and tridents, the fairies with javelins. During the action the red disappears from the face of the moon, and it resumes its natural color.*)

(*Seeing the change.*) Stay—'tis past. Hark.

(*Queen* STALACTA *is heard singing beneath the waters. All bend forward and listen to her song.*)

(*After song.*) 'Tis she, our queen.

(*All kneel. Music.* STALACTA *rises from the waters and steps on shore, assisted by* DRAGONFIN.)

STALACTA. Arise, my loving subjects.

(*All rise.*)

DRAGONFIN. (*Pantomines.*) Mistress, but now the light in yon great sapphire died out and stains of blood flushed in the face of the pale moon. You have 'scaped some deadly peril.

STALACTA. Thou art right. Listen, all. Tonight, while wandering in the fastnesses of the Hartz, without my protecting talisman, I heedlessly trod within one of the charmed circles of our enemy, the arch-fiend Zamiel.

ALL. Ha!

STALACTA. On the instant I was transformed into a white

dove with shorn pinions. From beneath the rank leaves of an adder-plant glided a huge serpent. Its eyes were burning coals, its tongue a living flame. I was paralyzed with fear and powerless to move. Nearer and nearer it came. I felt its stifling breath displace the purer air—I saw its venomed fangs glist'ning in the pale moonlight. Rising from out its deadly coil preparing itself to strike, when suddenly a youth, a mortal, strangely present in that wild, weird spot, seeing the danger of the trembling bird, seized a dead bough, which chance had fashioned like a Holy Cross, and smote the foul thing dead. Then he bore me safely from the charmed spot and gave me life and liberty.

DRAGONFIN. Revenge, revenge on the minions of Zamiel! (*Goes quietly off.*)

ALL. Revenge—revenge!

STALACTA. Nay, let no thought other than of joy mingle with this happy time. Remember, 'tis my natal hour, and I would have it, as in the past, a festal one. Let the invisible harmonies of this our realm breathe sweetest concord only. —And you, bright Crystaline, with your fair sisters, chase with flying feet the silver hours. (*Seats herself on bank.*)

(*Music. The Fairies form for dance. After the first pose, a loud, prolonged warning note, as if from a shell, is heard outside. All start in alarm, and hold the attitude of listening. The sound is repeated.*)

(*Music—hurry. The pose is broken and the fairies, gnomes and amphibea, the latter seizing their arms, form in alarm on either side. DRAGONFIN appears quickly.*)

(*STALACTA, who at the first sound has sprung to her feet.*) Speak, what danger threatens?

DRAGONFIN. The sentinel shells, played upon by the watchful winds, give alarm. Two daring mortals, armed with the enchanted magnet of the Black Crook, approach the secret entrance. Already they have passed the white whirlpool in safety. They come to despoil our realm of its glittering wealth.

STALACTA. Fear not, the talisman they bear is powerless against the spells that guard the portal.

ALL. Ho—ho—ho!

(*Echoes without and above. Music. Chorus—by gnomes, amphibea and fairies.*)

"Rejoice, rejoice, rejoice!
Sprites of the golden realm, rejoice.
Daring mortals mock our power
Flushed with the drink that the heart makes bold
They madly rush on the fatal hour.
Dark spells arise! Smite their longing eyes
That they never may gaze on the glittering prize!
    Rejoice, rejoice, rejoice!
Sprites of the golden realm rejoice!

STALACTA. My faithful subjects—your Queen commends your zeal with which you would guard from mortal sight our beauteous realm. But ere these rash intruders perish, I would gratify a strange desire. Speed hence, good Dragonfin. Catch me their shadows from the bosom of the moon-lighted lake and cast them upon my faithful mirror. I would look upon them ere they fade forever.

(*Music.* DRAGONFIN *prostrates himself before* STALACTA, *springs into the water and disappears.*)

Begin the spell!

(*Music. This is either* spoken *by her or* sung *by fairy-chorus.*)

    "Mortal shadows dimly cast
        By the moonbeams' mystic ray
    On the bosom of the lake
        Hither, hither, fly away,
    Flitting through the silver sheen
        Come at summons of our Queen
    Guardian spirits, let them pass,
        Cast their shadows on the glass."

(*Music.* DRAGONFIN *springs from the water, and after prostrating himself before the Queen, rises and points to the water.*)

(*Music. Fairies wave their wands. A small arched-headed frame of gold and coral stalactites rises at the distant entrance of the Grotto, showing small figures of* RODOLPHE *and* GREPPO *in boat, the former at the prow, gazing anxiously forward, the latter aft, in the attitude of paddling.*)

(STALACTA *who turns when the picture is fully shown. Chord of music.*)

(*Starting.*) Ha—'tis he! He must not perish. Invisible spirits, avert this peril.

"Shades of mortals hovering near
Join your masters—disappear."
(*Music—hurry. The mirror and figures quickly sink.*)
Dragonfin, come hither. Fly with swiftest speed to the
rocks beneath the waters of the guarded entrance. When
the frail bark which now approaches shall be rent asunder
by the relentless spells that guard our realm, be it your
task to snatch from death these daring mortals and bear
them safely hither.

ALL. (*All start forward inquiringly, exclaiming.*) Mistress!

STALACTA. Nay, question me not, away, away,
Slaves of my power, obey, obey.
(*Music—hurry.* DRAGONFIN *bows low, springs into the water and disappears.*)
(*Music. A small boat, with two mechanical figures or small doubles of* RODOLPHE *and* GREPPO *as they appeared in the mirror, appears from the distant entrance of the cavern, and moves very slowly across. When it reaches the center it sinks at the sound of the gong and flash of lightning at back.*)
(*Music—hurry. All the gnomes, amphibea, etc., utter exclamations of delight and indulge in extravagant antics, until checked by a gesture from* STALACTA.)
(*Soft music.* DRAGONFIN *rises slowly from the water, supporting on either side* RODOLPHE *and* GREPPO, *the latter gulping and grasping violently for breath as his head appears. They step on shore,* RODOLPHE *and* GREPPO *lost in bewilderment.* DRAGONFIN *bows low before* STALACTA. *The other amphibea and gnomes make a demonstration of attack.*)
(*Stepping between.*) Forbear! Who moves again 'till I alone command shall perish.
(*They retire.*)

RODOLPHE. (*Rubbing his eyes.*) Is this a phantasm—this glittering gold, yon flashing gems, these strange fantastic shapes? Have I then passed the portal of an unknown world, or am I dreaming?

STALACTA. Welcome, brave mortal, to our bright domain. And you, my subjects, know and greet your Queen's preserver.
(*Music. Gnomes and amphibea cluster around* RODOLPHE *and* GREPPO, *rolling at their feet and indulging in various*

grateful antics, after which the fairies surround them and evince their delight.)

RODOLPHE. (*Still bewildered.*) If this indeed be not a dream, tell me, Bright Being, you whose simple motion seems to sway the moves and passions of this Elfin Band, who art thou, and where am I?

STALACTA. I am called Stalacta, Queen of this dazzling realm. The glittering wonders that assail thine eyes are not creations of phantastic dreams but nature's handiwork, wrought with the cunning fingers in a bounteous mood.

GREPPO. (*Who has picked up a large mass of gold at the back, comes forward.*) 'Tis true, 'tis true. Behold the shining nugget.

STALACTA. Who is thy droll companion?

RODOLPHE. My simple henchman, a faithful guide and servitor.

STALACTA. I bid him welcome, for his master's sake.

GREPPO. Thanks, thanks, your Resplendent Majesty, thanks, thanks.

RODOLPHE. You spoke of service done; have we then met before?

STALACTA. Yes, once.

RODOLPHE. Indeed? When?

STALACTA. This very night.

RODOLPHE. Tonight?

STALACTA. Tonight, in the glen of firs, but not as now—then, a poor, weak, fluttering, charm-encompassed bird, you snatched me trembling from the jaws of death, broke the dark spell of transformation, and gave to me the priceless boon of liberty.

RODOLPHE. I do remember—

GREPPO. And so do I. Phew, how the sparks flew when Master smashed the head of the scaly monster, and such a smell of brimstone, I do believe it was one of Beelzebub's own imps in disguise.

STALACTA. Again thou art welcome. This is my natal hour. Wilt view the sports of this, our carnival?

RODOLPHE. Most willingly.

STALACTA. And while the revels proceed, thou shalt tell me thy story.

(*Music—ballet. Seats are brought forward by amphibea.* STALACTA *and* RODOLPHE *sit.* GREPPO *amuses himself with*

DRAGONFIN. *Gnomes and amphibea present him from time to time with nuggets of gold and jewels, which he thrusts into his pockets until they become greatly distended, during which action the diminutive sprites reappear in shells on the water, floating to and fro, fishing. The fairies form for dance. Grand ballet action by principals and full corps de ballet, during which the fishers in the shells are seen to catch small silver fish.*)

GREPPO. (*After the dance terminates.*) Ha, ha. Dancing. All very well in its way. But there's the sport for me, fishing! Look, Master, look. See the little rogues hook the silly shiners. Oh, if there is one thing in the world I love more than another, it is fishing—such fun to feel the greedy rascals snatch and see them wriggle. There's another—oh, I can't stand it any longer! Fishing is like the measles, it's catching. (*Turning to amphibea and gnomes.*) Would any of you handsome gentlemen oblige me with a spare hook and line.

(DRAGONFIN *nods assent and brings him rod and line.*)

Well, upon my word! I am very much obliged to your Scaly Magnificence. I'll do as much for you someday. By the way, is your Amphibious Majesty fond of fish?

(DRAGONFIN *nods affirmatively.*)

What kind?

(DRAGONFIN, *business of indicating that he likes large ones.*)

Like large ones, eh? All right, I'll make you a present of the first ten-pounder that I catch.

(*Music. He fishes from the shore and catches two small fishes, the last quite diminutive. Amphibea, gnomes and fairies laugh boisterously as each fish is drawn forth.*)

(*Coming down, chapfallen.*) Pshaw—mere sprats and sardines—not my kind at all. This is too much like taking advantage of confiding innocence. (*To* DRAGONFIN.) Couldn't your Finny Excellency oblige me with a more tempting bait, something that would seduce some big, greedy, wiggly, waggly fellow, into taking a nibble?

(DRAGONFIN *nods affirmatively. Music.* DRAGONFIN *goes to the margin of the water and draws forth a large crab, which he places on the hand of* GREPPO. *It seizes him by the fingers to the great delight of the amphibea, gnomes and fairies. He struggles frantically to extricate himself,*

and is finally released by DRAGONFIN, *who baits the hook
with the crab and gives him the rod and line.*)
(*Taking* DRAGONFIN *apart confidentially.*) I don't know
about this. Excuse me for asking a question, but as an
unprejudiced observer, don't you think this style of bait
more likely to bite the fish than the fish to bite the bait?
(DRAGONFIN *shakes his head and indicates that a large fish
will take it.*)
All right. Here goes then.
(*Music. He casts the line into the water. A moment after
it is violently seized and a frantic struggle ensues, during
which he is nearly drawn overboard two or three times.
Suddenly an amphibious monster springs from the water
and pursues* GREPPO *around, off and on the stage to the
great delight of the amphibea, gnomes and fairies, who
indulge in boisterous laughter.*)
(GREPPO, *in his terror, throws himself at the feet of*
STALACTA *for protection. She rises and waves her hand.
The monster retires and is pacified by* DRAGONFIN.)
GREPPO. (*Coming forward.*) Really, my fishy-fleshy friend,
you must excuse me. I beg ten thousand pardons. I hadn't
the remotest idea in the world that any of you bottle-green
gentlemen were lying around loose on the bottom, watching for a supper of raw crabs. Indeed I hadn't.
(*The monster growls and makes a start at him.*)
(*Music.* DRAGONFIN *interposes and pacifies the monster by
patting him on the back. Then, taking its hand, passes it
into that of* GREPPO.)
GREPPO. (*Shaking the monster's hand cordially.*) All right,
I accept your apology. (*Then turning to* DRAGONFIN.) Now
you're what I call a true friend—a friend in need, you stick
by a fellow when he hasn't the courage to stick by himself.
This is the second time you've done me a service. Once in
saving me from too much water and now in saving me
from too much luck, and I'll let you see that I can be
grateful. You like fish?
(DRAGONFIN *nods affirmatively.*)
(GREPPO *passing the monster over to him.*) Consider him
yours.
(*All the amphibea, gnomes and fairies laugh and go up.*)
STALACTA. (*Rising and leading* RODOLPHE *forward.*) Thy
story claims for thee my pity and my aid.

RODOLPHE. And Hertzog the Black Crook—

STALACTA. Is a vile sorcerer whose dark, unhallowed spells were wrought for thy destruction.

RODOLPHE. How?

STALACTA. Beneath the entrance to this charmed spot, intertwined amid the branches of the coraline, are whole hecatombs of human bones, the whitened relics of adventurous mortals who like thyself have sought the realm. Until tonight no human eye has ever seen the dazzling splendor of this wondrous dome. No human footsteps save thine own and his who follows thee have ever pressed these sands of gold. Had not thy coming been to me foreshadowed and all my power been interposed to snatch thee from the impending doom, then thou too had'st joined the hapless throng that mouldering lies beneath yon depths.

RODOLPHE. Then is thy debt to me already paid.

STALACTA. Not so—I am still thy debtor and must ever be. Thou art environed by danger and need the power of my protection. Return unto the outer world again, thy happiness is there. She whom thou lovest is worthy of thy love, therefore return.

RODOLPHE. Amina, dear Amina.

STALACTA. In the secret cell of these caverns, whose walls are solid gold, lie countless hoards of richest treasure, gleaned for ages by the tireless gnomes. In the crystal depths of these waters sparkle gems richer by far than human eyes have ever gazed upon. Of these thou shalt bear with thee the choicest. Behold my gift.

(*Music. A jeweled stalactiform etagere with strong light from calcium falling upon it rises in front of ground-piece, bearing upon its different shelves rich vases filled with gold and various-colored jewels which* DRAGONFIN, *gnomes, and amphibea remove, performing a series of grotesque evolutions to marked music. Etagere sinks—after which music.* STALACTA *waves her wand; a golden boat studded with jewels glides on.*)

This bark, protected by a potent spell, shall bear thee safely to your neighboring shore. My faithful gnomes shall be thy treasure bearers. But ere we part, take thou this jeweled circlet. (*Gives him a ring from her finger.*) Should danger threaten—as perchance it will, for baffled malice has a thousand stings—press but thy lips upon the gem and thou wilt find me by thy side.

(*Music.* RODOLPHE *kneels and kisses her hand. She raises him.*)

Farewell.

(*Music. He slips into the boat.* GREPPO, *bearing a large mass of gold, affectionately embraces* DRAGONFIN, *shakes hands with the gnomes and amphibea, kisses the fairies, bows low to* STALACTA *and gets into the boat. A dolphin, glittering in green and gold, rises from waters with principal danseuse bearing vase of treasure; other dolphins float with diminutive sprites bearing treasure. Copious shower of gold, the other sprites on the water catching the flakes in shells of silver. Poses by gnomes, amphibea and fairies. The whole scene brilliantly lighted. Slow curtain.*)

ACT III

Scene 1

A lapse of six months.

Illuminated gardens of Wolfenstein by moon-light, with terrace and illuminated castle at back. This scene, standing as it does the entire act, should be elaborate and beautiful. Music.

Masqueraders in ball costumes discovered promenading. Grand Ballet divertissement, after which the masquers gradually disappear at different entrances.

Enter from the terrace DAME BARBARA, *masked, falutingly dressed and carrying a huge fan. She is followed by* CARLINE.

BARBARA. (*Unmasking and coming forward.*) Phew, what a relief. Thank the saints his Countship's birthday comes but once a year. Another such festival would be the death of me. Ah! I'm stewed, fried, broiled and roasted. (*Fans herself vigorously.*)

CARLINE. (*Aside.*) And still as tough as Dame Gretchen's gander, what was twenty-one last Easter. (*Aloud.*) Why, Madam Barbara, I thought you enjoyed it.

BARBARA. So I do, child, so I do; particularly the masquerading. One has so many pleasant things whispered in one's ear; but I can't say so much for the waltzing. It's such a terrible thing to take the starch out of one's linen.

CARLINE. La, Madam Barbara, what's a little starch? Nothing. If I waltzed as gracefully as you
(BARBARA *makes a gesture of satisfaction.*)
and had such an inviting waist—
(BARBARA *pinches her waist.*)
I'd keep at it until I was as limp as a boiled cabbage leaf.

BARBARA. Then you—you think me graceful, eh?

CARLINE. (*Aside.*) As a hippopotamus. (*Aloud.*) As a sylph. You were the envy of all the ladies and the admiration of all the other sex. Did you notice that courtly gentleman in the blue mask?

BARBARA. And what of *him?*

CARLINE. Nothing, only he was frantic to get an introduction to you.

BARBARA. No! Was he?

CARLINE. Yes indeed, Madam. And when his Lordship, the Count, engaged the lady Amina for a moment, he turned to me and slipping a golden crown into my palm with one hand, pressing his heart with the other and pointing to you with the other, asked with a sweet, sighing, silvery voice, trembling with emotion: "Who is that lovely being?"

BARBARA. No—did he?

CARLINE. Yes indeed, Madam. (*Aside.*) The saints forgive me for lying. (*Aloud.*) And Mynheer von Puffengruntz, who overheard him, turned pea-green with jealousy.

BARBARA. (*Fanning herself and pressing her hand upon her heart.*) Be still, little trembler, be still. I declare, my silly heart is fluttering like a poor little starling in a gold cage.

CARLINE. (*Aside.*) More like a big buzzard in a steel trap.

BARBARA. Carline, take my fan, child. (*Gives it.*) The exertion will make my complexion too ruddy.

CARLINE. So it will, Madam, and ruddy complexions are not genteel—allow *me.* (*Fans her vigorously.*)

BARBARA. Not so violent, girl, you'll disarrange my hair. Gently, very gently, a sort of sportive zephyr.

CARLINE. I understand, Madam, you want a mild sort of tickling sensation, something like one feels on one's neck when a gentleman whispers in one's ear—

BARBARA. (*Languidly.*) Y-e-s. (*Sighs.*) And he called me a- a- what did he call me?

CARLINE. A swan-like creature. (*Aside.*) A goose.

BARBARA. (*Sighs.*) Who can he be, I wonder.

CARLINE. Nobody appears to know exactly. I heard his Lordship, the Count, whisper to the Baron von Stuffencram that he suspected the mysterious blue mask to be no other than the young prince Leopold. —Once, while dancing, his domino came open at the breast and I saw a collar of jewels fit for an emperor. However, as everybody is to unmask at the grand banquet, we will then know all about him.

BARBARA. Eh, what, the Prince Leopold?

CARLINE. So his Lordship, the Count, thinks.

BARBARA. Why, he is already affianced, as everybody knows, to the young Princess Frederica.

CARLINE. Dear me, so he is—how unfortunate.

BARBARA. Poor young man—how I pity him. What a terrible thing it is to be of royal blood and not have the liberty to choose for one's self. Heigh-ho! I know it is a sad, cruel, wicked thing to blight a young and budding affection, but as the right honorable foster-mother that-*is*-to-be of her right honorable Ladyship that-is-to-be, I mustn't encourage his highness in a hopeless passion. (*Displays herself.*)

(*Enter* VON PUFFENGRUNTZ.)

VON PUFFENGRUNTZ. (*At back, admiringly.*) There she is! What a grace, what a dignity, what a walk. (*Coming forward.*) Ah—a—a.

BARBARA. (*Sighing.*) There's another victim to love's cruel dart; my fan, child.

CARLINE. (*Giving it.*) Be careful, use it gently, Madam. Remember your complexion. (*Aside.*) What a lovely couple—powder and puff.

VON PUFFENGRUNTZ. (*Aside.*) What a golden opportunity. (*Aloud.*) Young woman, as I left the grand hall I heard your mistress asking for you.

CARLINE. (*Aside.*) Of course, I understand—cunning old walrus. (*Aloud.*) May I retire, Madam?

BARBARA. Yes, certainly, child, that is, if her Ladyship requires you. (*Coquettes with her dress, etc.*)

CARLINE. (*Aside.*) I thought so, willing old pelican. She's beginning to dress her feathers already. Never mind. I shall have another flirtation with the prince's equerry, the drollest and most agreeable fellow in the world, and *such* a rogue. (*Exits.*)

(VON PUFFENGRUNTZ *gazes admiringly at* BARBARA *and sighs.*)

BARBARA. (*Casting sidelong glances at him.*) Heigh-ho! There he is. My charms tonight have completed the conquest. He is fast-bound in the bonds of rosy cupid. I see a proposal in one eye and a marriage settlement in the other. But I mustn't draw him in too suddenly. These men are like trout; they must be played with a little.

VON PUFFENGRUNTZ. Full moon of the festival, why have you so cruelly robbed the grand hall of your light, and left us to grope about in the dull glimmer of the sickly stars?

BARBARA. Don't talk to me about moonshine and sickly stars, you heartless, gay deceiver.

VON PUFFENGRUNTZ. Deceiver?

BARBARA. Deceiver! Didn't I see you gallivanting with the Fräulein von Skragneck, the rich Burgomaster's daughter?

VON PUFFENGRUNTZ. Politeness, my dear Madam Barbara, merely politeness, on my honor. The fact is I—I had the misfortune to tread on the lady's favorite bunion, and what you mistook for tenderness was only an apology—an apology, believe me, my dear Madam Barbara, only an apology.

BARBARA. Oh, you men, you deceiving men! You are always ready with an excuse.

VON PUFFENGRUNTZ. On the honor of a von Puffengruntz, I swear I speak the truth. The Fräulein von Skragneck indeed! Haven't I got eyes? Ah, cruel fair one, compared with her and all others, you are as the stately sunflower in a meadow of dandelions. As—as the queenly holly-hock in a garden of chickweed.

(*Music—tremulo-piano.*)

(DRAGONFIN, *ascends quickly, steps forward and listens.*)

BARBARA. (*Aside.*) It's coming at last. I know it's coming. (*Pressing her heart.*) What a strange flutter. I hope I'm not going to faint. Dear me, what poor weak, silly crea-

tures we are. I must nerve myself for the trying occasion.
How fortunate it is that I happen to have my smelling-
salts about me. (*Draws flask from her pocket, turns her
back to* VON PUFFENGRUNTZ, *and drinks.*)

VON PUFFENGRUNTZ. (*Aside.*) She's moved. She's overcome
with emotion. She turns to hide her blushes. She yields,
and now, like a conqueror, I'll gather in the fruits of
victory.

(*He kneels with difficulty at the feet of* BARBARA. *His face
is half-averted, and he is about to take her hand, when
DRAGONFIN glides quietly back of and between them,
extends his left hand to* VON PUFFENGRUNTZ *and takes
BARBARA's in the other. They both sigh.* VON PUFFENGRUNTZ
squeezes the hand of DRAGONFIN, *who shakes with suppressed laughter.*)

Poor, frightened thing, how she trembles.

BARBARA. (*Aside.*) Dear me, how strangely the tender passion affects him. He's shaking like an aspen and his hand
is as cold as ice.

VON PUFFENGRUNTZ. Bewitching siren, listen to the voice of
love.

BARBARA. Oh, Mynheer von Puffengruntz, how can you?

VON PUFFENGRUNTZ. Don't call me von Puffengruntz. Call me
Maximilian, call me *your* Maximilian. (*Squeezes* DRAGON-
FIN's *hand.* DRAGONFIN *squeezes* BARBARA's *hand.*)

BARBARA. Oh, don't, you naughty man, you—you hurt my
hand.

VON PUFFENGRUNTZ. No, did I? Queen of Love and Beauty,
then let me heal the bruise.

(*Kisses the hand of* DRAGONFIN *rapturously, who, at the
same time kisses* BARBARA's.)

And now that I've healed it, let me call it mine. (*Looks
for the first time attentively at the hand; continues the
inspection up the arm until he encounters the grinning
face of* DRAGONFIN, *when in speechless terror he drops the
hand, makes various floundering attempts to regain his
feet and exits, hurriedly.*)

BARBARA. (*Aside.*) Shall I keep him a little longer with
Cupid's dart sticking in his bosom, or shall I end his
misery. (*Aloud.*) Ahem, you'll—you'll never be a naughty
boy again?

(DRAGONFIN *squeezes her hand.*)

And you'll promise never to tread on the Fräulein von Skragneck's favorite bunion. (DRAGONFIN *squeezes her hand.*) (*Aside.*) Poor fellow, joy has made him speechless, he can only answer with a squeeze of the hand. (*Aloud.*) Well then, Maximilian, I'm yours! (*Falls into* DRAGONFIN'S *arms; looks up into his face.*) (*Music. She utters a piercing scream and rushes off.*) (DRAGONFIN *imitates and indulges in extravagant antics until music changes—when he starts, inclines his ear to the ground and listens—rises, moves cautiously, starts, points off, shakes his clenched hand threateningly, and quickly disappears.*)

HERTZOG. (*Entering hurriedly and disturbed.*) Foiled, tricked, crossed in the hour of my victory! A life desperately played for and fairly won, snatched from the jaws of death. He lives, my chosen victim lives, and flushed with triumph and vast hoards of gold, stalks boldly forth to mock me. Oh, curse the interposing power that stepped between us, a withering palsy light upon her arm and blight and pestilence infect the air she breathes! Oh, impotent, oh driveling fool! To work, to work. A soul once tampered with must be pursued, not cast aside to tempt another, so runs the bond which I've sealed. 'Tis well, 'tis well. I'll track him as the sleuth-hound tracks the stag. He must, he *shall* be mine. (*Music. Exit hurriedly.*) (*March of Amazons.*)

(*Re-enter masquers, who cross and disappear.*)

(*Enter* CARLINE, *laughing immoderately. She is followed by* GREPPO, *who is dressed in a smart, but outré livery.*)

CARLINE. No, no, Master Equerry, that won't do. You are very clever, very droll, and you tell very funny stories, but that last joke is a trifle too much.

GREPPO. But my dear Susetta.

CARLINE. (*Laughing.*) There, there, I knew you were not in earnest—my name's not Susetta.

GREPPO. Of course it isn't, it's—it's—what is it?

CARLINE. No, it isn't "What-is-it"—it's Carline.

GREPPO. Of course it is, but you see, I always mean Carline
when I say Susetta. Therefore Susetta—that is, my dear
Carline—when I tell you I love you—

CARLINE. (*Laughing.*) I don't believe a word you say. Why,
you arrived here scarcely three hours ago, and you've
already been making love to half the girls in the castle.

GREPPO. It's a mistake, my dear Susetta—I mean Carline—
altogether a mistake. I had my eye on you from the first,
and any little outside pleasantry you may have happened
to notice was only to get my hand in.

CARLINE. And this is only to keep it in, I suppose. No, no,
I'm not so simple as I look, and I tell you, clever Master
Equerry, it won't do.

GREPPO. But my dear Carline, allow me to tell you that I'm
not an equerry.

CARLINE. No?

GREPPO. (*Drawing himself up.*) I'm Consulting Secretary—
Confidential Advisor—Portable Treasury and Principal Dis-
bursing Officer to his Highness the Prince—(*Aside.*) Everybody takes master to be a prince and it's no part of my
business to undeceive them. Besides, if he isn't a prince,
he deserves to be, and I ought to be his Prime Minister.

CARLINE. Dear Me! Consulting Secretary!

GREPPO. Consulting Secretary.

CARLINE. Confidential Advisor?

GREPPO. Confidential Advisor.

CARLINE. Portable Treasury!

GREPPO. Portable Treasury. Behold! (*Showing two glittering
purses.*) Here are two purses, my master's and my own.
From this (*Showing one nearly empty.*) by the Prince's
orders came the gold I scattered among the servants in the
courtyard. With this (*Showing full one.*) I intend to
endow the maiden of my choice.

CARLINE. And you really mean—

GREPPO. That you are she.

CARLINE. No!

GREPPO. Yes.

CARLINE. I'm afraid to trust you.

GREPPO. Allow me to make a deposit. (*Gives purse.*)

CARLINE. (*Examining and admiring purse.*) Full of glittering
gold. Oh, dear, you've taken away my breath.

GREPPO. No, have I? Permit me to return it to you. (*Kisses
her.*)

(*Duet is introduced here.*)

Now listen, my dear little Carline. I· have a secret and as there should be no secrets between man and wife—that is man and wife that-*are*-to-be—I'm going to share it with you.

CARLINE. A secret, dear Greppo?

GREPPO. *Dear* Greppo! Oh, say that again.

CARLINE. (*With increased tenderness.*) Well then, dear Greppo.

GREPPO. Oh, thank you. You needn't repeat it again. At present that's as much as I can stand 'till I get used to it.

CARLINE. Well then, the secret.

GREPPO. Yes. In the first place, do you love your mistress, Carline?

CARLINE. Love her? I'd die for her.

GREPPO. No, no, no, no. I don't want you to go quite so far as that. I'm not ambitious to be a widower before I've had my honeymoon.

CARLINE. Well then, I love her dearly.

GREPPO. That's better. And she loves my mas— that is, young Rodolphe the painter?

CARLINE. Better than her own life, poor dear lady.

GREPPO. And would marry him but for this ruffianly Count Wolfenstein?

CARLINE. Yes—but the secret.

GREPPO. (*With caution.*) Well then, you must know—
(*Music.*)
Hark—somebody's coming.

(*Enter* RODOLPHE *and* AMINA. *He is brilliantly dressed, wearing a collar and other ornaments of glittering jewels, blue mask and domino.* AMINA *also wears mask and domino.*)

AMINA. Someone is here.

RODOLPHE. Fear not, they are our own people. (*Comes forward with* AMINA.) Leave us, good Greppo, and take your companion with you.

GREPPO. Yes, good Master. Come along Carline.

CARLINE. Surely I've heard that voice before?

GREPPO. (*Taking her arm.*) Hush, that's the secret I was going to share with you, and if you'll take a stroll with me in the "ramble" that leads to the "lovers' paradise," I'll tell you all about it.

CARLINE. Yes, *dear* Greppo.

GREPPO. Oh, don't.

(*Music. Exeunt.* RODOLPHE *and* AMINA *unmask.*)

AMINA. Oh, dear Rodolphe, is this a dream?

RODOLPHE. What's *past* seems so, but day has dawned on our long clouded night and this is the awaking.

AMINA. Your story is indeed most wondrous. But oh, dear Rodolphe, I tremble for your life. If you should be discovered, the vengeance of the ruthless Wolfenstein, backed by his horde of fierce retainers, would be terrible.

RODOLPHE. Fear not, I will defend my right with my life. The same kind power that interposed between me and destruction protects us still. You shall be saved. All is ready for our flight. On the border of the forest, beyond the boundary of the gardens, swift horses are concealed. After midnight, the moon, veiling her face behind the Brocken, will cast a deep shadow over the valley. When all is quiet, I will be beneath your window; the rest is easy. Carline and my faithful Greppo will accompany us.

AMINA. (*Throwing her arms around him.*) Oh my Rodolphe, my more than life, coming thus suddenly from the darkness of my despair into the sunlight of this new-born hope dazzles me. My eyelids close, I cannot look this great joy in the face. I fear to call it mine.

RODOLPHE. Fear?

AMINA. Fear with that fear which springs from woman's love.

RODOLPHE. (*Kissing her.*) Be calm, sweet love, be brave, and all will yet be well.

(*Music—piano. Laughter heard outside.*)

Hark, the masquers come this way; let's mingle with the throng. (*They mask and cross the stage.*)

(*Music—louder.*)

(*Masquers enter laughing and chattering, remaining at back while so engaged; after all are on, music changes to hurry.*)

(HERTZOG, *with drawn sword, enters hurriedly, followed quickly by guards,* WOLFENSTEIN *with drawn sword,* WULFGAR, BRUNO, *and, last,* VON PUFFENGRUNTZ *with*

BARBARA, *the two latter remaining on terrace.* HERTZOG *glaring on* RODOLPHE.)

WOLFENSTEIN. Let no one stir. Guard every avenue that leads from hence. (*To guests.*) Bear with me, friends, there's treason in our midst.

ALL. Treason?

WOLFENSTEIN. 'Tis said a serf, a wretch, usurping the semblance of a noble prince and bent on outrage, has dared to mingle with this goodly throng. If this be false, to all I'll make amends for this rude breaking in upon the general joy. If it be true, 'tis fit we know it. Therefore I do command that all shall here unmask.

AMINA. Lost—lost!

ALL. Aye, let all unmask.

(*All unmask.* RODOLPHE *in doing so throws off his domino, draws his sword and places himself before* AMINA. *Chord of music.*)

WOLFENSTEIN. 'Tis true. Yield, audacious miscreant!

RODOLPHE. Never, while life remains!

WOLFENSTEIN. Upon him, guards, hew him to pieces!

(*Music. Ladies scream,* AMINA *faints and falls into the arms of* GREPPO *who enters.* WOLFENSTEIN *and guards are rushing upon* RODOLPHE.)

GREPPO. The ring, Master, the ring!

(RODOLPHE *kisses the ring. Lights flash.* STALACTA *springs up in glittering mail, with helmet, sword and shield, followed by* DRAGONFIN, *armed with a trident. Fairies and nymphs as amazons, with breastplates, helmets, shields and javelins. Gnomes and amphibea with knobbed clubs and tridents.*)

(*Exciting action.*)

(WOLFENSTEIN, *guards, and gentlemen shrink back appalled.* HERTZOG *stands, the embodiment of baffled rage.* VON PUFFENGRUNTZ *on terrace, faints and falls into the arms of* BARBARA, *who fans him. Tableau and quick curtain.*)

ACT IV

Scene 1

A lapse of six months.
An apartment in the Castle of Wolfenstein.
Music.
Enter BARBARA.

BARBARA. Alas, that things should ever fall so ill! 'Tis now
six months since that never-to-be-forgotten night, and still
no news of the lost Mistress of Wolfenstein. Nor yet of
his Lordship, who has sworn an oath never to return to
the castle until he has brought her back and revenged
himself on the horrible monster who has stolen her. And
that graceless baggage, Carline, too, to go off at the same
time, leaving all the cares of the household to fall on my
poor shoulders. And then, to make matters worse, spells
and witchcraft turn all things upside down. The cows
milk vinegar, the wells are dry, the hens lay addled eggs—

VON PUFFENGRUNTZ. (*Entering with very red nose and
tipsy.*) And all the wine's turned sour.

BARBARA. (*Looking ruefully at him.*) There's another comfort. To think that I, the right honorable foster-mother
that WAS to have been, to her right honorable Ladyship
that WAS to have been, for whom many a young and
tender heart has sighed in vain, should ever have thrown
herself away upon a wine butt.

VON PUFFENGRUNTZ. (*Hic.*) A wine butt, Madam von
Puffengruntz?

BARBARA. Aye, a wine butt—a beer-barrel, a brute that hasn't
drawn a sober breath since the day after we were married,
now more than three months ago.

VON PUFFENGRUNTZ. (*Hic.*) A beer-barrel?

BARBARA. (*Savagely.*) I said a beer-barrel!

VON PUFFENGRUNTZ. (*Hic.*) Certainly, of course. Just whichever you please, my dear. Wine butt or beer-barrel, it's
all the same to me. You know you will cackle.

BARBARA. Cackle!

VON PUFFENGRUNTZ. (*Hic.*) Cackle, my dear. You know I never have a moment's peace, you're not even quiet when you're asleep. You snore, Madame von Puffengruntz, you snore loud enough to split the drum of my ear and rip out the seams of my night-cap.

BARBARA. Snore, you wretch! I, snore?

VON PUFFENGRUNTZ. (*Hic.*) Yes, my dear, and have the nightmares. (*Hic.*) I don't like a wife that snores, and I hate a wife that has the nightmares. In future we are going to have separate apartments. Hereafter I intend to sleep alone.

BARBARA. Alone?

VON PUFFENGRUNTZ. (*Hic.*) I said, alone!

BARBARA. Am I awake? Who and what do you take me for?

VON PUFFENGRUNTZ. (*Hic.*) I took you for a gentle spice—a sort of seasoning to the dull life I lead here in the castle, but, damn it, Madame, you have turned out to be all the condiments in one. A bottom layer of mustard, a top dressing of cayenne pepper, and a subterranean lake of vinegar in the middle.

BARBARA. (*Enraged and approaching him—he retreats.*) Cackle! Snore! Nightmare! Separate apartments! Cayenne pepper! You wretch—you sot—you villain—I'll pepper you. (*Pulls his wig off.*) There—take that and that and that. (*Beats him over the head with it, till both off.*)

Scene 2

The retreat of RODOLPHE *in the forest of Bohemia.*
Music.
At opening—distant sound of hunter's horn and echo.
Enter RODOLPHE *and* AMINA, *followed by* GREPPO; *the two first are in hunting costume.*

RODOLPHE. (*Showing his spear and horn to* GREPPO.) I weary with the chase. Call together our people and bid them lead our horses to where the forest path crosses the brook—there we will join them.

GREPPO. 'Tis wisely resolved, good master. The sun declines—night comes on apace, and we are yet some three good

miles from home. Besides, I'm hollow as a drum; more-
over, in early Autumn ven'son keeps not overlong and the
fat haunch of yonder noble buck cries out for speedy
roasting. Pray do not tarry long. (*Exit.*)

RODOLPHE. Well, dear love, tomorrow ends the year of our
probation. Tomorrow, at the holy altar's foot, I call you
mine.

AMINA. Tomorrow—how brief the time, and yet how long till
then! Oh, Rodolphe, will it come to us? There seems to be
a lurking danger in the air—a cloud between us and the
coming light.

RODOLPHE. Fear not—here in the deep seclusion of our forest
home we are safe from all pursuit.
(*Distant horn, and echo at back.*)
Hark, 'tis Greppo calling in the huntsmen. Let's on to
meet them.
(*Music. They are crossing stage when they are suddenly
confronted by* HERTZOG, WOLFENSTEIN *and* WULFGAR, *who
enter quickly. Chord.*)

WOLFENSTEIN. Ha—ha—ha. At last, we meet!

RODOLPHE. (*Starting back and drawing his sword.*) Entrapped! Fly Amina—seek safety with our people. My arms
shall bar pursuit.

AMINA. No, Rodolphe, we will die together.

WOLFENSTEIN. Alive—take him alive! Yield!

RODOLPHE. (*Standing on his defense.*) He who takes my
sword must win it.

HERTZOG. Put up thy blade; she whom thou would'st invoke
is powerless to aid.

RODOLPHE. False wretch, but that another's life hangs on the
slender thread of mine, and though coward numbers
swarmed on every side, I'd try this issue with my single
sword. But know thou, thou still art juggled with the
power I once invoked, potent still.
(*Music. He kisses ring.*)

(STALACTA *springs from the thicket in glittering full armor
with* DRAGONFIN.)

Behold, we meet on equal ground!

WOLFENSTEIN. Though environed by a thousand fiends, my
hate would find a way to reach you.

(*Music.*)

(*Grand triple-sword combat.* RODOLPHE *and* WOLFENSTEIN, STALACTA *and* HERTZOG, DRAGONFIN *and* WULFGAR. HERTZOG, *wounded and dismayed, flies.* AMINA, *who during the combat has knelt in prayer, throws herself into the arms of* RODOLPHE. *They both kneel at the feet of* STALACTA. DRAGONFIN *indulges in grotesque exultation over the bodies of* WOLFENSTEIN *and* WULFGAR.)

Scene 3

Music.
Enter RODOLPHE, *supporting* AMINA.

RODOLPHE. Look up—Amina, all danger's past. Courage. Ere long we'll meet our people.

AMINA. And you are safe?

RODOLPHE. Safe. Come, poor trembling dove. Courage, Courage.
(*Music. Exit. Music.*)

(*Enter* HERTZOG, *infuriated.*)

HERTZOG. Let one vast curse fill all the air. Am I then juggled with? Malignant powers, obey your master's call. Viewless spirits of evil, work now your direst spells! As toppling mountains crush the mighty pines, crush thou the power that thwarts and mocks me! Zamiel, mighty master, I invoke thy aid.
(*Music. Thunder.*)

(*Two fiends, enter quickly, bearing lighted flambeaux.*)

FIENDS. Your will?

HERTZOG. Summon your infernal legions. Pursue yon flying pair. Fire the forest—girdle them with a belt of flame—close every avenue of escape. Away—away.
(*Music. Thunder. Fiends salaam and rush off, followed by* HERTZOG.)

Scene 4

Burning forest. A grand and comprehensive conflagration scene.
Music.
At opening of scene, loud crackling noise (torpedoes) and red fire on both sides.
RODOLPHE *and* AMINA *enter. As they attempt to escape they are drawn back by Fiends with flaming torches.*

AMINA. (*In agony.*) I burn, I suffocate.
RODOLPHE. Courage, courage. The ring, the ring.
(*He kisses the ring. Gong sounds, a rock opens, disclosing a grotto of silver stalactites. They quickly enter.* HERTZOG *and Fiends spring forward, as* STALACTA *steps forth from the opening, holding aloft a glittering cross.* HERTZOG *and Fiends shrink back. Tableau.*)

Scene 5

The forest by night. Lights down, sound of hunter's horn and very faint echo.
GREPPO *enters.*

GREPPO. What's the use? Now what *is* the use? The oftener I call, the fainter comes the answer. Here it is, quite dark—Master waiting for the horses and I wandering about like a Jack-o'Lantern, following the horn of some goblin huntsman. There's some devil's work going on—I know there's some devil's work going on. (*Starting.*) I beg his infernal majesty's pardon—I hope I haven't said anything to offend, but strange sights and sounds are in the air. Birds that ought to have been to roost an hour ago fly screaming from tree to tree. The dismal screech-owl from his hole in the oak answers the croak of the dreary monk-raven. And just now I saw a big fat buck scampering through the forest with his tail on fire. Oh, dear, oh dear, what fearful omens, and I'm to be married tomorrow! If anything should happen to me—if my poor dear darling little Carline should happen to be left a widow before she's made a wife—if I should never taste—that is if 'I should never know—Oh, Lord, it won't bear thinking of! I'll try once more.

(*Winds the horn. Echo without, scarcely audible.*)

Worse and worse. Oh Lord, Oh Lord! I want to go home! (*Exit.*)

Scene 6

Pandemonium. ZAMIEL *in council, seated on an illuminated throne of skulls and flame. Lesser thrones, one occupied by* REDGLARE, *with pen and open book, another by a secretary, writing. At the foot of the central throne, two dwarf demon pages with wands, in attendance.*

Music.

Fiends discovered in a chorus of demoniacal yells and fiendish laughter, dancing around a flaming chasm. After the action is continued a brief time, ZAMIEL *waves his scepter.*

Demons separate.

ZAMIEL. 'Tis well. Let silence reign awhile. How stands the record of the dying year? Has every seed brought sinful fruit? Is all the harvest gathered in—is every bond fulfilled?

REDGLARE. All—all save one.

ZAMIEL. Who plays the laggard.

REDGLARE. One who sought to rival thy great power—Hertzog, the Black Crook.

ALL THE FIENDS. Ho, ho, ho.

(*Echoed without and above, followed by a single wild blast of infernal music.*)

ZAMIEL. If when the brazen tongue of clamorous Time, now trembling on the midnight's verge, proclaims the appointed hour, the wail of no fresh soul by him betrayed breaks on the air of Hell, let him be summoned.

(*Music.*)

(*The demons utter a wild wail of delight and resume the dance. The gong strikes twelve. At the first stroke, the demons cease dancing and hold separate pictures of exultation. At the termination of each stroke a single brazen* blast of demoniacal music. At the twelfth stroke, loud and continued thunder. Demons utter a wild cry. ZAMIEL *rises and waves his scepter.*)

(*If possible, the scene backs away and discloses vistas of Pandemonium teeming with infernal life and wreaths of flame, from which appear illuminated heads of demons, skeletons and nondescript monsters.*)

(*Gong sounds.* HERTZOG *is dragged on by Fiends, and is dashed into the flaming chasm. Demons howl and dance around.*)

Scene 7

Subterranean gallery of emerald and crystal stalactites. Music.

Characteristic march. Grand procession of amphibea and gnomes bearing in their arms and upon their heads salvers, shells, and quaint vases filled with gold and jewels. They are followed by amazons in armor, led by STALACTA. *They march, double the march, and vary the evolutions, 'till the transformation is ready, when they exit and the scene breaks away to*

Scene 8

Music.

An elaborate mechanical and scenical construction of the Realms of STALACTA, *occupying the entire stage. This scene must be of gradually-developing and culminating beauty, introducing during its various transformations* STALACTA, *the entire host of fairies, sprites, water nymphs, amphibea, gnomes, etc., bearing treasure.* RODOLPHE, AMINA, GREPPO *and* CARLINE.

Calcium lights, brilliant fires, and slow curtain.

SHENANDOAH

Preface to SHENANDOAH

Shenandoah is one of the few successful nineteenth-century plays about the Civil War. Two years before its appearance, William Gillette's spy thriller *Held by the Enemy* (1886) had for the first time demonstrated the theatrical possibilities of the Civil War. Presumably because of the success of this play, Howard refused to change the scene of his own play to the Crimea, as Lester Wallack had advised him to do. *Shenandoah* first played in Boston, in 1888, with little success, but Howard's reward came the following year. Charles Frohman took it over and started its sensational run at the New York Star Theatre, on September 9, 1889. This production launched Frohman's career, and it earned Howard royalties that in the first year alone came to more than $100,000.

At that time Bronson Howard (1842–1908) was already "the first American dramatist of his day," as the playwright Augustus Thomas later called him. Born into the family of a prominent Detroit merchant, Howard achieved success and fame in 1870 with a comedy, *Saratoga*. Thereafter his influence in the American theatre grew rapidly, and despite the relative obscurity of his name today, his importance in our theatre annals is great. He was effective in having the copyright laws improved to benefit dramatists. He was the first American playwright to make his living entirely on royalties— a feat that considerably raised the stature of all playwrights. A recognized spokesman for and leader in his profession, he founded and later became President of the first society for dramatic authors (subsequently known as the Society of American Dramatists and Composers). Finally, although individual works by other playwrights dealing with native characters and themes had had some success earlier, Howard was the first dramatist whose works dealt almost exclusively with the American milieu.

Saratoga was a comic treatment of such a milieu. Produced by Augustin Daly, it is a farcical comedy of manners in which the hero is engaged to and pursued by four girls at once. While its scene was American, however, its type characters were easily movable to a resort setting in England, where it played under the title of *Brighton*. Among his other important plays is *The Banker's Daughter* (1878), a more serious work that deals with a girl who gives up the man she loves and marries one she does not love, all for the sake of her father. This play, originally produced as *Lillian's Last Love* in 1873, is of importance because it became the subject of "The Autobiography of a Play," a notable document on drama and theatre that was first delivered as an address at Harvard University in 1886. In it, Howard traces the extensive development and revisions of the play, and reveals the profound knowledge of audiences and certain unfailing "laws of dramatic construction" needed to turn a play into a popular success.* The next year (1887) Howard came out with a somewhat melodramatic satire of Wall Street that realized close to half a million dollars in royalties, *The Henrietta*.

Even though *Shenandoah* was evidently based on one of Howard's early comedies—it was advertised as a "New Military Comedy"—much of the play is somber. The third act, for example, ends with a stream of bedraggled and wounded soldiers finally being rallied into enthusiasm by the sensational appearance of General Sheridan. But Howard was primarily a writer of comedy, and even in this play comic characters and situations abound. Among the former are the gruff Major-General Buckthorn and his romantically militarized daughter Jenny, her reserved lover Heartsease, and the low-comic figures of Sergeant Barket and Old Margery. Comic situations abound particularly in the scenes between the lovers (of whom there are four sets). The characters, action, and setting are often romantic, occasionally verging on the sentimental and the melodramatic. Among those involved in such actions are the friends Kerchival West and Robert Ellingham, who find themselves on opposing sides in the war that starts at the end of the first act; their sisters

---

* "The Autobiography of a Play" is reprinted in *Papers on Playmaking*, A Dramabook paperback (1957) edited by Brander Matthews. Brief biographies of Howard may be found in the *Dictionary of American Biography* and in a collection of addresses published by the American Dramatists Club, *In Memoriam, Bronson Howard* (1910).

Madeline and Gertrude, each of whom is in love with her brother's friend; the villain Edward Thornton, who fails to seduce Constance Haverill but succeeds in arousing General Haverill's suspicions of his wife; and Lieutenant Frank Bedloe, General Haverill's errant son who is sent to his death by his father. Throughout, however, Howard endeavored to represent the effect on human beings of sectional and partisan conflicts. What is striking is the extent to which Howard transcended the stereotyped Civil War romance and melodrama, best represented by Gillette's popular *Secret Service* (1895), to create a play that is still moving and entertaining.

The setting of the play is both romantic and realistic. The first act has for its backdrop the Charleston bay, harbor, and city lights; the Ellingham Residence, setting of the second act, overlooks a striking stage panorama that includes the Shenandoah Valley and Three Top Mountain. At the same time, Howard strove for realism, particularly in regard to historical and military details, as is emphasized by the stage directions in the play and the following extracts from the Program, reprinted in Samuel French's edition of *Shenandoah* (1897):

In ACT I, just before the opening of the war, HAVERILL is a Colonel in the Regular Army. KERCHIVAL WEST and ROBERT ELLINGHAM are Lieutenants in his regiment, having been classmates at West Point.

ACT I

CHARLESTON HARBOR IN 1861. AFTER THE BALL

The citizens of Charleston knew almost the exact hour at which the attack on Fort Sumter would begin, and they gathered in the gray twilight of the morning to view the bombardment as a spectacle.—*Nicolay, Campaigns of the Civil War, Vol. I.*

"I shall open fire in one hour."—*Beauregard's last message to Major Anderson. Sent at* 3:20 A.M., *April* 12, 1861.

ACTS II AND III

The Union Army, under General Sheridan, and the Confederate Army, under General Early, were encamped

facing each other about twenty miles south of Winchester, on Cedar Creek. * * * Gen. Sheridan was called
to Washington. Soon after he left, a startling despatch
was taken by our own Signal Officers from the Confederate Signal Station on Three Top Mountain.—*Pond,
Camp. Civ. War, Vol. XI.*

On the morning of Oct. 19th, the Union Army was
taken completely by surprise. Thoburn's position was
swept in an instant. Gordon burst suddenly upon the
left flank. The men who escaped capture streamed
through the camps along the road to Winchester.—
Pond, supra.

Far away in the rear was heard cheer after cheer.—
Three years in the Sixth Corps.

ACT IV

WASHINGTON, 1865. RESIDENCE OF GENERAL BUCKTHORN
I feel that we are on the eve of a new era, when there
is to be great harmony between the Federal and Confederate.—*Gen. Grant's Memoirs.*

The Cavalry Trumpet Signals in Acts II. and III. are
given accurately as provided in the U.S. Cavalry Tactics.
The Torch Signals are also strictly correct, in accordance
with the Service Code.

M.M.

SHENANDOAH
by Bronson Howard

Characters

KERCHIVAL WEST, Colonel in Sheridan's Cavalry
MADELINE WEST, his sister
ROBERT ELLINGHAM, Colonel in Confederate Army
GERTRUDE ELLINGHAM, his sister
GENERAL JOHN HAVERILL, in Sheridan's Cavalry
MRS. CONSTANCE HAVERILL, his wife
LIEUTENANT FRANK BEDLOE, General Haverill's son, in Sheridan's Cavalry
MRS. EDITH HAVERILL, his wife
EDWARD THORNTON, Captain in Secret Service, Confederate Army
MAJOR-GENERAL FRANCIS BUCKTHORN, Commander of the 19th U.S. Army Corps
JENNY BUCKTHORN, his daughter
CAPTAIN HEARTSEASE, in Sheridan's Cavalry, loves Jenny Buckthorn
SERGEANT BARKET, General Buckthorn's orderly
OLD MARGERY, housekeeper in General Buckthorn's home
JANNETTE, maid in General Buckthorn's home
MAJOR HARDWICK, Surgeon in Confederate Army
CAPTAIN LOCKWOOD, U.S. Army Signal Corps
LIEUTENANT OF SIGNAL CORPS, U.S. Army
LIEUTENANT OF INFANTRY, U.S. Army
CORPORAL DUNN, U.S. Army
PRIVATE BENSON, U.S. Army
GENERAL SHERIDAN, U. S. Cavalry Commander

OFFICERS, SOLDIERS, SERVANTS

ACT I

CHARLESTON HARBOR IN 1861. "AFTER THE BALL."

SCENE. *A Southern Residence on the shore of Charleston Harbor. Interior.—Large double doors up center, open. Large, wide window, with low sill, extends down right side of the stage. Veranda is seen through the doors and the window. A wide opening on the left with a corridor beyond. Furniture and appointments quaint and old-fashioned, but an air of brightness and of light; the general tone of the walls and upholstery that of the old Colonial period in its more ornamental and decorative phase, as shown in the early days of Charleston. Old candlesticks and candelabra, with lighted candles nearly burned down. Beyond the central doors and the window there is a lawn, with southern foliage, extending down to the shores of the harbor; a part of the bay lies in the distance, with low-lying land beyond. The lights of Charleston are seen over the water along the shore. The gray twilight of early morning gradually steals over the scene as the Act progresses.*

As the curtain rises, KERCHIVAL WEST *sitting in a chair, feet extended and head thrown back, a handkerchief over his face.* ROBERT ELLINGHAM *strolls in on veranda, beyond the window, smoking. He looks to the right, starts and moves to the window; leans against the upper side of the window and looks across.*

ROBERT. Kerchival!

KERCHIVAL. (*Under handkerchief.*) Eh? H'm!

ROBERT. Can you sleep at a time like this? My own nerves are on fire.

KERCHIVAL. Fire? Oh—yes—I remember. Any more fire-works, Bob?

ROBERT. A signal rocket from one of the batteries, now and then. (*Goes up beyond the window.* KERCHIVAL *arouses himself, taking handkerchief from his eyes.*)

KERCHIVAL. What a preposterous hour to be up. The ball was over an hour ago, all the guests are gone, and it's nearly four o'clock. (*Looks at his watch.*) Exactly ten minutes of four. (*Takes out a cigar.*) Our Southern friends assure us that General Beauregard is to open fire on Fort Sumter this morning. I don't believe it. (*Lighting cigar and rising, he looks out through the window.*) There lies the old fort—solemn and grim as ever, and the flag-staff stands above it, like a warning finger. If they do fire upon it—(*Shutting his teeth for a moment and looking down at the cigar in his hand.*)—the echo of that first shot will be heard above their graves, and Heaven knows how many of our own, also; but the flag will still float!—over the graves of both sides.

(ROBERT *enters from the central door and approaches him.*)

Are you Southerners all mad, Robert?
ROBERT. Are you Northerners all blind?
(KERCHIVAL *sits down.*)
We Virginians would prevent a war if we could. But your people in the North do not believe that one is coming. You do not understand the determined frenzy of my fellow Southerners. Look! (*Pointing toward the rear of the stage.*) Do you see the lights of the city, over the water? The inhabitants of Charleston are gathering, even now, in the gray, morning twilight, to witness the long-promised bombardment of Fort Sumter. It is to be a gala day for them. They have talked and dreamed of nothing else for weeks. The preparations have become a part of their social life—of their amusement—their gayeties. This very night at the ball—here—in the house of my own relatives—what was their talk? What were the jests they laughed at? Sumter! War! Ladies were betting bonbons that the United States would not dare to fire a shot in return, and pinning ribbons on the breasts of their "heroes." There was a signal rocket from one of the forts, and the young men who were dancing here left their partners standing on the floor to return to the batteries—as if it were the night before another Waterloo. The ladies themselves hurried away to watch the "spectacle" from their own verandas. You won't see the

truth! I tell you, Kerchival, a war between the North and South is inevitable!

KERCHIVAL. And if it does come, you Virginians will join the rest.

ROBERT. Our State will be the battle ground, I fear. But every loyal son of Virginia will follow her flag. It is our religion!

KERCHIVAL. My State is New York. If New York should go against the old flag, New York might go to the devil. That is my religion.

ROBERT. So differently have we been taught what the word "patriotism" means!

KERCHIVAL. You and I are officers of the same regiment of the United States Regular Army, Robert; we were classmates at West Point, and we have fought side by side on the plains. You saved my scalp once; I'd have to wear a wig, now, if you hadn't. I say, old boy, are we to be enemies?

ROBERT. (*Laying his hand over his shoulder.*) My dear old comrade, whatever else comes, our friendship shall be unbroken!

KERCHIVAL. Bob! (*Looking up at him.*) I only hope that we shall never meet in battle!

ROBERT. In battle? (*Stepping down front.*) The idea is horrible!

KERCHIVAL. (*Rising and crossing to him.*) My dear old comrade, one of us will be wrong in this great fight, but we shall both be honest in it.

(*He gives his hand;* ROBERT *grasps it warmly, then turns away.*)

ROBERT. Colonel Haverill is watching the forts, also; he has been as sad to-night as we have. Next to leaving you, my greatest regret is that I must resign from his regiment.

KERCHIVAL. You are his favorite officer.

ROBERT. Naturally, perhaps; he was my guardian.

(*Enter* HAVERILL *from the rear. He walks down, stopping in the center of the stage.*)

HAVERILL. Kerchival! I secured the necessary passports to the North yesterday afternoon; this one is yours; I brought it down for you early in the evening.

(KERCHIVAL *takes paper and goes to window.*)
I am ordered direct to Washington at once, and shall start
with Mrs. Haverill this forenoon. You will report to Captain Lyon, of the 2d Regiment, in St. Louis. Robert! I have
hoped for peace to the last, but it is hoping against hope.
I feel certain, now, that the fatal blow will be struck this
morning. Our old regiment is already broken up, and you,
also, will now resign, I suppose, like nearly all your fellow
Southerners in the Service.

ROBERT. You know how sorry I am to leave your command,
Colonel!

HAVERILL. I served under your father in Mexico; he left me,
at his death, the guardian of you and your sister, Gertrude.
Even since you became of age, I have felt that I stood in
his place. But you must be your sister's only guardian now.
Your father fell in battle, fighting for our common country,
but you—

ROBERT. He would have done as I shall do, had he lived. He
was a Virginian!

HAVERILL. I am glad, Robert, that he was never called upon
to decide between two flags. He never knew but one, and
we fought under it together. (*Exit.*)

ROBERT. Kerchival! Something occurred in this house to-night
which—which I shouldn't mention under ordinary circumstances, but I—I feel that it may require my further attention, and you, perhaps, can be of service to me. Mrs.
Haverill, the wife of the Colonel—

KERCHIVAL. Fainted away in her room.

ROBERT. You know?

KERCHIVAL. I was one of the actors in the little drama.

ROBERT. Indeed!

KERCHIVAL. About half-past nine this evening, while the
ladies were dressing for the ball, I was going upstairs; I
heard a quick, sharp cry, sprang forward, found myself
at an open door. Mrs. Haverill lay on the floor inside, as
if she had just reached the door to cry for help, when she
fell. After doing all the unnecessary and useless things I
could think of, I rushed out of the room to tell your sister,
Gertrude, and my own sister, Madeline, to go and take
care of the lady. Within less than twenty minutes afterwards, I saw Mrs. Haverill sail into the drawing-room, a
thing of beauty, and with the glow of perfect health on her

cheek. It was an immense relief to me when I saw her. Up to that time I had a vague idea that I had committed a murder.

ROBERT. Murder!

KERCHIVAL. M-m. A guilty conscience. Every man, of course, does exactly the wrong thing when a woman faints. When I rushed out of Mrs. Haverill's room, I left my handkerchief soaked with water upon her face. I must ask her for it, it's a silk one. Luckily, the girls got there in time to take it off; she wouldn't have come to if they hadn't. It never occurred to me that she'd need to breathe in my absence. That's all I know about the matter. What troubles you? I suppose every woman has a right to faint whenever she chooses. The scream that I heard was so sharp, quick and intense that—

ROBERT. That the cause must have been a serious one.

KERCHIVAL. Yes! So I thought. It must have been a mouse.

ROBERT. Mr. Edward Thornton has occupied the next room to that of Mrs. Haverill to-night.

KERCHIVAL. (*Quickly.*) What do you mean?

ROBERT. During the past month or more he has been pressing, not to say insolent, in his attentions to Mrs. Haverill.

KERCHIVAL. I've noticed that myself.

ROBERT. And he is an utterly unscrupulous man; it is no fault of mine that he was asked to be a guest at this house to-night. He came to Charleston, some years ago, from the North, but if there are any vices and passions peculiarly strong in the South, he has carried them all to the extreme. In one of the many scandals connected with Edward Thornton's name, it was more than whispered that he entered a lady's room unexpectedly at night. But, as he killed the lady's husband in a duel a few days afterwards, the scandal dropped.

KERCHIVAL. Of course; the gentleman received ample satisfaction as an outraged husband, and Mr. Thornton apologized, I suppose, to his widow.

ROBERT. He has repeated the adventure.

KERCHIVAL. Do—you—think—that?

ROBERT. I was smoking on the lawn, and glanced up at the window; my eyes may have deceived me, and I must move cautiously in the matter; but it couldn't have been imagination; the shadow of Edward Thornton's face and head appeared upon the curtain.

KERCHIVAL. Whew! The devil!

ROBERT. Just at that moment I, too, heard the stifled scream.

(*Enter* EDWARD THORNTON.)

THORNTON. Gentlemen!

ROBERT. Your name was just on my tongue, Mr. Thornton.

THORNTON. I thought I heard it, but you are welcome to it. Miss Gertrude has asked me to ride over to Mrs. Pinckney's with her, to learn if there is any further news from the batteries. I am very glad the time to attack Fort Sumter has come at last!

ROBERT. I do not share your pleasure.

THORNTON. You are a Southern gentleman.

ROBERT. And you are a Northern "gentleman."

THORNTON. A Southerner by choice; I shall join the cause.

ROBERT. We native Southerners will defend our own rights, sir; you may leave them in our keeping. It is my wish, Mr. Thornton, that you do not accompany my sister.

THORNTON. Indeed!

ROBERT. Her groom, alone, will be sufficient.

THORNTON. As you please, sir. Kindly offer my excuses to Miss Gertrude. You and I can chat over the subject later in the day, when we are alone. (*Moving up stage.*)

ROBERT. By all means, and another subject, also, perhaps.

THORNTON. I shall be entirely at your service. (*Exit to veranda.*)

ROBERT. Kerchival, I shall learn the whole truth, if possible, to-day. If it is what I suspect—what I almost know—I will settle with him myself. He has insulted our Colonel's wife and outraged the hospitality of my friends. (*Walking to right.*)

KERCHIVAL. (*Walking to left.*) I think it ought to be my quarrel. I'm sure I'm mixed up in it enough.

MADELINE. (*Without, calling.*) Kerchival!

ROBERT. Madeline.

(*Aside, starting,* KERCHIVAL *looks across at him sharply.*)

KERCHIVAL. (*Aside.*) I distinctly saw Bob give a start when he heard Madeline. Now, what can there be about my sister's voice to make a man jump like that?

GERTRUDE. (*Without.*) Brother Robert!

KERCHIVAL. Gertrude!

(*Aside, starting,* ROBERT *looks at him sharply.*) How the tones of a woman's voice thrill through a man's soul!

(*Enter* MADELINE.)

MADELINE. Oh, Kerchival—here you are.

(*Enter* GERTRUDE, *from the apartment, in a riding habit, with a whip.*)

GERTRUDE. Robert, dear! (*Coming down to* ROBERT; *they converse in dumb show.*)
MADELINE. Where are your field glasses? I've been rummaging all through your clothes, and swords, and sashes, and things. I've turned everything in your room upside down.
KERCHIVAL. Have you?
MADELINE. I can't find your glasses anywhere. I want to look at the forts. Another rocket went up just now. (*Runs up the stage and stands on piazza looking off.*)
KERCHIVAL. A sister has all the privileges of a wife to upset a man's things, without her legal obligation to put them straight again. (*Glances at* GERTRUDE.) I wish Bob's sister had the same privileges in my room that my own has.
GERTRUDE. Mr. Thornton isn't going with me, you say?
ROBERT. He requested me to offer you his apologies.
KERCHIVAL. May *I* accompany you?
(ROBERT *turns to window on right.*)
GERTRUDE. My groom, old Pete, will be with me, of course; there's no particular need of anyone else. But you may go along, if you like. I've got my hands full of sugar plums for Jack. Dear old Jack—he always has his share when we have company. I'm going over to Mrs. Pinckney's to see if she's had any more news from General Beauregard; her son is on the General's staff.
MADELINE. (*Looking off to right.*) There's another rocket from Fort Johnson; and it is answered from Fort Moultrie. Ah! (*Angrily.*) General Beauregard is a bad, wicked man! (*Coming down.*)
GERTRUDE. Oh! Madeline! You are a bad, wicked Northern girl to say such a thing.
MADELINE. I *am* a Northern girl.
GERTRUDE. And I am a Southern girl. (*They face each other.*)
KERCHIVAL. (*Dropping into a chair.*) The war has begun.

(ROBERT *has turned from the window; strolls across stage, watching the girls.*)

GERTRUDE. General Beauregard is a patriot.

MADELINE. He is a Rebel.

GERTRUDE. So am I.

MADELINE. Gertrude!—You—you—

GERTRUDE. Madeline!—You—

MADELINE. I—I—

GERTRUDE. I—

BOTH. O—O-h! (*Bursting into tears and rushing into each other's arms, sobbing, then suddenly kissing each other vigorously.*)

KERCHIVAL. I say, Bob, if the North and South do fight, that will be the end of it.

GERTRUDE. I've got something to say to you, Madeline, dear. (*Confidentially and turning with her arms about her waist. The girls sit down talking earnestly.*)

ROBERT. Kerchival, old boy! There's—there's something I'd like to say to you before we part to-day.

KERCHIVAL. I'd like a word with you, also!

MADELINE. You don't really mean that, Gertrude—with me?

ROBERT. I'm in love with your sister, Madeline.

KERCHIVAL. The devil you are!

ROBERT. I never suspected such a thing until last night.

GERTRUDE. Robert was in love with you six weeks ago.

(MADELINE *kisses her.*)

KERCHIVAL. *I've* made a discovery, too, Bob.

MADELINE. *I've* got something to say to *you,* Gertrude.

KERCHIVAL. I'm in love with *your* sister.

ROBERT. (*Astonished.*) You are?

MADELINE. Kerchival has been in love with you for the last three months.

(GERTRUDE *offers her lips—they kiss.*)

KERCHIVAL. I fell in love with her the day before yesterday. (*The two gentlemen grasp each other's hands warmly.*)

ROBERT. We understand each other, Kerchival. (*Turns up the stage and stops at door.*) Miss Madeline, you said just now that you wished to watch the forts. Would you like to walk down to the shore?

MADELINE. Yes!

(*Rising and going up to him. He takes one of her hands in his own and looks at her earnestly.*)

ROBERT. This will be the last day that we shall be together, for the present. But we shall meet again—sometime—if we both live.

MADELINE. If we both live! You mean—if *you* live. You must go into this dreadful war, if it comes.

ROBERT. Yes, Madeline, I must. Come let us watch for our fate.

(*Exeunt to veranda.*)

KERCHIVAL. (*Aside.*) I must leave Charleston to-day. (*He sighs.*) Does she love me?

GERTRUDE. I am ready to start, Mr. West, when you are.

KERCHIVAL. Oh! Of course, I forgot. (*Rising.*) I shall be delighted to ride at your side.

GERTRUDE. At my side! (*Rising.*) There isn't a horse in America that can keep by the side of my Jack, when I give him his head, and I'm sure to do it. You may follow us. But you can hardly ride in that costume; while you are changing it, I'll give Jack his bonbons. (*Turning to window.*) There he is, bless him! Pawing the ground, and impatient for me to be on his back. Let him come, Pete. (*Holding up bonbons at window.*) I love you.

KERCHIVAL. Eh? (*Turning suddenly.*)

GERTRUDE. (*Looking at him.*) What?

KERCHIVAL. You were saying—

GERTRUDE. Jack!

(*Looking out. Head of a large black horse appears through window.*) You dear old fellow. (*Feeds him with bonbons.*) Jack has been my boy ever since he was a little colt. I brought you up, didn't I, Jack? He's the truest, and kindest, and best of friends; I wouldn't be parted from him for the world, and I'm the only human he'll allow to be near him.

KERCHIVAL. (*Earnestly.*) You are the only woman, Miss Gertrude, that I—

GERTRUDE. Dear Jack!

KERCHIVAL. (*Aside.*) Jack embarrasses me. He's a third party.

GERTRUDE. There! That will do for the present, Jack. Now go along with Pete! If you are a very good boy, and don't let Lieutenant Kerchival West come within a quarter of a mile of me, after the first three minutes, you shall have some more sugar plums when we get to Mrs. Pinckney's. (*An old Negro leads horse away.* GERTRUDE *looks around at* KERCHIVAL.) You haven't gone to dress, yet; we shall be late. Mrs. Pinckney asked a party of friends to witness the bombardment this morning, and breakfast together

on the piazza while they are looking at it. We can remain
and join them, if you like.

KERCHIVAL. I hope they won't wait for breakfast until the
bombardment begins.

GERTRUDE. I'll bet you an embroidered cigar-case, Lieutenant, against a box of gloves that it will begin in less than
an hour.

KERCHIVAL. Done! You will lose the bet. But you shall have
the gloves; and one of the hands that go inside them shall
be—(*Taking one of her hands; she withdraws it.*)

GERTRUDE. My own—until some one wins it. You don't believe
that General Beauregard will open fire on Fort Sumter this
morning?

KERCHIVAL. No; I don't.

GERTRUDE. Everything is ready.

KERCHIVAL. It's so much easier to get everything ready to do
a thing than it is to do it. I have been ready a dozen times,
this very night, to say to you, Miss Gertrude, that I—that
I— (*Pauses.*)

GERTRUDE. (*Looking down and tapping her skirt with her
whip.*) Well?

KERCHIVAL. But I didn't.

GERTRUDE. (*Glancing up at him suddenly.*) I dare say, General Beauregard has more nerve than you have.

KERCHIVAL. It is easy enough to set the batteries around
Charleston Harbor, but the man who fires the first shot
at a woman—

GERTRUDE. Woman!

KERCHIVAL. At the American flag—must have nerves of steel.

GERTRUDE. You Northern men are so slow, to—

KERCHIVAL. I have been slow; but I assure you, Miss Gertrude, that my heart—

GERTRUDE. What subject are we on now?

KERCHIVAL. You were complaining because I was too slow.

GERTRUDE. I was doing nothing of the kind, sir!—let me
finish, please. You Northern men are so slow, to believe
that our Southern heroes—Northern *men* and Southern
heroes—you recognize the distinction I make—you won't
believe that they will keep their promises. They have
sworn to attack Fort Sumter this morning, and—they—will
do it. This "American Flag" you talk of is no longer our
flag: it is foreign to us!—It is the flag of an enemy!

KERCHIVAL. (*Tenderly and earnestly.*) Am I your enemy?

GERTRUDE. You have told me that you will return to the North, and take the field.

KERCHIVAL. Yes, I will. (*Decisively.*)

GERTRUDE. You will be fighting against my friends, against my own brother, against me. We *shall* be enemies.

KERCHIVAL. (*Firmly.*) Even that, Gertrude—(*She looks around at him, he looks squarely into her eyes as he proceeds*)—if you will have it so. If my country needs my services, I shall not refuse them, though it makes us enemies! (*She wavers a moment, under strong emotion, and turns away; sinks upon seat, her elbow on back of it, and her tightly-clenched fist against her cheek, looking away from him.*)

GERTRUDE. I will have it so! I am a Southern woman!

KERCHIVAL. We have more at stake between us, this morning, than a cigar-case and a box of gloves. (*Turning up stage.*)

(*Enter* MRS. HAVERILL *from apartment.*)

MRS. HAVERILL. Mr. West! I've been looking for you. I have a favor to ask.

KERCHIVAL. Of me?—with pleasure.

MRS. HAVERILL. But I am sorry to have interrupted you and Gertrude.

(*As she passes down* KERCHIVAL *moves up stage.* GERTRUDE *rises.*)

(*Apart.*) There are tears in your eyes, Gertrude, dear!

GERTRUDE. (*Apart.*) They have no right there.

MRS. HAVERILL. (*Apart.*) I'm afraid I know what has happened. A quarrel! and you are to part with each other so soon. Do not let a girl's coquetry trifle with her heart until it is too late. You remember the confession you made to me last night?

GERTRUDE. (*Apart.*) Constance! (*Starting.*) That is my secret; more a secret now than ever.

MRS. HAVERILL. (*Apart.*) Yes, dear; but you do love him.

(GERTRUDE *moves up stage.*)

GERTRUDE. You need not ride over with me, Mr. West.

KERCHIVAL. I can be ready in one moment.

GERTRUDE. I choose to go alone! Old Pete will be with me; and Jack, himself, is a charming companion.

KERCHIVAL. If you prefer Jack's company to mine—

GERTRUDE. I do. (*Exit on veranda.*)

KERCHIVAL. Damn Jack! But you will let me assist you to mount. (*Exit after her.*)

MRS. HAVERILL. We leave for the North before noon, but every hour seems a month. If my husband should learn what happened in my room to-night, he would kill that man. What encouragement could I have given him? Innocence is never on its guard—but, (*Drawing up.*) the last I remember before I fell unconscious, he was crouching before me like a whipped cur! (*Starts as she looks out of window.*) There is Mr. Thornton, now—Ah! (*Angrily.*) No—I must control my own indignation. I must keep him and Colonel Haverill from meeting before we leave Charleston. Edward Thornton would shoot my husband down without remorse. But poor Frank! I must not forget him, in my own trouble. I have but little time left to care for his welfare.

(*Re-enter* KERCHIVAL.)

KERCHIVAL. You said I could do you a favor, Mrs. Haverill?

MRS. HAVERILL. Yes, I wanted to speak with you about General Haverill's son, Frank. I should like you to carry a message to Charleston for me as soon as it is light. It is a sad errand. You know too well the great misfortune that has fallen upon my husband in New York.

KERCHIVAL. His only son has brought disgrace upon his family name, and tarnished the reputation of a proud soldier. Colonel Haverill's fellow officers sympathize with him most deeply.

MRS. HAVERILL. And poor young Frank! I could hardly have loved the boy more if he had been my own son. If he had not himself confessed the crime against the bank, I could not have believed him guilty. He has escaped from arrest. He is in the City of Charleston. I am the only one in all the world he could turn to. He was only a lad of fourteen when his father and I were married, six years ago; and the boy has loved me from the first. His father is stern and bitter now in his humiliation. This note from Frank was handed to me while the company were here last evening. I want you to find him and arrange for me to meet him, if you can do it with safety. I shall give you a letter for him.

KERCHIVAL. I'll get ready at once; and I will do all I can for the boy.

MRS. HAVERILL. And—Mr. West! Gertrude and Madeline have told me that—that—I was under obligations to you last evening.

KERCHIVAL. Don't mention it. I merely ran for them, and I—I'm very glad you didn't choke—before they reached you. I trust you are quite well now?

MRS. HAVERILL. I am entirely recovered, thank you. And I will ask another favor of you, for we are old friends. I desire very much that General Haverill should not know that—that any accident occurred to me to-night—or that my health has not been perfect.

KERCHIVAL. Certainly, madam!

MRS. HAVERILL. It would render him anxious without cause.

KERCHIVAL. (*Aside.*) It looks as if Robert was right; she doesn't want the two men to meet.

(*Enter* HAVERILL, *a white silk handkerchief in his hand.*)

HAVERILL. Constance, my dear, I've been all over the place looking for you. I thought you were in your room. But—by the way, Kerchival, this is your handkerchief; your initials are on it.

(KERCHIVAL *turns and stares at him a second.* MRS. HAVERILL *starts slightly and turns front.* HAVERILL *glances quickly from one to the other, then extends his hands toward* KERCHIVAL, *with the handkerchief.* KERCHIVAL *moves to him and takes it.* MRS. HAVERILL *drops into chair.*)

KERCHIVAL. Thank you.

(*Walks up and exits with a quick glance back.* HAVERILL *looks at* MRS. HAVERILL, *who sits nervously, looking away. He then glances up after* KERCHIVAL. *A cloud comes over his face and he stands a second in thought. Then, with a movement as if brushing away a passing suspicion, he smiles pleasantly and approaches* MRS. HAVERILL; *leans over her.*)

HAVERILL. My fair Desdemona! (*Smiling.*) I found Cassio's handkerchief in your room. Have you a kiss for me? (*She looks up, he raises her chin with a finger and kisses her.*) That's the way I shall smother you.

MRS. HAVERILL. (*Rising and dropping her head upon his breast.*) Husband!

HAVERILL. But what is this they have been telling me?

MRS. HAVERILL. What have they said to you?

HAVERILL. There was something wrong with you in the early part of the evening; you are trembling and excited, my girl!

MRS. HAVERILL. It was nothing, John; I—I—was ill, for a few moments, but I am well now.

HAVERILL. You said nothing about it to me.

MRS. HAVERILL. Do not give it another thought.

HAVERILL. Was there anything besides your health involved in the affair? There was. (*Aside.*) How came this handkerchief in her room?

MRS. HAVERILL. My husband! I do not want to say anything more—at—at present—about what happened to-night. There has never been a shadow between us—will you not trust me?

HAVERILL. Shadow! You stand in a bright light of your own, my wife; it shines upon my whole life—there can be no shadow there. Tell me as much or as little as you like, and in your own time. I am sure you will conceal nothing from me that I ought to know. I trust my honor and my happiness to you, absolutely.

MRS. HAVERILL. They will both be safe, John, in my keeping. But there is something else that I wish to speak with you about; something very near to your heart—your son!

HAVERILL. My son!

MRS. HAVERILL. He is in Charleston.

HAVERILL. And not—in prison? To me he is nowhere. I am childless.

MRS. HAVERILL. I hope to see him to-day; may I not take him some kind word from you?

HAVERILL. My lawyers in New York had instructions to provide him with whatever he needed.

MRS. HAVERILL. They have done so, and he wants for nothing; except that I will seek out the poor young wife—only a girl herself—whom he is obliged to desert, in New York.

HAVERILL. His marriage was a piece of reckless folly, but I forgave him that.

MRS. HAVERILL. I am sure that it was only after another was dependent on him that the debts of a mere spendthrift were changed to fraud—and crime.

HAVERILL. You may tell him that I will provide for her.

MRS. HAVERILL. And may I take him no warmer message from his father?

HAVERILL. I am an officer of the United States Army. The name which my son bears came to me from men who had borne it with honor, and I transmitted it to him without a blot. He has disgraced it, by his own confession.

MRS. HAVERILL. *I* cannot forget the poor mother who died when he was born; her whose place I have tried to fill, to both Frank and to you. I never saw her, and she is sleeping in the old graveyard at home. But I am doing what she would do to-day, if she were living. No pride—no disgrace—could have turned her face from him. The care and the love of her son has been to me the most sacred duty which one woman can assume for another.

HAVERILL. You have fulfilled that duty, Constance. Go to my son! I would go with you, but he is a man now; he could not look into my eyes, and I could not trust myself. But I will send him something which a man will understand. Frank loves you as if you were his own mother; and I—I would like him to—to think tenderly of me, also. He will do it when he looks at this picture. (*Taking a miniature from his pocket.*)

MRS. HAVERILL. Of me!

HAVERILL. I have never been without it one hour, before, since we were married. He will recognize it as the one that I have carried through every campaign, in every scene of danger on the Plains; the one that has always been with me. He is a fugitive from justice. At times, when despair might overcome him, this may give him nerve to meet his future life manfully. It has often nerved me, when I might have failed without it. Give it to him, and tell him that I sent it. (*Giving her the miniature.*) I could not send a kinder message, and he will understand it.

(*Turning, he stands a moment in thought.* THORNTON *appears at window, looking at them quietly, over his shoulder, a cigar in his hand.* MRS. HAVERILL *sees him, and starts with a suppressed breath, then looks at* HAVERILL, *who moves away. He speaks aside.*)

My son! My son! We shall never meet again. (*Exit, in thought.*)

(MRS. HAVERILL *looks after him earnestly, then turns and looks at* THORNTON, *drawing up to her full height.* THORN-TON *moves up stage, beyond window.*)

MRS. HAVERILL. Will he dare to speak to me again?

(*Enter* THORNTON; *he comes down the stage quietly. He has thrown away cigar.*)

THORNTON. Mrs. Haverill! I wish to offer you an apology.

MRS. HAVERILL. I have not asked for one, sir!

THORNTON. Do you mean by that, that you will not accept one?

MRS. HAVERILL. (*Aside.*) What can I say? (*Aloud.*) Oh, Mr. Thornton!—for my husband's sake, I—

THORNTON. Ah! You are afraid that your husband may become involved in an unpleasant affair. Your solicitude for his safety, madame, makes me feel that my offense to-night was indeed unpardonable. No gentleman can excuse himself for making such a mistake as I have made. I had supposed that it was Lieutenant Kerchival West, who—

MRS. HAVERILL. What do you mean, sir?

THORNTON. But if it is your husband that stands between us—

MRS. HAVERILL. Let me say this, sir: Whatever I may fear for my husband, he fears nothing for himself.

THORNTON. He knows? (*Looking at her, keenly.*)

(*Enter* KERCHIVAL WEST, *now in riding suit. He stops, looking at them.*)

You are silent. Your husband does know what occurred to-night; that relieves my conscience. (*Lightly.*) Colonel Haverill and I can now settle it between us.

MRS. HAVERILL. No, Mr. Thornton! My husband knows nothing, and, I beg of you, do not let this horrible affair go further. (*Sees* KERCHIVAL.)

KERCHIVAL. Pardon me. (*Stepping forward.*) I hope I am not interrupting you. (*Aside.*) It *was* Thornton. (*Aloud.*) You said you would have a letter for me to carry, Mrs. Haverill.

MRS. HAVERILL. Yes, I—I will go up and write it at once. (*As she leaves she stops and looks back. Aside.*) I wonder how much he overheard.

KERCHIVAL. (*Quietly.*) I suppose eight o'clock will be time enough for me to go?

MRS. HAVERILL. Oh, yes! (*Glancing at him a moment.*)— quite. (*Exit.*)

KERCHIVAL. (*Quietly.*) Mr. Thornton! You are a scoundrel! Do I make myself plain?

THORNTON. You make the fact that you desire to pick a quarrel with me quite plain, sir; but I choose my own quarrels and my own enemies.

KERCHIVAL. Colonel Haverill is my commander, and he is beloved by every officer in the regiment.

THORNTON. On what authority, may I ask, do you—

KERCHIVAL. The honor of Colonel Haverill's wife is under our protection.

THORNTON. Under your protection? You have a better claim than that, perhaps, to act as her champion. Lieutenant Kerchival West is Mrs. Haverill's favorite officer in the regiment.

KERCHIVAL. (*Approaching him.*) You dare to suggest that I—

THORNTON. If I accept your challenge, I shall do so not because you are her protector, but my rival.

KERCHIVAL. Bah! (*Striking him sharply on the cheek with glove. The two men stand facing each other a moment.*) Is it my quarrel now?

THORNTON. I think you are entitled to my attention, sir.

KERCHIVAL. My time here is limited.

THORNTON. We need not delay. The Bayou La Forge is convenient to this place.

KERCHIVAL. I'll meet you there, with a friend, at once.

THORNTON. It will be light enough to see the sights of our weapons in about one hour.

(*They bow to each other, and* THORNTON *goes out.*)

KERCHIVAL. I've got ahead of Bob.

GERTRUDE. (*Without.*) Whoa! Jack! Old boy! Steady, now— that's a good fellow.

KERCHIVAL. She has returned. I *must* know whether Gertrude Ellingham loves me—before Thornton and I meet. He is a good shot.

GERTRUDE. (*Without, calling.*) O—h! Pete! You may take Jack to the stable. Ha—ha—ha! (*Appears at window; to* KERCHIVAL.) Old Pete, on the bay horse, has been doing his best to keep up with us; but Jack and I have led him such a race! Ha—ha—ha—ha! (*Disappearing beyond the window.*)

KERCHIVAL. Does she love me?

GERTRUDE. (*Entering at the rear and coming down.*) I have

the very latest news from the headquarters of the Confederate Army in South Carolina. At twenty minutes after three this morning General Beauregard sent this message to Major Anderson in Fort Sumter: "I shall open fire in one hour!" The time is up!—and he will keep his word! (*Turning and looking out of the window.* KERCHIVAL *moves across to her.*)

KERCHIVAL. Gertrude! I must speak to you; we may never meet again; but I must know the truth. I love you. (*Seizing her hand.*) Do you love me? (*She looks around at him as if about to speak; hesitates.*) Answer me! (*She looks down with a coquettish smile, tapping her skirt with her riding whip.*) Well? (*A distant report of a cannon, and low rumbling reverberations over the harbor.* GERTRUDE *turns suddenly, looking out.* KERCHIVAL *draws up, also looking off.*)

GERTRUDE. A low—bright—line of fire—in the sky! It is a shell. (*A second's pause; she starts slightly.*) It has burst upon the fort. (*Looks over her shoulder at* KERCHIVAL, *drawing up to her full height.*) Now!—do you believe that we Southerners are in deadly earnest?

KERCHIVAL. We Northerners are in deadly earnest, too. I have received my answer. (*He crosses quickly and then turns.*) We are—enemies! (*They look at each other for a moment.*) (*Exit* KERCHIVAL.)

GERTRUDE. Kerchival! (*Moving quickly half across stage, looking after him eagerly, then stops.*) Enemies! (*Drops into the chair sobbing bitterly. Another distant report, and low, long reverberations as the curtain descends.*)

ACT II

The Ellingham Homestead in the Shenandoah Valley. Exterior. Three Top Mountain seen in the distance. A corner of the house, with projecting end of the veranda. Low wall extends from the veranda across stage to center, then with

a turn to right it is continued off stage. A wide opening in
wall at center, with a low, heavy stone post, with flat top, on
each side. Beyond wall and opening, a road runs across stage.
At the back of this road elevation of rock and turf. This slopes
up to rear, is level on top about twelve feet, then slopes
down to road, and also out behind wood, at right. The level
part in center rises to about four feet above stage. Beyond
this elevation in the distance is a broad valley, with Three
Top Mountain rising on right. Foliage appropriate to North-
ern Virginia. Rustic seats and table are on the right. A low
rock near the stone post. When curtain rises it is sunset. As
act proceeds this fades into twilight and then brightens into
moonlight. At rise of curtain a trumpet signal is heard, very
distant. GERTRUDE *and* MADELINE *are standing on elevation.*
GERTRUDE *is shading her eyes with her hand and looking off*
to left. MADELINE *stands a little below her, on the incline,*
resting her arm about GERTRUDE'S *waist, also looking off.*

GERTRUDE. It is a regiment of Union Cavalry. The Federal
troops now have their lines three miles beyond us, and
only a month ago the Confederate Army was north of
Winchester. One army or the other has been marching up
and down the Shenandoah Valley for three years. I wonder what the next change will be. We in Virginia have had
more than our share of the war. (*Looking off.*)

MADELINE. You have, indeed, Gertrude. (*Walking down to
a seat.*) And we at home in Washington have pitied you
so much. But everybody says that there will be peace in
the valley after this. (*Dropping into seat.*)

GERTRUDE. Peace! (*Coming down.*) That word means something very different to us poor Southerners from what it
means to you.

MADELINE. I know, dear; and we in the North know how you
have suffered, too. We were very glad when General
Buckthorn was appointed to the command of the Nineteenth Army Corps, so that Jenny could get permission for
herself and me to come and visit you.

GERTRUDE. The old General will do anything for Jenny, I
suppose.

MADELINE. Yes. (*Laughing.*) We say in Washington that
Jenny is in command of the Nineteenth Army Corps herself.

GERTRUDE. I was never more astonished or delighted in my life than when you and Jenny Buckthorn rode up, this morning, with a guard from Winchester; and Madeline, dear, I—I only wish that my brother Robert could be here, too. Do you remember in Charleston, darling—that morning—when I told you that—that Robert loved you?

MADELINE. He—(*Looking down.*)—he told me so himself only a little while afterwards, and while we were standing there, on the shore of the bay—the—the shot was fired which compelled him to enter this awful war—and me to return to my home in the North.

GERTRUDE. I was watching for that shot, too. (*Turning.*)

MADELINE. Yes—(*Rising.*)—you and brother Kerchival—

GERTRUDE. We won't talk about that, my dear. We were speaking of Robert. As I told you this morning, I have not heard from him since the battle of Winchester, a month ago. Oh, Madeline! The many, many long weeks, like these, we have suffered, after some terrible battle in which he has been engaged. I do not know, now, whether he is living or dead.

MADELINE. The whole war has been one long suspense to me. (*Dropping her face into her hands.*)

GERTRUDE. My dear sister! (*Placing her arm about her waist and moving to left.*) You are a Northern girl, and I am a Rebel—but we are sisters.

(*They go up veranda and out. An old countryman comes in. He stops and glances back, raises a broken portion of the capstone of the post, and places a letter under it.* GERTRUDE *has stepped back on veranda and is watching him. He raises his head sharply, looking at her and bringing his finger to his lips. He drops his head again, as with age, and goes out.* GERTRUDE *moves down to stage and up to road, looks to right and left, raises broken stone, glancing back as she does so, then takes the letter and moves down.*)

Robert is alive! It is his handwriting! (*She tears open the wrapper.*) Only a line from him! and this—a dispatch—and also a letter to me! Why, it is from Mrs. Haverill—from Washington—with a United States postmark. (*Reads from a scrap of paper.*)

"The enclosed dispatch must be in the hands of Captain Edward Thornton before eight o'clock to-night. We have

signaled to him from Three Top Mountain, and he is waiting for it at the bend in Oak Run. Our trusty scout at the
Old Forge will carry it if you will put it in his hands."
The scout is not there, now; I will carry it to Captain
Thornton myself. I—I haven't my own dear horse to depend on now; Jack knew every foot of the way through
the woods about here; he could have carried a dispatch
himself. I can't bear to think of Jack; it's two years since
he was captured by the enemy—and if he is still living—
I—I suppose he is carrying one of their officers. No! Jack
wouldn't fight on that side. He was a Rebel—as I am. He
was one of the Black Horse Cavalry—his eyes always
flashed towards the North. Poor Jack! my pet. (*Brushing
her eyes.*) But this is no time for tears. I must do the best
I can with the gray horse. Captain Thornton shall have the
dispatch. (*Reads from note.*)
"I also enclose a letter for you. I found it in a United
States mail-bag which we captured from the enemy."
Oh—that's the way Mrs. Haverill's letter came—Ha—ha—
ha—by way of the Rebel army! (*Opens it; reads.*)
"My Darling Gertrude: When Colonel Kerchival West was
in Washington last week, on his way from Chattanooga, to
serve under Sheridan in the Shenandoah Valley, he called
upon me. It was the first time I had seen him since the
opening of the war. I am certain that he still loves you,
dear."
(*Kisses letter eagerly, then draws up.*) It is quite im-
material to me whether Kerchival West still loves me or not.
(*Reads.*)
"I have kept your secret, my darling."—Ah! My secret!—
"but I was sorely tempted to betray the confidence you
reposed in me at Charleston. If Kerchival West had heard
you say, as I did, when your face was hidden in my bosom,
that night, that you loved him with your whole heart—"—
Oh! I could bite my tongue out now for making that confession—(*Looks down at letter with a smile.*) "I am
certain that he still loves you."
(*A Trumpet Signal. Kisses letter repeatedly. Signal is repeated louder than at first. She starts, listening.*)

(JENNY BUCKTHORN *runs in, on veranda.*)

JENNY. Do you hear, Gertrude, they are going to pass this very house.
(*A Military band is playing "John Brown" in the distance. A chorus of soldiers is heard.*)
I've been watching them through my glass; it is Colonel Kerchival West's regiment.

GERTRUDE. (*Eagerly, then coldly.*) Colonel West's! It is perfectly indifferent to me whose regiment it is.

JENNY. Oh! Of course. (*Coming down.*) It is equally indifferent to me; Captain Heartsease is in command of the first troop.
(*Trumpet Signal sounds.*)
Column right! (*Runs up to the road. Looking off to left.*) They are coming up the hill.

GERTRUDE. At my very door! And Kerchival West in command! I will not stand here and see them pass. The dispatch for Captain Thornton! I will carry it to him as soon as they are gone.
(*Exit up veranda; band and chorus increasing in volume.*)

JENNY. Cavalry! That's the branch of the service I was born in; I was in a fort at the time—on the Plains. Sergeant Barket always said that my first baby squall was a command to the garrison; if any officer or soldier, from my father down, failed to obey my orders, I court-martialed him on the spot. I'll make 'em pass in review. (*Jumping up on rustic seat.*) Yes! (*Looking off to left.*) There's Captain Heartsease himself, at the head of the first troop. Draw sabre! (*With parasol.*) Present!
(*Imitating the action. Band and chorus are now full and loud; she swings parasol in time. A Trumpet Signal. Band and chorus suddenly cease.*)
Halt! Why, they are stopping here. (*Trumpet Signal sounds.*) Dismount! I—I wonder if they are going to—I do believe—
(*Looking eagerly. Trumpet Signal.*)
Assembly of Guard Details! As sure as fate, they are going into camp here. We girls will have a jolly time. (*Jumping down.*) Ha—ha—ha—ha! Let me see. How shall I receive Captain Heartsease? He deserves a court-martial, for he stole my lace handkerchief—at Mrs. Grayson's reception—in Washington. He was called away by orders to the West

that very night, and we haven't met since. (*Sighs.*) He's
been in lots of battles since then; I suppose he's forgotten
all about the handkerchief. We girls, at home, don't forget
such things. We aren't in battles. All we do is to—to scrape
lint and flirt with other officers.

(*Enter* CAPTAIN HEARTSEASE, *followed by* COLONEL ELLING-
HAM; *stops at gate.*)

HEARTSEASE. This way, Colonel Ellingham.
(*They enter. As they come down* HEARTSEASE *stops sud-
denly, looking at* JENNY, *and puts up his glasses.*)
Miss Buckthorn!
JENNY. Captain Heartsease!
HEARTSEASE. (*Very quietly and with perfect composure.*)
I am thunderstruck. The unexpected sight of you has
thrown me into a fever of excitement.
JENNY. Has it? (*Aside.*) If he gets so excited as that in battle
it must be awful. (*Aloud.*) Colonel Ellingham!
ROBERT. Miss Buckthorn! You are visiting my sister? I am
what may be called a visitor—by force—myself.
JENNY. Oh! You're a prisoner!
ROBERT. I ventured too far within the Union lines to-night,
and they have picked me up. But Major Wilson has kindly
accepted my parole, and I shall make the best of it.
JENNY. Is Major Wilson in command of the regiment?
HEARTSEASE. Yes. Colonel West is to join us at this point,
during the evening.
ROBERT. I am very glad you are here, Miss Buckthorn, with
Gertrude.
JENNY. Somebody here will be delighted to see you, Colonel.
ROBERT. My sister can hardly be pleased to see me as a
prisoner.
JENNY. Not your sister.
(*Passing him and crossing to veranda. Turns and beckons
to him. Motions with her thumb, over her shoulder. He
goes up steps of the veranda and turns.*)
ROBERT. What do you mean?
JENNY. I mean this—(*Reaching up her face, he leans down,
placing his ear near her lips*)—somebody else's sister! When
she first sees you, be near enough to catch her.
ROBERT. I understand you! Madeline!

(*Exit on veranda.* JENNY *runs up steps after him, then stops and looks back at* HEARTSEASE *over railing.* HEARTSEASE *takes a lace handkerchief from his pocket.*)

JENNY. I do believe that's my handkerchief.

(*A guard of Sentries marches in and across stage in road. Corporal in command orders halt and a sentry to post, then marches guard out. Sentry stands with his back to audience, afterwards moving out and in, appearing and disappearing during the Act.*)

HEARTSEASE. Miss Buckthorn! I owe you an apology. After I left your side, the last time we met, I found your handkerchief in my possession. I assure you, it was an accident.

JENNY. (*Aside, pouting.*) I thought he *intended* to steal it. (*Aloud.*) That was more than a year ago. (*Then brightly.*) Do you always carry it with you?

HEARTSEASE. Always; there. (*Indicating his left breast pocket.*)

JENNY. Next to his heart!

HEARTSEASE. Shall I return it to you?

JENNY. Oh, if a lace handkerchief can be of any use to you, Captain, during the hardships of a campaign—you—you may keep that one. You soldiers have so few comforts—and it's real lace.

HEARTSEASE. Thank you. (*Returning handkerchief to his pocket.*) Miss Buckthorn, your father is in command of the Nineteenth Army Corps. He doesn't like me.

JENNY. I know it.

HEARTSEASE. But you are in command of him.

JENNY. Yes; I always have been.

HEARTSEASE. If ever you decide to assume command of any other man, I—I trust you will give *me* your orders.

JENNY. (*Aside, starting back.*) If that was intended for a proposal, it's the queerest-shaped one I ever heard of. (*Aloud.*) Do you mean, Captain, that—that you—I must command myself now. (*Shouldering her parasol.*) 'Bout—face! March! (*Turning squarely around, marching up and out, on veranda.*)

HEARTSEASE. I have been placed on waiting orders. (*Stepping up stage and looking after her; then very quietly and without emotion.*) I am in an agony of suspense. The sight of that girl always arouses the strongest emotions of my nature.

(*Enter* COLONEL KERCHIVAL WEST, *looking at paper in his hand. Sentinel, in road, comes to a salute.*)

Colonel West!

KERCHIVAL. Captain!

HEARTSEASE. You have rejoined the regiment sooner than we expected.

KERCHIVAL. (*Looking at paper.*) Yes; General Haverill is to meet me here at seven o'clock. Major Wilson tells me that some of your company captured Colonel Robert Ellingham, of the Tenth Virginia.

HEARTSEASE. He is here under parole.

KERCHIVAL. And this is the old Ellingham homestead. (*Aside.*) Gertrude herself is here, I suppose; almost a prisoner to me, like her brother; and my troops surround their home. She must, indeed, feel that I am her enemy now. Ah, well, war is war. (*Aloud.*) By the bye, Heartsease, a young Lieutenant, Frank Bedloe, has joined our troop?

HEARTSEASE. Yes; an excellent young officer.

KERCHIVAL. I sent for him as I came through the camp. Lieutenant Frank "Bedloe" is the son of General Haverill.

HEARTSEASE. Indeed! Under an assumed name!

KERCHIVAL. He was supposed to have been killed in New Orleans more than a year ago; but he was taken prisoner instead.

HEARTSEASE. He is here.

KERCHIVAL. I should never have known him with his full beard and bronzed face. His face was as smooth as a boy's when I last met him in Charleston.

(*Enter* LIEUTENANT FRANK BEDLOE; *he stops, saluting.*)

FRANK. You wished me to report to you, Colonel?

KERCHIVAL. You have been assigned to the regiment during my absence.

FRANK. Yes, sir.

(KERCHIVAL *moves to him and grasps his hand; looks into his eyes a moment before speaking.*)

KERCHIVAL. Frank Haverill.

FRANK. You—you know me, sir?

KERCHIVAL. I saw Mrs. Haverill while I was passing through Washington on Saturday. She told me that you had escaped from prison in Richmond, and had re-entered the service. She did not know then that you had been assigned to my regiment. I received a letter from her, in Winchester, this morning, informing me of the fact, and asking for my good offices in your behalf. But here is the letter. (*Taking a letter from wallet and giving it to him.*) It is for you rather than for me. I shall do everything I can for you, my dear fellow.

FRANK. Thank you, sir. (*He opens letter, dropping envelope upon table.*) Kind, thoughtful and gentle to my faults, as ever—(*Looking at letter*)—and always thinking of my welfare. My poor little wife, too, is under her protection. Gentlemen, I beg of you not to reveal my secret to my father.

KERCHIVAL. General Haverill shall know nothing from us, my boy, you have my word for that.

HEARTSEASE. Nothing.

KERCHIVAL. And he cannot possibly recognize you. What with your full beard, and thinking as he does, that you are—

FRANK. That I am dead. I am dead to him. It would have been better if I had died. Nothing but my death—not even that—can wipe out the disgrace which I brought upon his name.

HEARTSEASE. General Haverill has arrived.

(*Enter* GENERAL HAVERILL, *with a Staff Officer.*)

FRANK. (*Moving down.*) My father!

HAVERILL. (*After exchanging salutes with the three officers, turns to Staff Officer, giving him a paper and brief instructions in dumb show. Officer goes out over incline. Another Staff Officer enters, salutes and hands him a paper, then stands up.*) Ah! The men are ready. (*Looking at paper, then to* KERCHIVAL.) Colonel! I have a very important matter to arrange with you; there is not a moment to be lost. I will ask Captain Heartsease to remain. (FRANK *salutes and starts up stage;* HAVERILL *looks at him, starting slightly; raises his hand to detain him.*) One moment; your name!

HEARTSEASE. Lieutenant Bedloe, General, of my own troop, and one of our best officers.

(HAVERILL *steps to* FRANK, *looking into his face a moment.*)

HAVERILL. Pardon me!

(*He steps down stage.* FRANK *moves away from him, then stops and looks back at him.* HAVERILL *stands up a moment in thought, covers his face with one hand, then draws up.*) Colonel West! We have a most dangerous piece of work for a young officer—

(FRANK *starts joyfully.*)

—to lead a party of men, whom I have already selected. I cannot *order* an officer to undertake anything so nearly hopeless; he must be a volunteer.

FRANK. Oh, sir, General! Let me be their leader.

HAVERILL. I thought you had passed on.

FRANK. Do not refuse me, sir.

(HAVERILL *looks at him a moment.* HEARTSEASE *and* KERCHIVAL *exchange glances.*)

HAVERILL. You are the man we need, my young friend. You shall go. Listen! We wish to secure a key to the cipher dispatches, which the enemy are now sending from their signal station on Three Top Mountain. There is another Confederate Signal Station in the valley, just beyond Buckton's Ford. (*Pointing to left.*) Your duty will be this: First, to get inside the enemy's line; then to follow a path through the woods, with one of our scouts as your guide; attack the Station suddenly, and secure their code, if possible. I have this moment received word that the scout and the men are at the fort, now, awaiting their leader. Major McCandless, of my staff, will take you to the place. (*Indicating Staff Officer.* FRANK *exchanges salutes with him.*)

My young friend! I do not conceal from you the dangerous nature of the work on which I am sending you. If—if you do not return, I—I will write, myself, to your friends. (*Taking out a note book.*) Have you a father living?

FRANK. My—father—is—is—he is—

HAVERILL. I understand you. A mother? Or—

KERCHIVAL. I have the address of Lieutenant Bedloe's friends, General.

HAVERILL. I will ask you to give it to me, if necessary. (*He extends his hand.*) Good-bye, my lad.

(FRANK *moves to him.* HAVERILL *grasps his hand, warmly.*) Keep a brave heart and come back to us.

(FRANK *moves up stage. Exit Staff Officer.*)

FRANK. He is my father still. (*Exit.*)

HAVERILL. My dead boy's face! (*Dropping his face into both hands.*)

HEARTSEASE. (*Apart to* KERCHIVAL.) He shall not go alone. (*Aloud.*) General! Will you kindly give me leave of absence from the command?

HAVERILL. Leave of absence! To an officer in active service— and in the presence of the enemy?

KERCHIVAL. (*Taking his hand. Apart.*) God bless you, old fellow! Look after the boy.

HAVERILL. A–h– (*With a sudden thought, turns.*) I think I understand you, Captain Heartsease. Yes; you may have leave of absence.

HEARTSEASE. Thank you.

(*He salutes.* HAVERILL *and* KERCHIVAL *salute. Exit* HEARTS-EASE.)

KERCHIVAL. Have you any further orders for me, General?

HAVERILL. I wish you to understand the great importance of the duty to which I have just assigned this young officer. General Sheridan started for Washington this noon, by way of Front Royal. Since his departure, we have had reason to believe that the enemy are about to move, and we must be able to read their signal dispatches, if possible. (*Sitting down.*) I have ordered Captain Lockwood, of our own Signal Corps, to report to you here, with officers and men. (*He takes up empty envelope on table, unconsciously, as he speaks, tapping it on table.*) If Lieutenant Bedloe succeeds in getting the key to the enemy's cipher, we can signal from this point–(*Pointing to elevation.*)–to our station at Front Royal. Men and horses are waiting there now, to carry forward a message, if necessary, to General Sheridan himself. (*He starts suddenly, looking at envelope in his hand; reads address. Aside.*) "Colonel Kerchival West"–in my wife's handwriting!

KERCHIVAL. I'll attend to your orders.

HAVERILL. Postmarked at Washington, yesterday. (*Reads.*) "Private and confidential." (*Aloud.*) Colonel West! I found a paragraph, to-day, in a paper published in Richmond, taken from a prisoner. I will read it to you. (*He takes a newspaper slip from his wallet and reads.*) "From the *Charleston Mercury.* Captain Edward Thornton, of the Confederate Secret Service, has been assigned to duty in the Shenandoah Valley. Our gallant Captain still bears upon his face the mark of his meeting, in 1861, with Lieutenant, now Colonel Kerchival West, who is also to serve in the valley, with Sheridan's Army. Another meeting between these two men would be one of the strange coincidences of the war, as they were at one time, if not indeed at present, interested in the same beautiful woman." (*Rises.*) I will ask you to read the last few lines, yourself. (*Crossing, he hands* KERCHIVAL *the slip.*)

KERCHIVAL. (*Reading.*) "The scandal connected with the lovely wife of a Northern officer, at the opening of the war, was over-shadowed, of course, by the attack on Fort Sumter; but many Charlestonians will remember it. The lady in defense of whose good name Captain Thornton fought the duel"—he defended her good name!—"is the wife of General Haverill, who will be Colonel West's immediate commander." (*Pauses a moment, then hands back slip.*) General! I struck Mr. Thornton, after a personal quarrel.

HAVERILL. And the cause of the blow? There is much more in this than I have ever known of. I need hardly say that I do not accept the statement of this scandalous paragraph as correct. I will ask you to tell me the whole story, frankly, as man to man.

KERCHIVAL. (*After a moment's thought.*) I will tell you—all— frankly, General.

(*Enters* SERGEANT BARKET.)

BARKET. Colonel Wist? Adjutant Rollins wishes to report—a prisoner—just captured.

HAVERILL. We will meet again later, to-night when the camp is at rest. We are both soldiers, and have duties before us, at once. For the present, Colonel, be on the alert; we must watch the enemy.
(*Moves up stage.* BARKET *salutes.* HAVERILL *stops and looks at envelope in his hands, reading.*)
"Private and confidential." (*Exit.*)

KERCHIVAL. Sergeant Barket! Lieutenant Bedloe has crossed
the enemy's line, at Buckton's Ford, with a party of men.
I wish you to ride to the ford yourself, and remain there,
with your horse in readiness and fresh. As soon as any
survivor of the party returns, ride back with the first news
at full speed.

BARKET. Yes, sir. (*Starting.*)

KERCHIVAL. You say a prisoner has been captured? Is it a
spy?

BARKET. Worse—a petticoat.

KERCHIVAL. A female prisoner! (*Dropping into seat.*)

BARKET. I towld the byes your honor wouldn't thank us fer
the catchin' of her. The worst of it is she's a lady; and
what's worse still, it's a purty one.

KERCHIVAL. Tell Major Wilson, for me, to let her take the
oath, and everything else she wants. The Government of
the United States will send her an apology and a new
bonnet.

BARKET. The young lady is to take the oath, is it? She says
she'll see us damned first.

KERCHIVAL. A lady, Barket?

BARKET. Well! she didn't use thim exact words. That's the
way I understand her emphasis. Ivery time she looks at
me, I feel like getting under a boom-proof. She was dashing through the woods on a gray horse, sur; and we had
the divil's own chase. But we came up wid her, at last,
down by the bend in Oak Run. Just at that moment we
saw the figure of a Confederate officer, disappearing among
the trays on the ither side.

KERCHIVAL. A—h!

BARKET. Two of us rayturned wid the girl; and the rist wint
after the officer. Nothing has been heard of thim yet.

KERCHIVAL. Have you found any dispatches on the prisoner?

BARKET. Well!—yer honor, I'm a bachelor, meself; and I'm
not familiar with the taypography of the sex. We byes are
in mortal terror for fear somebody might order us to go
on an exploring expedition.

KERCHIVAL. Tell them to send the prisoner here, Barket, and
hurry to Buckton's Ford yourself, at once.

BARKET. As fast as me horse can carry me, sir, and it's a good
one. (*Exit.*)

KERCHIVAL. I'd rather deal with half the Confederate army
than with one woman, but I must question her. They

captured her down by the Bend in Oak Run. (*Taking out
map, and looking at it.*) I see. She had just met, or was
about to meet, a Confederate officer at that point. It is
evident that she was either taking him a dispatch or was
there to receive one. Oak Run.

(CORPORAL DUNN *and two soldiers enter, with* GERTRUDE
as a prisoner. They stop, KERCHIVAL *sits, studying map.*
GERTRUDE *glances at him and marches down with her head
erect; she stops, with her back to him.*)

CORPORAL DUNN. The prisoner, Colonel West!

KERCHIVAL. Ah! Very well, Corporal; you can go.

(*Rising; he motions the guard to retire.* CORPORAL DUNN
gives the necessary orders and exit with guard.)
Be seated, madam.

(GERTRUDE *draws up, folding her arms and planting her
foot, spitefully.* KERCHIVAL *shrugs his shoulders. Aside.*)
I wish they'd capture a tigress for me, or some other
female animal that I know how to manage better than I
do a woman. (*Aloud.*) I am very sorry, madam; but, of
course, my duty as a military officer is paramount to all
other considerations. You have been captured within the
lines of this army, and under circumstances which lead
me to think that you have important dispatches upon your
person. I trust that you will give me whatever you have,
at once. I shall be exceedingly sorry if you compel me to
adopt the extreme—and the very disagreeable course—for
both of us—of having—you—I—I hesitate even to use the
word, madam—but military law is absolute—having you—

GERTRUDE. Searched! If you dare, Colonel West! (*Turning
to him suddenly and drawing up to her full height.*)

KERCHIVAL. Gertrude Ellingham! (*Springs across to her, with
his arms extended.*) My dear Gertrude!

GERTRUDE. (*Turning her back upon him.*) Not "dear Gertrude" to you, sir!

KERCHIVAL. Not?—Oh! I forgot.

GERTRUDE. (*Coldly.*) I am your prisoner.

KERCHIVAL. Yes. (*Drawing up firmly, with a change of manner.*) We will return to the painful realities of war. I am
very sorry that you have placed yourself in a position like
this, and, believe me, Gertrude—(*With growing tenderness.*)—I am still more sorry to be in such a position myself.
(*Resting one hand on her arm, and his other arm about
her waist.*)

GERTRUDE. (*After looking down at his hands.*) You don't like the position? (*He starts back, drawing up with dignity.*) Is that the paramount duty of a military officer?

KERCHIVAL. You will please hand me whatever dispatches or other papers may be in your possession.

GERTRUDE. (*Looking away.*) You will *force* me, I suppose. I am a woman; you have the power. Order in the guard! A Corporal and two men—you'd better make it a dozen— I am dangerous! Call the whole regiment to arms! Beat the long roll! I won't give up, if all the armies of the United States surround me.

(*Enter* GENERAL BUCKTHORN.)

KERCHIVAL. General Buckthorn! (*Saluting.*)

BUCKTHORN. Colonel West.

GERTRUDE. (*Aside.*) Jenny's father!

(BUCKTHORN *glances at* GERTRUDE, *who still stands looking away. He moves down to* KERCHIVAL.)

BUCKTHORN. (*Apart, gruffly.*) I was passing with my staff, and I was informed that you had captured a woman bearing dispatches to the enemy. Is this the one?

KERCHIVAL. Yes, General.

BUCKTHORN. Ah! (*Turning, he looks at her.*)

GERTRUDE. I wonder if he will recognize me. He hasn't seen me since I was a little girl. (*She turns toward him.*)

BUCKTHORN. (*Turning to* KERCHIVAL *and punching him in the ribs.*) Fine young woman!—(*He turns and bows to her very gallantly, removing his hat. She bows deeply in return.*) A-h-e-m! (*Suddenly pulling himself up to a stern, military air; then gruffly to* KERCHIVAL, *extending his hand.*) Let me see the dispatches.

KERCHIVAL. She declines positively to give them up.

BUCKTHORN. Oh! Does she? (*Walks up stage thoughtfully, and turns.*) My dear young lady! I trust you will give us no further trouble. Kindly let us have those dispatches.

GERTRUDE. (*Looking away.*) I have no dispatches, and I would not give them to you if I had.

BUCKTHORN. What! You defy my authority? Colonel West, I command you! Search the prisoner!

(GERTRUDE *turns suddenly towards* KERCHIVAL, *facing him defiantly. He looks across at her, aghast. A moment's pause.*)

KERCHIVAL. General Buckthorn—I decline to obey that order.

BUCKTHORN. You—you decline to obey my order! (*Moves down to him fiercely.*)

KERCHIVAL. (*Apart.*) General! It is the woman I love.

BUCKTHORN. (*Apart.*) Is it? Damn you, sir! I wouldn't have an officer in my army corps who *would* obey me, under such circumstances. I'll have to look for those dispatches myself.

KERCHIVAL. (*Facing him, angrily.*) If you dare, General Buckthorn!

BUCKTHORN. (*Apart.*) Blast your eyes! I'd kick you out of the army if you'd *let* me search her; but it's my military duty to swear at you. (*To* GERTRUDE.) Colonel West has sacrificed his life to protect you.

GERTRUDE. His life!

BUCKBHORN. I shall have him shot for insubordination to his commander, immediately. (*Gives* KERCHIVAL *a huge wink, and turns up stage.*)

GERTRUDE. Oh, sir! General! I have told you the truth. I have no dispatches. Believe me, sir, I haven't so much as a piece of paper about me, except—

BUCKTHORN. Except? (*Turning sharply.*)

GERTRUDE. Only a letter. Here it is. (*Taking letter from bosom of her dress.*) Upon my soul, it is all I have. Truly, it is.

BUCKTHORN. (*Taking letter.*) Colonel West, you're reprieved. (*Winks at* KERCHIVAL, *who turns away, laughing.* BUCK-THORN *reads letter.*) "Washington"—Ho—ho! From within our own lines—"Colonel Kerchival West"—

KERCHIVAL. Eh?

GERTRUDE. Please, General!—Don't read it aloud.

BUCKTHORN. Very well! I won't.

KERCHIVAL. (*Aside.*) I wonder what it has to do with me.

BUCKTHORN. (*Reading. Aside.*) "If Kerchival West had heard you say, as I did—m—m—that you loved him with your whole heart—" (*He glances up at* GERTRUDE, *who drops her head, coyly.*) This is a very important military document. (*Turns to the last page.*) "Signed, Constance Hav-erill." (*Turns to front page.*) "My dear Gertrude!" Is this Miss Gertrude Ellingham?

GERTRUDE. Yes, General.

BUCKTHORN. I sent my daughter, Jenny, to your house, with an escort, this morning.

GERTRUDE. She is here.

BUCKTHORN. (*Tapping her under the chin.*) You're an arrant
little Rebel, my dear; but I like you immensely. (*Draws up
suddenly, with an Ahem!, then turns to* KERCHIVAL.)
Colonel West, I leave this dangerous young woman in your
charge.

(KERCHIVAL *approaches.*) If she disobeys you in any way,
or attempts to escape—read that letter! (*Giving him letter.*)

GERTRUDE. Oh! General!

BUCKTHORN. But not till then.

KERCHIVAL. (*Tenderly, taking her hand.*) My—prisoner!

GERTRUDE. (*Aside.*) I could scratch my own eyes out—or his,
either—rather than have him read that letter.

(*Enter* CORPORAL DUNN, *with a guard of four soldiers and*
CAPTAIN EDWARD THORNTON *as a prisoner.*)

KERCHIVAL. Edward Thornton!

GERTRUDE. They have taken him, also! He has the dispatch!

CORPORAL DUNN. The Confederate Officer, Colonel, who was
pursued by our troops at Oak Run, after they captured
the young lady.

BUCKTHORN. The little witch has been communicating with
the enemy!

KERCHIVAL. (*To* GERTRUDE.) You will give me your parole
of honor until we next meet?

GERTRUDE. Yes. (*Aside.*) That letter! I *am* his prisoner.
(*Walks up steps, looking back at* CAPTAIN THORNTON, *and
then leaves stage.*)

KERCHIVAL. We will probably find the dispatches we have
been looking for now, General.

BUCKTHORN. Prisoner! You will hand us what papers you may
have.

THORNTON. I will hand you nothing.

BUCKTHORN. Colonel!

(KERCHIVAL *motions to* THORNTON, *who looks at him
sullenly.*)

KERCHIVAL. Corporal Dunn!—search the prisoner.

(DUNN *steps to* THORNTON, *taking him by the shoulder and
turning him rather roughly so that* THORNTON's *back is to
the audience.* DUNN *throws open his coat, takes paper from
his breast, hands it to* KERCHIVAL, *who gives it to* BUCK-
THORN.)

Proceed with the search.

(DUNN *continues search.* BUCKTHORN *drops upon seat, lights match and looks at paper.*)

BUCKTHORN. (*Reading.*) "General Rosser will rejoin General Early with all the cavalry in his command, at—" This is important.

(*Continues to read with matches. The* CORPORAL *hands a packet to* KERCHIVAL. *He removes covering.*)

KERCHIVAL. (*Starting.*) A portrait of Mrs. Haverill! (*Touches* CORPORAL DUNN *on shoulder quickly and motions him to retire.* DUNN *falls back to the guard.* KERCHIVAL *speaks apart to* THORNTON, *who has turned front.*) How did this portrait come into your possession?

THORNTON. That is my affair, not yours!

BUCKTHORN. Anything else, Colonel?

KERCHIVAL. (*Placing miniature in his pocket.*) Nothing?

THORNTON. (*Apart, over* KERCHIVAL's *shoulder.*) A time will come, perhaps, when I can avenge the insult of this search, and also this scar. (*Pointing to a scar on his face.*) Your aim was better than mine in Charleston, but we shall meet again; give me back that picture.

KERCHIVAL. Corporal! Take your prisoner!

THORNTON. Ah!

(*Springs viciously at* KERCHIVAL; CORPORAL DUNN *springs forward, seizes* THORNTON *and throws him back to Guard.* KERCHIVAL *walks to right,* DUNN *stands with his carbine leveled at* THORNTON, *looks at* KERCHIVAL, *who quietly motions him out.* CORPORAL DUNN *gives orders to men and marches out, with* THORNTON.)

BUCKTHORN. Ah! (*Still reading with matches.*) Colonel! (*Rising.*) The enemy has a new movement on foot, and General Sheridan has left the army! Listen! (*Reads from dispatches with matches.*) "Watch for a signal from Three Top Mountain to-night."

KERCHIVAL. We hope to be able to read that signal ourselves.

BUCKTHORN. Yes, I know. Be on your guard. I will speak with General Haverill, and then ride over to General Wright's headquarters. Keep us informed.

KERCHIVAL. I will, General.

(*Saluting.* BUCKTHORN *salutes and exit.*)

"Watch for a signal from Three Top Mountain to-night." (*Looking up at Mountain.*) We shall be helpless to read it unless Lieutenant Bedloe is successful. I only hope the poor boy is not lying dead, already, in those dark woods beyond the ford. (*Turns down, taking miniature from pocket.*) How came Edward Thornton to have this portrait of Mrs. Haverill in his possession?

(GERTRUDE *runs in on veranda.*)

GERTRUDE. Oh, Colonel West! He's here! (*Looks back.*) They are coming this way with him.

KERCHIVAL. Him! Who?

GERTRUDE. Jack.

KERCHIVAL. Jack!

GERTRUDE. My own horse!

KERCHIVAL. Ah, I remember! He and I were acquainted in Charleston.

GERTRUDE. Two troopers are passing through the camp with him.

KERCHIVAL. He is not in your possession?

GERTRUDE. He was captured at the battle of Fair Oaks, but I recognized him the moment I saw him; and I am sure he knew me, too, when I went up to him. He whinnied and look so happy. You are in command here— (*Running down.*)—you will compel them to give him up to me?

KERCHIVAL. If he is in my command, your pet shall be returned to you. I'll give one of my own horses to the Government as a substitute, if necessary.

GERTRUDE. Oh, thank you, my dear Kerchival! (*going to him; he takes her hand, looking into her eyes.*) I—I could almost—

KERCHIVAL. Can you almost confess, at last, Gertrude, that you—love me? (*Tenderly; she draws back, hanging her head, but leaving her hand in his.*) Have I been wrong? I felt that that confession was hovering on your tongue when we were separated in Charleston. Have I seen that confession in your eyes since we met again to-day—even among the angry flashes which they have shot out at me? During all this terrible war—in the camp and the trench— in the battle—I have dreamed of a meeting like this. You are still silent?

(*Her hand is still in his. She is looking down. A smile steals over her face, and she raises her eyes to his, taking his hand in both her own.*)

GERTRUDE. Kerchival! I—

(*Enter* BENSON. *She looks around over her shoulder.*
KERCHIVAL *looks up. A trooper leading a large black
horse, now caparisoned in military saddle, bridle, follows*
BENSON *across; another trooper follows.*)
Jack! (*Runs up the stage, meeting horse.* KERCHIVAL
turns.)

KERCHIVAL. Confound Jack! That infernal horse was always
in my way!

GERTRUDE. (*With her arm about horse's neck.*) My darling
old fellow! Is he not beautiful, Kerchival? They have taken
good care of him. How soft his coat is!

KERCHIVAL. Benson, explain this!

BENSON. I was instructed to show this horse and his leader
through the lines, sir.

KERCHIVAL. What are your orders, my man?
(*Moving up, trooper hands him paper. He moves down
a few steps, reading it.*)

GERTRUDE. You are to be mine again, Jack, mine! (*Resting
her cheek against horse's head and patting it.*) The Colonel
has promised it to me.

KERCHIVAL. Ah! (*With a start, as he reads paper.* GERTRUDE
raises her head and looks at him.) This is General Sheridan's horse, on his way to Winchester, for the use of the
General when he returns from Washington.

GERTRUDE. General Sheridan's horse? He is mine!

KERCHIVAL. I have no authority to detain him. He must go on.

GERTRUDE. I have hold of Jack's bridle, and you may order
your men to take out their sabres and cut my hand off.

KERCHIVAL. (*Approaches her and gently takes her hand as it
holds the bridle.*) I would rather have my own hand cut
off, Gertrude, than bring tears to your eyes, but there is
no alternative!
(GERTRUDE *releases bridle and turns front, brushing her
eyes, her hand still held in his, his back to audience. He
returns order and motions troopers out; they move out,
with horse.* KERCHIVAL *turns to move.* GERTRUDE *starts
after horse; he turns quickly to check her.*)
You forget—that—you are my prisoner.

GERTRUDE. I *will* go!

KERCHIVAL. General Buckthorn left me special instructions—
(*Taking out wallet and letter.*)—in case you declined to
obey my orders—

GERTRUDE. Oh, Colonel! Please don't read that letter. (*Stands near him, dropping her head. He glances up at her from letter. She glances up at him and drops her eyes again.*) I will obey you.

KERCHIVAL. (*Aside.*) What the deuce can there be in that letter?

GERTRUDE. Colonel West! Your men made me a prisoner this afternoon; to-night you have robbed me, by your own orders, of—of—Jack is only a pet, but I love him; and my brother is also a captive in your hands. When we separated in Charleston you said that we were enemies. What is there lacking to make those words true to-day? You *are* my enemy! A few moments ago you asked me to make a confession to you. You can judge for yourself whether it is likely to be a confession of—love—or of hatred!

KERCHIVAL. Hatred!

GERTRUDE. (*Facing him.*) Listen to my confession, sir! From the bottom of my heart—

KERCHIVAL. Stop!

GERTRUDE. I will not stop!

KERCHIVAL. I command you.

GERTRUDE. Indeed!

(*He throws open the wallet in his hand and raises letter.*) Ah!

(*She turns away; turns again, as if to speak. He half opens letter. She stamps her foot and walks up steps of veranda. Here she turns again.*)

I tell you, I—

(*He opens letter. She turns, and exits with a spiteful step.*)

KERCHIVAL. I wonder if that document orders me to cut her head off! (*Returning it to wallet and pocket.*) Was ever lover in such a position? I am obliged to cross the woman I love at every step.

(*Enter* CORPORAL DUNN, *very hurriedly.*)

DUNN. A message from Adjutant Rollins, sir! The prisoner, Captain Thornton, dashed away from the special guard which was placed over him, and he has escaped. He had a knife concealed, and two of the Guard are badly wounded. Adjutant Rollins thinks the prisoner is still

within the lines of the camp—in one of the houses or the
stables.

KERCHIVAL. Tell Major Wilson to place the remainder of the
Guard under arrest, and to take every possible means to
recapture the prisoner.

(CORPORAL DUNN *salutes, and exit.*)

So! Thornton has jumped his guard, and he is armed. I
wonder if he is trying to get away, or to find me. From
what I know of the man, he doesn't much care which he
succeeds in doing. That scar which I gave him in Charleston is deeper in his heart than it is in his face.

(*A signal light suddenly appears on Three Top Mountain.
The "Call."*) Ah!—the enemy's signal!

(*Enter* CAPTAIN LOCKWOOD, *followed by the* LIEUTENANT
OF SIGNAL CORPS.)

Captain Lockwood! You are here! Are your signalmen with
you?

LOCKWOOD. Yes, Colonel; and one of my Lieutenants.

(LIEUTENANT *is looking up at signal with his glass.* CAP-
TAIN LOCKWOOD *does same.*)

(HAVERILL *enters, followed by two Staff Officers.*)

HAVERILL. (*As he enters.*) Can you make anything of it,
Captain?

LOCKWOOD. Nothing, General! Our services are quite useless
unless Lieutenant Bedloe returns with the key to their
signals.

HAVERILL. A—h! We shall fail. It is time he had returned, if
successful.

SENTINEL. (*Without.*) Halt! Who goes there?

(KERCHIVAL *runs up stage and half way up incline, looking
off.*)

Halt!

(*A shot is heard without.*)

BARKET. (*Without.*) Och!—Ye murtherin spalpeen!

KERCHIVAL. Sentinel! Let him pass; it is Sergeant Barket.

SENTINEL. (*Without.*) Pass on.

KERCHIVAL. He didn't give the countersign. News from
Lieutenant Bedloe, General!

BARKET. (*Hurrying in, up the slope.*) Colonel Wist, our brave
byes wiped out the enemy, and here's the papers.

KERCHIVAL. Ah! (*Taking papers.—Then to* LOCKWOOD.) Is
that the key?

LOCKWOOD. Yes. Lieutenant!
(LIEUTENANT *hurries up to elevation, looking through his
glass.* LOCKWOOD *opens book.*)

HAVERILL. What of Lieutenant Bedloe, Sergeant?

BARKET. Sayreously wounded, and in the hands of the inimy!

HAVERILL. (*Sighing.*) A—h.

BARKET. (*Coming down stone steps.*) It is reported that
Captain Heartsease was shot dead at his side.

KERCHIVAL. Heartsease dead!

LIEUTENANT OF SIGNAL CORPS. (*Reading Signals.*) Twelve—
Twenty-two—Eleven.

BARKET. Begorra! I forgot the Sintinil entirely, but he didn't
forget me. (*Holding his left arm.*)

HAVERILL. Colonel West! We must make every possible
sacrifice for the immediate exchange of Lieutenant Bedloe,
if he is still living. It is due to him. Colonel Robert Ellingham is a prisoner in this camp; offer him his own exchange
for young Bedloe.

KERCHIVAL. He will accept, of course. I will ride to the front
with him myself, General, and show him through the lines.

HAVERILL. At once!
(KERCHIVAL *crosses front and exit on veranda.*)
Can you follow the dispatch, Captain?

LOCKWOOD. Perfectly; everything is here.

HAVERILL. Well!

LIEUTENANT OF SIGNAL CORPS. Eleven—Twenty-two—One—
Twelve.

LOCKWOOD. (*From book.*) "General Longstreet is coming
with—"

HAVERILL. Longstreet!

LIEUTENANT OF SIGNAL CORPS. One—Twenty-one.

LOCKWOOD. "With eighteen thousand men."

HAVERILL. Longstreet and his corps!

LIEUTENANT OF SIGNAL CORPS. Two—Eleven—Twenty-two.

LOCKWOOD. "Sheridan is away!"

HAVERILL. They have discovered his absence!

LIEUTENANT OF SIGNAL CORPS. Two—Twenty-two—Eleven—
One—Twelve—One.

LOCKWOOD. "We will crush the Union Army before he can return."

HAVERILL. Signal that dispatch from here to our Station at Front Royal. Tell them to send it after General Sheridan—and ride for their lives.

(LOCKWOOD *hurries out.*)

Major Burton! We will ride to General Wright's head-quarters at once—our horses!

(*Noise of a struggle is heard without.*)

BARKET. What the devil is the row out there?

(*Exit, also one of Staff Officers.*)

HAVERILL. (*Looking off to left.*) What is this! Colonel West wounded!

(*Enter* KERCHIVAL WEST, *his coat thrown open, with* ROBERT, BARKET *assisting.*)

ROBERT. Steady, Kerchival, old boy! You should have let us carry you.

KERCHIVAL. Nonsense, old fellow! It's a mere touch with the point of the knife. I—I'm faint—with the loss of a little blood—that's all. Bob!—I—

(*Reels suddenly and is caught by* ROBERT *as he sinks to ground, insensible.*)

ROBERT. Kerchival. (*Kneeling at his side.*)

HAVERILL. Go for the Surgeon!

(*To Staff Officer, who goes out quickly on veranda.*)

How did this happen?

(*Enter* CORPORAL DUNN *and Guard, with* THORNTON. *He is in his shirt sleeves and disheveled, his arms folded. They march down.*)

Captain Thornton!

ROBERT. We were leaving the house together; a hunted ani-mal sprang suddenly across our path, like a panther. (*Looking over his shoulder.*) There it stands. Kerchival!—my brother!

CORPORAL DUNN. We had just brought this prisoner to bay, but I'm afraid we were too late.

HAVERILL. This is assassination, sir, not war. If you have killed him—

THORNTON. Do what you like with me; we need waste no words. I had an old account to settle, and I have paid my debt.

ROBERT. General Haverill! I took these from his breast when he first fell.

(*Handing up wallet and miniature to* HAVERILL. HAVERILL *starts as he looks at miniature.* THORNTON *watches him.*)

HAVERILL. (*Aside.*) My wife's portrait!

THORNTON. If I have killed him—your honor will be buried in the same grave.

HAVERILL. Her picture on his breast! She gave it to him—not to my son!

(*Dropping into seat.* CAPTAIN LOCKWOOD *enters with a Signalman, who has a burning torch on a long pole; he hurries up elevation.* CAPTAIN LOCKWOOD *stands below, facing him. Almost simultaneously with entrance of the Signalman,* GERTRUDE *runs in on veranda.*)

GERTRUDE. They are calling for a surgeon! Who is it? Brother! —you are safe. Ah! (*Uttering a scream, as she sees* KER-CHIVAL, *and falling on her knees at his side.*) Kerchival! Forget those last bitter words I said to you. Can't you hear my confession? I do love you. Can't you hear me? I love you!

(*Signalman is swinging the torch as curtain descends,* LOCKWOOD *looking out to right.*)

ACT III

Same scene. It is now bright daylight, with sunshine flecking foreground and bathing distant valley and mountains. JENNY BUCKTHORN *is sitting on low stone post, in center of stage, looking toward left. She imitates a Trumpet Signal on her closed fists.*

JENNY. What a magnificent line! Guides-posts! Every man and every horse is eager for the next command. There comes the flag!

(*As scene progresses trumpet signals are heard without and she follows their various meanings in her speech.*)

To the standard! The regiment is going to the front. Oh! I do wish I could go with it. I always do, the moment I hear the trumpets. Boots and Saddles! Mount! I wish I was in command of the regiment. It was born in me. Fours

right! There they go! Look at those horses' ears! Forward.
(*A military band is heard without, playing "The Battle
Cry of Freedom."* JENNY *takes attitude of holding a bridle
and trotting.*)
Rappity—plap—plap—plap, etc.
(*Imitates the motions of a soldier on horseback, stepping
down to rock at side of post; thence to the ground and
about the stage, with the various curvettings of a spirited
horse. A chorus of soldiers is heard without, with band.
The music becomes more and more distant.* JENNY *gradually stops as music is dying away, and stands, listening. As
it dies entirely away, she suddenly starts to an enthusiastic
attitude.*)
Ah! If I were only a man! The enemy! On Third Battalion,
left, front, into line, march! Draw sabres! Charge! (*Imitates a trumpet signal. As she finishes, she rises to her full
height, with both arms raised, and trembling with enthusiasm.*) Ah! (*Suddenly drops her arms and changes to an
attitude and expression of disappointment—pouting.*) And
the first time Old Margery took me to Father, in her arms,
she had to tell him I was a girl. Father was as much dis-
gusted as I was. But he'd never admit it; he says I'm as
good a soldier as any of 'em—just as I am.

(*Enter* BARKET, *on veranda, his arm in a sling.*)

BARKET. Miss Jenny!
JENNY. Barket! The regiment has marched away to the front,
and we girls are left here, with just you and a corporal's
guard to look after us.
BARKET. I've been watching the byes mesilf. (*Coming down.*)
If a little military sugar-plum like you, Miss Jenny, objects
to not goin' wid 'em, what do you think of an ould piece
of hard tack like me? I can't join the regiment till I've
taken you and Miss Madeline back to Winchester, by your
father's orders. But it isn't the first time I've escorted you,
Miss Jenny. Many a time, when you was a baby, on the
Plains, I commanded a special guard to accompany ye's
from one fort to anither, and we gave the command in a
whisper, so as not to wake ye's up.
JENNY. I told you to tell Father that I'd let him know when
Madeline and I were ready to go.

BARKET. I tould him that I'd as soon move a train of army
mules.

JENNY. I suppose we must start for home again to-day?

BARKET. Yes, Miss Jenny, in charge of an ould Sargeant wid
his arm in a sling and a couple of convalescent throopers.
This department of the United States Army will move to
the rear in half an hour.

JENNY. Madeline and I only came yesterday morning.

BARKET. Whin your father got ye's a pass to the front, we all
thought the fightin' in the Shenandoey Valley was over. It
looks now as if it was just beginning. This is no place for
women, now. Miss Gertrude Ellingham ought to go wid
us, but she won't.

JENNY. Barket! Captain Heartsease left the regiment yesterday, and he hasn't rejoined it; he isn't with them, now, at
the head of his company. Where is he?

BARKET. I can't say where he is, Miss Jenny. (*Aside.*) Lyin'
unburied in the woods, where he was shot, I'm afraid.

JENNY. When Captain Heartsease does rejoin the regiment,
Barket, please say to him for me, that—that I—I may have
some orders for him, when we next meet. (*Exit, on
veranda.*)

BARKET. Whin they nixt mate. They tell us there is no such
thing as marriage in Hiven. If Miss Jenny and Captain
Heartsease mate there, they'll invint somethin' that's
mighty like it. While I was lyin' wounded in General
Buckthorn's house at Washington, last summer, and ould
Margery was taking care of me, Margery tould me, confidentially, that they was in love wid aitch ither; and I
think she was about right. I've often seen Captain Heartsease take a sly look at a little lace handkerchief, just before
we wint into battle. (*Looking off stage.*) Here's General
Buckthorn himself. He and I must make it as aisy as we
can for Miss Jenny's poor heart.

(*Enter* GENERAL BUCKTHORN.)

BUCKTHORN. Sergeant Barket! You haven't started with those
girls yet?

BARKET. They're to go in half an hour, sir.

BUCKTHORN. Be sure they do go. Is General Haverill here?

BARKET. Yes, sur; in the house with some of his staff, and the
Surgeon.

BUCKTHORN. Ah! The Surgeon. How is Colonel West, this
morning, after the wound he received last night?

BARKET. He says, himself, that he's as well as iver he was;
but the Colonel and Surgeon don't agray on that subject.
The dochter says he mustn't lave his room for a month.
The knife wint dape; and there's somethin' wrong inside
of him. But the Colonel, bein' on the outside himsilf, can't
see it. He's as cross as a bear, baycause they wouldn't let
him go to the front this morning, at the head of his regiment. I happened to raymark that the Chaplain was prayin'
for his raycovery. The Colonel said he'd court-martial him
if he didn't stop that—quick; there's more important things
for the Chaplain to pray for in his official capacity. Just at
that moment the trumpets sounded, "Boots and Saddles."
I had to dodge one of his boots, and the Surgeon had a
narrow escape from the ither one. It was lucky for us both
his saddle wasn't in the room.

BUCKTHORN. That looks encouraging. I think Kerchival will
get on.

BARKET. Might I say a word to you, sur, about Miss Jenny?

BUCKTHORN. Certainly, Barket. You and old Margery and
myself have been a sort of triangular mother, so to speak,
to the little girl since her own poor mother left her to our
care, when she was only a baby, in the old fort on the
Plains. (*Unconsciously rests his arm over* BARKET's *shoulder, familiarly, and then suddenly draws up.*) Ahem!
(*Gruffly.*) What is it? Proceed.

BARKET. Her mother's bosom would have been the softest
place for her poor little head to rest upon, now, sur.

BUCKTHORN. (*Touching his eyes.*) Well!

BARKET. Ould Margery tould me in Washington that Miss
Jenny and Captain Heartsease were in love wid aitch ither.

BUCKTHORN. (*Starting.*) In love!

BARKET. I approved of the match.

BUCKTHORN. What the devil!

(BARKET *salutes quickly and starts up stage and out.*
BUCKTHORN *moves up after him, and stops at post.* BARKET
stops in road.)

BARKET. So did ould Margery.

BUCKTHORN. (*Angrily.*) March!

(BARKET *salutes suddenly and marches off.*)
Heartsease! That young jackanapes! A mere fop; he'll never make a soldier. My girl in love with—bah! I don't believe it; she's too good a soldier, herself.

(*Enter* HAVERILL, *on veranda.*)

Ah, Haverill!

HAVERILL. General Buckthorn! Have you heard anything of General Sheridan since I sent that dispatch to him last evening?

BUCKTHORN. He received it at midnight and sent back word that he considers it a ruse of the enemy. General Wright agrees with him. The reconnaissance yesterday showed no hostile force, on our right, and Crook reports that Early is retreating up the valley. But General Sheridan may, perhaps, give up his journey to Washington, and he has ordered some changes in our line, to be executed this afternoon at four o'clock. I rode over to give you your instructions in person. You may order General McCuen to go into camp on the right of Meadow Brook, with the second division.

(HAVERILL *writing in his note-book.*)

(*Enter* JENNY, *on veranda.*)

JENNY. Oh, Father! I'm so glad you've come. I've got something to say to you.
(*Running down and jumping into his arms, kissing him. He turns with her, and sets her down, squarely on her feet and straight before him.*)

BUCKTHORN. And I've got something to say to you—about Captain Heartsease.

JENNY. Oh! That's just what I wanted to talk about.

BUCKTHORN. Fall in! Front face! (*She jumps into military position, turning towards him.*) What's this I hear from Sergeant Barket? He says you've been falling in love.

JENNY. I have. (*Saluting.*)

BUCKTHORN. Young woman! Listen to my orders. Fall out! (*Turns sharply and marches to* HAVERILL.) Order the Third Brigade of Cavalry, under Colonel Lowell, to occupy the left of the pike.

JENNY. Father! (*Running to him and seizing tail of his coat.*) Father dear!

BUCKTHORN. Close in Colonel Powell on the extreme left— (*Slapping his coat-tails out of* JENNY's *hands, without looking around.*)—and hold Custer on the second line, at Old Forge Road. That is all at present. (*Turning to* JENNY.) Goodbye, my darling! (*Kisses her.*) Remember your orders! You little pet! (*Chuckling, as he taps her chin; draws up suddenly and turns to* HAVERILL.) General! I bid you good-day.

HAVERILL. Good-day, General Buckthorn.

(*They salute with great dignity.* BUCKTHORN *starts up stage;* JENNY *springs after him, seizing his coat-tails.*)

JENNY. But I want to talk with you, Father; I can't fall out. I—I—haven't finished yet.

(*Clinging to his coat, as* BUCKTHORN *marches out rapidly, in road, holding back with all her might.*)

HAVERILL. It may have been a ruse of the enemy, but I hope that General Sheridan has turned back from Washington. (*Looking at his note-book.*) We are to make changes in our line at four o'clock this afternoon. (*Returning book to his pocket, he stands in thought.*) The Surgeon tells me that Kerchival West will get on well enough if he remains quiet; otherwise not. He shall not die by the hand of a common assassin; he has no right to die like that. My wife gave my own picture of herself to him—not to my son—and she looked so like an angel when she took it from my hand! They were both false to me, and they have been true to each other. I will save his life for myself.

(*Enter* GERTRUDE, *on veranda.*)

GERTRUDE. General Haverill! (*Anxiously, coming down.*) Colonel West persists in disobeying the injunctions of the Surgeon. He is preparing to join his regiment at the front. Give him your orders to remain here. Compel him to be prudent!

HAVERILL. (*Quickly.*) The honor of death at the front is not in reserve for him.

GERTRUDE. Eh? What did you say, General?

HAVERILL. Gertrude! I wish to speak to you, as your father's old friend; and I was once your guardian. Your father was my senior officer in the Mexican War. Without his care I should have been left dead in a foreign land. He, himself, afterwards fell fighting for the old flag.

GERTRUDE. The old flag. (*Aside.*) My father died for it, and he—(*Looking toward left.*)—is suffering for it—the old flag!

HAVERILL. I can now return the kindness your father did to me, by protecting his daughter from something that may be worse than death.

GERTRUDE. What do you mean?

HAVERILL. Last night I saw you kneeling at the side of Kerchival West; you spoke to him with all the tender passion of a Southern woman. You said you loved him. But you spoke into ears that could not hear you. Has he ever heard those words from your lips? Have you ever confessed your love to him before?

GERTRUDE. Never. Why do you ask?

HAVERILL. Do not repeat those words. Keep your heart to yourself, my girl.

GERTRUDE. General! Why do you say this to me? And at such a moment—when his life—

HAVERILL. His life! (*Turning sharply.*) It belongs to me!

GERTRUDE. Oh!

KERCHIVAL. (*Without.*) Sergeant!

(*He steps into road, looking back.* HAVERILL *comes down.*) See that my horse is ready at once. General! (*Saluting.*) Are there any orders for my regiment beyond those given to Major Wilson, in my absence, this morning? I am about to ride on after the troops and reassume my command.

HAVERILL. (*Quietly.*) It is my wish, Colonel, that you remain here under the care of the Surgeon.

KERCHIVAL. My wound is a mere trifle. This may be a critical moment in the campaign, and I cannot rest here. I must be with my own men.

HAVERILL. (*Quietly.*) I beg to repeat the wish I have already expressed.

(KERCHIVAL *walks to him, and speaks apart, almost under his breath, but very earnest in tone.*)

KERCHIVAL. I have had no opportunity, yet, to explain certain matters, as you requested me to do yesterday; but whatever there may be between us, you are now interfering with my duty and my privilege as a soldier; and it is my right to be at the head of my regiment.

HAVERILL. (*Quietly.*) It is my positive order that you do not reassume your command.

KERCHIVAL. General Haverill, I protest against this—

HAVERILL. (*Quietly.*) You are under arrest, sir.

KERCHIVAL. Arrest!

GERTRUDE. Ah!

(KERCHIVAL *unclasps his belt and offers his sword to* HAVERILL.)

HAVERILL. (*Quietly.*) Keep your sword; I have no desire to humiliate you; but hold yourself subject to further orders from me.

KERCHIVAL. My regiment at the front!—and I under arrest! (*Exit.*)

HAVERILL. Gertrude! If your heart refuses to be silent—if you feel that you must confess your love to that man—first tell him what I have said to you, and refer him to me for an explanation. (*Exit.*)

GERTRUDE. What can he mean? He would save me from something worse than death, he said. "His life—It belongs to me!" What can he mean? Kerchival told me that he loved me—it seems many years since that morning in Charleston—and when we met again, yesterday, he said that he had never ceased to love me. I will not believe that he has told me a falsehood. I have given him my love, my whole soul and my faith. (*Drawing up to her full height.*) My perfect faith!

(JENNY *runs in, to road, and up slope. She looks down hill, then toward left and enters.*)

JENNY. A flag of truce, Gertrude. And a party of Confederate soldiers, with an escort, coming up the hill. They are carrying someone; he is wounded.

(*Enter, up the slope, a Lieutenant of Infantry with an escort of Union Soldiers, their arms at right shoulder, and a party of Confederate Soldiers bearing a rustic stretcher.* LIEUTENANT FRANK BEDLOE *lies on stretcher.* MAJOR HARDWICK, *a Confederate Surgeon, walks at his side.* MADELINE *appears at veranda, watching them.* JENNY *moves down to left.* GERTRUDE *stands with her back to audience. Lieutenant gives orders in a low tone, and front escort moves toward right, in road. Confederate bearers and Surgeon pass through gate. Rear escort moves on in road, under Lieutenant's orders. Bearers halt in the front of stage; on a sign from Surgeon, they leave stretcher on ground, stepping back.)*

MAJOR HARDWICK. Is General Haverill here?

GERTRUDE. Yes; what can we do, sir?

MADELINE. The General is just about mounting with his staff, to ride away. Shall I go for him, sir?

MAJOR HARDWICK. Say to him, please, that Colonel Robert Ellingham, of the Tenth Virginia, sends his respects and sympathy. He instructed me to bring this young officer to this point, in exchange for himself, as agreed upon between them last evening.

(*Exit* MADELINE.)

JENNY. Is he unconscious or sleeping, sir?

MAJOR HARDWICK. Hovering between life and death. I thought he would bear the removal better. He is waking. Here, my lad! (*Placing his canteen to the lips of* FRANK, *who moves, reviving.*) We have reached the end of our journey.

FRANK. My father!

MAJOR HARDWICK. He is thinking of his home.

(FRANK *rises on one arm, assisted by Surgeon.*)

FRANK. I have obeyed General Haverill's orders, and I have a report to make.

GERTRUDE. We have already sent for him. (*Stepping to him.*) He will be here in a moment.

FRANK. (*Looking into her face, brightly.*) Is not this—Miss—Gertrude Ellingham?

GERTRUDE. You know me? You have seen me before?

FRANK. Long ago! Long ago! You know the wife of General Haverill?

GERTRUDE. I have no dearer friend in the world.

FRANK. She will give a message for me to the dearest friend I have in the world. My little wife! I must not waste even the moment we are waiting. Doctor! My note-book!

(*Trying to get it from his coat. Surgeon takes it out. A torn and blood-stained lace handkerchief also falls out.* GERTRUDE *kneels at his side.*)

Ah! I—I—have a message from another—(*Holding up handkerchief.*)—from Captain Heartsease.

(JENNY *makes a quick start towards him.*)

He lay at my side in the hospital, when they brought me away; he had only strength enough to put this in my hand, and he spoke a woman's name; but I—I—forget what it is. The red spots upon it are the only message he sent.

(GERTRUDE *takes handkerchief and looks back at* JENNY, *extending her hand.* JENNY *moves to her, takes the handkerchief and turns back, looking down on it. She drops her face into her hands and goes out sobbing on veranda.*)

(*Enter* MADELINE *on veranda.*)

MADELINE. General Haverill is coming. I was just in time. He was already on his horse.

FRANK. Ah! He is coming. (*Then suddenly.*) Write! Write! (GERTRUDE *writes in note-book as he dictates.*) "To—my wife—Edith:—Tell our little son, when he is old enough to know—how his father died; not how he lived. And tell her who filled my own mother's place so lovingly— she is your mother, too—that my father's portrait of her, which she gave to me in Charleston, helped me to be a better man!" And—Oh! I must not forget this—"It was taken away from me while I was a prisoner in Richmond, and it is in the possession of Captain Edward Thornton, of the Confederate Secret Service. But her face is still beside your own in my heart. My best—warmest, last—love—to you, darling." I will sign it.

(GERTRUDE *holds book, and he signs it, then sinks back very quietly, supported by Surgeon.* GERTRUDE *rises and walks away.*)

MADELINE. General Haverill is here.

(*Surgeon lays fold of blanket over* FRANK'S *face and rises.*)

GERTRUDE. Doctor!

MAJOR HARDWICK. He is dead.

(MADELINE, *on veranda, turns and looks away. Lieutenant orders the guard, "Present Arms."*)

(*Enter* HAVERILL, *on veranda. He salutes guard as he passes. Lieutenant orders, "Carry Arms."* HAVERILL *comes down.*)

HAVERILL. I am too late?

MAJOR HARDWICK. I'm sorry, General. His one eager thought as we came was to reach here in time to see you.

(HAVERILL *moves to bier, looks down at it, then folds back blanket from face. He starts slightly as he first sees it.*)

HAVERILL. Brave boy! I hoped once to have a son like you. I shall be in your father's place to-day, at your grave. (*Replaces blanket and steps back.*) We will carry him to his comrades in the front. He shall have a soldier's burial, in sight of the mountain-top beneath which he sacrificed his young life; that shall be his monument.

MAJOR HARDWICK. Pardon me, General. We Virginians are your enemies, but you cannot honor this young soldier more than we do. Will you allow my men the privilege of carrying him to his grave?

(HAVERILL *inclines his head. Surgeon motions to Confederate Soldiers, who step to bier and raise it gently.*)

HAVERILL. Lieutenant!

(*The Lieutenant orders guard "Left Face." Confederate bearers move through gate, preceded by* MAJOR HARDWICK. HAVERILL *draws his sword, reverses it, and moves up behind bier with bowed head. Lieutenant orders "Forward March," and the cortège disappears. While the girls are still watching it, heavy sound of distant artillery is heard, with booming reverberations among hills and in valley.*)

MADELINE. What is that sound, Gertrude?

GERTRUDE. Listen!

(*Another and more prolonged distant sound, with long reverberations.*)

MADELINE. Again! Gertrude!

(GERTRUDE *raises her hand to command silence; listens. Distant cannon again.*)

GERTRUDE. It is the opening of a battle.

MADELINE. Ah! (*Running down stage. The sounds are heard again, prolonged.*)

GERTRUDE. How often have I heard that sound! (*Coming down.*) This is war, Madeline! You are face to face with it now.

MADELINE. And Robert is there! He may be in the thickest of the danger—at this very moment.

GERTRUDE. Yes. Let our prayers go up for him; mine do, with all a sister's heart.

(KERCHIVAL *enters on veranda, without coat or vest, his sash about his waist, looking back as he comes in.*)

Kerchival!

KERCHIVAL. Go on! Go on! Keep the battle to yourselves. I'm
out of it.
(*The distant cannon and reverberations are rising in volume.*)

MADELINE. I pray for Robert Ellingham—and for the *cause*
in which he risks his life!
(KERCHIVAL *looks at her, suddenly; also* GERTRUDE.)
Heaven forgive me if I am wrong, but I am praying for
the enemies of my country. His people are my people, his
enemies are my enemies. Heaven defend him and his, in
this awful hour.

KERCHIVAL. Madeline! My sister!

MADELINE. Oh, Kerchival! (*Turning and dropping her face
on his breast.*) I cannot help it—I cannot help it!

KERCHIVAL. My poor girl! Every woman's heart, the world
over, belongs not to any country or any flag, but to her
husband—and her lover. Pray for the man you love, sister—
it would be treason not to. (*Passes her before him to left
of stage. Looks across to* GERTRUDE.) Am I right?
(GERTRUDE *drops her head.* MADELINE *moves up veranda
and out.*)
Is what I have said to Madeline true?

GERTRUDE. Yes! (*Looks up.*) Kerchival!

KERCHIVAL. Gertrude! (*Hurries across to her, clasps her in
his arms. He suddenly staggers and brings his hand to his
breast.*)

GERTRUDE. Your wound! (*Supporting him as he reels and
sinks into seat.*)

KERCHIVAL. Wound! I have no wound! You do love me!
(*Seizing her hand.*)

GERTRUDE. Let me call the Surgeon, Kerchival.

KERCHIVAL. You can be of more service to me than he can.
(*Detaining her. Very heavy sounds of battle; she starts,
listening.*)
Never mind that! It's only a battle. You love me!

GERTRUDE. Be quiet, Kerchival, dear. I do love you. I told you
so, when you lay bleeding here, last night. But you could
not hear me. (*At his side, resting her arm about him,
stroking his head.*) I said that same thing to—to—another,
more than three years ago. It is in that letter that General
Buckthorn gave you.

(KERCHIVAL *starts.*)
No—no—you must be very quiet, or I will not say another
word. If you obey me, I will repeat that part of the letter,
every word; I know it by heart, for I read it a dozen times.
The letter is from Mrs. Haverill.

KERCHIVAL. (*Quietly.*) Go on.

GERTRUDE. "I have kept your secret, my darling, but I was
sorely tempted to betray the confidence you reposed in
me at Charleston. If Kerchival West—(*Retires backward
from him as she proceeds.*)—had heard you say, as I did,
when your face was hidden in my bosom, that night, that
you loved him with your whole heart—"

KERCHIVAL. Ah!
(*Starting to his feet. He sinks back. She springs to support
him.*)

GERTRUDE. I will go for help.

KERCHIVAL. Do not leave me at such a moment as this. You
have brought me a new life. (*Bringing her to her knees
before him and looking down at her.*) Heaven is just opening before me. (*His hands drop suddenly and his head falls
back.*)

GERTRUDE. Ah! Kerchival! You are dying!
(*Musketry. A sudden sharp burst of musketry, mingled
with the roar of artillery near by.* KERCHIVAL *starts, seizing*
GERTRUDE'S *arm and holding her away, still on her knees.
He looks eagerly toward left.*)

KERCHIVAL. The enemy is close upon us!

(BARKET *runs in, up slope.*)

BARKET. Colonel Wist! The devils have sprung out of the
ground. They're pouring over our lift flank like Noah's
own flood. The Union Army has started back for Winchester, on its way to the North Pole; our own regiment,
Colonel, is coming over the hill in full retrate.

KERCHIVAL. My own regiment! (*Starting up.*) Get my horse,
Barket. (*Turns.*) Gertrude, my life! (*Embraces* GER-
TRUDE.)

BARKET. Your horse is it? I'm wid ye! There's a row at Finne-
gan's ball, and we're in it. (*Springs to road, and runs out.*)

KERCHIVAL. (*Turns away. Stops.*) I am under arrest.
(*Retreat begins. Fugitives begin to straggle across stage
from left.*)

GERTRUDE. You must not go, Kerchival; it will kill you.

KERCHIVAL. Arrest be damned! (*Starts up toward center, raising his arms above his head with clenched fist, and rising to full height.*) Stand out of my way, you cowards! (*They cower away from him as he rushes out among them. The stream of fugitives passing across the stage swells in volume.* GERTRUDE *runs through them and up to elevation, turning.*)

GERTRUDE. Men! Are you soldiers? Turn back! There is a leader for you! Turn back! Fight for your flag—and mine!— the flag my father died for! Turn back! (*Looks out toward the left and then turns toward front.*) He has been marked for death already, and I—I can only pray. (*Dropping to her knees.*)

(*The stream of fugitives continues, now over elevation also. Rough and torn uniforms, bandaged arms and legs; some limping and supported by others, some dragging their muskets after them, others without muskets, others using them as crutches. There is a variety of uniforms, both cavalry and infantry; flags are draggled on the ground, the rattle of near musketry and roar of cannon continue; two or three wounded fugitives drop down beside hedge.* PRIVATE BENSON *staggers in and drops upon a rock near post. Artillerists, rough, torn and wounded, drag and force a field-piece across.* CORPORAL DUNN, *wounded, staggers to top of elevation. There is a lull in sounds of the battle. Distant cheers heard without.*)

CORPORAL DUNN. Listen, fellows! Stop! Listen! Sheridan! General Sheridan is coming!

(*Cheers from those on stage.* GERTRUDE *rises quickly. The wounded soldiers rise, looking over hedge. All on stage stop, looking eagerly toward left. Cheers without come nearer, with shouts of "Sheridan! Sheridan!"*)

The horse is down; he is worn out.

GERTRUDE. No! He is up again! He is on my Jack! Now, for your life, Jack, and for me! You've never failed me yet.

(*Cheers without now swell to full volume and are taken up by those on stage. The horse sweeps by with* GENERAL SHERIDAN.)

Jack! Jack!! Jack!!!

(*Waving her arms as he passes. She throws up her arms and falls backward, caught by* DUNN. *The stream of men is reversed and surges across stage to left, in road and on elevation, with shouts, and throwing up of hats. Field-piece is forced up slope with a few bold, rough movements; artillerists are loading it, and stream of returning fugitives is still surging by in road as curtain falls.)*

ACT IV

Residence of GENERAL BUCKTHORN, *in Washington. Interior. Fireplace slanting upward from left toward center of stage. On right toward center there is a small alcove. On left there is an opening to hall with a stair-case beyond. There is a door on right and a wide opening with portières leads on left toward another room. There is an upright piano toward front of stage on right and an armchair and low stool before the fireplace. A small table is set for tea. It is afternoon;* MRS. HAVERILL, *in an armchair, is resting her face upon her hand, and looking into fire.* EDITH *is on a low stool at her side, sewing a child's garment.*

EDITH. It seems hardly possible that the war is over, and that General Lee has really surrendered. There is music in the streets nearly all the time, now, and everybody looks so cheerful and bright.
(*Distant fife and drums are heard playing "Johnnie Comes Marching Home."* EDITH *springs up and runs up to window, looking out.*)
More troops returning! The old tattered battle-flag is waving in the wind, and people are running after them so merrily. Every day, now, seems like a holiday. The war is over. All the women ought to feel very happy, whose—whose husbands are—coming back to them.

MRS. HAVERILL. Yes, Edith; those women whose—husbands are coming back to them. (*Still looking into fire.*)

EDITH. Oh! (*Dropping upon stool, her head upon arm of chair.*)

MRS. HAVERILL. (*Resting her arm over her.*) My poor, little darling! *Your* husband will not come back.

EDITH. Frank's last message has never reached me.

MRS. HAVERILL. No; but you have one sweet thought always with you. Madeline West heard part of it, as Gertrude wrote it down. His last thought was a loving one, of you.

EDITH. Madeline says that he was thinking of you, too. He knew that you were taking such loving care of his little one, and of me. You have always done that, since you first came back from Charleston, and found me alone in New York.

MRS. HAVERILL. I found a dear, sweet little daughter. (*Stroking her head.*) Heaven sent you, darling! You have been a blessing to me. I hardly know how I should have got through the past few months at all without you at my side.

EDITH. What is your own trouble, dear? I have found you in tears so often; and since last October, after the battle of Cedar Creek, you—you have never shown me a letter from —from my—Frank's father. General Haverill arrived in Washington yesterday, but has not been here yet. Is it because I am here? He has never seen me, and I fear that he has never forgiven Frank for marrying me.

MRS. HAVERILL. Nonsense, my child; he did think the marriage was imprudent, but he told me to do everything I could for you. If General Haverill has not been to see either of us, since his arrival in Washington, it is nothing that you need to worry your dear little head about. How are you getting on with your son's wardrobe?

EDITH. Oh! Splendidly! Frankie isn't a baby any longer; he's a man, now, and he has to wear a man's clothes. (*Holding up a little pair of trousers, with maternal pride*). He's rather young to be dressed like a man, but I want Frank to grow up as soon as possible. I long to have him old enough to understand me when I repeat to him the words in which General Haverill told the whole world how his father died! (*Rising.*) And yet, even in his official report to the Government, he only honored him as Lieutenant Bedloe. He has never forgiven his son for the disgrace he brought upon his name.

MRS. HAVERILL. I know him so well—(*Rising.*)—the unyielding pride, that conquers even the deep tenderness of his nature. He can be silent, though his own heart is breaking. (*Aside.*) He can be silent, too, though *my* heart is breaking. (*Dropping her face in her hand.*)

EDITH. *Mother!* (*Putting her arm about her.*)

(*Enter* JANNETTE.)

JANNETTE. A letter for you, Madam.

MRS. HAVERILL. (*Taking note. Aside.*) He has answered me.
(*Opens and reads letter, and inclines her head to* JAN-
NETTE, *who goes out to hall. Aloud.*)
General Haverill will be here this afternoon, Edith. (*Exit.*)

EDITH. There is something that she cannot confide to me, or
to anyone. General Haverill returned to Washington yesterday, and he has not been here yet. He will be here to-day.
I always tremble when I think of meeting him.
(GENERAL BUCKTHORN *appears in hall.*)

BUCKTHORN. Come right in; this way, Barket. Ah, Edith!

BARKET. (*Entering.*) As I was saying, sur—just after the battle
of Sayder Creek began—

BUCKTHORN. (*To* EDITH.) More good news! The war is, indeed, over now!

BARKET. Whin Colonel Wist rode to the front to mate his
raytrating rigiment—

BUCKTHORN. General Johnston has surrendered his army,
also; and that, of course, does end the war.

EDITH. I'm very glad that all the fighting is over.

BUCKTHORN. So am I; but my occupation, and old Barket's,
too, is gone. Always at work on new clothes for our little
soldier?

EDITH. He's growing so, I can hardly make them fast enough
for him. But this is the time for his afternoon nap. I must
go now, to see if he is sleeping soundly.

BUCKTHORN. Our dear little mother! (*Tapping her chin.*) I
always claim the privilege of my white hair, you know.
(*She puts up her lips; he kisses her. She goes out.*) The
sweetest young widow I ever saw!
(BARKET *coughs.* BUCKTHORN *turns sharply;* BARKET *salutes.*)
Well! What the devil are you thinking about now?

BARKET. The ould time, sur. Yer honor used to claim the same
privilege for brown hair.

BUCKTHORN. You old rascal! What a memory you have! You
were telling me for the hundredth time about the battle of
Cedar Creek; go on. I can never hear it often enough.
Kerchival West was a favorite of mine, poor fellow!

BARKET. Just afther the battle of Sayder Creek began, when

the Colonel rode to the front to mate his raytrating rigiment—

BUCKTHORN. I'll tell Old Margery to bring in tea for both of us, Barket.

BARKET. For both of us, sur?

BUCKTHORN. Yes; and later in the evening we'll have something else, together. This is a great day for all of us. I'm not your commander to-day, but your old comrade in arms—(*Laying his arm over* BARKET's *shoulder*)—and I'm glad I don't have to pull myself up now every time I forget my dignity. Ah! you and I will be laid away before long, but we'll be together again in the next world, won't we, Barket?

BARKET. Wid yer honor's permission. (*Saluting.*)

BUCKTHORN. Ha—ha—ha! (*Laughing.*) If we do meet there, I'm certain you'll salute me as your superior officer. There's old Margery, now. (*Looking toward door and calling.*) Margery! Tea for two!

MARGERY. (*Without.*) The tay be waiting for ye, sur; and it be boilin' over wid impatience.

BUCKTHORN. Bring up a chair, Barket. (*Sitting down in armchair.*)

BARKET. (*Having placed table and drawing up a chair.*) Do you know, Gineral, I don't fale quite aisy in my moind. I'm not quite sure that Margery will let us take our tay together. (*Sits down, doubtfully.*)

BUCKTHORN. I hadn't thought of that. I—(*Glancing to right.*) —I hope she will, Barket. But, of course, if she won't— she's been commander-in-chief of my household ever since Jenny was a baby.

BARKET. At Fort Duncan, in Texas.

BUCKTHORN. You and Old Margery never got along very well in those days; but I thought you had made it all up; she nursed you through your wound, last summer, and after the battle of Cedar Creek, also.

BARKET. Yis, sur, bliss her kind heart, she's been like a wife to me; and that's the trouble. A man's wife is such an angel when he's ill that he dreads to get well; good health is a misfortune to him. Auld Margery and I have had anither misunderstanding.

BUCKTHORN. I'll do the best I can for both of us, Barket. You were telling me about the battle of—

BARKET. Just afther the battle of Sayder Creek began, whin Colonel Wist rode to the front to mate his raytrating rigiment—

(*Enter* OLD MARGERY, *with a tea-tray. She stops abruptly, looking at* BARKET. *He squirms in his chair.* BUCKTHORN *rises and stands with his back to mantel.* OLD MARGERY *moves to table, arranges things on it, glances at* BARKET, *then at* BUCKTHORN, *who looks up at ceiling, rubbing his chin.* OLD MARGERY *takes up one of the cups, with saucer.*)

OLD MARGERY. I misunderstood yer order, sur. I see there's no one here but yerself. (*Going.*)

BUCKTHORN. Ah, Margery! (*She stops.*) Barket tells me that there has been a slight misunderstanding between you and him.

OLD MARGERY. Day before yesterday, the ould Hibernian dhrone had the kitchen upside down, to show anither old milithary vagabond loike himself how the battle of Sayder Creek was fought. He knocked the crame pitcher into the basket of clane clothes, and overturned some raspberry jam and the flat-irons into a pan of fresh eggs. There *has* been a misunderstanding betwane us.

BUCKTHORN. I see there has. I suppose Barket was showing his friend how Colonel Kerchival West rode forward to meet his regiment, when he was already wounded dangerously.

OLD MARGERY. Bliss the poor, dear young man! He and I was always good frinds, though he was something of a devil in the kitchen himself, whin he got there. (*Wiping her eye with one corner of her apron.*) And bliss the young Southern lady that was in love wid him, too. (*Changing cup and wiping other eye with the corner of her apron.*) Nothing was iver heard of ayther of thim after that battle was over, to this very day.

BUCKTHORN. Barket was at Kerchival's side when he rode to the front.

(OLD MARGERY *hesitates a moment, then moves to table, sets down cup and marches out.* BUCKTHORN *sits in armchair again, pouring tea.*)

I could always find some way to get Old Margery to do what I wanted her to do.

BARKET. You're a great man, Gineral; we'd niver have con-
quered the South widout such men.

BUCKTHORN. Now go on, Barket; you were interrupted.

BARKET. Just afther the battle of Sayder Creek began, whin—

(*Enter* JANNETTE, *with a card, which she hands to* BUCK-
THORN.)

BUCKTHORN. (*Reading card.*) Robert Ellingham! (*Rises.*) I
will go to him. (*To* JANNETTE.) Go upstairs and tell Miss
Madeline to come down.

JANNETTE. Yes, sir. (*Going.*)

BUCKTHORN. And, Jannette, simply say there is a caller; don't
tell her who is here.

(*Exit* JANNETTE. BUCKTHORN *follows her out to hall.*)
Ellingham! My dear fellow! (*Extending his hand and disappearing.*)

BARKET. Colonel Ellingham and Miss Madeline—lovers! That's
the kind o' volunteers the country nades now!

(*Enter* BUCKTHORN *and* ROBERT.)

BUCKTHORN. (*As he enters.*) We've been fighting four years
to keep you out of Washington, Colonel, but we are delighted to see you within the lines, now.

ROBERT. I am glad, indeed, General, to have so warm a
welcome. But can you tell me anything about my sister,
Gertrude?

BUCKTHORN. About your sister? Why, can't you tell us? And
have you heard nothing of Kerchival West on your side of
the line?

ROBERT. All I can tell you is this: As soon as possible after
our surrender at Appomattox, I made my way to the
Shenandoah Valley. Our home there is utterly deserted. I
have hurried down to Washington in the hopes that I might
learn something of you. There is no human being about
the old homestead; it is like a haunted house—empty, and
dark, and solitary. You do not even know where Gertrude
is?

BUCKTHORN. We only know that Kerchival was not found
among the dead of his own regiment at Cedar Creek,
though he fell among them during the fight. The three
girls searched the field for him, but he was not there. As
darkness came on, and they were returning to the house,

Gertrude suddenly seized the bridle of a stray horse, sprang upon its back and rode away to the South, into the woods at the foot of Three Top Mountain. The other two girls watched for her in vain. She did not return, and we have heard nothing from her since.

ROBERT. Poor girl! I understand what was in her thoughts, and she was right. We captured fourteen hundred prisoners that day, although we were defeated, and Kerchival must have been among them. Gertrude rode away, alone, in the darkness, to find him. I shall return to the South at once and learn where she now is.

(JANNETTE *has re-entered, down the stairs.*)

JANNETTE. Miss Madeline will be down in a moment. (*Exit in hall.*)

BARKET. (*Aside.*) That name wint through his chist like a rifle ball.

BUCKTHORN. Will you step into the drawing-room, Colonel? I will see Madeline myself, first. She does not even know that you are living.

ROBERT. I hardly dared ask for her. Is she well?

BUCKTHORN. Yes; and happy—or soon will be.

ROBERT. Peace, at last!

(*Exit to apartment.* BUCKTHORN *closes portières.*)

BUCKTHORN. I ought to prepare Madeline a little, Barket; you must help me.

BARKET. Yis, sur, I will.

(*Enter* MADELINE, *down the stairs.*)

MADELINE. Uncle! Jannette said you wished to see me; there is a visitor here. Who is it?

BARKET. Colonel Robert Ellingham.

MADELINE. Ah! (*Staggering.*)

BUCKTHORN. (*Supporting her.*) You infernal idiot! I'll put you in the guard-house!

BARKET. You wanted me to help ye, Gineral.

MADELINE. Robert is alive—and here? (*Rising from his arms, she moves to portières, holds them aside, peeping in; gives a joyful start, tosses aside portières and runs through.*)

BUCKTHORN. Barket! There's nothing but that curtain between us and Heaven.

BARKET. I don't like stayin' out o' Hiven, myself, sur. Gineral! I'll kiss Ould Margery—if I die for it! (*Exit.*)

BUCKTHORN. Kiss Old Margery! I'll give him a soldier's funeral.

(*Enter* JENNY *from hall, demurely.*)

Ah! Jenny, my dear! I have news for you. Colonel Robert Ellingham is in the draw-room.

JENNY. Oh! I am delighted. (*Starting.*)

BUCKTHORN. A-h-e-m!

JENNY. Oh!—exactly. I see. I have some news for *you*, papa. Captain Heartsease has arrived in Washington.

BUCKTHORN. Oh! My dear! I have often confessed to you how utterly mistaken I was about that young man. He is a soldier—as good a soldier as you are. I'll ask him to the house.

JENNY. (*Demurely.*) He is here now.

BUCKTHORN. Now?

JENNY. He's been here an hour; in the library.

BUCKTHORN. Why! Barket and I were in the library fifteen minutes ago.

JENNY. Yes, sir. We were in the bay-window; the curtains were closed.

BUCKTHORN. Oh! exactly; I see. You may tell him he has my full consent.

JENNY. He hasn't asked for it.

BUCKTHORN. Hasn't he? And you've been in the bay-window an hour? Well, my darling—I was considered one of the best Indian fighters in the old army, but it took me four years to propose to your mother. I'll go and see the Captain. (*Exit.*)

JENNY. I wonder if it will take Captain Heartsease four years to propose to me. Before he left Washington, nearly two years ago, he told everybody in the circle of my acquaintance, except me, that he was in love with me. I'll be an old lady in caps before our engagement commences. Poor dear mother! The idea of a girl's waiting four years for a chance to say, "Yes." It's been on the tip of my tongue so often, I'm afraid it'll pop out, at last, before he pops the question.

(*Enter* BUCKTHORN *and* HEARTSEASE *from the hall.*)

BUCKTHORN. Walk right in, Captain; this is the family room. You must make yourself quite at home here.

HEARTSEASE. Thank you. (*Walking down toward right.*)

BUCKTHORN. My dear! (*Apart to* JENNY.) The very first thing he said to me, after our greeting, was that he loved my daughter.

JENNY. Now he's told my father!

BUCKTHORN. He's on fire!

JENNY. Is he? (*Looking at* HEARTSEASE, *who stands quietly stroking his mustache.*) Why doesn't he tell *me?*

BUCKTHORN. You may have to help him a little; your mother assisted me. When you and Jenny finish your chat, Captain—(*Lighting a cigar at the mantel.*)—you must join me in the smoking room.

HEARTSEASE. I shall be delighted. By the way, General—I have been in such a fever of excitement since I arrived at this house—

JENNY. (*Aside.*) Fever? Chills!

HEARTSEASE. That I forgot it entirely. I have omitted a very important and a very sad commission. I have brought with me the note-book of Lieutenant Frank Bedloe—otherwise Haverill—in which Miss Gertrude Ellingham wrote down his last message to his young wife.

JENNY. Have you seen Gertrude?

BUCKTHORN. (*Taking book.*) How did this note-book come into your possession?

HEARTSEASE. Miss Ellingham visited the prison in North Carolina where I was detained. She was going from hospital to hospital, from prison to prison, and from burial-place to burial-place, to find Colonel Kerchival West, if living—or some record of his death.

BUCKTHORN. Another Evangeline! Searching for her lover through the wilderness of this great war!

HEARTSEASE. I was about to be exchanged at the time, and she requested me to bring this to her friends in Washington. She had not intended to carry it away with her. I was not exchanged, as we then expected, but I afterwards escaped from prison to General Sherman's Army.

BUCKTHORN. I will carry this long-delayed message to the widowed young mother. (*Exit.*)

JENNY. I remember so well, when poor Lieutenant Haverill took out the note-book and asked Gertrude to write for him. He—he brought me a message at the same time.
(*Their eyes meet. He puts up his glasses. She turns away, touching her eyes.*)

HEARTSEASE. I—I remember the circumstances you probably allude to; that is—when he left my side—I—I gave him my —I mean your—lace handkerchief.

JENNY. It is sacred to me!

HEARTSEASE. Y-e-s—I would say—is it?

JENNY. (*Wiping her eyes.*) It was stained with the life-blood of a hero!

HEARTSEASE. I must apologize to you for its condition. I hadn't any chance to have it washed and ironed.

JENNY. (*Looking around at him, suddenly; then, aside.*) What could any girl do with a lover like that? (*Turning up stage.*)

HEARTSEASE. (*Aside.*) She seems to remember that incident so tenderly! My blood boils!

JENNY. Didn't you long to see your—your friends at home— when you were in prison, Captain?

HEARTSEASE. Yes—especially—I longed especially, Miss Buck-thorn, to see—

JENNY. *Yes!—to see—*

HEARTSEASE. But there were lots of jolly fellows in the prison. (JENNY *turns away.*)
We had a dramatic society, and a glee club, and an orchestra. I was one of the orchestra. I had a banjo, with one string; I played one tune on it, that I used to play on the piano, with one finger. But, Miss Buckthorn, I am a prisoner again, to-night—your prisoner.

JENNY. (*Aside.*) At last!

HEARTSEASE. I'll show you how that tune went. (*Turns to piano and sits.*)

JENNY. (*Aside.*) Father said I'd have to help him, but I don't see an opening.
(HEARTSEASE *plays part of an air with one finger and strikes two or three wrong notes.*)

HEARTSEASE. There are two notes down there, somewhere, that I never could get right. The fellows in prison used to dance while I played—(*Playing.*)—that is, the lame ones did; those that weren't lame couldn't keep the time.

JENNY. You must have been in great danger, Captain, when you escaped from prison.

HEARTSEASE. Y-e-s. I was badly frightened several times. One night I came face to face, on the road, with a Confederate Officer. It was Captain Thornton.

JENNY. Oh! What did you do?

HEARTSEASE. I killed him.

(*Very quietly, and trying tune again at once. Enter* JAN-NETTE, *from hall; she glances into room and goes up stairs.*)

I used to skip those two notes on the banjo. It's very nice for a soldier to come home from the war, and meet those— I mean the one particular person—that he—you see, when a soldier loves a woman, as—as—

JENNY. (*Aside.*) As he loves me. (*Approaches him.*)

HEARTSEASE. As soldiers often do—

(*Plays; she turns away, petulantly; he plays tune through correctly.*) That's it!

JENNY. (*Aside.*) I'm not going to be made love to by piece-meal, like this, any longer. (*Aloud.*) Captain Heartsease! Have you anything in particular to say to me? (*He looks up.*)

HEARTSEASE. Y-e-s. (*Rising.*)

JENNY. Say it! You told my father, and all my friends, that you were in love with me. Whom are you going to tell next?

HEARTSEASE. I *am* in love with you.

JENNY. It was my turn.

HEARTSEASE. (*Going near to her.*) Do you love me?

JENNY. (*Laying her head quietly on his breast.*) I must take time to consider.

HEARTSEASE. (*Quietly.*) I assume that this means "Yes."

JENNY. It isn't the way a girl says "No."

HEARTSEASE. My darling!

JENNY. Why! His heart is beating as fast as mine is!

HEARTSEASE. (*Quietly.*) I am frantic with joy.

(*Kisses her. She hides her face on his breast. Enter* MRS. HAVERILL, *down-stairs, followed by* JANNETTE. MRS. HAV-ERILL *stops suddenly.* JANNETTE *stands in doorway.* HEARTSEASE *inclines his head to her, quietly looking at her over* JENNY.)

I am delighted to see you, after so long an absence; I trust
that we shall meet more frequently hereafter.

JENNY. (*Looking at him*). Eh?

HEARTSEASE. (*Looking down at her.*) I think, perhaps, it
might be as well for us to repair to another apartment, and
continue our interview, there!

JENNY. (*Dropping her head on his breast again.*) This room
is very comfortable.

MRS. HAVERILL. Jenny, dear!

(JENNY *starts up; looks from* MRS. HAVERILL *to* HEARTS-
EASE.)

JENNY. Constance! I—'Bout face! March!

(*She turns and goes out.*)

MRS. HAVERILL. I am glad to see you again, Captain, and
happy as well as safe.

HEARTSEASE. Thank you, Madam. I am happy. If you will
excuse me, I will join—my father—in the smoking-room.
(MRS. HAVERILL *inclines her head, and* HEARTSEASE *walks
out.*)

MRS. HAVERILL. Jannette! You may ask General Haverill to
come into this room.

(*Exit* JANNETTE. MRS. HAVERILL *walks down stage, reading a note.*)

"I have hesitated to come to you personally, as I have
hesitated to write to you. If I have been silent, it is because
I could not bring my hand to write what was in my mind
and in my heart. I do not know that I can trust my tongue
to speak it, but I will come."

(*Enter* HAVERILL, *from hall; he stops.*)

HAVERILL. Constance!

MRS. HAVERILL. My husband! May I call you husband? After
all these months of separation, with your life in almost
daily peril, and my life—what? Only a weary longing for
one loving word—and you are silent.

HAVERILL. May I call you wife? I do not wish to speak that
word except with reverence. You have asked me to come
to you. I am here. I will be plain, direct and brief. Where
is the portrait of yourself, which I gave you, in Charleston,
for my son?

MRS. HAVERILL. Your son is dead, sir; and my portrait lies
upon his breast, in the grave.

(HAVERILL *takes miniature from his pocket and holds it towards her in his extended hand. She starts back.*)

He gave it to you? And you ask me where it is?

HAVERILL. It might have lain in the grave of Kerchival West!

MRS. HAVERILL. Ah!

HAVERILL. Not in my son's. I found it upon *his* breast.

(*She turns front, dazed.*)

Well! I am listening! It was not I that sought this interview, madam; and if you prefer to remain silent, I will go. You know, now, why I have been silent so long.

MRS. HAVERILL. My only witnesses to the truth are both dead. I shall remain silent. (*Turning towards him.*) We stand before each other, living, but not so happy as they. We are parted, forever. Even if you should accept my unsupported word—if I could so far forget my pride as to give it to you—suspicion would still hang between us. I remain silent. (HAVERILL *looks at her, earnestly, for a moment, then approaches her.*)

HAVERILL. I cannot look into your eyes and not see truth and loyalty there. Constance!

MRS. HAVERILL. No, John! (*Checking him.*) I will not accept your blind faith! (*Moving.*)

HAVERILL. (*Looking down at picture in his hand.*) My faith is blind; blind as my love! I do not wish to see!

(*Enter* EDITH. *She stops and looks at* HAVERILL. *He raises his head and looks at her.*)

EDITH. This is General Haverill? (*Dropping her eyes.*) I am Edith, sir.

HAVERILL. (*Gently.*) My son's wife. (*Kisses her forehead.*) You shall take the place he once filled in my heart. His crime and his disgrace are buried in a distant grave.

EDITH. And you have not forgiven him, even yet?

MRS. HAVERILL. Is there no atonement for poor Frank's sin— not even his death? Can you only bury the wrong and forget the good?

HAVERILL. The good?

MRS. HAVERILL. Your own words to the Government, as his commander!

HAVERILL. What do you mean?

MRS. HAVERILL. "The victory of Cedar Creek would have been impossible without the sacrifice of this young officer."

HAVERILL. My own words, yes—but—

EDITH. "His name must take its place forever, in the roll of names which his countrymen honor."

HAVERILL. Lieutenant Bedloe!

MRS. HAVERILL. Haverill! You did not know?

HAVERILL. My—son.

EDITH. You did not receive mother's letter?—after his death?

HAVERILL. My son! (*Sinking upon a chair.*) I left him alone in his grave, unknown; but my tears fell for him then, as they do now. He died before I reached him.

EDITH. Father! (*Laying her hand gently on his shoulder.*) You shall see Frank's face again. His little son is lying asleep upstairs; and when he wakes up, Frank's own eyes will look into yours. I have just received his last message. I will read it to you. (*Opens the note-book and reads.*) "Tell our little son how his father died, not how he lived. And tell her who filled my own mother's place so lovingly." (*She looks at* MRS. HAVERILL, *moves to her and hides her face in her bosom.*) My mother!

MRS. HAVERILL. Edith—my child! Frank loved us both.

EDITH. (*Reading.*) "Father's portrait of her, which she gave to me in Charleston—(HAVERILL *starts.*)—helped me to be a better man."

HAVERILL. (*Rising to his feet.*) Constance!

EDITH. (*Reading.*) "It was taken from me in Richmond, and it is in the possession of Captain Edward Thornton."

HAVERILL. One moment! Stop! Let me think! (EDITH *looks at him.*) Thornton was a prisoner—and to Kerchival West. A dispatch had been found upon him—he was searched! (*He moves to her and takes both her hands in his own, bowing his head over them.*) My head is bowed in shame.

MRS. HAVERILL. Speak to me, John, as you used to speak! Tell me you still love me!

HAVERILL. The—the words will come—but they are—choking me—now. (*He presses her hand to his lips.*)

MRS. HAVERILL. We will think no more of the past, except of what was bright in it. Frank's memory, and our own love, will be with us always.

(*Enter* BUCKTHORN, *followed by* HEARTSEASE.)

BUCKTHORN. Haverill! You are back from the war, too. It begins to look like peace in earnest.

HAVERILL. Yes. Peace and home.
(*Shaking hands with him.* MRS. HAVERILL *joins* EDITH.)

(*Enter* BARKET.)

BARKET. Gineral!
(BUCKTHORN *moves to him.* HAVERILL *joins* MRS. HAVERILL *and* EDITH. BARKET *speaks apart, twisting one side of his face.*)
I kissed her!
BUCKTHORN. Have you sent for a surgeon?
BARKET. I felt as if the inimy had surprised us agin, and Sheridan was sixty miles away.
HAVERILL. This is old Sergeant Barket.
(BARKET *salutes.*)
You were the last man of us all that saw Colonel West.
BARKET. Just afther the battle of Sayder Creek began—whin Colonel Wist rode to the front to mate his retraying rigiment—the byes formed in line, at sight of him, to raysist the victorious inimy. It was just at the brow of a hill—about there, sur—(*Pointing with his cane.*) and—here! (*Takes the tray from table and sets it on carpet, then lays slices of bread in a row.*) That be the rigiment.
(*All are interested.* MADELINE *and* ROBERT *enter, and look on.* BARKET *arranges two cups and saucers in a row.*)
That be the inimy's batthery, sur.

(*Enter* MARGERY. *She goes to the table, then looks around, sharply at* BARKET.)

OLD MARGERY. Ye ould Hibernian dhrone! What are yez doin' wid the china on the floor? You'll break it all!
BUCKTHORN. Ah—Margery! Barket is telling us where he last saw Colonel Kerchival West.
OLD MARGERY. The young Colonel! The tay-cups and saucers be's the inimy's batthery? Yez may smash 'em, if ye loike!
BUCKTHORN. Go on, Barket.
(JENNY *and* HEARTSEASE *have entered, as* BARKET *proceeds, the whole party lean forward, intensely interested.* GERTRUDE *enters in the hall, looks in, beckons as if to some one without, and* KERCHIVAL *follows. They move to center of stage, back of the rest and listen unseen.*)
BARKET. Just as the rigiment was rayformed in line, and

Colonel Wist was out in front—widout any coat or hat, and wid only a shtick in his hand—we heard cheers in the rear. Gineral Sheridan was coming! One word to the men—and we swept over the batthery like a whirlwind! (*Slashing his cane through cups and saucers.*)

OLD MARGERY. Hoo-roo!

BARKET. The attack on the lift flank was checked. But when we shtopped to take breath, Colonel Wist wasn't wid us. (GERTRUDE *turns lovingly to* KERCHIVAL. *He places his arm about her.*)

Heaven knows where he is now. Afther the battle was over, poor Miss Gertrude wint off by hersilf into the wilderness to find him.

KERCHIVAL. My wife! You saved my life, at last. (*Embracing her.*)

BARKET. They'll niver come together in this world. I saw Miss Gertrude, myself, ride away into the woods and disappear behind a school-house on the battle-field, over there.

GERTRUDE. No, Barket—(*All start and look.*)—it was the little church; we were married there this morning!

MARGARET FLEMING

Preface to MARGARET FLEMING

Margaret Fleming was a *succès d'estime*, warmly encouraged and supported by important literary figures of the day. After a trial run in Lynn, Massachusetts, in July, 1890, however, managers in Boston and New York would not lease their theatres for the production of a play they considered too daring in theme and treatment, particularly at the third-act curtain. Its author finally rented a small Boston auditorium, where *Margaret Fleming* had its first production—a three-week run beginning on May 4, 1891, and then another three-week run in October. According to William Dean Howells, "It became the talk of the whole city wherever cultivated people met." He further wrote, in *Harper's Magazine* (August 1891): "The power of this story as presented in Mr. Herne's every-day phrase, and in the naked simplicity of Mrs. Herne's acting of the wife's part, was terrific. It clutched at the heart. It was common; it was pitilessly plain; it was ugly; but it was true, and it was irresistible." But such realism, which had naturally found champions in Howells, Hamlin Garland, and others, was precisely that which repelled mass audiences.

Both in theme and in dramaturgy the play was considerably ahead of its time. Contemporaneous with the plays of Henrik Ibsen, *Margaret Fleming* shows the influence of the great Norwegian, who was, in fact, one of Herne's idols. The "problem" in the play is less neatly solved that it would have been by Ibsen. But it is there, in the form of the rising ghost of Philip's adultery and its effects on himself and Margaret. *Margaret Fleming* is thus America's first modern drama of ideas, a play that frankly discusses problems heretofore shunned, and does so without the traditional melodrama. Also strongly reminiscent of Ibsen is the dramaturgy, which constitutes an equally significant turning point in American theatre history. What distinguishes *Margaret Fleming* from the other plays in this volume—and indeed from the other plays produced before it—are the absence of heroes, villains,

soliloquies, and asides; dramatic climaxes that are devoid
of violent action or words; frequent anticlimactic curtains;
lifelike details in action and setting; and other devices of the
"realistic" drama that have remained dominant (or have
become clichés) in our age.

After the trial run, where he had played Philip, Herne
played the part of Joe Fletcher—and "deliciously," according
to Howells. *Margaret Fleming* was given a special matinée
performance at Palmer's Theatre in New York on December
9, 1891, but was coldly received by New York audiences and
critics alike. The play never achieved popularity, even after
Herne rewrote the last act. Its earlier version is not extant,
but Hamlin Garland, in an article in *The Arena* (October
1891), incidentally furnishes the following interesting account of what happened in that version, after Margaret's
blindness and the daring third-act curtain:

> . . . It all ends in the flight of Fleming, and the destruc-
> tion of their home. Several years later a chain of events
> brings wife and husband together in the office of the
> Boston Inspector of Police. Joe Fletcher, a street peddler,
> and husband of Maria, the sister of Lena Schmidt, was
> the means of bringing them together again. Fleming
> runs across Joe on the Common, and Joe takes him to
> see Maria. Margaret has found Maria and her child,
> which Maria had taken. Philip's altercation with Maria
> brings them into the police office. After explanations, the
> inspector turns to the husband and wife, and voicing
> conventional morality, advises them to patch it up.
> "When you want me, ring that bell," he says, and leaves
> them alone. There is a hush of suspense, and then
> Fleming, seeing the work he had wrought in the blind
> face before him, speaks.
>
> PHILIP. Margaret!
> MARGARET. Well!
> PHILIP. This is terrible.
> MARGARET. You heard the inspector. He calls it a "com-
> mon case."
> PHILIP. Yes, I was wondering whether he meant that or
> only said it.
> MARGARET. I guess he meant it, Philip. We'll be crowded
> out of his thoughts before he goes to bed to-night.

❋ ❋ ❋

MARGARET. Ah, well, it's done now, and—

PHILIP. Yes, it's done. For four years I've been like an escaped prisoner that wanted to give himself up and dreaded the punishment. I'm captured at last, and without hope or fear,—I *was* going to say without shame,—I ask you, my judge, to pronounce my sentence.

MARGARET. That's a terrible thing to ask me to do, Philip. . . . (*She hesitates.*)

PHILIP. Of course you'll get a divorce?

MARGARET. Don't let us have any more ceremonies, Philip. . . . I gave myself to you when you asked me to. We were married in my mother's little home. Do you remember what a bright, beautiful morning it was?

PHILIP. Yes.

MARGARET. That was seven years ago. To-day we're *here!* . . .

❋ ❋ ❋

MARGARET. I *am* calm. My eyes have simply been turned in upon myself for four years. I see clearer than I used to.

PHILIP. Suppose I could come to you some day and say, Margaret, I'm *now* an honest man. Would you live with me again?

MARGARET. The wife-heart has gone out of me, Philip.

PHILIP. I'll wait, Margaret. Perhaps it may come back again. Who knows?

❋ ❋ ❋

PHILIP. Is it degrading to forgive?

MARGARET. No; but it is to condone. Suppose *I* had broken faith with you?

PHILIP. Ah, Margaret!

MARGARET. I know! But suppose I had? Why should a wife bear the whole stigma of infidelity? Isn't it just as revolting in a husband? . . . Then can't you see that it is simply impossible for me to live with you again?

PHILIP. That's my sentence. . . . We'll be friends?

MARGARET. Yes, friends. We'll respect each other as
friends. We never could as man and wife.

As they clasp hands, something latent, organic rushes
over her. She masters it, puts his hand aside: "Ring
that bell!"

Herne rewrote this last act into the present version, with
its promise of an eventual reconciliation of the Flemings, for
the McVicker's Theatre production in Chicago in 1892, and
it has been thus performed in the few revivals and in the
amateur productions that it still receives occasionally. The
script of this later version, too, is lost, but Mrs. Herne, who
not only created the part of Margaret but was also closely
associated with the composition of the play, later recon-
structed it for publication in its present form.

Born in Cohoes, New York, in 1839, James A. Herne
(originally Ahern) was a prominent actor, playwright, and
stage manager. He became the leading man for Lucille
Western, to whose sister Helen he had been briefly married.
While managing Maguire's New Theatre in San Francisco
he began dramatizing some of the novels of Dickens, who
was a strong influence on Herne's work. There also began
his association with David Belasco, at the time (1874) a bit
player in Herne's *Rip Van Winkle*; they collaborated on a
number of plays, including the long popular *Hearts of Oak*
(1879). By then Herne had become stage manager and
leading actor at San Francisco's Baldwin Theatre, where he
met the Irish-born player Katharine Corcoran (1857–1943),
whom he married in 1878. An excellent actress, who was
Herne's leading lady in most of his plays, Mrs. Herne also
inspired—to the point of suggesting "scenes, lines, and stage
business," according to Hamlin Garland—his playwriting,
which in time became less and less melodramatic and more
realistic.

Herne had great faith in art, which he persistently attempted to elevate in his own profession. The Syndicate that
was formed in 1896 and almost totally dominated American
theatres for a decade was not, of course, given to artistic
experimentation. Herne therefore joined others who were
striving to establish something like André Antoine's Théâtre
Libre in Paris and Otto Brahm's Freie Bühne in Berlin. They

called for the "establishment of a distinctively American Theatre," where "the Drama shall be considered a Work of Art, and produced as such—independent of cheap popularity." *Margaret Fleming* was hailed by his associates in this unsuccessful project, and Herne himself invested—and lost—thousands of dollars in his attempts to make the play popular. He formulated his artistic creed, "Art for Truth's Sake," a manifesto published in *The Arena* (February 1897). But it was the maudlin and the melodramatic that was popular, and Herne's *Shore Acres* (1892)—in which he played the sentimental Yankee Uncle Nat—was more attuned to such tastes and made a fortune for him. Among his other plays in which he and Mrs. Herne starred are *The Reverend Griffith Davenport* (1899), a Civil War drama that had little commercial success, and his last play, *Sag Harbor* (1899), a very successful revamping of *Hearts of Oak*, in which Herne took the part of Captain Marble. It was during the run of this play that he died, in New York City, on June 2, 1901.

For Herne's biography and a study of his work and milieu, see Herbert J. Edwards and Julie A. Herne's *James A. Herne, The Rise of Realism in the American Drama* (University of Maine, 1964).

M.M.

MARGARET FLEMING
By James A. Herne

Characters

PHILIP FLEMING, a mill owner
MARGARET FLEMING, his wife
LUCY, their baby
BOBBY, office boy
MR. FOSTER, manager of the mill
WILLIAMS, foreman
JOE FLETCHER
DOCTOR LARKIN
MARIA BINDLEY, the nursemaid
JANE, the maid
HANNAH, the cook
MRS. BURTON
CHARLIE BURTON, her 10-year-old son
INFANT

Setting: Canton, Massachusetts;
May and June, 1890.

ACT I

SCENE 1

It is a morning in Spring in PHILIP FLEMING'S *private office
at the mill. Bright sunlight floods the room at first. Later it
becomes cloudy until at the end of the act, rain is falling
fitfully. The room is handsomely furnished. There is a table
in the center at the back between two windows. Above the
table and attached to the wall is a cabinet with a mirror in
the door. In the right corner is an umbrella-stand and hat-
rack beside a door leading to the street. There are two windows below the door. A little to the right of the center of the
room is an armchair, and in the same position on the left is a
flat-top office desk, with a chair on either side. Behind it on
the left is a door leading to the mill. There is a bunch of
flowers on the desk, and two silver frames holding pictures of*
MARGARET *and* LUCY. *There are also pictures on the wall,
including one of the mill and one of* PHILIP'S *father as a
young man.*

As the curtain rises, BOBBY *enters from the left with a
desk-basket of mail, which he places on the desk. He re-
arranges the chairs slightly. As he is about to go out a key
is heard in the door on the right.* BOBBY *pauses expectantly.*
PHILIP FLEMING, *carrying an umbrella and a rain-coat, enters
from the street door on the right. He is a well dressed,
prosperous, happy-looking man about thirty-five. He hangs
up his hat and coat, and places his umbrella in the stand.
Then he glances carelessly into the hat-rack mirror and
runs his hand lightly over his hair.*

PHILIP. (*In a friendly manner.*) Good morning, Bobby.
BOBBY. (*Grinning appreciatively.*) Good morning, sir.
    (PHILIP *goes to his desk and, shifting one or two articles
    out of his way, begins the duties of the day.*)
PHILIP. Did you get wet this morning in that big shower?
BOBBY. Yes, sir, a little, but I'm all right now.

461

(PHILIP *glances rapidly through the letters and with an eager manner selects two large envelopes, opens one, glances through a document it contains and places it in his inside coat-pocket with a satisfied smile.*)

PHILIP. (*Chatting, as he continues his work.*) Still doing the four mile sprint?

BOBBY. Yes, sir. Oh, I like it, sir—when it don't rain.

(PHILIP *opens other letters rapidly, glancing with a quick, comprehensive eye through each before placing it in the growing heap on the desk.*)

PHILIP. How about the bicycle?

BOBBY. Well, sir, Mr. Foster says he thinks he'll be able to recommend me for a raise pretty soon, if I keep up my record.

PHILIP. (*Looking at him quizzically.*) A raise, Bobby?

BOBBY. Yes, Mr. Fleming, and my mother says I can save all I get and I guess I'll have a bicycle pretty soon then.

PHILIP. How long have you been here?

BOBBY. Six months the day after tomorrow.

PHILIP. (*Smiling kindly.*) I guess I'll have to talk to Foster, myself.

BOBBY. Oh, thank you, Mr. Fleming.

(PHILIP *opens a letter which appears to disturb him. He pauses over it with a worried frown.*)

PHILIP. Ask Mr. Foster to come here at once, please.

(*As* BOBBY *starts to go.*)

And tell Williams I want to see him.

BOBBY. Yes, sir.

(*He goes out the door on the left. There is a moment's pause, and then* FOSTER *enters from the same door. He is a bright, active young man about twenty-eight or thirty.*)

PHILIP. Good morning, Foster.

FOSTER. Good morning, Mr. Fleming.

PHILIP. Here's a letter from the receiver for Reed and Vorst. He wants to know if we'll accept an immediate settlement of forty percent.

FOSTER. (*Becoming serious.*) Gee, Mr. Fleming, I don't see how we can. I was depending on at least fifty percent to carry us through the summer. It's always a dull season, you know, and—

PHILIP. Why, we have more orders now than we had this time last year.

FOSTER. Yes, I know, sir. But, I was going to speak to you. The Cotton Exchange Bank doesn't want to renew those notes.

PHILIP. Doesn't, eh? Well, then, we'll have to accept Reed and Vorst's offer.

FOSTER. I think it would be a mistake just now, sir. If we hold out they've got big assets.

PHILIP. Can't be helped. I'm hard-pressed. We're short of ready money.

FOSTER. I don't understand it. We've had a better winter than we've had for years.

PHILIP. (*Smiling.*) That last little flier I took wasn't as successful as the former ones.

FOSTER. You've been too lenient with the retailers.

PHILIP. "Live and let live" 's my motto.

FOSTER. I'd hate to see anything happen to the mill.

PHILIP. Nothing's going to happen. Let me do the worrying. Our credit's good. I'll raise the money tomorrow.

FOSTER. I hope so, sir. Anything else?

PHILIP. (*Giving him the letters.*) Wire the answers to these right away. That's all.

FOSTER. All right, sir. (*He goes out.*)

(PHILIP *takes up a large sheet of paper which contains a report from one of the departments of the mill. He scans it closely and makes some calculations upon a sheet of paper.* WILLIAMS *enters.*)

PHILIP. (*Looking up.*) Good morning, Williams.

(WILLIAMS *is quite an old man, but has the attitude of one who knows his business and can do things. He stands with bent shoulders and arms hanging limp. He is chewing tobacco, and speaks with a quick, sharp, New England accent.*)

WILLIAMS. Good morning, Mr. Fleming.

PHILIP. (*Holding the report in his hand.*) Williams, a short time ago you told me that the main supply belt in the finishing room was only repaired a few times during the last six months. I find here from your report that it has broken down about twice a week since last January. How long does it take to make a repair?

WILLIAMS. Oh, sometimes about ten minutes—other times again, twenty minutes. We have done it in five minutes.

PHILIP. There are about one hundred and ten operators in that room?

WILLIAMS. One hundred and seven.

PHILIP. Why, you should have reported this condition the first week it arose. Poor economy, Williams. (*He makes a few, rapid calculations upon the back of a report.*) Twelve hundred dollars lost time. (*He shakes his head.*) We could have bought a new belt a year ago and saved money in the bargain.

WILLIAMS. I told Mr. Baker several times, sir, in the beginning and he didn't seem to think anything of it.

PHILIP. Well, report all such details to me in the future.

(*He writes a few lines rapidly and rings the bell.* BOBBY *enters briskly.*)

Tell Mr. Foster to get those firms over long distance, and whichever one can make the quickest delivery to place orders there—see?

BOBBY. Yes, sir. (*He has a soiled card in his hand, which he offers to* PHILIP *with a grin.*) A man outside told me to hand you his visiting card.

WILLIAMS. Is that all, sir?

PHILIP. Yes. (*He smiles as he reads the card.*) Joe Fletcher! Tell him to come in.

(*He resumes work at his desk.* WILLIAMS *goes out.*)

BOBBY. Yes, sir. (*He follows* WILLIAMS.)

(*After a moment* JOE FLETCHER *enters. He is a man of middle age, well made but heavy and slouching in manner. He has a keen, shrewd eye in a weak and dissipated face, which is made attractive, nevertheless, by a genial and ingratiating smile. He is wearing a shabby linen coat called a "duster," which hangs, crushed and limp, from his neck to his ankles. Strung from his left shoulder is a cord hung with sponges of various sizes. Several lengths of chamois are dangling with the sponges across his breast and back, draping his right hip and leg. In one hand he has a weather-beaten satchel. He carries by a leather thong a heavy stone hanging from a cracked plate. There are two holes in the rim of the plate through one of which runs the thong by which it is carried. The other, the big stone, is fastened to it with a piece of chain. He carries it unconscious of its weight. There is a pervading sense of intimacy between the man and his equipment, and from his*

*battered hat to his spreading shoes the stains of the road,
like a varnish, bind them together in a mellow fellowship.*)

PHILIP. Hello, Joe. (*He looks at him with humorous curiosity.*)

JOE. (*Light-heartedly.*) How d'do, Mr. Fleming. (*His voice
is broken and husky. He gives a little, dry cough now and
then in an ineffectual attempt to clear it. He crosses to the
corner of the table, and shows by his step that his feet are
sore and swollen.*)

PHILIP. What are you doing now, Joe?

JOE. (*Indicating his effects. While he talks he places the
stone against a corner of the table on the floor, and puts
the valise on the edge of the table.*) Traveling merchant;
agent for Brummell's Giant Cement; professional corn doctor—soft and hard corns—calluses—bunions removed instantly, ingrowing nails treated 'thout pain or loss of blood
—*or* money refunded. Didn't ye read m'card? (*He coughs.*)

PHILIP. (*Laughing.*) Well, not all of it, Joe.

JOE. (*Reminiscently.*) Inventor of Dr. Fletcher's famous
cough mixture, warranted to cure coughs—colds, hoarseness and loss o' voice. An infallible remedy fur all chronic
conditions of the *pul-mon-*ary organs. (*He coughs again.*)
When not too fur gone. (*He takes a labelled bottle, containing a brown mixture from his inside pocket, shakes it
and holds it up proudly before* PHILIP.) Kin I sell ye a
bottle? (*He smiles ingratiatingly.*)

PHILIP. (*Smiling but shaking his head.*) No, Joe, I guess not
today.

JOE. (*Opening the satchel insinuatingly.*) Mebbe a few
boxes o' corn salve? It's great. (PHILIP *shakes his head.*)
Would ye like to consider a box o' cement?

PHILIP. (*Still smiling.*) No, but I'll take one of those big
sponges.

JOE. I thought I could sell ye something.

(*He unhooks a large sponge and lays it upon the desk.*
PHILIP *hands him a bill. He takes it carelessly, looks at it,
shakes his head regretfully and puts it into his pocket.
Then he feels in his other pocket and taps his vest
pockets.*) Gosh, I'm sorry, but I ain't got a bit of change.

PHILIP. Oh, never mind the change, Joe. (*He laughs indulgently.*)

JOE. (*Regretfully.*) Well, I'd feel better if *I* hed the change.

(JOE *has been standing to the left of the desk.*) Kin I set down fur a minnit, Mr. Fleming? M'feet gets so tired.

PHILIP. Yes, Joe, sit down.

JOE. I got pretty wet a while ago in that shower. My, but it did come down.

PHILIP. (*Warmly.*) Perhaps you'd like a hot drink?
(*He indicates with a nod of the head, the cabinet back of* JOE, *as the latter is about to sit down.* JOE *shows a lively interest.*)

JOE. (*Glancing at* PHILIP *with a shy twinkle in his eye.*) Oh, kin I, Mr. Fleming? Thank ye. (*He shuffles over to the cabinet, opens the door and gloats over the vision of joy which greets him. He selects a bottle.*)

PHILIP. Hold on, Joe. Wait for some hot water.

JOE. (*Hastily.*) No, thank ye. I'm afraid I'd be like the Irishman in the dream.

PHILIP. What was that, Joe?

JOE. (*As he pours out a generous portion.*) Well, the Irishman was dreaming that he went to see the priest, and the priest asked him to have a drink. "I will, thank ye kindly," says Pat. "Is it hot or cold, ye'll have it?" says the priest? "Hot, if ye plaze, yer Riverence," says Pat, and while they were waiting fur the hot water, Pat wakes up. "Bad luck to me," says he, "why didn't I take it cold?" (*He drains the glass, smacks his lips and chuckles.*) My, but that's good stuff! Mr. Fleming, are ye as fond of it yourself as ye used to be?

PHILIP. (*Smiling and shaking his head.*) No, Joe. I've got through with all that foolishness. I've sowed my wild oats.

JOE. (*Chuckling as he sits in the chair.*) You must have got a pretty slick crop out o' yourn.

PHILIP. Every man gets a pretty full crop of those, Joe, before he gets through.

JOE. Ye've turned over a new leaf, eh?

PHILIP. Yes—married.

JOE. Married?

PHILIP. Yes, and got a baby.

JOE. Thet so! Did ye marry out'n the mill?

PHILIP. Oh, no. She was a Miss Thorp, of Niagara. (*He hands the picture of the child to* JOE.)

JOE. (*Showing interest immediately, and gazing at the picture, while gradually a gentle responsive smile plays over his features. He says, admiringly.*) By George! that's a great baby! (*He gives a chuckling laugh at it.*) Boy?

PHILIP. (*Proudly.*) No. Girl!

JOE. Thet so! Should a thought you'd a wanted a boy. (*With sly significance, and chuckling at his own joke.*) Ye've hed so many girls.

PHILIP. (*He laughs lightly.*) Tut, tut, Joe, no more of that for me. (*He hands him the frame containing* MARGARET'S *picture.*) My wife.

JOE. (*His expression becoming grave as the sweetness and dignity of the face touches him. He takes a long breath.*) My, but that's a fine face. Gee, if she's as good as that, you're a lucky man, Mr. Fleming.

PHILIP. Yes, Joe, I've got more than I deserve, I guess. (*He becomes serious for the first time and a shadow flits over his face. He sighs.*)

JOE. (*Sympathetically.*) Oh, I understand just how you feel. I'm married m'self. (*He sits down facing the audience, his hands clasped, his thumbs gently rolling over each other. A far-away tender look comes into his eyes.*)

PHILIP. (*Surprised.*) Married?

(JOE *nods his head.*)

Where's your wife?

JOE. Left me. (*He gives a sigh of self pity.*)

PHILIP. (*Touched.*) Left you! (*He shakes his head compassionately, then the thought comes to him.*) If my wife left me I'd kill myself.

JOE. (*Philosophically.*) Oh, no, no, ye wouldn't. You'd get over it, just as I did. (*He sighs.*)

PHILIP. How did it happen? What did you do?

JOE. (*Innocently.*) Not a durn thing! She was a nice, German woman, too. She kept a gent's furnishing store down in South Boston, and I married her.

PHILIP. (*Recovering himself and speaking gaily.*) Oh, Joe. (*He shakes his head in mock reproval.*) You married her for her money, eh? (*He laughs at him.*)

JOE. (*Ingenuously.*) No, I didn't, honest. I thought I might get a whack at the till once in a while, but I didn't.

PHILIP. (*Quizzing him.*) Why not, Joe?

JOE. She fixed me up a pack and sent me out on the road to sell goods, and when I got back, she was gone. There was a new sign on the store, "Isaac Litchenstein, Ladies and Gents' Drygoods." (*He draws a big sigh.*)

PHILIP. And you've never seen her since?

JOE. (*Shaking his head sadly.*) No, siree, never!

PHILIP. (*Serious again, impressed by* JOE.) That's pretty tough, Joe.

(BOBBY *enters.*)

BOBBY. Doctor Larkin would like to see you, sir.

JOE. (*Gathering himself and his merchandise together.*) Well, I guess I'll get out and drum up a few sales. Much obliged to you, Mr. Fleming.

PHILIP. Oh, stop at the house, Joe. Mrs. Fleming might want something. It's the old place on Linden Street.

JOE. Got a dog?

PHILIP. Yes.

JOE. That settles it.

PHILIP. Only a pug, Joe.

JOE. Oh, a snorer. I'll sell him a bottle of cough mixture.

(*As* DR. LARKIN *enters.*)

Hello, Doc! How are you? Raining?

(JOE *goes to the door on the right, crossing the* DOCTOR *who is walking toward* PHILIP *on the left.*)

DOCTOR. (*Looking at him, mystified.*) Good morning, sir. No, it's not raining.

(JOE *goes out.* DR. LARKIN *is a tall, gaunt man who looks older than he is, with quite a stoop in his shoulders. He has dark brown hair and a beard, streaked with grey, and soft, kind blue eyes. He carries the medicine satchel of a homeopathic physician. His manner is usually distant and cold but extremely quiet and gentle. In the opening of this scene he is perturbed and irritated, later he becomes stern and authoritative.*)

PHILIP. Good morning, Doctor Larkin.

DOCTOR. (*Turning to* PHILIP.) Who is that fellow? (*He looks after* JOE *as he goes out.*)

PHILIP. Don't you remember him? That's Joe Fletcher. (PHILIP *is standing to the right of the desk, and* DOCTOR LARKIN *at the left center of the stage.*)

DOCTOR. Is that Joe Fletcher? Why he used to be quite a decent sort of fellow. Wasn't he a foreman here in your father's time?

PHILIP. Yes, he was one of the best men in the mill.

DOCTOR. (*Shaking his head.*) He is a sad example of what

liquor and immorality will bring a man to. He has indulged his appetites until he has no real moral nature left.

PHILIP. (*Lightly.*) Oh, I don't think Joe ever had much "moral nature."

(*The sunlight leaves the room. It is growing cloudy outside.*)

DOCTOR. Every man has a moral nature. In this case it is love of drink that has destroyed it. There are some men who are moral lepers, even lacking the weakness of the tippler as an excuse.

PHILIP. Have you been to the house, doctor? About midnight Margaret thought little Lucy had a fever. She was going to call you up—but—

DOCTOR. (*Abruptly.*) She would not have found me in at midnight.

PHILIP. Ah, is that so? Someone very ill?

(*The telephone rings.*)

Excuse me, doctor. Hello. Oh, is that you, Margaret? How is Lucy now? Good! I knew she'd be all right. Yes, of course. Do—bring her. (*To the* DOCTOR.) She's bringing baby to the 'phone. Hello, Lucy. Many happy returns of the day. Good-bye. Yes, I'll be home at twelve sharp. Apple pie? Yes, of course, I like it. That is, *your* apple pie. (*He leaves the phone with a joyous air.*) This is baby's birthday, you know, doctor.

DOCTOR. I've just left a baby (*He speaks bitterly, looking at* PHILIP *significantly.*) that should never have had a birth-day.

PHILIP. (*Without noticing the* DOCTOR's *manner, he goes to the cabinet and, taking a box of cigars, offers the box to the* DOCTOR.) Why, Doctor, you're morbid today. Take a cigar, it will quiet your nerves.

(*The rain begins to fall, beating heavily agains the windows.*)

DOCTOR. No, thank you. (*With a subtle shade of repugnance in his tone.*) I'll smoke one of my own.

(PHILIP *smiles indulgently, goes to the desk, sits in the chair to the left of it, lights a cigar, leans back luxuriously, with his hands in his pockets, and one leg over the other, and tips back the legs of the chair.*)

PHILIP. (*Carelessly.*) What's the matter, doctor? You used to respect my cigars.

DOCTOR. (*Hotly.*) I used to respect you.

PHILIP. (*Rather surprised but laughing good-naturedly.*) Well, doctor, and don't you now? (*He is bantering him.*)

DOCTOR. (*Quietly but sternly.*) No, I don't.

PHILIP. (*Smoking placidly.*) Good Lord—why?

DOCTOR. (*His satchel resting upon his knees, his hands clasping the metal top, he leans over a trifle and, looking impressively into* PHILIP'S *face, says, in a low, calm voice.*) At two o'clock last night Lena Schmidt gave birth to a child.

PHILIP. (*Becoming livid with amazement and fear, and staring blankly before him, the cigar dropping from his parted lips.*) In God's name, how did they come to send for you?

DOCTOR. Doctor Taylor—he called me in consultation. He was frightened after the girl had been in labor thirty-six hours.

PHILIP. (*Murmuring to himself.*) Thirty-six hours! Good God! (*There is a pause, then he partly recovers himself.*) I suppose she told you?

DOCTOR. She told me nothing. It was a lucky thing for you that I was there. The girl was delirious.

PHILIP. Delirious! Well, I've done all I could for her, doctor.

DOCTOR. Have you? (*His tone is full of scorn.*)

PHILIP. She's had all the money she wanted.

DOCTOR. Has she? (*He speaks in the same tone.*)

PHILIP. I tried to get her away months ago, but she wouldn't do it. She was as stubborn as a mule.

DOCTOR. Strange she should want to remain near the father of her child, isn't it?

PHILIP. If she'd done as I told her to, this thing would never have happened.

DOCTOR. You'd have forced some poor devil to run the risk of state's prison. By God, you're worse than I thought you were.

PHILIP. Why, doctor, you must think I'm—

DOCTOR. I don't think anything about it. I know just what brutes such men as you are.

PHILIP. Well, I'm not wholly to blame. You don't know the whole story, doctor.

DOCTOR. I don't want to know it. The *girl's* not to blame. She's a product of her environment. Under present social conditions, she'd probably have gone wrong anyhow. But you! God Almighty! If we can't look for decency in men like you—representative men—where in God's name are we to look for it, I'd like to know?

PHILIP. If my wife hears of this, my home will be ruined.

DOCTOR. (*Scornfully.*) Your home! Your home! It is just such damn scoundrels as you that make and destroy homes.

PHILIP. Oh, come now, doctor, aren't you a little severe?

DOCTOR. Severe! Severe! Why, do you realize, if this thing should become known, it will stir up a stench that will offend the moral sense of every man, woman and child in this community?

PHILIP. Well, after all, I'm no worse than other men. Why, I haven't seen the girl for months.

DOCTOR. Haven't you? Well, then suppose you go and see her now.

PHILIP. (*He springs to his feet.*) I'll do nothing of the sort.

DOCTOR. Yes, you will. She shan't lie there and die like a dog.

PHILIP. (*He walks around the room greatly perturbed.*) I tell you I'll not go!

DOCTOR. Yes, you will.

PHILIP. (*He comes over to the* DOCTOR *and looks down upon him.*) What'll you do if I don't?

DOCTOR. I don't know, but you'd best go and see that girl.

PHILIP. (*He turns away.*) Well, what do you want me to say to her?

DOCTOR. Lie to her as you have before. Tell her you love her.

PHILIP. I never lied to her. I never told her I loved her.

DOCTOR. Faugh!

PHILIP. I tell you I never did!

DOCTOR. (*Rising from his chair.*) You'd better get Mrs. Fleming away from here until this thing blows over. When I think of a high-minded, splendid little woman like her married to a man like you—ugh! (*The* DOCTOR *goes out quickly.*)

(PHILIP, *left alone, walks about like an old man, seems dazed for a moment, then goes mechanically to the telephone.*)

PHILIP. Linden, 3721. Margaret. (*He speaks in a broken, hushed voice.*) Margaret! Yes, it's I, Philip. Yes! Well, I'm tired. No, I can't come home now. I will not be home to luncheon. I have a business engagement. No, I cannot break it off. It's too important. Eh? Why, with a man from

Boston. Yes, certainly, I will, just as soon as I can get away. Yes, dear—I will—good-bye.

(*Just before he finishes,* FOSTER *enters.*)

Hello, Foster.

FOSTER. (*Consulting a memorandum.*) I couldn't get the Harry Smith Company, New York, until noon, sir. They say that the belting can be shipped by fast express at once. The Boston people want ten cents a square foot more than they ask, but we can save that in time and express rates.

PHILIP. When would the New York shipment get here?

FOSTER. At the earliest, tomorrow afternoon.

PHILIP. White and Cross can ship at once, you say?

FOSTER. Yes, sir.

PHILIP. Well, give them the order. Their stuff is better, anyhow. Have a covered wagon at the station for the four-ten train. Keep enough men over time tonight to put it up.

FOSTER. Yes, sir, the sooner it's done, the better.

PHILIP. Yes, Williams is getting old. He's not the best man for that finishing room. Put him where you can keep an eye on him. He's all right. I have an appointment and will not be in the office again today. Get the interest on those notes off.

FOSTER. Yes, I've attended to that already. Anything else?

PHILIP. No.

FOSTER. All right, sir. Good morning.

(PHILIP *who has braced himself for this, relaxes again. The rain continues. He goes about the room, lights a cigar, puts on a raincoat, looks at his watch, buttons his coat, all the while sunk in deep thought. He takes his umbrella and hat and goes out quietly, shutting the door so that the click of the latch is heard, as the curtain falls.*)

SCENE 2

The scene is the living room in MARGARET'S *home. At the back large glass doors open on to a spacious porch with a garden beyond. There is a fireplace with logs burning, in the corner on the left, and beside it a French window opening on the garden. Below it is a door leading to another room. There is another door on the right going to the main part of the house. There is a table in the center, a baby grand piano*

*on the lower right, and a baby carriage close by the doors
at the back. The room is furnished in exquisite taste, showing
in its distinct character the grace and individuality of a well-
bred woman.*

*MARGARET is seated in a low rocking-chair near the fire
with the baby in her lap. A large bath towel is spread
across her knees. She is exquisitely dressed in an evening
gown.*

*MARIA BINDLEY, the nursemaid, is dressed in a black dress,
cap and apron. She is a middle-aged German woman,
dark in complexion, and of medium build and height. She
speaks with a not too pronounced German accent. She is
gathering up the baby's garments which are scattered about
MARGARET's feet. She is furtively weeping and makes an
occasional effort to overcome her emotion. MARGARET is
putting the last touches to the baby's night toilet. She is
laughing and murmuring mother talk to her.*

*A shaded lamp is burning on the table to the right. The
effect of the light is subdued. The glare of the fire is the
high note, making a soft radiance about MARGARET and
the child. MARIA is in the shadow, except as she flits into
the light whenever she moves near MARGARET. The sound
of the rain beating against the windows is heard now and
then.*

MARGARET. (*In a low, laughing tone.*) No—no—no! You little
beggar. You've had your supper! (*She fastens the last two
or three buttons of her dress.*) No more! Time to go to
sleep now! No use staying awake any longer for naughty
father. Two—whole—hours—late! No, he doesn't care a bit
about you; not a bit! (*She shakes her head.*) No, nor me
either. Never mind, darling, we'll punish him well for this.
Yes, we will. Perhaps we'll leave *him* some day, and then
we'll see how he likes being left alone. Naughty, bad
father—isn't he? *Yes he is!* Staying away all day! Never
mind, ladybird—hush, go to sleep now—Mother loves her!
Go to sleep—close your eyes. (*This is all said in a cooing,
soothing voice. She begins to sing a lullaby.*) Go—to—
sleep—blossom—go to sl—
(MARIA *comes close to* MARGARET *and picks up two little
socks. As she rises, she sniffs in an effort to suppress her*

tears. This attracts MARGARET's *attention, and immediately she is all commiseration.*)

MARGARET. Don't cry, Maria—please don't—it distresses me to see you cry.

MARIA. (*Smiling a little at* MARGARET's *sympathy. As she talks, she smooths the socks and folds them.*) I cannot help it, Mrs. Fleming—I am an unhappy woman. I try not to cry, but I cannot keep back de tears. (*She puts the socks in the basket on the table.*) I have had an unhappy life— my fadder vas a brute. (*She picks up the dress and shakes it.*) My first husband, Ralph Bindley, vas a goot, honest man. (*She puts the dress in the basket.*) Und my second husband vas dot tramp vot vas here dis morning. Vat I have told you aboudt already. (*She gathers together the other garments.*) Und now my sister—my little Lena—is dying.

MARGARET. (*In dismay.*) Dying! Why, you didn't tell me *that*, Maria!

MARIA. Vell, she is not dying yust this very moment, but the doctor says she vill never leave dot bed alive. My sweet little Lena! My lovely little sister. I have nursed her, Mrs. Fleming, yust like you nurse your baby now.

MARGARET. (*Holding the child to her breast.*) What did you say her name was?

MARIA. (*Working mechanically and putting the things neatly away.*) Lena,—Lena Schmidt. She does not go by my name—she goes by my fadder's name.

MARGARET. And, you say, she ran away from you?

MARIA. Ya—I tried to find her every place. I hunted high und low, but she does not come, und von day I meet an olt friend on Vashington Street, Chris Anderson, und Chris, he tell me that two or three weeks before he see her by the public gartens. Und she vas valking by the arm of a fine, handsome gentleman—und she look smiling and happy, und Chris, he says dot he knows *dot* gentleman— *dot* he vas a rich man vot lives down in Canton where Chris vonce worked when he comes to dis country first.

MARGARET. And didn't you ask the man's name?

MARIA. Ach, I forget. Und Chris go back to de olt country, und I never find out. Und den I tink maybe she is married to dot man—und she is ashamed of me and dot miserable husband of mine. I say to myself, "I vill go and see—und find oudt if she is happy." Den I vill go far away, where she vill never see me again. Und I come here to Canton, und at last I find her—und Ach Gott! She is going to be a mutter—und she is no man's vife! (*She has been weeping silently but has continued to work, only pausing at some point in her story that moved her.*)

MARGARET. (*Deeply touched.*) Did she tell you the man's name?

MARIA. Ach! No! You could not drag dot oudt of her mit red-hot irons. She says she loves dis man, und she vill make him no trouble. But, by Gott, I vill find dot man oudt, und I vill choke it from his troat. (*She is beside herself with vindictive passion.*)

MARGARET. (*Terrified at her ferocity and crushing her child to her breast.*) Oh, Maria—don't—please don't! You frighten me!

MARIA. (*At once all humility.*) Excuse me, Mrs. Fleming. I did not mean to do dot.

MARGARET. (*Kindly.*) You need not remain any longer. I can manage baby myself. You had best go to your sister at once. If I can be of any help to you, please tell me, won't you?

MARIA. Ya, Mrs. Fleming, I tank you. Und if she is vorse maybe I stay all night.

MARGARET. Yes, certainly. You need not come back tonight.

MARIA. (*Very softly and humbly.*) I am much obliged to you, Mrs. Fleming.

MARGARET. (*As* MARIA *is going.*) Oh! You had best take my raincoat.

MARIA. Ah, you are very goot, Mrs. Fleming. (*She has finished her work and is going but hesitates a moment and turns back.*) If you please, don't tell Mr. Fleming about me und my poor sister!

MARGARET. (*Slightly annoyed.*) Decidedly not! Why should I tell such things to him?

MARIA. Vell—men don't have sympathy mit peoples like us. He is a fine gentleman, und if he knowed about *her*—he might not like to have *me* by his vife und child. He might tink *I* vas as badt as she was. Good night, Mrs. Fleming.

MARGARET. Good night, Maria. No need to hurry back in the morning. (*There is a wistful sympathy in her face. As her eyes rest upon the door through which* MARIA *has passed, she is lost in thought. Presently a door slams, then she is all alert with expectation. There is a moment's pause, she listens then quickly puts the child in the baby carriage and runs to the door.)* Is that you, Philip?

JANE. (*Outside.*) No, ma'am, it is not Mr. Fleming. It was only the post man.

(MARGARET *turns away with a sigh of disappointment, goes to the French window and peers out at the rain. The* MAID *enters with several letters, leaves them on the table and goes out.* MARGARET *turns from the window, brushes the tears away impatiently, and drifts purposelessly across the room toward the right, her hands clasped behind her back. Finding herself at the piano she listlessly sits before it and plays a plaintive air, softly. Then suddenly she dashes into a prelude to a gay love song. As she sings half through a stanza, the song gradually loses spirit. Her hands grow heavy over the keys, her voice breaks, and the words come slow and faltering. She ends by breaking into tears, with her head lowered and her fingers resting idly upon the keys. The child attracts her and she goes quickly to her. She laughs through her tears into the wide-open eyes, and begins scolding her for not going to sleep. Soft endearing notes come and go in her voice. A tender joy takes possession of her spirit. She takes the child in her arms.*)

MARGARET. Well, my lady, wide awake! Come, come, no more nonsense, now! No. Go to sleep! Late hours—will—certainly spoil—your beauty. Yes! Close up your eyes—quick! Come! There, that's nice. She's a sweet, good child! (*She hums.*) Go—to—sleep! (*She sways slowly from right to left, then swinging with a rhythmic step with the lullaby, she lilts softly.*) Blow, blow, Blossom go—into the world below—I am the west wind wild and strong—blossoms must go when they hear my song. (*She puts out the lamp, leaving the room in the warm glare of the firelight.*) Go, little blossom, go—into the world below. Rain, rain, rain is here. Blossoms must learn to weep.

(*She reaches the French window. As she turns* PHILIP *is seen through the filmy curtains. He enters unnoticed.*)

I am the east wind, bleak and cold, poor little blossoms their petals must fold. Weep, little blossoms, weep, into your cradles creep.

(*She is unconscious of* PHILIP's *presence. His raincoat and hat are dripping wet. He is pale and weary, his manner is listless and abstracted and he looks as though he had been wandering about in the rain for hours. He drifts into the room.* MARGARET *turns around and takes a step, her eyes upon the child, then her lullaby grows indistinct as she notices that the baby is asleep. Another step takes her into* PHILIP's *arms. She gives a cry of alarm.*)

MARGARET. . . Oh, Philip! You frightened me! Why did you do that?

PHILIP. Why are you in the dark, Margaret? (*He goes toward her as if to take her in his arms.*) Dearest!

MARGARET. (*Drawing back from him with a shade of petulance.*) You're all wet. Don't come near baby. She was wakeful. I've put her to sleep. Where have you been all day?

PHILIP. Didn't I tell you over the 'phone I had an engagement?

MARGARET. (*As she flits swiftly into the room on the left.*) Did it take you all day to keep it? (*She remains in the room long enough to put the child in the crib and then returns.*)

PHILIP. Yes. A lot of things came up—that I didn't expect. I've been detained. (*He is still standing where she left him.*)

MARGARET. (*Turning up the lamp.*) Why, dear, look! Your umbrella is dripping all over the floor.

PHILIP. (*Noticing the little puddle of water.*) Oh, how stupid of me! (*He hurries out the door on the right, removes his hat and raincoat, leaves the umbrella, and returns quickly.*) (MARGARET, *meanwhile has mopped up the water. Then she turns on the lamp on the table to the right.*)

MARGARET. (*Reproachfully.*) We've been awfully lonesome here all day, baby and I!

PHILIP. (*By the fire.*) Forgive me, sweetheart. I've had a very hard day.

MARGARET. Did you forget it was Lucy's birthday?

PHILIP. (*Smiling gravely.*) No, I didn't forget. You have both been in my mind the whole day.

MARGARET. (*Glowing with love and a welcome that she refused to give until now.*) Oh, Philip! (*She throws herself in his arms.*) It's good to get you back. So good!
(*After a moment she rings the bell. The* MAID *answers.*) Jane, I wish you would serve dinner in here.

JANE. Yes, Mrs. Fleming.

PHILIP. (*Drawing her close to him again.*) Dear little wife!
(*As though a long time had passed since he parted from
her.*)

JANE. (*Coming in with a tray containing food and silver, and
going to the center table.*) Shall I lay the table here, Mrs.
Fleming?

MARGARET. No—here—cosy—by the fire.
(JANE *dresses the table deftly and without bustle. She
goes away and returns with the dinner.*)
You need not return, Jane. I'll ring if we need you.

JANE. Very well, Mrs. Fleming. (*She goes off.*)

PHILIP. (*Sitting to the right of the table, and taking a large
envelope from his pocket, he withdraws a bank book and
hands it to* MARGARET, *who is about to sit down on the
left.*) Here, Margaret—I want you to look over that.

MARGARET. (*Taking the book and reading the cover.*) Margaret Fleming in account with Boston Providence Savings
Bank. (*She opens the book and reads.*) "By deposit, May
3, 1890, $5,000." Five thousand dollars! Oh, Philip!

PHILIP. (*Smiling complacently.*) There's something else.

MARGARET. Yes? (PHILIP *nods his head, and hands her a
large envelope which he has taken from his pocket. She
looks at it and reads.*) "Margaret Fleming, guardian for
Lucy Fleming." (*She takes a document from the envelope.*) A certificate for $20,000 worth of United States
bonds, maturing 1930. Why, Philip! How wonderful. But,
can you afford it?
(*He smiles and nods his head, and then begins to serve
the dinner.* MARGARET, *in childish joy, rushes to the door
of the room where the child is.*)
Oh, baby! Lucy! You are rich, rich! (*She stops and peeps
in.*) Oh, my, I must not wake her. *The little heiress!* (*She
sits at the table and begins to serve.*)

PHILIP. (*Handing her another envelope. Tenderly.*) For you,
Margaret!

MARGARET. (*Taking it and becoming breathless as she reads
it.*) It's a deed for this house and all the land! Ah, Philip,
how generous you are, and this is what has kept you away
all day! And I was cross with you. (*Tears come to her
eyes.*) Forgive me, dear, please do. (*She goes to him and
kneels by his side.*) But, why do you do all this? What
need? What necessity for me to have a deed of property
from you?

PHILIP. Well, things have not been going just our way at the mill. The new tariff laws may help some, but I doubt it. At all events, before anything serious—

MARGARET. (*A little awed.*) Serious?

PHILIP. Well, you never can be sure. At any rate, in times of stress a business man should protect his family.

MARGARET. Is there danger—of—trouble?

PHILIP. No! I hope not. I think I'll be able to tide it over.

MARGARET. But, dear—you—this property, is worth a lot of money. Why not sell it? Wouldn't that be a great help? A resource in case—

PHILIP. Sell the home?

MARGARET. No, sell the house. The home is where we are. (*She rises and stands partly back of his chair with her arms about his neck.*) Where *love is*—no matter *where*, just so long as we three are there together. A big house—a little house—of course, I do love this place, where you were born, and baby— (*Taking a long breath.*) It's very precious—but— (*She has moved back to the head of the table and now lays down the deed.*) I cannot take it, dear. It frightens me. It's too valuable—all this—land—no—let us guard it together and if bad times come, it will be—a fine thing to have—

PHILIP. (*Protesting.*) Now, my dear!

MARGARET. I don't want the responsibility. Suppose something happened to me. (*She sits at the table, on the left.*)

PHILIP. Ah—Margaret—

MARGARET. (*Laughing.*) Well—I just said "suppose."

PHILIP. (*Laughing.*) Well—*don't say* it. We'll think of nothing "suppose." *Nothing*, but bright—*beautiful* things.

MARGARET. Come dear, eat. I should think you were famished. You've touched nothing yet.

PHILIP. I don't feel hungry. I'm tired—awfully tired.

MARGARET. No wonder, after all you've been through today. I'll make you a cup of tea.

(*She rings the bell.* JANE *enters.*)

Boiling water, Jane, please, and bring the tea things. (*While she is busy over the tea things she stops and looks at him quizzically.*) Who was that tramp you sent here this morning?

PHILIP. (*Innocently.*) What tramp?

MARGARET. Why, the one with the plate and the big stone—

the cough medicine,—the sponges and *the voice*. (*She imitates* JOE.)

PHILIP. (*Laughing.*) Ah, he's not a tramp—that's Joe Fletcher.

MARGARET. Did you know that he was Maria's husband?

PHILIP. (*Amazed.*) What! Maria's husband? What did he say to her?

MARGARET. (*Smiling reminiscently.*) He didn't say much— *She* did all the talking.

PHILIP. What did *she* say?

MARGARET. I don't know. She spoke in German. I think, she was swearing at him. When I came she had him by the ears and was trying to pull his head off. Then she got him to the floor and threw him down the front steps. It was the funniest thing I ever saw. I couldn't help laughing, yet my heart ached for her.

PHILIP. Poor Joe! That's the second time she's thrown him out.

MARGARET. She never did that before?

PHILIP. He says she did.

MARGARET. Well, she didn't. He robbed her and left her.

PHILIP. What?

MARGARET. She went out on the road to sell goods and left him in charge of the shop. When she came back he was gone and he had sold out the place to a secondhand dealer.

PHILIP. (*In wonderment.*) What a liar that fellow is!

MARGARET. Well, if he told you any other story—he certainly is. (*She notices a change in his face.*) Why, Philip! You look awfully white! Are you ill? Are you keeping anything from me? Oh, please tell me—do. Let me share your trouble. (*She goes to him, and puts her arms about his shoulders, with her face against his as she finishes the last line.*)

PHILIP. No—no—dear heart—nothing! There's nothing more to tell. I'm very tired.

MARGARET. Oh, how selfish of me. You should have gone to bed the moment you came.

PHILIP. I'll be all right in the morning. I must have caught a chill. (*He shudders.*) My blood seems to be congealed.

MARGARET. (*Alarmed.*) Oh, my dear—my poor boy! It was a dreadful thing you did. (*He starts guiltily.*) Going about in the rain all day. (*She goes swiftly into the room on the left and returns with a handsome dressing gown and slip-*

pers. PHILIP *has gone over to the fire.*) I must give you some aconite. A hot drink—and a mustard foot bath. (*She fusses over him, helps him to get into his dressing gown, and warms his slippers by the fire.*)

PHILIP. I don't think I need anything, dear, but a hot drink, perhaps, and a night's rest. I'll be all right in the morning. I think I'll take a little brandy.

MARGARET. (*Quickly.*) I'll get it for you, dear. Keep by the fire. (*She rushes out the door on the right, and returns quickly with a silver tray holding a cut-glass decanter of brandy and a glass. She pours out some and holds up the glass.*) Is that enough?

PHILIP. Plenty—thank you! (*He drinks it, while* MARGARET *replaces the tray on the small table at the back.*)

MARGARET. Now, dear, I'll look after that mustard bath.

PHILIP. (*Protesting.*) Oh, Margaret, please don't bother. I really don't need it.

MARGARET. (*Laughing at him.*) Yes, you do. (*She shakes her finger threateningly at him.*) You might just as well make up your mind that you've got to have it.

PHILIP. (*Smiling resignedly.*) All right—"*boss.*"

MARGARET. (*Laughing at him as she starts to go.*) You know, Philip, dear, you gave me the strangest feeling when you stood there—the rain dripping from you—you didn't look a bit like yourself. (*She gives an apologetic laugh.*) You gave me a dreadful fright. Just like a spirit! A lost spirit. (*She laughs again.*) Now, wasn't that silly of me? (*She runs off to the right, still laughing.*)

(PHILIP *sits in the fire light looking sadly after her, as the curtain falls.*)

ACT II

The scene is the same as the Second Scene of the First Act. The large doors at the back are open showing a luxuriant garden in brilliant sunshine. The baby is in her carriage by the garden door. MARGARET, *in a dainty house dress, is seated in a low chair in the center of the room, mending one of the baby's dresses.* DR. LARKIN, *sitting at the table on the left with his back turned to her, is folding little packages of medicine.* MARGARET *looks happy and contented as she chats with him.*

DOCTOR. You say you have no pain in the eyes?

MARGARET. No pain at all . . . only, once in awhile there is . . . a . . . sort of dimness.

DOCTOR. Yes, a dimness.

MARGARET. As if my eyes were tired.

DOCTOR. Yes!

MARGARET. When I read too long, or . . .

DOCTOR. (*Turning about and looking at her.*) Do you know what would be a good thing for you to do?

MARGARET. What, doctor?

DOCTOR. Wear glasses.

MARGARET. Why, doctor, aren't you dreadful! (*She laughs at him.*) Why, I'd look a sight.

DOCTOR. Well, it would be a good idea, all the same. You should wear glasses when you are reading or sewing, at least.

MARGARET. (*Laughing gaily at him.*) Well, I'll do nothing of the sort. Time enough for me to wear glasses, years and years from now.

DOCTOR. (*Smiling indulgently.*) It would be a good thing to do now. How is "Topsy" this morning?

MARGARET. (*Glancing proudly in the direction of the baby.*) Oh, she's blooming.

DOCTOR. Mrs. Fleming, any time you want to sell that baby, Mrs. Larkin and I will give you ten thousand dollars for her.

MARGARET. (*Laughing and beaming with pride.*) Yes . . . doctor . . . *when* we *want* to sell her. How is Mrs. Larkin?

DOCTOR. She's doing very nicely. I'm going to try to get her up to the mountains this summer. (*He finishes the packages.*) There . . . take one of these powders three times a day. Rest your eyes as much as possible. Don't let anything fret or worry you, and keep out-doors all you can. (*He closes the bag after putting a couple of bottles and a small medicine case in it.*)

MARGARET. Oh, doctor, aren't you going to leave something for Philip?

DOCTOR. (*Giving a dry, little grunt.*) Hum! I forgot about

him. (*Standing by the table, he takes a small case from his satchel removes two large bottles of pellets from it, fills two phials from them and makes a number upon the cork of each with a fountain pen.*) You say he was pretty wet when he came home last night?

MARGARET. Yes, and tired out. He had a very hard day, I think. I never saw him so completely fagged. It seemed to me he had been tramping in the rain for hours. I gave him a good scolding too, I tell you. I doctored him up as well as I could and put him to bed. (*Smiling contentedly.*) He's as bright as a lark this morning, but all the same, I insisted upon his remaining home for a rest.

DOCTOR. You take good care of him, don't you? (*He beams upon her kindly.*)

MARGARET. (*Playfully.*) I've got to . . . he's all I have, and men like Philip are not picked up every day, now, I tell you.

DOCTOR. (*Drily.*) No, men like Philip Fleming are certainly not to be found easily.

MARGARET. I hope there's nothing wrong with him. I was worried last night. You know, he has been working awfully hard lately.

DOCTOR. (*Kindly.*) Now, don't fret about imaginary ills. He's probably a little overworked. It might be a good idea to have him go away for a week or two.

MARGARET. (*Entering into the suggestion.*) Yes . . . a little trip somewhere would help him a lot, I'm sure.

DOCTOR. (*Holding up his finger.*) But you must go with him, though.

(MARGARET, *by this time, is standing up, with the baby's dress tucked under her arm. She takes stitches as she talks.*)

MARGARET. (*Eagerly.*) Of course! I wouldn't let him go alone. Somebody might steal him from me. (*She smiles.*)

DOCTOR. (*Snapping the clasp of his satchel, vehemently murmurs under his breath.*) Hum! They'd bring him back mighty quick, I guess. (*He turns to her.*) Give him these. Tell him to take two alternately every hour.

MARGARET. (*Taking the phials, and nodding her head as if to remember.*) Two every hour—thank you.

(PHILIP *enters from the garden, gaily humming an air. He has a freshly plucked rose in his hand.*)

PHILIP. Good morning, doctor.

DOCTOR. (*Coldly.*) Good morning.

MARGARET. (*Noticing the rose, regretfully.*) Oh, Philip, you plucked that rose.

PHILIP. Yes, isn't it lovely? It's the first of the season. (*He smells it.*)

MARGARET. Yes, and I've been watching it. I wanted it to open yesterday for baby's birthday.

PHILIP. (*Playfully.*) It saved itself for today for baby's mother. (*He puts it on her breast.*)

MARGARET. (*Pleased.*) Well, I'd rather it had bloomed yesterday for her. Excuse me, doctor, I must run into the kitchen. We have a new cook and she needs watching.

PHILIP. (*Gaily.*) And she's a dandy. (*He breaks into a chant.*) Oh, I'm glad we've got a new cookie. I'm glad we've got a new cook. She's . . .

MARGARET. (*Laughing at him.*) Hush! Hush! Philip, stop— be quiet! (*She puts her hand over his mouth. He tries to sing through her fingers.*) She'll hear you. Oh, doctor, isn't he terrible? He's poking fun at her all the time, but she is funny, though. (*She runs off joyously to the right.*)

PHILIP. What a glorious morning, after yesterday.

DOCTOR. (*Eyeing him coldly.*) Yes—it is—you're in high feather this morning, eh?

PHILIP. (*Cheerily.*) Of course I am. What's the good in worrying over things you can't help?

DOCTOR. Have you seen . . . ?

PHILIP. (*Quickly.*) Yes. (*In a low voice.*) I've made arrangements for her to go away as soon as she is well enough.

DOCTOR. *Humph!*

PHILIP. It's a terrible mess. I'll admit I never realized what I was doing, but I shall make things all right for this girl, and her child. (*He sits on the edge of the table to the left. The* DOCTOR *is standing to the right of him.*) Doctor, I'm going to tell my wife this whole, miserable story.

DOCTOR. (*Aghast.*) What?

PHILIP. (*Hastily interrupting.*) Ah, not now—in the future. When we both have grown closer together. When I have shown her by an honest and decent life that I ought to be forgiven—when I feel sure of her faith and confidence— then I shall confess and ask her to forgive me.

DOCTOR. (*Shaking his head.*) That would be a mighty hazardous experiment. You would draw a woman's heart strings closer and closer about you—and then deliberately tear them asunder. Best keep silent·forever.

PHILIP. There would be no hazard. I know Margaret—of course if she found me out now—I admit it—it would be a terrible thing, but—

DOCTOR. (*Abruptly.*) You'd better get Mrs. Fleming away from here for a few weeks.

PHILIP. (*Surprised.*) Away? (*He smiles confidently.*) What need?

DOCTOR. She is threatened with a serious affection of the eyes.

PHILIP. (*His smile fading away, then recovering quickly and laughing lightly.*) Aren't you trying to frighten me, doctor?

DOCTOR. (*Annoyed by his levity.*) I don't care anything about you, but, I tell you, your wife has a tendency to an affection of the eyes called glaucoma.

PHILIP. (*Interested.*) Glaucoma? Affection of the eyes? Why, Margaret has magnificent eyes.

DOCTOR. Yes, she has magnificent eyes, but, her child is the indirect cause of the development of an inherent weakness in them.

PHILIP. In what way?

DOCTOR. Conditions incident to motherhood. Shock. She is showing slight symptoms now that if aggravated would cause very serious consequences.

PHILIP. (*Puzzled.*) I do not understand.

DOCTOR. The eye—like other organs—has its own special secretion, which keeps it nourished and in a healthy state. The inflow and outflow of this secretion is equal. The physician sometimes comes across a patient of apparently sound physique, in whom he will find an abnormal condition of the eye where this natural function is, through some inherent weakness, easily disturbed. When the patient is subject to illness, great physical or mental suffering—the too great emotion of a sudden joy or sorrow—the stimulus of any one of these causes may produce in the eyes a super-abundant influx of this perfectly healthy fluid and the fine outflowing ducts cannot carry it off.

PHILIP. Yes. What then?

DOCTOR. The impact continues—until the result—is—

PHILIP. Yes? What is the result?

DOCTOR. Blindness.

PHILIP. (*Awed.*) Why—that is horrible—is there no remedy?

DOCTOR. Yes. A very delicate operation.

PHILIP. Always successful?

DOCTOR. If performed under proper conditions—yes.

PHILIP. And my wife is in danger of this? (*He walks up and down the room.*)

DOCTOR. There is no danger whatever to Mrs. Fleming, if the serenity of her life is not disturbed. There are slight, but nevertheless serious symptoms that must be remedied at once, with ordinary care. She will outgrow this weakness. Perhaps you will understand now, how necessary it is that she leave Canton for a few weeks.

PHILIP. (*Deeply impressed by the* DOCTOR's *recital.*) Yes, I do. I will set about getting her away at once. I can leave the mill for a while in Foster's hands.

DOCTOR. Yes, he is an honest, capable fellow. Above all things, do not let Mrs. Fleming suspect that there is anything serious the matter. Keep her cheerful.

PHILIP. Ah, Margaret is the sunniest, happiest disposition—nothing troubles her.

DOCTOR. Well, you keep her so.

(PHILIP *takes out his cigar case and offers it to the* DOCTOR. *The latter refuses laconically.*)

Thank you, I have my own.

(*He has taken a cigar from his vest pocket.* PHILIP *strikes a match and offers it to the doctor. At the same time, the* DOCTOR *is lighting his cigar with his own match, ignoring* PHILIP's *attention.* PHILIP *shrugs his shoulders indulgently, lights his cigar and good-naturedly watches the* DOCTOR, *who takes up his satchel and leaves the room hastily with a curt.*)

Good morning.

PHILIP. (*Genially.*) Good morning, Dr. Larkin. (*He sits in the armchair to the right and comfortably contemplates the convolutions of the cigar smoke.*)

(*The closing of the front door is heard.* JOE FLETCHER *appears at the French window, stealthily peering into the room. He sees* PHILIP *and coughs.*)

JOE. Hello, Mr. Fleming!

PHILIP. (*Looking up.*) Hello, Joe—come in.

JOE. (*In a whisper.*) Is it safe?

PHILIP. (*Laughing.*) Yes, I guess so.

JOE. (*Slouching inside.*) Where's Maria?

PHILIP. Gone out.

JOE. (*Relieved.*) Say, that was a damn mean trick you played on me yesterday.

PHILIP. What trick?

JOE. Sending me up here—you knew durn well she'd go fer me.

PHILIP. (*Laughing.*) I didn't know Maria was your wife, honest I didn't.

JOE. Oh, tell that to the marines. I want my sign. (*As* PHILIP *looks puzzled.*) The sample of giant's cement with the plate.

PHILIP. (*Remembering.*) Oh, yes. (*He chuckles to himself, goes to the door at the right and brings back the cracked plate with the big stone hung to it.* JOE *takes it and turns to go.*) Why did you lie to me yesterday?

JOE. I didn't lie to you.

PHILIP. You told me your wife ran away from you.

JOE. So she did.

PHILIP. *She* says you robbed her and left her.

JOE. She's a liar, and I'll tell it to her face.

PHILIP. (*Laughing.*) Come, Joe, you wouldn't dare.

JOE. She's a liar. I'm not afraid of her.

PHILIP. She made you run yesterday.

JOE. (*Holding up the sign.*) Didn't she have this? What chance has a fellow got when a woman has a *weapon* like this?

PHILIP. (*Laughing at him.*) And you were in the war.

JOE. Yes, and I was in the war! The Johnnies didn't fight with things like this.

PHILIP. (*Enjoying the situation.*) Come, Joe, I believe she'd make you run without that.

JOE. She's a liar. I can lick her. (*With conviction.*) I have licked her. (*He grows bolder.*) An' I'll lick her again.

PHILIP. (*Laughing heartily.*) Come, Joe, that'll do. The best way for you to lick 'er is there.

(*He points to the decanter upon the side table.* JOE *gazes upon it tenderly and chuckles with unctuous satisfaction.*)

JOE. That's a great joke, Mr. Fleming. *Kin* I? (*He shuffles over to the decanter.*)

PHILIP. Yes, go ahead.

(JOE *pours the liquor into a glass.* MARIA *walks hastily in through the window and sees* PHILIP.)

MARIA. (*Diffidently.*) Excuse me, Mr. Fleming, I did not

know you vas here. I always come in dot way mit de baby.
(JOE *is in the act of carrying the glass to his lips. He hears*
MARIA's *voice and stands terrified.* MARIA *sees him and
becomes inflamed with indignation. She puts her hands
on her hips and glares at him.*)
Vell, you dom scoundrel!

JOE. (*Soothingly extending a hand to her.*) There now,
Maria, keep cool. Don't lose your temper.

MARIA. (*Mocking him.*) Yah, don't lose my temper. Didn't
I tell you never to darken dis house again? Du Teufel aus
Hölle! (*She makes a lunge at him. He dodges and hops on
tip-toe from side to side in a zig-zag.*)

JOE. Just a minute, Maria! (*He gulps.*) I can—I can explain—
the whole—thing.

(*He makes a desperate bolt, but* MARIA *is on his heels.
He stumbles and falls sprawling upon his hands and face,
with his head to the front, in the center of the room. She
swoops upon him, digs her hands into the loose folds of
his coat between the shoulders and drags him to his feet.
He limps with fright, puffing and spluttering, awkwardly
helping himself and dropping the sign.*)
Maria, for God's sake, don't! I ain't ever done anything
to you.

MARIA. (*Dragging him toward the window.*) Ach, Gott! No,
you have never done nutting to me.

JOE. I'll make it all right with you. Let me go. I want my
sign! Ugh!

(*She throws him through the French window. He stumbles
and staggers out of sight.* MARIA *picks up the sign and
flings it after him. All the time she is scolding and weeping
with anger.*)

MARIA. Don't you dare come here no more to a decent house,
you loafer. You can't explain nutting to me, you tief—you
loafer— (*She sinks into the chair at the right of the table,
leans her arms across the table, buries her face in them
and sobs bitterly. All her fury has vanished and she is
crushed and broken.*)

PHILIP. (*Laughing and calling after* JOE.) Joe, come back!
Joe! (*He goes out through the window.*) Joe!

MARGARET. (*Rushing in and up to the garden door, afraid
some harm has come to the child.*) What on earth is the
matter? An earthquake?

MARIA. (*Sobbing.*) No. Mrs. Fleming. It vas dot miserable husband of me.

MARGARET. What?

MARIA. Yah, I yust came in now, und I find him dere drinking of Mr. Fleming's brandy.

MARGARET. Good gracious—what did you do, Maria?

MARIA. I skipped dot gutter mit him, I bet my life. (*She is still weeping.*)

MARGARET. (*A smile flickering about her lips.*) There, Maria, don't cry. Don't let him trouble you so. How is your sister?

MARIA. Vorse, Mrs. Fleming.

MARGARET. Worse. Oh, I'm so sorry.

MARIA. Yah. I don't tink she vill ever leave dot bed alive. My poor little Lena. Mrs. Fleming, I ask you—mebbe you vill come to see her. She talks about you all de time now.

MARGARET. (*Surprised.*) Talks about me? Why, how does she know me?

MARIA. Vell, she ask about you—a lot—und I tell her of you and your beautiful home und your little baby, und now she says she'd like yust once to look into your face.

MARGARET. (*Hesitating a moment.*) Well, I'll go. If I only could do anything for her, poor girl.

MARIA. Yah, she is a poor girl, Mrs. Fleming. Mebbe she vill tell you the name of dis man vot—

MARGARET. (*With repugnance.*) Oh, no, no! I don't want to know the brute, or his name.

MARIA. (*Vindictively.*) Oh, Gott! If I vould know it—

MARGARET. (*Breaking in upon her, kindly.*) But, I'll go to see her.

MARIA. Tank you, Mrs. Fleming. You are a goodt lady.

MARGARET. Where did you say she lives?

MARIA. (*Still quietly weeping.*) Forty-two Millbrook Street. By Mrs. Burton's cottage.

MARGARET. Very well.

(PHILIP's *voice is heard outside, laughing.*)
Oh, there's Mr. Fleming. Come, Maria, don't let him see you crying. Come, go to the kitchen and tell Hannah—
(*She has urged* MARIA *to her feet and is pressing her toward the door.*)

MARIA. Is dot new girl come?

MARGARET. Yes.

MARIA. Hannah is her name?

MARGARET. (*Pressing her.*) Yes, tell her to make you a nice cup of tea, and then you'd best go back to your sister.

MARIA. Tank you, Mrs. Fleming. I don't want no tea. Mebbe she needs me. I go right back to her. You'll come sure, Mrs. Fleming?

MARGARET. (*Putting her through the door on the right as* PHILIP *comes in through the window on the left.*) Yes, I'll come in a little while.

PHILIP. Oh, Margaret, I wish you'd been here. (*He begins to laugh.*) Such a circus. The funniest thing I ever saw.

MARGARET. Yes, Maria told me. Poor thing. I'm sorry for her. (PHILIP *laughs. She goes to her work basket which is on the center table, and takes out the two phials.* PHILIP *crosses to the right and* MARGARET *goes to him.*)

Here, dear—some medicine Dr. Larkin left for you.

PHILIP. (*Pushing her hand away gently.*) Oh, I don't want any medicine. There's nothing the matter with me. (*He begins to chuckle again.*) If you could—

MARGARET. (*Shaking him by the lapels of his jacket.*) Yes, there is a great deal the matter with you. (*She looks at him seriously and he becomes serious.*) Doctor says you're all run down. You've got to have a rest. Here, now, take two of these pellets, alternating every hour.

(*He takes the phials and puts them in his vest pocket.*)

Take some now!

PHILIP. Oh! Now? Must I?

MARGARET. (*Shaking him.*) Yes, this minute.

(*He takes two pellets and pretends to choke. She shakes him again.*)

Look at your watch. Note the time.

PHILIP. Yes'm.

MARGARET. Well, in an hour, take two from the other phial.

PHILIP. Yes'm. (*He lights a fresh cigar, and* MARGARET *gives a cry of reproval.*)

MARGARET. Philip! What are you doing? (*She rushes at him and takes the cigar from him.*) Don't you know you mustn't smoke when you are taking medicine.

PHILIP. Why not?

MARGARET. It'll kill the effect of it. You may smoke in an hour.

PHILIP. I've got to take more medicine in an hour?

MARGARET. Well, I guess you'll have to give up smoking.

PHILIP. What!

MARGARET. Until you're well.

PHILIP. But, I'm well now.

MARGARET. (*Going through the door on the left.*) *Until you have stopped taking those pellets!*

PHILIP. All right. I'll forget them.

MARGARET. Philip!

PHILIP. (*Going to the baby in the garden doorway.*) The cigars! What are you doing?

MARGARET. Changing my gown. I'm going out.

PHILIP. Where are you going?

MARGARET. Oh, just a little errand.

PHILIP. Well, hurry back.

MARGARET. Yes, I won't be long. (*She gives a little scream.*) Oh!

PHILIP. What's the matter?

MARGARET. Nothing. Stuck a pin into my finger, that's all.

PHILIP. My! You gave me a shock. (*He puts his hand to his heart playfully.*)

MARGARET. (*Laughing.*) Sorry. Did you see my gloves?

PHILIP. Yes.

MARGARET. Where?

PHILIP. On your hands, of course.

MARGARET. Now, don't be silly!

PHILIP. (*Playing with the baby.*) Margaret, you know, baby's eyes are changing.

MARGARET. No.

PHILIP. Yes. They're growing like yours.

MARGARET. Nonsense. She has your eyes.

PHILIP. (*Eyeing the baby critically.*) No, they're exactly like yours. She's got my nose though.

MARGARET. (*Giving a little cry of protest.*) Oh, Philip—don't say that.

PHILIP. Why?

MARGARET. It would be terrible if she had your nose. Just imagine my dainty Lucy with a great big nose like yours.

PHILIP. (*Feeling his nose.*) Why, I think I have a very nice nose.

MARGARET. (*Coming in, laughing.*) Oh, yes, it's a good enough nose—as noses go—but— (*She touches the bell.*)

PHILIP. (*Noticing her gown.*) Your new suit?

MARGARET. (*Gaily.*) Yes. Like it?

PHILIP. It's a dandy. Turn around.

(*She dances over to him and twirls about playfully.*)
Wait, there's a thread. (*He picks it off her skirt.*)
(JANE *enters.*)

MARGARET. Jane, please tell Hannah to come here.

JANE. Yes, ma'am. (*She goes.*)

(PHILIP *begins to chuckle.*)

MARGARET. Now, Philip, I implore you to keep still. Please don't get me laughing while I'm talking to her.

PHILIP. (*Indignantly.*) I'm not going to say anything.

(HANNAH *appears. She is very large, stout and dignified.*)

MARGARET. (*Hurriedly, in haste to be off.*) Hannah! I'm going out and I shall not be able to look after the baking of the bread. When the loaves have raised almost to the top of the pans put them in the oven.

HANNAH. (*Who has been studying admiringly* MARGARET'S *costume.*) Yes, Ma'am. I does always put the bread in when it's almost up to the top in the pans.

MARGARET. And bake them just one hour.

HANNAH. Ah! Yes, ma'am. I always bakes 'em an hour.

(PHILIP *smothers a laugh in a cough.* MARGARET *stares at him.*)

MARGARET. And, have luncheon on at half past twelve, please.

HANNAH. Yes, I always has the lunch on at half past twelve, sharp.

MARGARET. (*Who has been putting on her gloves.*) Thank you, Hannah, that's all. Well, I'm off. (*To* PHILIP.) Good-bye, dear. (*She starts off hastily.*)

HANNAH. Good-bye, ma'am. (*She goes out.*)

MARGARET. (*Pausing to look at* PHILIP *as he plays with the baby in the carriage.*) Oh, how dear you both look there together.

PHILIP. (*Looking at his watch.*) You'd best hurry if you want to get back at *half past twelve, sharp.* (*He imitates* HANNAH.)

MARGARET. (*Rapturously gazing at them.*) Oh, if I could paint, what a picture I would make of you two!

PHILIP. Are you going?

MARGARET. Yes, I'm going. (*She notices* PHILIP *giving the baby his watch, and giving a little scream of alarm, she rushes at him.*) Philip, what are you doing?

PHILIP. That's all right. She won't hurt it.

MARGARET. Suppose she'd swallow it.

PHILIP. Well!

MARGARET. (*Mocking him.*) Well! .There, put it in your
pocket. And have some sense. (*She picks up the rattle and
the big rubber ball and puts them in his hands.*) There,
you can play with these. (*They both laugh with the fun
of it all.*)

PHILIP. Oh! Go on Margaret, and hurry home.

MARGARET. (*Kissing him and the baby.*) All right. Won't be
long. Don't forget your medicine, and please don't smoke
when my back is turned. (*She dances out through the
French window, over-flowing with fun and animation. This
scene must be played rapidly, with a gay, light touch.*)

ACT III

The scene is a neat, plainly furnished sitting-room in MRS.
BURTON's *cottage. The walls are covered with old-fashioned
wall-paper of a faded green color. Sunlight streams in
through two windows at the back. In one there is a small
table holding a few pots of geraniums, and in the second, a
hanging basket of ivy. A few straggling vines creep about
the window-frame. There are doors at the left center, down
left and on the right. In the center of the room stands a table
with a chair to the right of it, and a few hair-cloth chairs are
here and there. A sofa stands against the left wall below the
door, and there is a low rocking-chair on the left.*

*The room is empty and after a moment the stillness is
broken by the wail of an infant. The hushed notes of a
woman's voice are heard from the open door on the left,
soothing the child. A low knock is heard at the door to the
right. The door opens slowly and* DOCTOR LARKIN *enters.*
MRS. BURTON *emerges from the room on the left with a
tiny baby wrapped in a soft white shawl in her arms. She
is a motherly woman, large and placid, with a benign
immobility of countenance. She speaks with a New England drawl.*

MRS. BURTON. Good morning, doctor. I didn't hear ye knock.

DOCTOR. How is your patient this morning?

MRS. BURTON. Why, ain't yer seen Dr. Taylor? Didn't he tell ye?

DOCTOR. No. She's—?

MRS. BURTON. (*Nodding her head.*) Yes.

DOCTOR. When did it happen?

MRS. BURTON. About an hour ago. She seemed brighter this morning. After her sister went out she slept for a while. When I came in the room she opened her eyes and asked me for a pencil and paper. I brought 'em to her and she writ for quite a spell. Then she lay back on the pillow. I asked her if she wouldn't take a little nourishment. She smiled and shook her head. Then she gave a long sigh—an' —an'—that was all there was to it.

DOCTOR. How's the child?

MRS. BURTON. Poor little critter— (*She looks down at it.*) I can't do nothing for it. I've tried everything. It ought to have mother's milk—that's all there is to it. Be quiet, you poor little motherless critter.

DOCTOR. It would be better for it if it had gone with her.

MRS. BURTON. Why, doctor, ain't ye awful?

DOCTOR. Why, what chance has that child got in this world? I'll send you something for it. (*He turns to go.*)

MRS. BURTON. Don't ye want to see her?

DOCTOR. No! What good can I be to her now, poor devil?
    (CHARLEY BURTON, *a sturdy lad of ten, breaks boisterously into the room from the door on the right, carrying a baseball and bat.*)

CHARLEY. Ma! Ma! Here's a woman wants to see Mrs. Bindley.

MRS. BURTON. (*Reprimanding him.*) Lady! And take your hat off.
    (DOCTOR LARKIN *and* MRS. BURTON *look expectantly toward the door.* MARGARET *enters slowly, her eyes bent upon her glove which she is unfastening.* DR. LARKIN *is dumbfounded at the sight of her. She takes a few steps toward him and looks up.*)

MARGARET. (*Pleasantly surprised at seeing him.*) Why, doctor! I didn't know that you were on this case.

DOCTOR. (*Confused.*) I'm not. Dr. Taylor—he—called me in consultation. But, what in the name of all that's wonderful brings you here?

MARGARET. Maria!

DOCTOR. What Maria? Not—

MARGARET. Yes, our Maria—this sick girl is her sister. (*She removes her hat and places it with her gloves on the table.*)

DOCTOR. (*In consternation.*) Her sister! Then you know?

MARGARET. I know that there is a poor sick girl here who wants—

DOCTOR. (*Going to her, brusquely.*) Mrs. Fleming, you'd best not remain here—the girl is dead. Go home.

MARGARET. (*Pityingly.*) Dead? Poor thing!

DOCTOR. Yes. Does your husband know you are here?

MARGARET. (*Shaking her head.*) Oh, no!

DOCTOR. Come, you must go home! (*He almost pushes her out of the room in his urgency.*)

MARGARET. (*Resisting him gently.*) Ah, no, doctor. Now that I am here, let me stay. I can be of some help, I know.

DOCTOR. No, you can be of no use. Everything has been done.

MARGARET. Well, I'll just say a word to Maria. Where is she?

DOCTOR. I don't know—I don't know anything about Maria.

MRS. BURTON. She's in there. (*She nods toward the door on the left.*)

(*The* DOCTOR *has crowded* MARGARET *almost through the door in his eagerness to have her out of the house. She is reluctantly yielding to him, when* MRS. BURTON'S *voice arrests her. She turns quickly and, looking over the* DOCTOR'S *shoulder, notices the child in* MRS. BURTON'S *arms. She impulsively brushes the* DOCTOR *aside and goes toward her, her face beaming with tender sympathy.*)

MARGARET. Oh, is this the baby?

MRS. BURTON. Yes'm.

MARGARET. (*Going close to her on tip-toes and gazing with maternal solicitude down upon the child.*) Poor little baby! What a dear mite of a thing it is.

MRS. BURTON. Yes'm.

MARGARET. (*Impulsively.*) Doctor, we must take care of this baby.

DOCTOR. (*Impatiently.*) You've got a baby of your *own*, Mrs. Fleming.

MARGARET. Yes, and that's why I pity this one. I suppose, I always did love babies, anyhow. They are such wonderful, mysterious little things, aren't they?

MRS. BURTON. Yes'm.

DOCTOR. (*Spurred by a growing sense of catastrophe.*) Mrs. Fleming, there is danger to your child in your remaining here.

MARGARET. (*Alarmed.*) Oh, doctor!

DOCTOR. I hated to tell you this before—but—there is contagion in this atmosphere.

MARGARET. (*Hastily taking her hat from the table.*) Doctor, why didn't you—
(*She is hurrying away when she is checked by a poignant moan. She turns a frightened face and sees* MARIA *coming from the room on the left with a letter in her hand.* MARIA'S *face is distorted by grief.*)

MARIA. Ah, Mrs. Burton, I have found out who dot man is. He is— (*She sees* MARGARET *and smiles bitterly upon her.*) So,—you have come, Mrs. Fleming?

MARGARET. (*Making a movement of sympathy.*) Maria!

MARIA. Vell, you may go back again. You can do nutting for her now. She is dead. (*Perversely.*) But, ven you do go, you vill take dot baby back mit you. He shall now have two babies instead of one.

MARGARET. (*Smiling.*) What do you mean, Maria? Who shall have two babies?

MARIA. (*Fiercely.*) Philip Fleming—dot's who.
(MARGARET *stares at her, only comprehending half what* MARIA *means.* DR. LARKIN *goes quickly to her.*)

DOCTOR. Come away, Mrs. Fleming—the woman is crazy. (*He tries to draw her away.*)

MARIA. (*Contemptuously.*) No, I ain't crazy! (*She shakes the letter at* MARGARET.) You read dot letter and see if I vas crazy!
(MARGARET, *in a dazed way, reaches for the letter, and tries to read it, turning it different ways.*)

MARGARET. I cannot make it out. (*She hands it to the doctor, and says helplessly.*) Read it—to me—doctor—please.

DOCTOR. (*Beside himself and snatching the letter.*) No, nor shall you. (*He makes a motion to tear the letter.*)

MARIA. (*Threateningly.*) Don't you tear dot letter, doctor.

MARGARET. (*Putting her hand out gently.*) You must not destroy that letter, doctor. Give it back to me. (DR. LARKIN *returns the letter reluctantly.* MARGARET *attempts to read it, fails, becomes impatient, and hands it to* MARIA, *helplessly.*) You read it to me, Maria.

(MARIA, *whose passion has subsided, takes the letter in an
awed manner and begins to read it. The* DOCTOR *is in a
daze.* MARGARET *sinks into the chair to the right of the
table. She has recovered her calm poise, but does not seem
to be at all the same* MARGARET.)

MARIA. (*Reading in a simple, unaffected manner.*)

Canton, June 10,

DEAR MR. FLEMING:

   You was good to come to see me, and I thank you. I
will not trouble you no more. I am sorry for what has
happened. I know you never loved me and I never asked
you to, but I loved you. It was all my fault. I will never
trouble you no more. You can do what you like with the
baby. I do not care. Do not be afraid, I shall never tell.
They tried to get me to but I never shall. Nobody will
ever know. No more at present, from your obedient
servant,

LENA SCHMIDT.

MARGARET. (*Turning to the* DOCTOR, *who is standing close to
her chair.*) Did you know—anything of this—doctor?

DOCTOR. (*Evasively.*) Well—I knew—something of it—but,
this girl may be lying. Such as she is—will say anything
sometimes.

MARIA. (*Fiercely.*) Don't you say dot, doctor. She would not
tell nutting to hurt him, not to save her soul.

DOCTOR. (*With finality.*) Well, now that you know the worst,
come away from here—come home.

MARIA. (*Bitterly.*) Oh! Ya! She can go home. She have
alvays got a home und a husband und fine clothes, because
she is his vife, but my poor sister don't have any of dese
tings, because she is only de poor mistress. But, by Gott,
she shall not go home unless she takes dot baby back mit
her.

DOCTOR. She shall do nothing of the sort.

MARIA. Vell, den, I vill take it, und fling it in his face.

MARGARET. (*Calmly, and rising from the chair.*) You shall
not go near him. You shall not say—one word to him!

MARIA. Von't I? Who is going to stop me? I vould yust like
to know dot?

MARGARET. (*Quite calmly.*) I am!

MARIA. (*Mockingly.*) You—you vill take his part, because

you are his vife! (*Fiercely.*) Vell! (*She draws a pistol from her dress pocket.*) Do you see dot gun? Vell, I buy dot gun, und I swore dot ven I find out dot man I vill have his life. Und, if you try to stop me, I vill lay you stiff und cold beside her.

MARGARET. (*Calmly, pityingly, holding out her hand as though to quiet her.*) Maria! Stop! How dare you talk like that to me? Give me that pistol.

(MARIA, *awed by* MARGARET'S *spirit, meekly hands her the weapon.*)

You think—I—am happy—because I am his wife? Why, you poor fool, that girl (*She points to the door on the left*) never in all her life suffered one thousandth part what I have suffered in these past five minutes. Do you dare to compare her to me? I have not uttered one word of reproach, even against her, and yet she has done me a wrong, that not all the death-bed letters that were ever written can undo. I wonder what I have ever done to deserve this! (*She loses control of herself and sinks sobbing, into the chair, her arms upon the table, and her head dropping upon them.*)

DOCTOR. (*Overcome by the situation, throws his arms about her and tries to draw her to her feet.*) For God's sake, Mrs. Fleming, let me take you out of this hell.

MARGARET. (*Gently resisting him.*) Ah, doctor, you cannot take *this hell* out of my breast. (*Suddenly her manner changes. She says with quick decision.*) Maria, get me a sheet of writing paper. Doctor, give me a pencil.

(DOCTOR LARKIN *puts his hand into his vest pocket.* MARIA, *who seems dazed, looks helplessly about as though the paper might be within reach. Then suddenly thinking of the letter in her hand, she tears off the blank half of it and quickly lays it on the table before* MARGARET.)

DOCTOR. (*Giving her the pencil.*) What are you going to do?

MARGARET. Send—for *him!*

DOCTOR. No—not here!

MARGARET. Yes—here— (*She writes nervously, mumbling what she writes.*) "Philip: I am waiting for you, here. That girl is *dead.*" (*She folds the letter.*) Where's that boy?

(MARIA *and* MRS. BURTON *both make a movement in search of* CHARLEY.)

MARIA. Charley! (*She goes to the door at the back and calls again in a hushed voice.*) Charley! (CHARLEY *enters. She*

whispers to him that the lady wants him.) You, go quick!
(CHARLEY *goes to* MARGARET.)

MARGARET. (*In tense nervousness.*) Charley, do you know
Mr. Fleming?

CHARLEY. Yes'm.

MARGARET. Do you know where he lives?

CHARLEY. Yes'm—on Canton Street.

MARGARET. Yes—go there—don't ring the bell—go through the
garden—you will find him there, playing with the baby.
Give him this.

CHARLEY. Any answer?

MARGARET. (*At nervous tension.*) No! Go quick! Quick! (*She
springs to her feet.*) Now, doctor—I want you to leave me!

DOCTOR. Mrs. Fleming, for God's sake don't see him here.

MARGARET. Yes, here—and—alone! Please go. (*The* DOCTOR
does not respond.) I don't want you or any other living
being to hear what passes between him and me, and,
(*She points to the room.*) *that dead girl.* Please go!

DOCTOR. Mrs. Fleming, as your physician, I order you to
leave this place at once.

MARGARET. No, doctor—I must see him, *here.*

DOCTOR. (*With gentle persuasion.*) Mrs. Fleming, you have
no right to do this. Think of your child.

MARGARET. (*Remembering.*) My baby! My poor, little innocent baby! Oh, I wish to God that she were dead. (*She
is beside herself and not realizing what she says. She
crosses to the left.*)

DOCTOR. (*Following her.*) Mrs. Fleming, in God's name, calm
yourself! I have tried to keep it from you, but, I am forced
to tell you— (*He is so deeply moved that he is almost
incoherent.*) If you continue in this way, dear lady, you
are exposing yourself to a terrible affliction—this trouble—
with your eyes. You are threatened with—if you keep up
this strain—a sudden blindness may fall upon you.

MARGARET. (*Appalled.*) Blind! Blind! (*She speaks in a low
terrified voice.*) Oh, no doctor, not *that*—not *now*—not until
after I've seen him.

DOCTOR. Not only that, but if you keep up this strain much
longer, it may cost you your life.

MARGARET. I don't care—what happens to me, only, let me
see him, and then, the sooner it all comes the better. (*She
crosses to the left with the* DOCTOR *following her.*)

DOCTOR. (*Growing desperate, and throwing his arms about*

her.) Mrs. Fleming, you must leave this place! Come home.

MARGARET. No. Doctor, please leave me alone. (*She draws herself from him.*) I tell you I've got to see him here. (*Then with a sweet intimacy, she goes to him.*) A woman has a strange feeling for the physician who brings her child into the world—I love you—I have always obeyed your orders, haven't I? (*She speaks brokenly.*)

DOCTOR. (*Quietly.*) Always.

MARGARET. Then, let me be the doctor now, and I order you to leave this house at once.

DOCTOR. (*Hopelessly.*) You are determined to do this thing?

MARGARET. (*With finality.*) Yes.

DOCTOR. Very well then—good-bye. (*He holds out his hand, which she takes mechanically. He holds her hand warmly for a moment. She clings to him as though afraid to let him go, then slowly draws away.*)

MARGARET. Good-bye!

(*The* DOCTOR *leaves the room quickly.* MARGARET *takes a step after him until she touches the left side of the table in the center. She stands there gazing into space, the calmness of death upon her face. The sunlight streaming through the window falls upon her.* MRS. BURTON *is sitting in a rocking-chair in the corner of the room.* MARIA *is sitting on the sofa at the left, weeping silently, with clasped hands, her arms lying in her lap, her body bent. She makes a plaintive moan before she speaks.*)

MARIA. Ah—Mrs. Fleming, you must not do dis ting. Vat vas I—vot was she, I'd like to know—dot ve should make dis trouble for you? You come here, like an angel to help us, und I have stung you like a snake in dot grass. (*She goes to* MARGARET *and falls upon her knees beside her.*) Oh, Mrs. Fleming, on my knees I ask you to forgive me.

(MARGARET *stands immobile at the table, her right hand resting upon its edge—her left hand partly against her cheek. She is lost in spiritual contemplation of the torment she is suffering. She shows impatience at the sound of* MARIA's *voice as though loath to be disturbed. She replies wearily.*)

MARGARET. I have nothing to forgive. Get up, Maria. You have done nothing to me—go away!

MARIA. (*In a paroxysm of contrition.*) Oh, I beg, Mrs. Fleming, dot you vill take dot gun and blow my brains out.

MARGARET. Don't go on like that, Maria! (MARIA's *weeping irritates her.*) Get up! Please go away. Go away, I say! (MARIA *slinks away quietly into the back room.* MARGARET *takes a long, sobbing breath, which ends in a sigh. She stares into space and a blank look comes into her face as though she were gazing at things beyond her comprehension. Presently the silence is broken by a low wail from the infant. It half arouses her.*)

MARGARET. What is the matter with that child? (*Her voice seems remote. Her expression remains fixed.*) Why don't you keep it quiet?

MRS. BURTON. (*In a hushed voice.*) It's hungry.

MARGARET. (*In the same mood, but her voice is a little querulous.*) Well, then, why don't you feed it?

MRS. BURTON. I can't get nothing fit for it. I've tried everything I could think of, but it's no use. (*She gets up and places the child upon the sofa to the left.*) There, be still, you poor little critter, an' I'll see what I ken get fer ye. (*As she goes to the door at the back,* MARGARET *speaks wearily.*)

MARGARET. Bring a lamp—it's getting dark here. (*She is still in the same attitude by the table. There is a silence, then the child's wail arouses her. She half turns her head in its direction—and tries to quiet it.*) Hush—child—hush— (*Then she reaches out her hand as if to pat it.*) There—there— poor little thing. Don't fret—it's no use to fret, child—be quiet now—there—there, now. (*She turns and slowly gropes her way to the sofa, sits on the edge of it, and feels for the child and gently pats it. She murmurs softly.*) Hush—baby —go to sleep.

(*There is a silence while a soft flood of sunshine plays about her. A pitying half smile flits across her face. She utters a faint sigh and again drifts away into that inner consciousness where she evidently finds peace. Again the child is restless—it arouses her and, hopeless of comforting it, she takes it in her arms. After a moment, she rises to her feet and stumbles toward the table. She knocks against the low chair. At the same moment,* PHILIP FLEMING *dashes breathlessly into the room through the door on the right. He pauses in horror as* MARGARET *raises her head, her eyes wide open, staring into his—her face calm and remote. She hushes the child softly, and sits in the low chair.* PHILIP *stands in dumb amazement watching her. The child begins to fret her again. She seems hopeless of comforting it. Then scarcely conscious of what she is doing, suddenly with an impatient, swift movement she unbuttons her dress to give nourishment to the child, when the picture fades away into darkness.*)

ACT IV

The scene is the same as the Second Act. The doors and window leading into the garden are open.

MARIA *is seated close to the open door, sewing. She occasionally looks into the garden as if guarding something. She is neatly dressed, fresh and orderly looking. Her manner is subdued. A bell rings and a closing door is heard. Then* DOCTOR LARKIN *enters.* MARIA *goes to meet him and scans his face anxiously.*

MARIA. Goot morning, doctor.

DOCTOR. Good morning. Well! Any news?

MARIA. (*Losing interest and shaking her head sadly.*) No, doctor. No vord from him yet. It is seven days now—I hoped—mebbe you might have some.

DOCTOR. No—nothing. How is Mrs. Fleming?

(MARIA *sits down to the left of the center of the room and the doctor to the right.*)

MARIA. Yust the same as yesterday, und the day before, und all the udder days. Ach, so bright, und so cheerful, but I tink all the same she is breaking her heart. Ach, ven I look into her sad eyes—vot cannot see me—I am ashamed to hold my head up. (*She brushes away the tears.*)

DOCTOR. Does she talk about him at all?

MARIA. No, she never speaks his name.

DOCTOR. How is the child?

MARIA. (*Brightening.*) She is fine. Dot little tooth came trough dis morning und she don't fret no more now.

DOCTOR. And, the *other* one?

MARIA. (*Indifferently.*) Oh, he's all right. I put him beside Lucy in her crib dis morning und she laughs and pulls at him und plays mit him yust like he vas a little kitten. Dis is no place for him, doctor. Ven Mr. Fleming comes home he vill fix tings, und I vill take him away by myself—vere she no more can be troubled mit him.

DOCTOR. Things will come out all right. You'd best keep quiet. Have nothing whatever to say in this matter.

MARIA. Ya. I make enough trouble already mit my tongue. You bet I keep it shut in my head now. Shall I call Mrs. Fleming? She is in the garden.

DOCTOR. She's there a great deal now, isn't she?

MARIA. Ya, she is always dere by the blossoms, und the babies. (*She goes to the door and says in slow, deferential voice.*) Mrs. Fleming, Doctor Larkin is here.

MARGARET. (*Outside.*) Yes, I'll come. (*She slowly emerges from the garden into the doorway, her arms filled with flowers. She is daintily dressed and there is a subtle dignity and reserve about her. She smiles cheerily.*) Good morning, doctor. Maria, there are some daffodils out by the yellow bed. Bring them, please. (*She slowly enters the room.*)

(*The DOCTOR goes to her and gently leads her to the table on the right where she puts the flowers, after carefully locating a place to lay them.*)

DOCTOR. Well, well, where did you get such a lot of roses? I couldn't gather so many in a month from my scrubby bushes. The bugs eat 'em all up.

MARGARET. Why don't you spray them? (MARIA *brings a large loose bunch of daffodils.*) Bring some jars, Maria.

DOCTOR. I did spray them.

MARGARET. When?

DOCTOR. When I saw the rose bugs.

MARGARET. (*Smiling.*) That's a fine time to spray bushes. Don't you know that the time to prevent trouble is to look ahead? From potatoes to roses, spray before anything happens—then nothing *will* happen.

DOCTOR. (*Laughing.*) Yes, of course, I know, but I forgot to do it until I saw two big, yellow bugs in the heart of every rose and all the foliage chewed up.

MARGARET. There's no use in it now. You are just wasting time. Start early next year before the leaves open.

DOCTOR. (*Admiringly.*) What a brave, cheery little woman you are.

MARGARET. What's the use in being anything else? I don't see any good in living in this world, unless you can live right.

DOCTOR. And this world needs just such women as you.

MARGARET. What does the world know or care about me?
(*The bell rings and the door opens and shuts.*)

DOCTOR. Very little, but it's got to feel your influence. (*He pats her hand.*)
(*The* MAID *enters.*)

MAID. Mr. Foster wishes to see you for a moment, Mrs. Fleming.

MARGARET. Tell him to come in.
(*The* MAID *goes out. In a moment* FOSTER *enters, flurried and embarrassed.*)
Good morning, Mr. Foster. (*She holds out her hands to him.*) Anything wrong at the mill?

FOSTER. Good morning, Mrs. Fleming. Oh, no—not at all, not at all. How do you do, doctor? (*He shakes hands with the* DOCTOR *with unusual warmth.*)

DOCTOR. (*Somewhat surprised and looking at him quizzically.*). Hello, Foster.

MARGARET. Will you sit down, Mr. Foster?

FOSTER. Thank you—yes, I will. What beautiful flowers. Mother says you have the loveliest garden in Canton.

MARGARET. (*Pleased.*) That's awfully nice of her. I had a delightful visit with her yesterday.

FOSTER. (*Nervously.*) Yes, she told me so.

MARGARET. We sat in the garden. What a sweet, happy soul she is.

FOSTER. (*Fussing with his hat and getting up and moving his chair close to the* DOCTOR's.) Yes. Mother always sees the bright side of the worst things.

MARGARET. She's very proud of you.

FOSTER. (*Laughing foolishly.*) Oh, yes, she is happy over anything I do. (*He looks at* MARGARET *furtively, then at the doctor. He evidently has something to say. Suddenly in a tense whisper he speaks to the doctor.*) Mr. Fleming has come back.

DOCTOR. Hush! Where is he? At the mill?

FOSTER. No. Here—outside.

DOCTOR. How does he look?

FOSTER. He's a wreck. He wants to see her.

DOCTOR. Well, tell her—I'll go— (*He rises.*)

FOSTER. No! (*He grabs him by the coat.*) For God's sake don't go. You tell her—you're her doctor.
(MARGARET *who has been busy with the flowers, becomes suddenly interested.*)

MARGARET. What are you two whispering about?

FOSTER. (*Laughing nervously.*) Oh, just a little advice, that's all. (*He goes to* MARGARET.) I'll say good morning, Mrs. Fleming. Glad to see you—er—looking—ah—so well. (*He shakes hands and rushes out.*)

(MARGARET *stands a little mystified. The* DOCTOR *approaches her gently.*)

DOCTOR. (*Very tenderly.*) Mrs. Fleming—I have something to say to you.

MARGARET. (*Standing tense and with ominous conviction.*) Philip is dead!

DOCTOR. No. He is not dead.

MARGARET. Where is he?

DOCTOR. *Outside.*

MARGARET. Why doesn't he come in?

DOCTOR. He's ashamed—afraid.

MARGARET. This is his home. Why should he be afraid to enter it? I will go to him. (*She starts toward the door, and then staggers. The* DOCTOR *puts an arm around her.*)

DOCTOR. There now. Keep up your courage. Don't forget, everything depends upon you.

MARGARET. (*Brokenly.*) I'm brave, doctor. I—perhaps it's best for you to tell him to come here.

DOCTOR. (*Patting her on the shoulder.*) Remember, you are very precious to us all. We cannot afford to lose *you.*

(MARGARET *stands by the table, calm and tense.* PHILIP *comes in from the right, carrying his cap in his hands. He looks weary and broken. He crosses behind* MARGARET *to the center of the stage and standing humbly before her, murmurs her name softly.*)

PHILIP. Margaret!

MARGARET. Well, Philip. (*After a slight pause.*) You have come back.

PHILIP. (*Humbly.*) Yes.

MARGARET. (*Gently.*) Why did you go away?

PHILIP. (*Overwhelmed with shame.*) I couldn't face you. I wanted to get away somewhere, and hide forever. (*He looks sharply at her.*) Can't you see me, Margaret?

MARGARET. (*Shaking her head.*) No!

PHILIP. (*Awed.*) You are blind! Oh!

(MARGARET *sits down in a chair by the table.* PHILIP *remains standing.*)

MARGARET. Don't mind. I shall be cured. Doctor Norton sees

me every day. He will operate as soon as he finds me normal.

PHILIP. You have been suffering?

MARGARET. Oh, no. (*After a pause.*) Philip, do you think that was right? To run away and hide?

PHILIP. I did not consider whether it was right or wrong. (*He speaks bitterly.*) I did not know the meaning of those words. I never have.

MARGARET. Oh, you are a man—people will soon forget.

PHILIP. (*Fiercely.*) I do not care about others. It is you, Margaret—will you ever forget? Will you ever forgive?

MARGARET. (*Shaking her head and smiling sadly.*) There is nothing to forgive. And, I want to forget.

PHILIP. (*Bewildered by her magnanimity, but full of hope.*) Then you will let me come back to you? You will help me to be a better—a wiser man?

MARGARET. (*Smilingly gently.*) Yes, Philip.
    (*A quick joy takes hold of* PHILIP. *He makes a warm movement to go to her, then checks himself, and approaches her slowly while speaking, overcome by the wonder and beauty of her kindness.*)

PHILIP. All my life, Margaret, I will make amends for what I have done. I will atone for my ignorance—Oh, my wife—my dear, dear wife. (*He hangs over her tenderly, not daring to touch her.*)
    (*At the word "wife"* MARGARET *rises, shrinking from him as though some dead thing was near her. A look of agony flits across her face.*)

MARGARET. No! Philip, not that! No! (*She puts out her hands to ward him off.*)

PHILIP. (*Beseechingly.*) Margaret!

MARGARET. (*Her face poignant with suppressed emotion, she confesses, brokenly.*) The wife-heart has gone out of me.

PHILIP. Don't—don't say that, Margaret.

MARGARET. I must. Ah, Philip, how I worshipped you. You were my idol. Is it my fault that you lie broken at my feet?

PHILIP. (*With urgency.*) You say you want to forget—that you forgive! Will you—?

MARGARET. Can't you understand? It is not a question of forgetting, or of forgiving— (*For an instant she is at a loss how to convince him.*) Can't you understand? Philip! (*Then suddenly.*) Suppose—I—had been unfaithful to you?

PHILIP. (*With a cry of repugnance.*) Oh, Margaret!

MARGARET. (*Brokenly.*) There! You see! You are a man, and you have your ideals of—the—sanctity—of—the thing you love. Well, I am a woman—and perhaps—I, too, have the same ideals. I don't know. But, I, too, cry "pollution." (*She is deeply moved.*)

PHILIP. (*Abashed.*) I did not know. I never realized before, the iniquity—of my—behavior. Oh, if I only had my life to live over again. Men, as a rule, do not consider others when urged on by their desires. How you must hate me.

MARGARET. No, I don't—I love you—I pity you.

PHILIP. Dear, not now—but in the future—some time—away in the future—perhaps, the old Margaret—

MARGARET. Ah, Philip, the old Margaret is dead. The truth killed her.

PHILIP. Then—there is no hope for me?

(*There is a dignity and a growing manliness in his demeanor as the scene progresses.*)

MARGARET. (*Warmly.*) Yes. Every hope.

PHILIP. Well, what do you want me to do? Shall I go away?

MARGARET. No. Your place is here. You cannot shirk your responsibilities now.

PHILIP. I do not want to shirk my responsibilities, Margaret. I want to do whatever you think is best.

MARGARET. Very well. It is best for us both to remain here, and take up the old life together. It will be a little hard for you, but you are a man—you will soon live it down.

PHILIP. Yes—I *will* live it down.

MARGARET. Go to the mill tomorrow morning and take up your work again, as though this thing had never happened.

PHILIP. Yes. All right. I'll do that.

MARGARET. Mr. Foster, you know, you have an unusually capable man there?

PHILIP. Yes, I appreciate Foster. He's a nice chap, too.

MARGARET. He has carried through a very critical week at the mill.

PHILIP. Don't worry, Margaret, everything will be all right there now. I will put my whole heart and soul into the work.

MARGARET. Then, you must do something for your child.

PHILIP. Yes, our dear child.

MARGARET. No, not our child—not Lucy. Your son.

PHILIP. My son?

MARGARET. Yes.

PHILIP. Where is he?

MARGARET. Here.

PHILIP. (*Resentfully.*) Who brought him here?

MARGARET. I did.

PHILIP. (*Amazed.*) You brought that child here?

MARGARET. Yes, where else should he go?

PHILIP. You have done that?

MARGARET. What other thing was there for me to do? Surely if he was good enough to bring into the world, he is good enough to find a shelter under your roof.

PHILIP. (*Moved by her magnanimity.*) I never dreamed that you would do that, Margaret.

MARGARET. Well, he is here. Now, what are you going to do with him?

PHILIP. (*Helplessly.*) What can I do?

MARGARET. Give him a name, educate him. Try to make atonement for the wrong you did his mother. You must teach him never to be ashamed of her, to love her memory—motherhood is a divine thing—remember that, Philip, no matter when, or how. You can do fine things for this unfortunate child.

PHILIP. (*Contemptuously.*) Fine things for him! I am not fit to guide a young life. A fine thing I have made of my own.

MARGARET. There is no use now lamenting what was done yesterday. That's finished. Tomorrow? What are you going to do with that?

PHILIP. There does not seem any "tomorrow" worth while for me. The past—

MARGARET. The past is dead. We must face the living future. Now, Philip, there are big things ahead for you, if you will only look for them. They certainly will not *come* to *you*. I will help you—we will fight this together.

PHILIP. Forgive me, please. I'll not talk like that any more.

MARGARET. Of course, there will be a lot of talk—mean talk—but they will get tired of that in the end. Where have you been all this time?

PHILIP. In Boston.

MARGARET. What have you been doing?

PHILIP. Nothing—I've been—in the hospital.

MARGARET. (*Stretching out her arms to him with an infinite tenderness.*) Ah, Philip, you have been ill?

PHILIP. No!

MARGARET. What was it. (*He is silent.*) Please tell me.

PHILIP. (*Rather reluctantly reciting his story.*) I was walking across the bridge over the Charles river one night—I was sick of myself—the whole world—I believed I should never see your face again. The water looked so quiet, it fascinated me. I just dropped into it and went down. It seemed like going to sleep. Then I woke up and I was in a narrow bed in a big room.

MARGARET. (*Breathless.*) The hospital?

PHILIP. Yes.

MARGARET. Oh, that was a cruel thing to do. Were they kind to you there?

PHILIP. Yes. There was an old nurse there—she was sharp. She told me not to be a fool, but to go back to my wife. She said—"If she's any good, she will forgive you." (*He smiles whimsically.*) Margaret, some day I am going to earn your respect, and then—I know, I shall be able to win you back to me all over again.

MARGARET. (*Smiling sadly.*) I don't know. That would be a wonderful thing. (*She weeps silently.*) A very wonderful thing. (*Then suddenly she springs to her feet.*) Ah, dreams! Philip! Dreams! And we must get to work.

(PHILIP *is inspired by her manner, and there is a quickening of his spirit, a response to her in the new vibration in his voice.*)

PHILIP. Work! Yes—I'll not wait until tomorrow. I'll go to the mill now.

MARGARET. That's fine. Do it.

PHILIP. Yes, I'll take a bath and get into some fresh clothing first.

MARGARET. Do. You must look pretty shabby knocking about for a week without a home.

PHILIP. Oh, I'll be all right. I'd like to see Lucy. (*He looks about.*) Where is she?

(MARGARET *is at the table occupied with the flowers.*)

MARGARET. They are both out there. (*She indicates with a turn of her head.*) In the garden.

(PHILIP *goes quickly to the door opening upon the garden and gazes out eagerly.* MARGARET, *at the table, pauses in in her work, gives a long sigh of relief and contentment. Her eyes look into the darkness and a serene joy illuminates her face. The picture slowly fades out as* PHILIP *steps buoyantly into the garden.*)

SELECTIVE BIBLIOGRAPHY

Anderson, John. *The American Theatre* (New York, 1938).

Clark, Barrett H., ed. *America's Lost Plays*, 20 vol. (Princeton, 1940–41; Bloomington, Indiana, 1963–65).

*Hartman, John Geoffrey. *The Development of American Social Comedy from 1787 to 1936* (Philadelphia, 1939).

*Hewitt, Barnard. *Theatre U.S.A. 1668–1957* (New York, 1959).

Hornblow, Arthur. *A History of the Theatre in America: From Its Beginnings to the Present Time*, 2 vol. (Philadelphia and London, 1919).

Hughes, Glenn. *A History of the American Theatre 1700–1950* (New York, 1951).

Hutton, Laurence. *Curiosities of the American Stage* (New York, 1891).

*Moody, Richard. *America Takes the Stage: Romanticism in American Drama and Theatre, 1750–1900* (Bloomington, 1955).

Morris, Lloyd. *Curtain Time: The Story of the American Theatre* (New York, 1953).

Moses, Montrose J. *The American Dramatist* (Boston, 1925).

—————— and John Mason Brown. *The American Theatre as Seen by Its Critics, 1752–1934* (New York, 1934).

Odell, George C.D. *Annals of the New York Stage*, 15 vol. (New York, 1927–49).

*Quinn, Arthur H. *A History of the American Drama from the Beginning to the Civil War* (New York, 1923 and 1943).

*——————. *A History of the American Drama from the Civil War to the Present Day*, 2 vol. (New York, 1927, 1937, and 1943).

Smith, Cecil. *Musical Comedy in America* (New York, 1950).

Taubman, Howard. *The Making of the American Theatre* (New York, 1965).

* Comprehensive bibliographies may be found in these volumes and in Richard Moody's extensive collection, *Dramas from the American Theatre 1762–1909* (Cleveland and New York, 1966).

PLAYS BY AMERICAN WOMEN:
1900–1930

Edited by Judith E. Barlow

These important dramatists did more than write significant new plays; they introduced to the American stage a new and vital character— the modern American woman in her quest for a forceful role in a changing American scene. It will be hard to remember that these women playwrights were ever forgotten.

A MAN'S WORLD Rachel Crothers
TRIFLES Susan Glaspell
PLUMES Georgia Douglas Johnson
MACHINAL Sophie Treadwell
MISS LULU BETT Zona Gale

Paper: ISBN: 1-55783-008-8

APPLAUSE
NEW YORK • LONDON